Community
Parks & Recreation
An Introduction

Christopher R. Edginton
Samuel V. Lankford
Rodney B. Dieser
Christopher L. Kowalski

Publishers: Joseph J. Bannon/Peter Bannon
Sales and Marketing Manager: Misti Gilles
Marketing Assistant: Kimberly Vecchio
Director of Development and Production: Susan M. Davis
Graphic Designer: Marissa Willison
Technology Manager: Mark Atkinson

Library of Congress Catalog Card Number: 2017941213
ISBN print edition: 978-1-57167-789-1
ISBN ebook: 978-1-57167-790-7
Printed in the United States.

SAGAMORE ◈ VENTURE

1807 N. Federal Dr.
Urbana, IL 61801
www.sagamorepub.com

For our families, our most important and immediate community.

Contents

Part I
History and Philosophical Foundations of Public Parks and Recreation

Part II
Managerial and Administrative Perspectives of Public Parks and Recreation Systems

Part III
Public Sector Service Provision in Parks and Recreation

About the Authors

Christopher R. Edginton is the R.J. McElroy Professor of Youth Leadership Studies, School of Kinesiology, Allied Health, and Human Services at the University of Northern Iowa. From 1991-2010, he served as professor and director of the School of Health, Physical Education and Leisure Services. In 1985, he founded the nationally award-winning Camp Adventure™ Child & Youth Services program. Since its inception, the program has provided contracted services for children and youth worldwide. From 2004–2014, he served as secretary general of the World Leisure Organization, a nongovernmental organization operating in consultative status with The United Nations. He is the cofounder of the Global Forum for Physical Education Pedagogy (GoFPEP), a worldwide social movement aimed at rethinking, reframing, and refocusing physical education pedagogy and the training of health and physical education teachers. Edginton has authored over 350 articles, over 30 books, and over 30 chapters in books. He has been identified as the leading proponent of the application of contemporary management concepts in the park and recreation field.

Samuel V. Lankford is professor and chair, Department of Recreation Administration, Fresno State University. Formerly he served as a professor and founding director of the Sustainable Tourism and the Environment Program at the University of Hawaii and University of Northern Iowa. He has a PhD with a focus in tourism planning and development and a master of urban and regional planning degree from the University of Oregon. He holds a master of arts in recreation and park planning and a BA in geography from CSU-Chico. He was a board member for *World Leisure* for six years, the president and treasurer for Hawaii and Recreation Association, and the Northern California Educator Representative for California Parks and Recreation Society. He was recognized as a Senior Fellow for the American Leisure Academy. Dr. Lankford has been a practicing planner in both staff and consulting roles in California, Oregon, Washington, Iowa, and Hawaii. He has conducted planning, needs assessments, community impact studies, carrying capacity studies, and market research in those states and other countries. He specializes in tourism and recreation development.

Rodney B. Dieser is a professor in the School of Kinesiology, Allied Health, and Human Services at the University of Northern Iowa (UNI), graduate coordinator of the master's of art degree in Philanthropy and Nonprofit Development at UNI, and works 10 hours a week as a licensed mental health counselor (tLMHC). He is also a certified therapeutic recreation specialist. Rod has published over 100 articles with over 60 being academic publications and has published three other textbooks. Rod has served as an associated editor for the *Therapeutic Recreation Journal* and *Leisure/Loisir* (academic journal of the Canadian Association for Leisure Studies) and has served as a guest editor for the *World Leisure Journal* and the *International Leisure Review*. His research and teaching interests include (1) cross-cultural therapeutic recreation/inclusive recreation and leisure service delivery; (2) leisure education intervention; (3) leisure and mental health; (4) historical and philosophical foundations of leisure, youth, and nonprofit human services, including Hull House, 1889-1953; and (5) the philanthropic labor and leisure endeavors of Bruce Springsteen.

Christopher L. Kowalski is an associate professor, School of Kinesiology, Allied Health, and Human Services, at the University of Northern Iowa. He joined the faculty of the Division of Leisure, Youth & Human Services in 2000. He also serves as a research coordinator for the Sustainable Tourism and Environment Program at the University of Northern Iowa. He holds a doctorate from the University of Northern Iowa, a master of science in recreation management from the University of Idaho, and a BA in psychology, sociology, and criminal justice from Creighton University (Nebraska). He has supervised community and youth recreation programs for over 20 years in Idaho, Iowa, Nebraska, and Texas, as well as abroad in Europe, Asia, and the Middle East. His research interests are coaching, youth leadership, and self-efficacy in the recreation field.

Preface

The inspiration for the development of the book *Community Parks & Recreation: An Introduction* was drawn from three sources. First and perhaps most important was the efforts of the senior authors in leading doctoral course work focused on the topic of community building. In this effort, two social constructs were used to discuss the topic of community. They were (1) sustainable environmental development and (2) social capital. In modern times, Rachel Carson's treatise, *Silent Spring* (1962), and Kenneth E. Boulding's essay, *The Economics of the Coming Spaceship Earth* (1966), addressed the importance of the interaction of the economy and the environment and gave way to the need for sustainable environmental development. Robert Putnam's book, *Bowling Alone: The Collapse and Revival of American Community* (2001), discusses the loss of social capital in American communities and the need for greater social bonding and social bridging.

The aforementioned social constructs are directly related to the work of community park and recreation organizations. The greening and beautification of communities as well as tying recreation services to clean economic development provide a direct connection between the work of public park and recreation departments and community development. Over the past 150 years, communities have focused their attention on enhancing quality of life, health, and wellness, and the greening of their environments through the provision of park and recreation services and amenities. Further, such services have galvanized communities to provide programs as mechanisms of social reform to address issues related to poverty, immigration, crowding, and the anonymity that comes from urban life. In contemporary times, the writings of Richard Florida, including his seminal book, *The Rise of the Creative Class* (2002), and *Who's Your City* (2008), have pointed to the importance of creating livable innovative community environments.

In our discussion with doctoral students, we asked them to consider what are the most important elements of a livable community? In what type of community would they like to live? How important are building social connections amongst family, friends, neighbors, colleagues, and others? How are such relationships developed and sustained? What types of organizations are more likely to create such opportunities for building one's social capital? What agencies in the community are concerned with addressing environmental degradation and on the flip side enhancing community beautification and greening? All of these questions pointed toward the importance of public parks and recreation and its community development efforts.

Second, as we reviewed the literature, it was interesting to note that few books in more contemporary times addressed the topic of community parks and recreation. As the profession of parks and recreation was historically tied to municipal services, we began to ask ourselves, is there a turn in the profession away from services offered at the local level? Although we did not come to a definitive conclusion regarding this matter, it became somewhat evident to us that much of the literature available to academics today was not in fact focused on municipal park and recreation services. Simply, it may be that job opportunities have been diminished in the public sector, and therefore the academic preparation of students is being directed elsewhere. With this effort, we hope to reenergize and rekindle a focus on community parks and recreation as an area of academic interest and study.

Third, we all had a deep interest in community parks and/or recreation services. At various times in one or more of our careers, we have served as playground leaders, recreation specialists, youth leaders, community therapeutic recreation specialists, recreation center directors, recreation supervisors, and/or director of parks and recreation. In preparing this book, it was as if we were coming full circle in our professional careers. We all started with a strong commitment to community parks and recreation, and this fact highlighted our commitment to the topic.

The book is organized into three major parts. Part I focuses on the "History and Philosophical Foundations of Public Parks and Recreation." The major intent of this section is to provide an underpinning to assist the student in understanding the major dimensions of public parks and recreation and its impact socially, culturally, environmentally, and economically. Part II of the book focuses on "Managerial and Administrative Aspects of Park and Recreation Systems." This section of the book provides practical strategies for administrative activities, planning, marketing, budgeting, engaging the public, and land acquisition. Part III of the book is focused on "The Public Sector Service Provision in Parks and Recreation." This section of the book focuses on program and service delivery, including chapters dealing with programming for community recreation, youth programming, programming for adults and seniors, programming special events, and community-based therapeutic recreation.

In the preparation of *Community Parks & Recreations: An Introduction,* each author was responsible for the preparation of four chapters. Therefore, we all equally shared in the authorship of the book. In addition, we all share the authorship of the final two chapters of the book. As such, there is no senior author, and each of our names could have been listed first or in some other order in the book.

Christopher R. Edginton
Samuel D. Lankford
Rodney B. Dieser
Christopher L. Kowalski

References

Boulding, K. E. (1966). The economics of the coming spaceship earth. Environmental quality issues in a growing economy. In H. Jarrett (Ed.), *Environmental quality in a growing economy* (pp. 3–14). Baltimore, MD: John Hopkins University Press.

Carson, R. (1994). *Silent spring.* First printing, 1962. Boston, MA: Houghton Mifflin.

Putnam, R. D. (2001). *Bowling alone: The collapse and revival of American community.* New York, NY: Simon and Schuster.

Florida, R. L. (2002). *The rise of the creative class: and how it's transforming work, leisure, community, and everyday life.* New York, NY: Basic Books.

Florida, R. (2008). *Who's your city?* New York, NY: Basic Books.

Acknowledgments

The authors would like to thank our doctoral students who have joined us in this journey of dialogue and discovery. At times, the conversation has been meaningful and relevant, leading to new insights and perspectives. Among those doctoral students we would like to acknowledge and thank are Amani Mohammed, Andrea Anderson, Chen Kong, Gale Carlson, Michelle Cook, Belinda Creighton-Smith, Amy Davison, Noha Fadlalddin, Tom Flack, Abubakarr Jalloh, Theodora Jn Baptiste, Elizabeth Majewski, Nate Newman, Michelle Rhoades, Junu Shrestha, Chris Denison, David Goodson, Don Briggs, Oksana Grybovych, Tony Ford, Jeff Farland, Brad Tan, Jim Hall, Wade Kooiman, Stanley Chiang, Ariana Cela, Jonell Pedescleaux, Germaine Jackson, and Tony Smothers. These individuals have enabled us to form an inspirational community of scholars.

We would also like to acknowledge support received from our colleagues in the College of Education to develop and continue our doctoral program in Allied Health, Recreation and Community Services. The program was previously identified as Leisure, Youth and Human Services, but we expanded the dimensions of the program to ensure that it was more inclusive and reflective of contemporary trends linking themes related to leisure and health, sustainable environmental development, social capital, and community development. Among those whom we would like to thank for their continued support are Mary Herring, Linda Fitzgerald, Rod Boody, Bill Callahan, and Vickie Robinson. All of these individuals have worked to reform the Doctorate of Education (EdD) to ensure that reflected guidelines established by the Carnegie Project on the Education Doctorate (CPED). CPED has worked to differentiate the doctorate of the EdD degree from the PhD degree as a degree that is focused on professional practice.

In addition, we would like to thank Al Oberlander and Scott Crawford of RDG Planning & Design for providing us with graphic illustrations and articles from projects with which they have been associated. We appreciate their support for this activity and also valued RDG's activities in designing the University of Northern Iowa's award-winning Wellness/Recreation Center. We would also like to acknowledge the contributions of Jack Carey and Millie Keith of the Freeport Park District and Mark Ripplinger of Cedar Falls, Iowa Parks and Recreation. We would like to thank Mike Nigbur from the City of Rochester (MN) Parks and Recreation Department for providing us the historical documents of this City's Parks and Recreation services and for outlining the collaborative work between Parks and Recreation Department and the prestigious Mayo Clinic. We would also like to thank Dr. Johanna Rian, Director, Mayo Clinic, Dolores Jean Lavins Center for Humanities in Medicine (Rochester MN Campus); Ryan Harren at the History Center of Olmstead County (Rochester MN); and Dr. Kenneth Mobily at The University of Iowa.

Chris Edginton would like to extend his appreciation to his wife, Susan, who has continuously supported his professional career for many, many years. Her work in managing Camp Adventure Child and Youth Services has been laudatory. The program has profited from her commitment, dedication, and passion for the program. The author would also like to thank his daughter, Carole. Carole is an adjunct instructor at the University of Northern

Iowa, Upper Iowa University, and Mount Mercy University. Every semester she teaches a full load of courses and is an outstanding professor. She has two daughters, Hanna and Lily. These are two very special granddaughters, with great interest in art and music. My son, David, is a Foreign Services Officer with the U.S. Department of State. His tours of duty have taken him to the United Arab Emirates, Uruguay, Bahrain, Iraq, New Zealand, and Saudi Arabia. David has two sons, Jacob and Joseph. Both boys are exceedingly handsome and very, very bright. I would also like to thank my coauthors, Sam Lankford, Rod Dieser, and Chris Kowalski for their commitment and dedication to this project. They were very responsive in ensuring that the project was completed in a timely fashion. As is the case with most intellectual journeys, it was stimulating and involved countless discussions and interactions leading to new insights in the parks and recreation field. Their efforts were greatly appreciated, and I value each of them as colleagues.

Many of us are grateful for the family, friends, and colleagues who form our personal community of support. In particular, Sam Lankford would like to acknowledge his supportive partner, Jill, and two bright children, Jordan and Jesse, who help to keep him connected to the topics he teaches and the experience base of his students. He is fortunate to live in proximity to his mother, father, and sister, who help him stay connected to his past. In addition, he has a whole cast of professional relationships that he has had the opportunity to collaborate with toward the betterment of the profession. Sam would like to thank his colleagues, Dr. Rod Dieser, Dr. Chris Kowalski, and Dr. Oksana Grybovych for their friendship and sense of community. Thank you to Dr. Fred Brooks, Dr. David Povey, Dr. Larry Neal, Dr. Dan Wheeler, Dr. Al Williams, Dr. Don De Graaf, and all the other PhD graduates from the University of Oregon's Department of Leisure Studies and Services; Joyce Spoehr and Willy Ching from the Hawaii Recreation and Parks Association; Ian Legaree of the Municipal and Community Affairs (MACA) of the Northwest Territories; and Manuel A. Mollinedo, the former Director of the City of Fresno Department of Parks, After School, Recreation and Community Services (PARCS). Thanks also go to the Dean of the College of Health and Human Services, Dr. Jody Hironaka-Juteau, faculty (Dr. L-Jay Fine, Dr. Nancy Nisbett, Dr. Michael Mahoney, and Dr. Jason Whiting) and staff of the Department of Recreation Administration at Fresno State, specifically Selena Winchell, Marlow Campos, and Simone Campos for their support, humor, and dedication. Thanks are also given to Sophie Karas, who provided important research materials for Sam's chapters. Appreciation is also given to Brandon Taylor, who is an instructor in recreation administration at CSU Fresno for discussing the need for this book and how the current books available do not treat community recreation in a comprehensive fashion. Finally, Sam would like to thank Dr. Christopher Edginton for his support, mentoring, inclusion in projects, and his friendship. He met Chris 30 years ago at the University of Oregon, where he was a graduate student in urban planning. Chris convinced him to pursue the PhD in recreation and leisure studies, and it has been an exciting journey. This is his community. Not all are so fortunate to experience the diversity in community he enjoys. This only underscores the need for us working in the field of leisure, parks, and recreation to embrace a community perspective. This book is focused on our need to build community, which moves us well beyond the provision of services.

Rod Dieser, who was raised in a poor, blue-color family with illiterate parents from "the old country," would like to extend his deep gratitude to his wife, Ricki, who was the first person who convinced him to attend university, go on to graduate school, and held his hand the first day he walked on a university campus. She has been holding my hand for over 25 years. He is grateful to his parents, John and Helen Dieser, who despite not having educational and financial resources, raised him to be thoughtful toward others and to appreciate and see the wisdom in "old world" culture and value diversity. He would like to extend his appreciation to his three sons, Chayce, Jonas, and Zachary, who have taught him the importance of empathy and the significance of simple things in life. He is thankful to his dog, Louie, who has helped his health by walking anywhere from 1 to 5 miles a day and is a good friend.

Chris Kowalski would like to thank his wife, Crystal, and their children, Norah and Lukas, for their support and encouragement throughout his professional career. It is a wonderful feeling to come home to a beautiful family who smile each time he walks in the door. Crystal, Norah, and Lukas's energy spur Chris on to be the best faculty member he can be at UNI. He would also like to recognize Kevin Roberts, Chris Guidry, and Dave Hirner for their friendship and camaraderie over the past 20 years; all three have remained true friends over the years. Finally, Chris would also like to acknowledge the lifelong support from his parents, Pat and Lana Kowalski.

In addition, we would like to acknowledge the efforts of Kristina Kofoot, Jennifer Stevens, Michelle Cook, and Joyce Levingston. In the preparation of any book, there is a great deal of clerical assistance, organization, and support that must be given to the effort. We would like to thank Kristina, Jennifer, Michelle, and Joyce for their commitment to this writing project. Without their help it would not have been possible.

We would also like to acknowledge the support that we have received from Sagamore–Venture for our writing efforts. Interestingly, we proposed this topic to Joe Bannon, and he indicated to us nearly simultaneously that Sagamore–Venture had such a title on their list of book acquisitions. Joe has always been supportive, encouraging, and has helped us with our writing efforts. We deeply appreciate his continued endorsement for our scholarly activities. We would also like to mention that his continued efforts of supporting the Academy of Leisure Sciences is noteworthy. Many individuals owe a great deal of gratitude to Joe for his continued efforts in supporting recreation, parks, leisure, and tourism higher education. We would also like to thank Peter Bannon at Sagamore–Venture. We enjoy greatly working with Peter and find him to be a valuable colleague. In addition, we would like to recognize the efforts of Susan Davis, Marissa Willison, Misti Gilles, and Kimberly Vecchio at Sagamore–Venture.

Christopher R. Edginton
Samuel V. Lankford
Rodney B. Deiser
Christopher L. Kowalski

Chapter One

Introduction to Community Parks & Recreation

CHAPTER OBJECTIVES

- To gain an understanding of the philosophical and foundational aspects of community parks and recreation
- To develop an appreciation of the role community parks and recreation professional as a public servant
- To understand the concept of community and the way in which public recreation services are organized and the strategies used to organize community resources
- To gain awareness of the ways in which public parks and recreation services are an asset to a community
- To understand the ways in which parks and recreation services contribute to community livability

INTRODUCTION

The soul of the community is reflected in the vitality of its public parks and recreation services. Community parks and recreation services impact very dramatically the quality of life, livability and health, and well-being of the members of any community. Community life and the activities engaged in by individuals and groups of people provide for a sense of belonging, meaningfulness, and relevance in the way people live their lives. Community parks and recreation programs, services, and facilities play a key role in creating opportunities for people to experience and enjoy life. They are often pivotal in assisting individuals in finding great value in their day-to-day living activities. As leisure has taken increased value in contemporary society, so have the services offered by community parks and recreation agencies.

Public parks and recreation agencies have a central role to play in the crafting of community life. Such services may provide a respite for individuals as well as stimulation for dealing with day-to-day challenges. As Edginton, DeGraff, Dieser, and Edginton have noted (2006):

> Leisure is freedom and contributes greatly to one's satisfaction in life….as a way of uplifting the spirit, improving our well-being, and enhancing our relationships with others' leisure…helps us shape our sense of self-worth, assist in the formulation and communication of values and norms, and aids us in improving the livability in our

lives and communities. Leisure is a way of energizing individuals to pursue those individual interests they value. While liberating individuals, leisure time affords opportunities to celebrate community living. It is a powerful medium that provides opportunities for us to enhance our social, cultural, and economic development. (p. xiii)

Specifically related to community parks and recreation, Butler (1976) defined recreation as "activities that lead to direct satisfaction on behalf of participants; recreation is the services that community parks and recreation agencies offer to community members."

As one can determine, public parks and recreation are an important part of enhancing community life. Leisure, whether viewed as free time, activity, or as a state of mind, can be enhanced when there are numerous, diverse, and high-quality community parks and recreation services available.

Community parks and recreation can be defined as any combination of leisure experiences and amenities that contribute to individual or a community's quality of life, health, and wellness, and sustainable environmental well-being. Parks and recreation services can be thought of as a developmental process that engages the community in positive, meaningful, and purposeful ways. In this book we use the terms *community* and *public* interchangeably. Community or public parks and recreation refers to government services and subdivisions of government that are offered closest to people. This includes municipal government, county government, and special districts.

In this chapter, a number of topics will be discussed. First, a discussion of philosophical foundations and perspectives related to community parks and recreation will be explored. This will be followed by a short discussion of mission statements from community parks and recreation departments. Key themes emerging from this analysis suggest that such agencies are committed to enhancing and improving quality of life, health and well-being, and stewardship of natural resources. Third, a discussion of the role of the parks and recreation professional as a public servant is included. Next, an explanation as to why parks and recreation services move people is explored. A discussion of the ways in which communities can be defined is next offered. This is followed by information regarding why community parks and recreation are an asset. In turn, useful information is presented on the ways in which the parks and recreation profession is involved in the building of the livability of communities. Also included is a discussion of strategies for organizing community resources, including social planning, community development, social marketing, and social action. Last, a presentation of the ways in which community parks and recreation services are organized is included.

PHILOSOPHICAL FOUNDATIONS AND PERSPECTIVES

"Parks are for people." This concept has resonated throughout the last 150 years of American and Canadian history. As Dustin, McAvoy, and Schultz (2002) have indicated, "From Yosemite to the Boston Common, recreation resources represents the democratic resources of the public good" (p. 6). They symbolize the fact that public parks and recreation areas belong to all. As they suggest, "in a nation committed to equality of conditions, public parks and playgrounds serve as an equalizing function" (p. 6). Regardless of one's socioeconomic status, all individuals have access to such public resources. Thus, public parks and recreation are in fact an expression America's democratic ideal. The core ideals and values of this concept include life, liberty, and the pursuit of happiness, which are embedded in our Declaration of Independence.

Complementing the aforementioned statement is one drawn from Texas A&M University professor John Crompton (2013), wherein he has proclaimed that "there are no great cities that do not have a great park system." This statement suggests that the infrastructure of any given great city must include the provision for parks and recreation services. In order for people to achieve a quality of life, they must have affordable access to public resources such as parks and recreation. As a result, such services have been woven into the fabric of community life over the past several decades. Public parks and recreation services are perceived to be an important element in any community's offering of its community services and are viewed as a standard element.

What then, are the general themes that community parks and recreation departments pursue? Such themes are not universally accepted but nonetheless provide insight into the roles of parks and recreation agencies and the professionals within such organizations. Many such organizations view their work as building a sense of community and promoting community *esprit de corps*. Parks and recreation agencies help individuals and communities find joy, zest, and encourage spirit in community life. Further, such organizations engage in the development of their community by promoting community development, which encourages social bonding and bridging. Parks and recreation agencies are often involved in enhancing social connectivity, unity, solidarity, connectedness, relatedness, and partnership building. Central to the work of parks and recreation agencies have been the contributions they make to the beautification and the settings of the community and to promoting and enhancing community livability. Drawing from the World Leisure Organization, parks and recreation organizations have become integral to the social, cultural, economic, and sustainable environmental well-being.

An essential component of community function is that of nurturing the human spirit. As Edginton, Hudson, Scholl, and Lauzon (2011) have noted, parks and recreation professionals work to "create hope in the lives of individuals" (p. 125). Their work involves providing people with the hope as they come to participate in leisure experiences that good things will happen to them. Edginton and Chen (2014) have offered the following:

> Creating hope is the central focus of the profession. We are the builders, creators, and developers of hope. An important element of the professional's vision and mission, hope motivates individuals in gaining the knowledge, skills, attitudes, and values that enrich their lives and those of others. Leisure provides opportunities for individuals to create shape and share their hope for increased well-being and a better quality of life. It is through creating hope that we build a confidence for fulfilling one's anticipated desires for the future. Hope builds confidence that [one's or a community's] needs and interest and desires can be fulfilled. (p. 173)

The many benefits that come from the prevision of community parks and recreation programs and services are in fact endless, including assisting individuals and communities in finding joy, happiness, and fulfillment. Benefits often focus on assisting individuals and communities in the development of their social, cultural, physical, cognitive, economic, and spiritual attributes. Figure 1.1 provides an analysis of the economic benefits of parks for cities. As one can see, not only do parks enhance environmental aesthetics and recreation benefits but also economic ones.

How Cities Use Parks for Economic Development

Parks provide intrinsic environmental, aesthetic, and recreation benefits to our cities. They are also a source of positive economic benefits. They enhance property values, increase municipal revenue, bring in homebuyers and workers, and attract retirees.

At the bottom line, parks are a good financial investment for a community. Understanding the economic impacts of parks can help decision makers better evaluate the creation and maintenance of urban parks. Key points include:

- Real property values are positively affected.

- Municipal revenues are increased.

- Affluent retirees are attracted and retained.

- Knowledge workers and talent are attracted to live and work.

- Homebuyers are attracted to purchase homes.

Figure 1.1. How cities use parks for economic development. (Lewis, 2007)

Parks and recreation professionals often operate from a holistic, humanistic, and activist role to engage in policy decision-making within communities. The parks and recreation profession is rooted in human services, and our advocacy activities are often in collaboration with other social and human services. There is a strong emphasis placed on working with people to identify needs and in turn assist them in assessing resources to meet such needs. Parks and recreation professionals work to teach individuals process and problem-solving skills from a community development perspective. It is the public's involvement that makes public parks and recreation relevant and vibrant in community life. A part of the professional activities of the parks and recreation professional is to engage in critical inquiry. As Edginton and Chen (2014) have written, parks and recreation professionals work to "inquire critically as to the conditions of human kind... critical inquiry should promote new solutions to problems...[and]... seek to improve the quality of life of all human beings by critically examining the conditions of society that lead to poverty, hatred, violence, and anomie" (p. 137). In the crafting of new solutions, the parks and recreation professional often operates as a social entrepreneur, bringing social inventions to solve problems to their communities.

MISSION STATEMENTS AND COMMUNITY PARKS AND RECREATION

What is the mission of community parks and recreation departments? A review of mission statements from multiple parks and recreation departments operating at municipal, county, and special districts levels reveal nearly 50 distinct philosophical perspectives that are used to guide the action of these types of organizations. Some of the more common statements include "quality of life, stewardship and preservation of natural resources and heritage sites, provision of beautiful spaces, health and wellness, and affordable and accessible services." Still other mission statements speak to the importance of the relationship between parks and recreation agencies and those whom they serve. Mission statements also reflect "the need to promote high-quality human services, treat people with courtesy and respect, and building partnerships with the community." Still others, promoting benefits such as "happiness, fun, learning, growth and development, providing safe and inviting places for people to gather, celebrate, contemplate, and engage in activity." Other mission statements reflect the importance of "leadership, professionalism, providing quality services, and commitment and a responsiveness to the needs of people as a way of enriching their lives." These themes parallel the National Recreation and Park Association's focus on conservation, health and wellness, social equity, as well as quality of life and the enhancement of sustainable environments through community parks and recreation (NRPA, 2017).

Figure 1.2 presents a mission and core value statement from the Chicago Park District. As one can see when reviewing this statement, a strong commitment is made to three primary themes. First is the enhancement of the quality of life through the provision of recreation and leisure opportunities. The second involves providing safe, inviting, and beautifully maintained parks and facilities. Last is the creation of a customer-friendly system. These primary mission-driven statements are supported by four core values: children first, best deal in town, built to last, and extra effort. Figure 1.3 is the City of Indianapolis Department of Parks and Recreation vision, mission, and values statement. As one can see in this document, the program emphasizes excellence as well as environmental initiatives and protecting parks, greenways, and open spaces. In addition, the statement emphasizes the importance of providing facilities and programs. The mission statement emphasizes fun, safe, and sustainable parks that enhance quality of life for individuals, neighborhoods, and communities.

PARKS AND RECREATION PROFESSIONALS AS PUBLIC SERVANTS

Public servants are those individuals who are involved in a government position usually based on merit. To be a public servant implies that one holds the public's welfare in trust. To be a public servant making the welfare of the community one's life work is viewed as a noble calling. Serving others is the highest vocation; individuals holding such responsible positions are empowered to enforce the organization's statutes, ordinances, codes, rules, and regulations. In more contemporary times, the parks and recreation professional as a public servant operates with integrity and excellence in a selfless, unselfish, generous, magnanimous, and self-effacing manner. He/she places concern for others above that of self.

The idea of government employees as merit-based public servants dates back to the Han dynasty in China. In the 18th century, the notion of civil service became an important element of the British Empire. Ultimately, a civil service system was established in the United States in 1871 for position in the government of the United States. In more contemporary times, the notion of the parks and recreation professional as a public servant has been adapted by Edginton, Hudson, Scholl, and Lauzon (2011) in discussing the works of Robert Greenleaf, who offers the idea of *servant leadership*. Greenleaf (1970) applies a theological perspective that to lead is to serve others first. Characteristics of servant leaders include the

Mission

The mission of the Chicago Park District is to:

- Enhance the quality of life in Chicago by becoming the leading provider of recreation   and leisure opportunities

- Provide safe, inviting and beautifully maintained parks and facilities

- Create a customer-focused and responsive park system that prioritizes the needs of children and families

Core Values

Children First. Our most important task is to bring children and families into our parks and give them great reasons to stay and play for a lifetime.

Best Deal in Town. We prioritize quality in our programs and accountability in our fiscal management to provide excellent and affordable recreation that invites everyone to come out and play.

Built to Last. We use our capital to renew our aging infrastructure and leverage partnerships that produce new parks and facilities that are forward-thinking and world class.

Extra Effort. We support innovation and welcome new ideas. We believe that professionalism, communication, technology, and team work serve as the foundation for great customer service and a productive workplace.

Figure 1.2. Chicago Park District Mission and Core Value Statement

willingness to listen, empathy, healing, awareness, persuasion, stewardship, commitment to the growth of others, and the building of community. As Greenleaf has written:

> The servant-leader is servant first....it begins with the natural feeling that one wants to serve, to serve first. Then conscious choice brings one to aspire to lead... The difference manifest itself in the care take by the servant—first to make sure that other people's highest priority needs are being served. The best test and the most difficult to administer, is, Do those served grow as people? Do they, while being served, become healthier, wiser, freer, more autonomous, more like themselves to become servants? And what is the effect on the least privileged in society; will they benefit or, at least not be further deprived? (1970, 1991, p. 7)

An important role of the community parks and recreation professional as a public servant is that of serving as an advocate. To be an advocate is to be a champion for others, advancing their interests and concerns. One can think of an advocate as an individual who works on behalf of a cause, in this case, the provision of high-quality parks and recreation services that are meaningful and relevant to those individuals to whom the programs areas

Our Vision

Indy Parks will be a national model of excellence and destination or facilities and programs, protecting parks, greenways, and open spaces and championing environmental initiatives.

Our Mission

Create, fun, safe, engaging, and sustainable parks that enhance the quality of life for individuals, neighborhoods, and communities.

Our Values

We are committed to public and employee safety. We strive to provide outstanding public service.

We support preservation of natural areas.

We encourage healthy living.

We cultivate and foster partnerships.

We are committed to professionalism, integrity, respect, and honesty.

We value stewardship and fiscal responsibility.

Figure 1.3. City of Indianapolis Parks and Recreation Department Vision, Mission, and Values Statement

and facilities are directed. At times, the parks and recreation professional as an advocate not only supports or promotes the interest of others, but also defends the same. Other roles of the community parks and recreation professional involve assisting individuals in solving their own problems; as such, they often act as an enabler, catalyst, coordinator, teacher, analyst, fact gatherer, and value clarifier (Edginton, Hudson, Dieser, & Edginton, 2004).

Community parks and recreation professionals often operate from a humanistic perspective. Such a philosophical perspective suggests that human nature is basically good. The focus of professionals employing this philosophical orientation would work to assist individuals and communities to focus on their strengths rather than their weaknesses. Further, a humanistic perspective advances the idea that human relations and interactions are of great value. This is central in many community parks and recreation programs as they provide opportunities for building civility, respect, graciousness, and reverence for others, and perhaps even for environmental resources. As choice is a central element in pursuing the leisure experience, humanists also understand and promote the idea that there are responsibilities that come from making decisions about one's leisure. Further, humanists advance the idea that there are differences in the way people may pursue their interests, but that it is important to respect and value the differences the exist in race, ethnicity, socioeconomic standing, beliefs, and culture. Such differences are to be celebrated and valued.

WHY PARKS AND RECREATION SERVICES MOVE PEOPLE

Parks and recreation services provide a critical role in enhancing the well-being and quality of life of individuals. The type, number, and options of recreation programs and services as well as the accessibility of greenspaces enhance the community in a very dramatic fashion. Parks and recreation services, according to Edginton and Chen (2014), promote "leisure-oriented themes, influence the promotion of the sustainable environment, provide opportunities for civic engagement, and encourage the social and cultural life of individuals" (p. 85). Such livable communities are often "well organized, designed, and planned in such a way as to promote a higher standard of living and great quality of life" (p. 85). They promote a sense of belonging through the provision "amenities, resources, and opportunities to experience leisure" (p. 85).

Drawing on the work of a well-known theory of motivation offered by Fredrick Herzberg, Edginton has depicted in Figure 1.4 what types of community services motivate people. Herzberg, utilizing Maslow's hierarchy of needs, has suggested that human needs can be placed on a continuum in two categories: hygiene factors and motivators. *Hygiene factors* refer to one's need for security, safety, and status. When these are not present in the environment, it creates dissatisfaction for individuals and the community. However, the presence of hygiene factors does not guarantee satisfaction in one's life or well-being. On the other hand, *motivators* refer to such factors as recognition, engaging and worthwhile

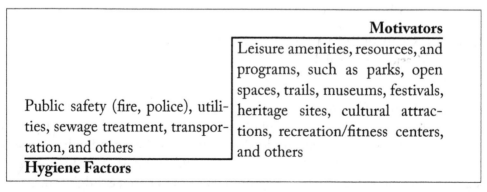

Figure 1.4. What Community Services Motivate People? *Source:* Edginton (2000)

opportunities, and opportunities for self-actualization. These factors can create satisfaction in one's life.

Edginton (2000) and Edginton and Chen (2014) have applied the Herzberg Hygiene-Motivation Model to a variety of services that may be found in a given community. For example, services that can be viewed in Figure 1.4 that can be thought of as hygiene factors include police, fire, sewage treatment, and transportation. When such services are missing in a community, people are dissatisfied and the livability of the community is disrupted. They are not motivators that lead to greater satisfaction in one's life or community. On the other hand, leisure amenities, or parks and recreation services programs and resources, including parks, open spaces, trails, museums, festivals, heritage sights, cultural attractions, and fitness/recreation centers produce greater satisfaction with one's life and are highly motivating to individuals.

WHAT IS A COMMUNITY?

To understand one's role as a parks and recreation professional operating within a local setting whether it be in a city, county, or within a special district, it is important to understand what constitutes a community. As a community-wide leader, the parks and recreation professional must be attuned to the needs, attitudes, and interest of those he/she serves. One must be knowledgeable of the characteristics or demographics of the community, its challenges and history. Further, it is important to gain a perspective of a community's culture—the ways in which people communicate, interact with one another, and build relationships between and among individuals and groups.

One can think of a community as a group of people who share a common interest, perspectives, and values. Community also implies a sense of place, a locality within which people live in proximity to one another, and/or are connected to one another in some fashion, even if it is an electronic one. Communities often emerge as individuals being connected socially, culturally, religiously, ethnically, or through some other characteristic. Communities often reflect the fact that harmonious bounds between people have emerged to define their interactions and behaviors. Smith (2001) has suggested that a community can be defined in three different ways as follows:

- **Place.** Territorial or place community can be seen as where people have something in common, and this shared element is understood geographically. Another way of naming this is as "locality."
- **Interest.** In interest of "elective" communities, people share a common characteristic other than place. They are linked together by factors such as religious belief, leisure interest, occupation, or ethnic origin.
- **Sense of Belonging.** Communities create a sense of belonging for individuals. They assist in helping individuals build their social capital (Putnam, 2000); that is, they serve as a form of communication and linking individuals together. They provide meaning to individuals in their lives.

All three of these ways of looking at community can be linked to one another. Certainly a place can provide a sense of belonging to an individual or facilitate their interest. It is interesting to note that community parks and recreation services all support the idea of community and the above-mentioned ways of viewing this concept. Parks and recreation areas and facilities create opportunities for individuals to share common experiences. Shared leisure interest joins people together around common community experiences whether it is participation in a club or festival or other social or cultural activity. Last, community parks and recreation programs and services develop opportunities for developing a sense of belonging.

WHY ARE COMMUNITY PARKS AND RECREATION AN ASSET?

An asset can be thought of as a community resource of social, cultural, economic, or environmental value. Communities across North America often advance their assets as a way of advertising the livability of their community, including its leisure amenities, such as green space and recreation programs and services for all ages. Community governmental parks and recreation departments, as well other nongovernmental organizations that provide similar types of programs, are often viewed as mainstays of government services and well in evidence among the nongovernment sector. Such programs and services are deemed to contribute to promoting higher quality of life and enriching and enhancing community well-being.

Too often, communities focus on their problems or deficits rather than building on their assets. Although every community has challenges, it is perhaps more important to find a way to build on the assets. Community parks and recreation services definitely can be viewed as an asset and often a viable and rich strength that may be employed to improve community life. Some of the ways in which community parks and recreation can be viewed as an asset are listed below.

Leadership

Community parks and recreation organizations include highly skilled professional individuals who can work to distill a focus or attention on a community concern, build partnerships, establish creative ways of addressing problems, building networks and engaging community resources to solve social, cultural, economic, and environmental challenges. In addition, parks and recreation departments assist in the organization of specialized groups of individuals or bodies to address particular areas of interest or concern. For example, it would not be unusual for a parks and recreation department to support the organization of an arts council, youth council or senior citizens group.

Areas and Facilities

Community parks and recreation organizations develop, build, and maintain a wide variety of leisure resources both physical structures and spaces. One can only think of the parks, open spaces, hiking and bike trails, pathways, greenways, wetlands, golf courses, playgrounds, gardens, botanical gardens, arboretums, grasslands, prairies, forest reserves, and common areas (such as plazas and squares). There are many recreation facilities associated with community parks and recreation organizations, including recreation centers, swimming pools, fitness centers, picnic shelters, nature centers, skateboard parks, boating facilities, fishing piers and platforms, museums, heritage/historical sights, shooting ranges, sport and playing fields, and many others.

Programs and Services

A wide array and scope of programs and services are offered by community parks and recreation services in a variety of different formats. Some of the program areas that are often associated with community parks and recreation departments include visual arts, graphic arts, and preforming arts; literary activities; aquatics; sports, games, and athletics; outdoor recreation; social recreation; self-improvement/educational activities; wellness activities; hobbies; travel and tourism; volunteer services; and festivals and special events.

Targeted Community Services

Parks and recreation departments often target their programs and services in such a way as to address the needs of a specific population. For example, there are few parks and recreation departments that don't offer services for senior citizens, early childhood education programs, or to disadvantaged or disabled populations. Youth programs are also targeted services offered historically by parks and recreation departments. Further, community parks and recreation departments often address in partnership with other community agencies programs for recycling and reuse of environmental resources.

Leisure Education Programs

Community parks and recreation departments serve as a major vehicle for educating the public regarding leisure. As Edginton and O'Neill (2010) have noted, "helping individuals make choices about their parks and recreation experiences often involves providing them with the background for such decision-making"; they further offer that "people need appropriate skills, knowledge, and attitudes to enjoy a given parks and recreation experience at its fullest" (p. 172).

Parks and recreation departments and their professional staff work to develop these assists engaging in whatever is needed to support the vision, mission, and goals of the department. Often such work involves assisting in identifying community assets and involving individuals and groups in program provision, especially working as volunteers. It is important to view the entire community as an asset and recognize that as Hampton and Heaven (2015) note, "everyone in a community can be a force for community improvement," and further offered, "every single person has capacities, abilities, and gifts. Living a good life depends on whether those capacities can be used, abilities expressed, and gifts given."

BUILDING COMMUNITY LIVABILITY

Central to the work of the parks and recreation profession is the building of the livability of the community. In fact, it could be argued that we are losing our sense of community. As Putnam (2000) argues, the involvement in community activities, organizations, and events has declined dramatically over the last several decades. He calls this a loss of social capital. Such social capital builds relationships among community members and is important in advancing cohesion and social support for the vitality of the community. Social capital also enables community development in terms of understanding the collective need for individuals to come to together to contribute to the life of the community. This is an important element in understanding the notion of community livability and its relationship to parks and recreation services.

Community livability is challenging to define, and as Edginton (2000) has noted,

The idea of livability is more difficult to define and perhaps even understand. Livability is often views from an individual, subjective perspective. Livability can be thought of as '...life that can be lived.' The term also refers to life that is fit or pleasant to live, habitable, or agreeable by nature. To live is to be alive, to have a joyful, pleasant, agreeable life. (p. 30)

The idea of livability is one of working to reenergize our sense of community and relationships with one another. "Community implies commonness—a life that is lived in association with others often with shared or compatible interest, values, and needs...a community is a place where people with common interest live, play, and work" (p. 31). In this sense, parks and recreation programs, services, and areas and facilities are important assets that contribute to building community life. Community livability at the turn of the century was also known as the "sociability" of community life. According to Rodgers, writing in *Atlantic Social Politics in a Progressive Age* (1998), the "Germans sought public leisure: the concert halls and outdoor musicals, the parks, the strange and alluring atmosphere of the open-air beer gardens; in effect, the Germans had created a culture of public enjoyment" (p. 88).

How do parks and recreation services contribute to community livability? A framework developed by the Nations in Bloom project (1999) suggests a number of components that are useful in promoting greater community liability. We refer to these as the *livability mix*. Components are discussed below.

Environmentally Sensitive Practices

We can think of such practices as ones in which sustainable environmental concerns are addressed. Not only is this reflected in the conservation and preservation of natural resources but also in the way in which we deal with other land, air, and water concerns. Parks and recreation departments have historically been champions of environmentally sensitive practices by providing greenspaces. Further, parks and recreation agencies have often led the charge to prevent degradation of the environment through the provision of educational programs and practices that protect environmental resources.

Enhancement of Community Attractiveness

The beautification of the community is another important role played by parks and recreation departments. Appealing landscapes, tree-lined streets, public street sculptures, art in public places, and other strategies for beautifying a community often are programs of community parks and recreation departments. Programs that emphases cleaning up a community are often ones that are organized and promoted by parks and recreation departments. Such activities often require the organization of volunteers to participate in such activities and the local parks and recreation department is a major vehicle for drawing together resources.

Opportunities for Leisure and Cultural Appreciation

Community parks and recreation departments are a major source creating opportunities for leisure and cultural appreciation. A wide array of programs, services, areas, and facilities that are accessible and affordable offer the foundation for opportunities. It is especially important that programs serve all age groupings and categories of individuals spanning from children to seniors. It is important that individual interests and values be represented in the leisure and cultural leisure opportunity offerings by community parks and recreation departments. Further, it is important to offer programs that range on a continuum from casual, informal drop-in programs to ones that are highly structured.

Programs that Provide Opportunities for Involvement of People

Parks and recreation services provide a means for individuals to be involved in the decisions that influence their lives. When programs emphasize a community development orientation wherein programs are self-directed activities, there is a greater opportunity for individuals to be involved. Further, parks and recreation programs provide many volunteer opportunities. Serving as a coach, befriending/mentoring, serving as an instructor, teaching/tutoring, helping youth find their voice, supporting the planning, organization, and implementation of large scale community events and festivals, leading outdoor education/recreation programs, trips, tours, and others.

Heritage Management

Communities can profit by preserving historical buildings and other cultural resources. As Edginton (2000) has noted, heritage management "provides a foundation for the community and a sense of who we are as individuals and as a community" (p. 38). History draws us together into a common heritage that can be shared. Not only does the preservation of historic buildings and cultural resources serve to advance the concept of community, it also provides an opportunity to celebrate the diversity of a place. Often communities are made up of divergent racial and ethnic groupings and supporting the historical and cultural heritage of these groups helps preserve and enhance their value to the community.

STRATEGIES USED IN COMMUNITY ORGANIZATION

In meeting social, cultural, and economic leisure needs, public parks and recreation agencies garner resources from society and provide leisure programs, services, areas, and facilities. Edginton, Hudson, Dieser, and Edginton (2004) have commented that there are four strategies that can be used by public parks and recreation departments in organizing community resources. These are *social planning, community development, social marketing,* and *social action*. Each of these strategies is built on a different set of assumptions in terms of goals, orientation to participants, professional roles, and basic strategies. The following is a brief summary of the aforementioned strategies.

Social Planning

Social planning is a rational and logical task-oriented strategy wherein the knowledge and expertise of the professional is used to plan and organize services. The basic strategy is one of fact finding to meet the community needs. The professional serves as a program planner and implementer. Participants are viewed as individuals who consume what professional diagnose for them to meet their needs and interest. Social planning is very similar to social marketing, which will be discussed in Chapter 7.

Community Development

Community development is built on the assumption that participants can serve as partners in the process of determining their leisure interest and needs. Basically, community development rests on the assumption that professionals can teach the processes that participants can utilize to plan, organize, and implement services. The professional serves as an enabler, catalyst, teacher, and value clarifier. The focus of the professional in dealing with community members is to assist them in thinking about the development of the community as well as developing their leadership skills and abilities. Commentary regarding community development is found in Chapters 1, 6, and 10.

Social Marketing

Social marketing is built on the assumption that the professional should work to satisfy participant needs. The goal of social marketing is to know and understand the participant's needs so well that services presell themselves. Much like social planning, the professional serves as an analyst, planner, promoter, and implementer. The professional works to adjust the traditional marketing mix of product, price, place, and promotion. We have added a fifth item to this mix—partnerships. Chapter 7 provides greater detail on the concept of social marketing.

Social Action

Social action is a strategy that addresses the needs of disadvantaged populations with an eye toward addressing issue of social inequality and injustice. The goal of social action is one of attempting to shift power through the distillation of issues. Professional roles include serving as an advocate, broker, agitator, negotiator, and/or organizer. Chapter 16 addresses some of the issues in dealing with disadvantaged populations.

Social Policy

Social policy is a strategy that attends to the improvement of a community's social and environmental well-being and welfare. Often parks and recreation professionals work to prevent or remedy challenges, such as environmental degradation, including air, water, and land pollution; delinquency; crime; childhood and adult obesity; or in a positive light, the need to improve community livability, beautification, greening, and its quality of life. In this strategy, the parks and recreation professional works to gather information, facts, and resources that can be used to craft and shape social policy so that boards of directors that are policy driven may act to address community problems and concerns. Chapters 3, 4, 12, and 16 address how parks and recreation can increase the well-being of society.

In this book we have emphasized the community development strategies as a way of gaining insight into the leisure needs and interests of the participants as well as the way in which community resources are utilized.

THE ORGANIZATION OF COMMUNITY PARKS AND RECREATION

There are three primary forms of government organization at the local level that enable the provision of public parks and recreation services. The most common form of organization is when parks and recreation services are a part of the municipal government of a city, town, or village. In the United States, there are over 10,000 cities, nearly 4,500 towns, and over 3,500 villages. Each one of these forms of municipal government may have some type of parks and recreation department or may provide related services. For example, public works departments may assume the responsibility for the maintenance of park areas, especially in smaller communities. The second form of organization for parks and recreation services is that which finds a county assuming the responsibility. In the United States there are 3,000 counties. Last, there are special governmental districts—park districts, or park and recreation districts—that provide parks and recreation services exclusively within some geographic area of jurisdiction.

Recreation and Parks as Part of a Municipal Government

Municipal governments make up the most common form of government in the United States. It is the government at the local level that is closest to the people being served. Its authority is derived from state statutes or codes that outline its authority and powers. Municipal governments often assume the responsibility of providing parks and recreation services. Expenditures for parks and recreation account for slightly over 2.1% of total local government spending. This amount has not changed dramatically in the last 15 years or so (U.S. Census Bureau, n.d.).

Recreation and Parks as a Part of County Government

Counties are another form of local government. They represent attempts to bring government close to people. County functions include assessing and collecting property taxes, registering voters, offering law enforcement, and record keeping. Counties are increasingly engaged in providing social or human services, including those related to parks and recreation, libraries, museums, and stadiums. The Henderson County (North Carolina) parks and recreation department offers a full range of recreation activities, including the operation of the Henderson County Athletics and Activity Center (HCAAC).

Recreation and Parks Operating as a Special District

Special purpose districts are independent governmental units that operate separately from other municipal or county governments. Such special districts operate within a designated geographic area, are governed by an independent board of directors, and have their own taxing and fiscal powers. Special districts are focused on specifically designed service areas. What makes a special district unique is the fact that it can focus its energies and attention toward a specific type of service, such as parks and recreation. The Bloomington (California) Recreation and Park District was established in 1972 by an act of the San Bernardino Board of Supervisors. The district maintains two community parks, an equestrian arena, sports fields, and a community center. The District also offers a summer swim program. As Bollens (1957) offers, special districts are

> ...organized entities, possessing a structural form, an official name, perpetual succession, and the rights to sue and be sued, to make contracts, and to obtain and dispose of property. They have officers who are popularly elected or are chosen by other public officials. They have a high degree of public accountability. Moreover, they have considerable fiscal and administrative independence from other governments. The financial and administrative criteria distinguish special districts and other governments from all dependent or subordinate districts and from most authorities which, lacking one or both of these standards, are not governmental units. (p. 1)

Home Rule Legislation

In various states throughout the United States, local subdivisions of government are provided with opportunity to organize their governance structure within their own administrative area. In other words, their administrative structure can be decentralized in such a way as to meet the particular needs of their community. Thus, various forms of organization and governance may emerge to provide parks and recreation services.

The basis for the authority to operate parks and recreation services as a part of a municipality, county, or as a special district is derived from state statutes and codes. Such statutes and codes are referred to as *enabling legislation*. This legislation gives appropriate officials the authority to implement services. The El Cerrito Park (California) and Recreation Commission draws its powers from municipal code section 2.04.240, which states that there shall be a parks and recreation commission, and its duties will include (1) to act in an advisory capacity to the council and the city manager on all matters pertaining to public recreation, including parks, playgrounds, landscaping within the boundaries of parks, playgrounds, and recreational facilities, child care, educational courses, and entertainment; (2) to make recommendations regarding the annual budget, within its scope of concern, to the city manager and the council; (3) To make recommendations to the council annually concerning fees for city-sponsored programs; (4) To assist in planning recreation programs for the residents of the city, to promote public interest therein, and to solicit the cooperation of other public and private agencies; and (5) To make recommendations to the council regarding present and future needs for parks and recreation facilities. In this case, the commission is operating an advisory capacity, and its authority comes from powers derived from the city council.

In the state of Iowa, Chapter 350 provides legislation that authorizes the establishment of county conservation boards. The purposes of Chapter 350 are to create a county conservation board and to authorize counties to acquire, develop, maintain, and make available to the inhabitants of the county, public museums, parks, preserves, parkways, playgrounds, recreational centers, forests, wildlife, and other conservation areas, and to promote and preserve the health and general welfare of the people, to encourage the orderly development and conservation of natural resources, and to cultivate good citizenship by providing adequate programs of public recreation. For example, the Black Hawk County (Iowa) Conservation Board (BHCCB) was authorized by the people of the county at the general election in 1956 for the purpose of purchasing and developing land for parks, hunting, and fishing access, and other recreational use within the county. The Illinois Park District Code (70 ILCS 1205/) established by the Illinois General Assembly provides for a variety of powers including, but not limited to the following: (1) means for organizing; (2) the annexation of property; (3) election powers and duties of officers; (4) taxing powers; (5) general powers including those related to swimming pools, airports, tennis courts, zoos, recreation and facilities, and the operation and management of harbors.

SUMMARY

This chapter has included an exploration of the philosophical and foundational elements associated with community parks and recreation. A democratic notion related to the ideal of the public good, public parks and recreation has contributed over time to enhancing quality of life, livability of communities, and the health and well-being of individuals and groups. Public parks and recreation play a key role in assisting individuals in finding meaningfulness and relevance during their leisure. Without question, such organizations play a critical role in crafting community life through the provision of high-quality programs, services, and areas and facilities.

There are numerous benefits that come about as a result of the provision of community parks and recreation. Some of these include assisting individuals in finding joy and happiness in their lives, building a sense of social connectivity, unity, solidarity, connectedness, relatedness, and partnership building. Such programs nurture the human spirit. They provide hope for individuals; in fact as has been noted the profession is about building, creating, and developing hope. Further, public parks and recreation provide opportunities for beautification of the community and the preservation and conservation of open spaces.

A public servant's orientation is one wherein the public's welfare is the focus of one's work. Serving others, operating with integrity and excellence in a selfless, unselfish, generous, magnanimous, and self-effacing manner is the hallmark of a public servant's orientation. Also, parks and recreation professionals often operate from a humanistic perspective and serve as advocates. Their role is one of promoting critical inquiry. This suggests that the professional will find ways to address problems and concerns and in fact reconstruct social order to meet emerging needs. Over the last 150 years, parks and recreation professionals have engaged in a great deal of social entrepreneurship resulting in numerous social inventions such as parks, playgrounds, and recreation centers. Although such inventions may not be unique to the United States, they have been adapted to our society and culture.

A community is a place where people share a common interest, perspective, and values. Communities can be defined in different ways including (1) as a place, (2) as people sharing common interest, and (3) a form of communication and linkage that promotes a sense of belonging. Parks and recreation organizations provide many assets to a community. For example, they offer leadership, areas and facilities, programs and services, targeted community services, and leisure education programs. Central to a strong community orientation is that of building the livability of the community. In the United States, we are losing our sense of community, and parks and recreation services promotes the idea of building social capital through community development. There are a number of ways in which government organizations at the local level provide public parks and recreation services. Among these include (1) recreation and parks as part of a municipal government, (2) recreation and parks as a part of county government, and (3) recreation and parks operating as a special district.

DISCUSSION QUESTIONS

1. What is community life and how is the term "the soul of the community" related to that concept?
2. What is the relationship between community parks and recreation services and promoting life satisfaction, community livability, and one's health and well-being?
3. How do recreation resources reflect the democratic ideals of the public good?
4. What are some of the benefits of community parks and recreation services?
5. Why do parks and recreation services move people?
6. What is a community?
7. What assumptions must be considered when organizing community resources?
8. Compare and contrast social planning, community development, social marketing, and social action.
9. Why are parks and recreation are services an asset?
10. At the local level of government, how are parks and recreation services organized?

REFERENCES

Boelens, L. (2009). *The urban connection: An actor-relational approach to urban planning.* Rotterdam, The Netherlands: O10-Publishers.

Butler, G. (1976). *Introduction to community recreation* (5th ed.). New York, NY: McGraw Hill.

Crompton, J. L. (2013). The economic benefits of state and local parks. Town hall meetings. Retrieved from www. agrilifecdn.tamu.edu/cromptonrpts/files/2011/06/state-and-local.ppt

Dustin, D. L., McAvoy, L. H., Schultz, J. H. (2002). *Stewards of access/Custodians of choice: A philosophical foundation for the park and recreation profession* (3rd ed.). Urbana, IL: Sagamore.

Edginton, C. R. (Ed.). (2000). Community livability: A model for Iowa. In C. R. Edginton (Ed.), *Enhancing the livability of Iowa communities: The role of recreation, natural resource development, and tourism.* Cedar Falls, IA: The University of Northern Iowa.

Edginton, C. R., & Chen, P. (2014). *Leisure as transformation.* Urbana, IL: Sagamore.

Edginton, C. R., DeGraaf, D. G., Dieser, R. B., & Edginton, S. R. (2006). *Leisure and life satisfaction foundation perspectives* (4th ed.). New York, NY: McGraw-Hill.

Edginton, C. R., Hudson, S. D., Dieser, R.B ., & Edginton, S. R. (2004). *Leisure programming: A service-centered and benefits approach* (4th ed.). Boston, MA: WCB/McGraw-Hill.

Edginton, C. R., Hudson, S. D., Scholl, K. G., & Lauzon, L. (2011). *Leadership for recreation, parks, and leisure services* (4th ed.). Urbana, IL: Sagamore.

Edginton, C. R., & O'Neill, J. (2010). Program and service management. In M. Moiseichik (Ed.), *Management of park and recreation agencies* (3rd ed.) Ashburn, VA: National Recreation and Parks Association.

Greenleaf, R. K. (1970, 1991). *The servant as leader.* Indianapolis, IN: Robert K Greenleaf Center for Servant-Leadership.

Hampton, C., & Heaven, C. (2015). Understanding and describing the community. In Assessing community needs and resources: Community tool box. Retrieved from http://ctb.ku.edu/en/table-of-contents/assessment/assessing-community-needs-and-resources/describe-the-community/main

Lewis, M. (2007). How cities use parks for economic development. Washington, D.C. American Planning Association. Retrieved from https://www.planning.org/cityparks/briefingpapers/economicdevelopment.htm

National Recreation and Park Association. (2017). About NRPA. Retrieved from http://www.nrpa.org/About-National-Recreation-and-Park-Association/

Putnam, R. D. (2000). *Bowling alone: The collapse and revival of American community.* New York, NY: Simon & Schuster.

Rodgers, D. T. (1998). *Atlantic crossings: Social politics in a progressive age.* Cambridge, MA: The Belkamp Press of Harvard University Press.

Rosen, M. S. (1999, September). Nations in bloom: An international challenge. *International Federation of Park and Recreation Administration, 8, 9.*

Smith, M. K. (2001). 'Community' in the encyclopedia of informal education. Retrieved from http://www.infed.org/community/community.htm.

U.S. Census Bureau. State and Local Government Finances. (n.d.). Retrieved from http://www.census.gov/govs/www/estimate.html.

Chapter Two

History of Public Parks and Recreation

CHAPTER OBJECTIVES

- To build an awareness and appreciation for the history of the parks and recreation movement
- To understand the factors that influence the development of events as well as the contributions of individuals to the parks and reaction movements and institutions
- To gain specific knowledge of the development of selected large landscape parks and selected metropolitan parks and recreation systems
- To gain knowledge of people and events during the development of the recreation movement
- To understand contemporary developments in the parks and recreation movement

INTRODUCTION

Public parks and recreation has a storied and impressive history with many significant contributions that have served to shape and influence the profession as well as the country as a whole. Individuals such as Fredrick Law Olmsted, Jane Addams, Ellen Star Gates, Joseph Lee, Henry Curtis, Luther Gulick, and Charles Eliot all have contributed dramatically to changing the social, cultural, and political fabric of American society and its institutions. Each of these individuals has in one way or another been responsible for the development of programs and/or facilities of historical significance. Their work brought hope to others and inspired the nation as a whole by providing model developments that could be replicated in other settings facing similar conditions or challenges. Many of these professionals were networked with one another crossing paths in their professional careers and activities.

The focus of the conversation is on the history of community or public parks and recreation. This movement, starting on the east coast of the United States, ultimately spread throughout the entire nation. Public parks and recreation has a rich history worthy of examination. An understanding of the past is valuable in gaining insights into the development of the profession. As is often said, one has to understand the past in order to shape the future. As George Santayana has noted, "Those who cannot remember the past are condemned to repeat it." By understanding the causes of various social, cultural, and political developments from a historical perspective, one may gain a greater appreciation of the future potential consequences of one's actions. In many ways, the past and the present are linked together and even perhaps the future if one can apply historical lessons.

Following is a discussion of the historical evolution of municipal parks, metropolitan/comprehensive park systems, settlement houses/recreation centers, playgrounds, and professional societies and associations. An effort will be undertaken to identify noteworthy individuals and events who have contributed to the historical evolution of the movement. As indicated, the history of public parks and recreation is a rich one worthy of investigation.

FACTORS INFLUENCING THE HISTORICAL DEVELOPMENT OF PARKS AND RECREATION

Toward the middle and end of the 1800s and into the 1900s, there was tremendous economic conflict and social disorder in the United States. The social and economic lives of people and the 60-hour work week created little opportunity for people to enjoy their lives and enhance their well-being through their recreational and leisure pursuits. Further, urbanization led to the swelling of populations in cities. The mass movement of individuals from rural communities into urban environments created the need for social and political reform to address emerging social, cultural, and economic conditions. For many, urban life was drab, as they were crowded into poor housing and slum tenements. Overcrowding, poor sanitation, and the lack of open space and recreation facilities all contributed to the need for social reform.

Many of the aforementioned challenges emerged as American society was transitioning from the agricultural era to the industrial society. This transformation required new ways of thinking, new strategies, and social inventions to address the needs of people as society moved from one era to another. The lack of play spaces, open areas, and ways in which public recreation structures could be provided all contributed to the need for social reform. In this period of time, especially in the late 1800s, a number of reform movements emerged. This period in American history is known as the *progressive era*. Many individuals critiqued societal conditions and offered suggestions about the way in which schools, government services, and living conditions could be improved. As Edginton and Chen (2014) have suggested,

> The…profession as we know it today emerged from the civic efforts that were employed [to address the need for social reform]…a parallel to this movement and as an extension of its efforts to provide common areas has been the development of parks and open space at the local…level…The concept of public open spaces emerged in the late 1800s. (p. 126–127)

Among the most notable individuals offering critique was social reformer and muckraking journalist Jacob Riis (Figure 2.1). His essay entitled, *How the Other Half Lives: Studies Among the Tenements of New York,* appeared in 1890 following the publication of an essay that appeared in *Scribner's* magazine in 1889. Riis drew attention to the plight of immigrants living in squalid conditions of destitution and despair (Stivers, 2000, p.18). He was able to draw into his circle of influence future president Theodore Roosevelt, who at the time was the president of the board of commissioners of the New York City police department.

It was in these social and cultural conditions that the public parks and recreation movement emerged. Stivers (2000) argues that there were two distinct areas of municipal reform that emerged during this period of time. She characterizes one category as "Bureau Men" and the other as "Reform Women" (p. 16). Bureau men were engaged in the application of scientific management techniques to the administration of city government. They chiefly saw city government as a business and sought to find structural reforms and systems to reform government. Their goal was to objectify the work of government, thus making it more efficient. They worked to systematize (budgeting), centralize executive control and neutralize (politics-administration dichotomy). Bureau Men saw themselves as individuals with the expertise to address problems, and the role of citizens was one of providing oversight to their activities. The countervailing perspective offered by Reform Women was to focus on improving living conditions and seeing the city as a home and citizens as neighbors to be involved in decision-

Figure 2.1. Jacob Riis. *Source:* Wikipedia (2016)

making processes. Their focus was on building new programs and social innovations to solve problems. Their prospective of administration was one of humanizing processes, linking agencies to people, and using discretionary judgment.

Leaders in our field and significant programs of social reform emerged out of these perspectives. For example, the New York Bureau of Municipal Research, which ultimately offered significant new methods of budgeting and openness in government, emerged to confront the politics of New York City's corrupt political machine Tammany Hall. One of its early leaders was Robert Moses, who later gained fame for his construction of parks and for the establishment of regional park commissions in New York. In fact, Moses was responsible for drafting the enabling legislation that allowed for such entities to exist. On the other hand, Reform Women were reflected in the work of such individuals as Jane Addams and Ellen Gates Starr (See Figures 2.2 and 2.3). They provided an alternative method to address the ills of industrialization and urbanization by organizing beautification programs, creating settlement houses, and examining other issues of the time. Their efforts aimed at public advocacy ranged from the local to the national level (p. 55).

Between the early 1850s and early 1900s, several significant social inventions emerged in the area of public parks and recreation. The first was that of large-scale landscape architecture city park as reflected in the development of Central Park in New York City. The second was the establishment of settlement houses, which was reflected in the development of Stanton Coit's neighborhood guild on New York City's lower east side in 1886. This was followed by the establishment of Hull House which was located in South Halsted Street in

Figure 2.2. **Jane Addams.** *Source:*
Biography.com (2014)

Figure 2.3. **Ellen Starr Gates.**
Source: Women in the Progressive
Era (n.d.)

Chicago in the same year. The playground movement was initiated in 1885 in Boston, Massachusetts, where the Boston Sand Gardens were organized. Further, in 1892, the Boston Park Commission established a metropolitan park system under the leadership of Charles Eliot. Also, Jens Jensen championed the establishment of a metropolitan park system for Chicago in 1904 which today is known as the Cook County Forest Preserve System. The first system of recreation centers (Field Houses and Public Baths) was established by the South Side Park District in Chicago in 1905.

MUNICIPAL PARKS

The concept of municipal parks in the United States is a relatively new phenomenon. Doell and Fitzgerald (1954) suggest that the "municipal park" was a late development and primarily used for multipurpose utilitarian purposes (p. 24). Parks or other open areas or spaces were identified as commons, plazas, squares, and or marketplaces. For example, the Santa Fe (New Mexico) Plaza was established in c. 1610 and served originally as a presidio, and included residents, barracks, a chapel, a prison, and government offices. In 1634, Boston established a commons area that was used for the grazing of animals, the quartering of soldiers, and today ultimately for recreation purposes. The Boston commons is often referred to as the oldest city park in America. In Canada, the Commons of Halifax is often referred to as the country's oldest park, founded in 1749.

In 1682, William Penn designated five open squares in the plan for Philadelphia that was developed by Surveyor General Thomas Holme. These squares were to be utilized for public affairs. Savannah, Georgia, included plans for markets, public gardens, and forest trees. General James Oglethorpe, the founder of the colony of Georgia, in visiting the city in 1736, was "greatly please by the public gardens, which comprised ten acres of undulating ground in a delightful situation near the river" (p. 25). The original plan for Savannah called for 24 small squares and open spaces in addition to the public squares and commons. When plans for Washington D.C. were developed by Major Pierre Charles L'Efant in 1736, his vision included a city with "spacious public parks, squares, fountains, walks and broad, tree-lined avenues" (LaGasse

& Cook, 1965, p. 9). In 1732, plans called for the development of parks in the Dutch colony on New Amsterdam, later known as New York City. At the time there was not a great deal of open space, and one such area, known as the Bowling Green Fence and Park, was set aside as open space. Today this space remains and has been used for various purposes, including serving as a cattle market, parade ground, and other recreational purposes since 1638. The last early development was the provision of a park at Fort Dearborn in 1839 in Chicago. Later this area became part of Grant Park, a large urban park located near the center of Chicago.

Central Park, New York City

The idea of a large landscape park in New York City was first introduced by William Cullen Bryant. Bryant, a journalist, was a strong advocate for a park in Central Manhattan. At the time, Andrew Jackson Downing, editor of the *Horticulturist,* was advocating for the development of public parks and gardens following visitations to Europe in the mid-1950s. The concept for Central Park was advanced to New York's common council in 1851, and acquisition of land proceeded between 1853 and 1856. Initially the governance of the park was handled by a board of commissioners, consisting of the mayor and the street commissioners. The first chief engineer of Central Park was a graduate of West Point, Egbert L Vielé. He developed a plan for the development of the park but was unable to accomplish much work. In 1857, Frederick Law Olmsted was named the superintendent of the park.

The Park Commissioners saw Central Park in the following light:

> While the Park is intended as a place for freedom and relaxation and for play and not for work, it has been constructed with no ideas of encouraging laziness or in any way the benefits of idlers and drones…its paramount objective is to offer facilities for a daily enjoyment of life to the industrious thousands who work steadily and continuously. (Miller, 2003, p. 18)

> The civic and business leaders of New York knew that a park was a defining characteristic of sophistication and culture. All the great cities of Europe had spacious public parks; London had Hyde Park, Regent's Park, and St. James Park; Paris had the Tuileries, the Jardin du Luxembourg, and the newly redesigned Bois de Boulogne. These parks had originally been properties of the crown, which had given the grounds over to the public beginning in the eighteenth century. Some New Yorkers asked themselves why these former monarchies did more for their subjects than their own republican form of government. (Miller, 2003, p. 19)

Olmsted is known as the father of landscape architecture. He had an enormous impact on not only the design of Central Park, but on other parks and public spaces throughout the United States and Canada. Olmsted was widely traveled, having journeyed to England to visit public gardens. He was particularly impressed with Birkenhead Park, designed by Joseph Paxton. Olmsted offered numerous articles that appeared in the *New York Daily Times* and prepared several books, including *A Journey in the Seaboard Slave States* (1856), *A Journey Through Texas* (1857), *A Journey in the Back Country in the Winter of 1853-1854* (1860), and a one-volume abridgment, *Journeys and Explorations in the Cotton Kingdom* (1861). During the Civil War, Olmsted directed the U.S. Sanitary Commission, which was a forerunner of the American Red Cross (See Figure 2.4).

Figure 2.4. **Frederick Law Olmsted.**
Source: Hall (1995)

Figure 2.5. **Calvert Vaux.** *Source:* Hall (1995)

In 1858, the Park Commission, following a competition, gave to Olmsted and his partner Calvert Vaux an award for further developing the resource (See Figure 2.5). As this was the first large public park in the United States, its design features would have a significant impact on the development of similar spaces in the United States. The landscape design of 778 acres when it was opened was called the "Greensward Plan." The development of the park involved 3,800 employees in 1859, and at the time was the largest public works project in the United States (See Figure 2.6). Olmsted's principles of design included the following: (1) Preserve the natural scenery and if necessary restore and emphasize it, (2) Avoid all formal design except in very limited areas without buildings, (3) Keep open lawns and meadows in large central areas, (4) Use native trees and shrubs especially in heavy border plantings, (5) Provide circulation by means of paths and roads laid in wide sweeping curves, and (6) Place the principal road so that it will approximately circumscribe the whole area. (Waugh, 1927) (See Figure 2.7).

Olmsted was also responsible for the development of many other park designs, parkways and many other recreation areas. Of particular note were his designs for Prospect Park in Brooklyn, the Buffalo park system (New York), Mount Royal (Montreal, Canada), and the Niagara Reservation at Niagara Falls. However, his work did not stop there, as he was involved in city planning (e.g., Riverside, Illinois), cemeteries, colleges, and school campuses, as well as private estates. Olmsted left a lasting legacy on the landscape of America. Olmsted designed parks and park systems in New York, California, Connecticut, New Jersey, Massachusetts, Illinois, Pennsylvania,

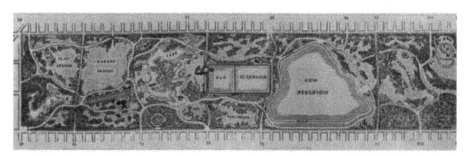

Figure 2.6. **Greensward-Olmsted and Vaux plan for Central Park.** *Source:* Clay (1972)

Michigan, Washington, DC, Rhode Island, Kentucky, Missouri, Wisconsin, and Quebec.

Over time, design concepts for parks changed dramatically. Over 100 years ago, the role was to bring the pastoral, idealized rural environment into the hectic city. The idea was to promote opportunities for contemplation, reflection, and a linkage to nature. Today this philosophy has been somewhat overcome. Doell and Fitzgerald (1954) state that as

Figure 2.7. Skating in Central Park. *Source:* Photographs of Old America (2009)

> Even the great masterpieces of idealized rural landscape created by Olmsted and others of the pioneers in park building had in many instances been transformed from places where 'city dwellers' could secure the genuine recreation coming from the peaceful enjoyment of an idealized rural landscape, to active recreation areas. Broad, open meadows had been appropriated for gold or baseball diamonds; the swift-moving automobile had usurped the pleasant carriage driveway, destroying the restful atmosphere of the area, and in some rare instances even the amusement devices of the commercial amusement park had even permitted entrance. In town parks had been appropriated either for children's playgrounds or for neighborhood playfields. (p. 36)

The idea of municipal parks has virtually gained universal acceptance across the United States. As Edginton, DeGraaf, Dieser, and Edginton (2002) have offered, park systems have expanded from a few communities to 100 systems in 1889 and then to 800 systems by 1902. Today, in the United States, there are over 3,000 park systems and many more parks. Without question, the works of Olmsted and Vaux had a tremendous impact on advancing this social invention, which was an expression of the American democratic ideal.

Golden Gate Park

The park movement spread across the continent in relatively short order. With the discovery of gold in California, San Francisco became an instant city. As Young (2004) notes, "…at least as early as 1854, San Franciscans began to grumble about the shortage of available green space in their swiftly expanding city"(p. 31). The initial plan for the city did not make provisions for a public park, only for small spaces. However, in contrast to New York City, San Francisco was not densely populated and had many open areas. By 1860, within the city, there were numerous small squares, plazas, parks, pleasure gardens, and private resorts. Thus, many of the citizens of the community felt there was a need to create a large public landscape park; however, the city was constrained by financial limitations.

In the mid-1860s, Fredrick Law Olmsted was employed as the manager of the Mariposa Estate, a gold mining company in and around Yosemite. Following the failure of the mining company and while remaining in Northern California, Olmsted designed a cemetery, grounds for the University of California, Berkley, and several private estates. During this time, Olmsted advocated for a large public park to be developed in San Francisco, arguing that the "…park would increase local prosperity, because real-estate values would rise; residents who might have moved away, 'particularly…citizens of wealth and large tax payers,' would remain; and new populations, 'particularly of wealthy citizens,' would be attracted" (Young, 2004, p. 46). Also, he argued that parks were especially valuable for women and children, as he suggested "a park was the place for all society to gather amicably" (p. 46). In 1866, Olmsted submitted a plan for an interconnected park system in San Francisco.

In 1868, the San Francisco Board of Supervisors began the process of discussing strategies for acquiring land and property to develop a large landscape park and interconnected park system that would be called "Golden Gate Park." This area ultimately included 1,017 acres, and is one of the largest public parks throughout the world (See Figure 2.8). Action started in earnest in 1870, when the San Francisco Park Commission called for bids to produce a land survey. The climatic conditions and coastal dunes of the area designated for the park presented a number of unique challenges. Olmsted and Vaux were solicited for advice and provided a design for the area. William Hammond Hall (See Figure 2.9), a young civil engineer, became the first superintendent for the park. Because of the topography, the new park required nearly 50,000 different tree and shrub plantings.

Figure 2.8. **Golden Gate Park.** *Source:* David Rumsey Map Collection (n.d.)

Figure 2.9. **William Hammond Hall.**
First Superintendent, Golden Gate Park.
Source: SFPix.com (n.d.)

By 1873, over 250,000 individuals visited the park. In 1875, these figures exceeded half a million visitors. Many visitors were able to visit the park by using the cable car system of San Francisco. The park included opportunities for people to bike, ride, and walk and relax. Many unique design features including a conservatory, lakes, formal gardens, children's playgrounds, Japanese tea garden, athletic fields (ultimately a stadium), tennis courts, temple of music, lawn bowling, rustic shelters, and paths and driveways. In 1894, Golden Gate Park was the site of the California Midwinter Exposition. Many structures were damaged or destroyed in Golden Gate Park as a result of the devastating earthquake that occurred in San Francisco in 1906.

John McLaren was appointed as the park superintendent in 1887. He had an enormous impact on the continued development of Golden Gate Park and was able to use his political skills as well as his knowledge of horticulture to advance his design and further development of the park area. He emphasized the use of natural elements in the park design. He "intentionally installed foliage that created a sense of eastern lushness to contrast with surrounding area's distinct aridity" (p. 168). He had millions of trees and forms of vegetation planted during his work as the superintendent of the park, and his design work was not limited to Golden Gate Park in San Francisco.

METROPOLITAN/COMPREHENSIVE PARK SYSTEMS

The plan included the designer's conception of Central Park as a part of a broader city plan for parks and greenspaces. As Doell and Fitzgerald (1954) offer from the Olmsted and Vaux plan,

The dominant and justifying purpose of Central Park was conceived to be that of permanently affording, in the densely populated central portion of an immense metropolis, a means to certain kinds of refreshment of the mind and nerves which most city dwellers greatly need and which they are known to derive in large measure from the enjoyment of suitable scenery. (p. 30)

This concept would later give way to the development of metropolitan interconnected park systems, such as those in Boston and Chicago. The work of Charles W. Eliot served to advance an interconnected park and open space system, which is known as the Boston Metropolitan Park System. In Chicago, the efforts of Jens Jensen resulted ultimately in the interrelated park, forest, and open spaces system that today is known as the Forest Preserve District of Cook County.

Boston Metropolitan Park System

The Boston Metropolitan Park System was initially established in 1893. Today the park system includes approximately 20,000 acres of parks, forest, river/ocean reservations, and parkways. It set into course the idea that parks and other spaces could be combined together into an integrated network. Charles W. Eliot was the chief advocate advancing this concept. Eliot saw the need for a new type of "public landscape; he suggested that there was a need for reservations, trusteeships, and rural landscape reservation…" (Morgan, 1999, p. x). His ideas were in contrast to his mentor and eventual partner Olmsted who emphasized "Green country parks, parkways, and pastoral retreats and places in which modern city dwellers could find spiritual replenishment through contemplation of nature" (Morgan, 1999 p. x). Elliot's work contrasted that of Olmsted, who emphasized large landscape parks, parkways, and pastoral venues that enabled individuals to engage in contemplation and spiritual regeneration (Morgan, 1999). Elliot's great genius was in seeing the need for reservations, trusteeships, and other types of landscapes reservations that reflected rural settings (Morgan, 1999).

The Boston Park Commission advanced the idea of creating a Metropolitan Park Commission. In petitioning the General court, they requested the following:

The undersigned petitioners respectfully represent that the seashores, the river-banks, the mountain-tops, and almost all the finest parts of the natural scenery of Massachusetts are possessed by private persons, whose private interest often dictate the destruction of said scenery or the exclusion of the public from enjoyment thereof. In the opinion of the undersigned, the scenes of natural beauty to which the people of the commonwealth are to-day of right entitled to resort for pleasure and refreshment are both too few in number and too small in area… (Doell & Fitzgerald, 1954, p. 34–35)

Building the rationale for the Metropolitan Park System (see Figure 2.10) was to expand public reserves so that they could include scenery that cut across regions or districts. As Eliot noted in his speech to his legislators (Doell & Fitzgerald, 1954),

The boundaries or our towns are very apt to bisect the prettiest passages of scenery, as where the line follows the channel of a river or brook the banks of which are beautiful. In these cases, it is at present practically certain that neither town would act to take the banks, for it would be senseless for one to act without the other, and one or the other is almost sure to feel that its burden of expense is out of proportion to the benefit to accrue to it. Under the park act, a board of park commissioners will seldom make open spaces near the boundary of their town or city, even though the best lands for the purpose are to be found there and even though a dense population

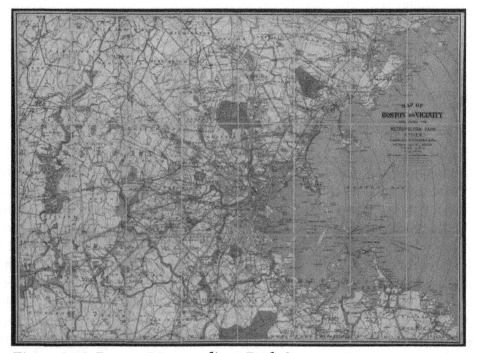

Figure 2.10. **Boston Metropolitan Park System.** *Source:* Digital Commonwealth (n.d.)

needs them there. Under the park act, no park board can take lands outside the arbitrary town boundary, ever though a fine site for a park lies adjacent to the boundary near their own center of population, and so remote from the population of the adjacent township that its park board will never want to buy or take the place. (p. 35)

Forest Preserve District of Cook County

The Forest Preserve District of Cook County operates nearly 70,000 acres in a network of open spaces that includes forest, prairies, wetlands, streams, and lakes. The forest preserve concept was initiated in 1911 for the purpose:

to acquire … and hold lands … containing one or more natural forests or lands connecting such forests or parts thereof, for the purpose of protecting and preserving the flora, fauna and scenic beauties within such district, and to restore, restock, protect, and preserve the natural forests and said lands together with their flora and fauna, as nearly as may be, in their natural state and condition, for the purpose of the education, pleasure, and recreation of the public. (p. 1)

In 1869, a plan was established for developing parks in a boulevard system in Chicago. This plan proposed linking together three independent commissions and there was a "… general feeling that proposed parks and parkways—a greenbelt throughout the city—would help boost Chicago's cosmopolitan character" (Grese, 1992, p. 29). Initially the influence of Olmsted and Vaux were felt as they were hired to develop designs for the area. Following this development and the implementation of the Columbian Exposition in 1893, Chicago pushed to be "The Capital of the Midwest" (p. 38). What followed in 1909 was what was known as Daniel Burnham and Edward H. Bennett's plan of Chicago. This plan called for ways to utilize the elements remaining from the Columbian Exposition, the need for new parks and ways to improve the lakefront.

In 1903, Jens Jensen offered a plan reflecting "a proposed system of forest parks and country pleasure roads" (Grese, 1992 p. 65) and one year later he proposed "a metropolitan park system for Chicago with interconnected parks/preserve lands, parkways and cemeteries" (Grese, 1992 p. 65). This enabled the establishment of an "outer park belt." His plan divided the Chicago metropolitan area into four areas. Jensen and his colleague Dwight Perkins advocated for the preservation of natural areas in Cook County. In 1904 they wrote,

Instead of acquiring space only, the opportunity exists for preserving country naturally beautiful. The bluffs and beaches along the Lake Shore, the Skokie, the North Chicago river valley, the Des Plaines Valley, Salt Creek, Flag Creek, Mt. Forest, the Sag Valley, Palos Heights, Blue Island Ridge, the Calumet River and Lake; all of these should be preserved for the benefit of the public in both the city and its suburbs, and for their own sake and scientific value, which, if ever lost, cannot be restored for generations…Another reason for acquiring these outer areas is the necessity of providing for future generations, which will extend to the borders of Cook County and intervening areas. (p. 63)

Figure 2.11 offers an illustration of the Forest Preserve System in the 1920s. Jensen's legacy is not only reflected in his landscape designs but also in the connection of spaces to create an environmental buffer. He was a strong advocate of insuring that individuals had access to nature for more passive forms of recreation (See Figure 2.12).

THE RECREATION MOVEMENT

At the turn of the century, an exploration of children's play was being undertaken. Authors such as Herbert Spencer, William James, Carl Groos, and G. Stanley Hall all offered theories of play; for example, Spence viewed play as surplus energy. These theories, while having little meaning for the average American, provided an underpinning to address the problems found in urban America. In particular, the tenement problem found people being packed into a single building and little play space being made available for children. Discussing the evolution of the play and recreation movement, Rainwater (1922) noted that,

At first the movement focused in the provision of common areas that were used for recreation. Later in the 1880s and early 1900s, there was great concern for the provision of play opportunities for children. This gave rise to a host of developments, including a provision for sand gardens, model playgrounds, small parks, recreation centers, and civic are and welfare that in turn led to neighborhood organizations that ultimately led to the organization of community-wider services... (p. 277)

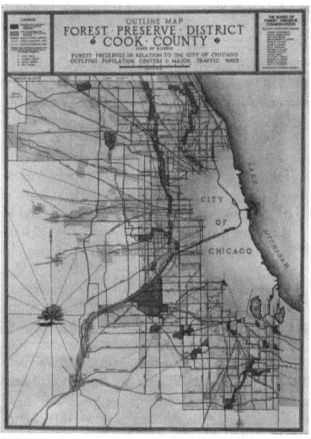

Figure 2.11. Forest Preserve District of Cook County map, circa late 1940s, early 1950s. *Source:* Vena (2013)

The Boston Sand Gardens, established in 1885, represent the initial effort at providing play spaces for children and generally speaking represent the beginning of the recreation movement. This development was supported through the efforts of the Massachusetts Emergency and Hygiene Association and was located in the yard of the children's mission on Parmenter street in Boston. Dr.

Figure 2.12. Jens Jensen. *Source:* Grese (1992)

Marie E. Zakrzewska "sent a letter describing the inexpensive sand piles used as highly effective play areas for children in the most congested parts of Berlin (German)" (Knapp, p. 20). Dr. Zakrzewska had traveled to America to work with Elizabeth Blackwell to establish the first women's and children's hospital in New York City. The Sand Gardens provided a focal point for children to engage in play and sing songs under the direction of women serving as volunteers. In a short period of time, the term *sand garden* was replaced with the term *playground*. In 1899, the Boston City Council provided financial support for the further development of playgrounds. In a short period of time, other cities throughout the United States developed playgrounds, including Baltimore, Brooklyn, Cleveland, Chicago, Denver, Milwaukee, Minneapolis, New York, Philadelphia, Pittsburgh, and Providence (Doell & Fitzgerald, 1954, p. 70).

In 1888, the city of New York passed a law that appropriated $1 million to acquire lands to develop playgrounds. Further, a state law was passed in New York in 1895 that decreed "Hereafter, no school house shall be constructed in the City of New York without an open-air playground attached to or used in connection with the same." The first municipally built playground occurred at Seward Park in 1903 and included surfacing, fences, recreation pavilion, and play and gymnastic equipment. In 1903, another significant development occurred in Chicago when voters of the South Side Park District passed a $5 million-dollar bond issue to support the acquisition and development of recreation resources. This development resulted in the crafting of large field houses "…which included gymnasiums, swimming pools, meeting halls, and club rooms" (Doell & Fitzgerald, 1954, p. 70). The development of these facilities created the opportunity of year-round programing and led to the extension of "drama, craft, club groups, and other interests" (p. 71). The indoor facilities were complemented with extensive outdoor resources including "playgrounds, athletic fields, bandstands, and outdoor swimming pools" (p. 71). This development served as a guidepost for park districts in the Chicago metropolitan area but also for other communities nationally. For example, in 1904, Los Angeles "created a board of playground commissioners and became the first city to administer recreation under a separate playground commission" (p. 71). By 1906, 41 cities noted having organized public recreation programs.

Of course, the training of playground leaders and or recreation professionals commenced soon after the establishment of playgrounds, field houses, and recreation centers. The major resource for the preparation of individuals was *The Normal Course in Play: Practical Material for Use in the Training of Playground and Recreation Workers* (1909). This training program was implemented in a variety of settings, including play institutes and colleges and universities. Clark W. Hetherington and Dr. Henry S. Curtis were responsible for providing leadership to a committee of 23 individuals who prepared the training materials. The purpose of the training program was "…to lay before the instructor [of the play course], in as vivid a way as possible the main facts about the play movement and program, its significance in the life of the community and individual, and the sources of information regarding it" (1926, p. v). The introduction of the book states that "it is the task of the instructor giving the course to adapt and interpret the material in a way which will make it most vital and will most effectively correlate it with other course which the educational institute offers. It was pointed out that correlating courses could include such study areas as psychology, sociology, child study, anthropology, civics, pedagogy, physical education, dramatics, and storytelling" (ibid).

Another significant development in the recreation movement was the establishment of settlement houses. The first being established by Stanton Coit on New York's lower east side in 1886 (Stivers, 2000). This short-lived experiment was followed in the same year by the establishment of Hull House by Jane Addams and Ellen Starr Gates in Chicago in 1889 (See Figure 2.13). "Addams and Starr, Coit, and a number of other Americans had visited Toynbee House (London, England), where they were stirred by the social action possibilities of living and working with poor people"(Stivers, 2000, p. 56). Settlement house activities were varied including many recreation programs and services as well as facilities such as playgrounds. For example, the grounds of Hull House included a model playground which was the first facility outside of the sand gardens established in 1893. Programs and services of the American settlement house movement usually included

Amateur dramatics, signing groups, art classes, and the like, but from the first, the settlers saw their primary mission as the development of an understanding of the conditions and causes of poverty, especially by the living with and learning from neighborhood residents themselves. By becoming neighbors of the poor, they would gradually become their friends; by sharing the experiences of the poor, they would be able to interpret neighborhood problems to those who currently did not understand them but might be able to make a difference. (p. 56)

Following this initial period of development, America moved to a wartime footing. During this period of time, the nature and scope of recreation programs expanded to meet the needs of entire communities across all age ranges and areas of interest. No longer was recreation viewed as a program only for children offered during the summer months only, a means of combatting juvenile delinquency and focused on games and sports. During World War I, the nation organized what was known as War Camp Community Services (See Figure 2.14). This was an effort at encouraging communities to garner their resources to provide recreation for military personnel. During the 1920s, there was a rapid expansion of pub-

---

In September of 1889, when Jane Addams, Ellen Gates Starr, and Mary Keyser opened Hull House in Chicago, these individuals had no idea what type of impact they would have on the play and recreation movement. Pioneers in community recreation, Hull House developed numerous original social, play, youth, and recreational programs. Among these include:

- Established first public playground in Chicago
- Established first baths in Chicago
- Established first public gymnasium in Chicago
- Established first little theater in Chicago
- Established first citizenship preparation course in Chicago
- Established first free arts exhibits in Chicago
- Established first public swimming pool in Chicago
- Established first Boy Scout troop in Chicago
- Developed first investigations in Chicago regarding social/recreational values of saloons, which eventually created coffee shops and recreation centers

Figure 2.13. Centennial Annual Report of the Hull House Foundation

lic recreation. President Calvin Coolidge called upon Americans to advance municipal as well as other ways of organizing public recreation. In 1924, Coolidge's "Conference on Outdoor Recreation" report offered 21 fundamentals for community recreation programs.

The 1930s and 1940s were depression years in the United States. Although resources were limited, many communities were able to expand their programs, areas, and facilities by working with the Works Progress Administration (WPA) (See Figure 2.15). The WPA brought to the attention of communities the attention of parks and recreation services. World War II again brought a focus on community recreation and the consolidation of services for industrial workers and military personnel. Following the war, there was an expansion of recreation systems nationwide. Programs for senior citizens became featured, and there was an effort to consolidate separate parks and recreation administrative entities into one integrated unit. The 1960s and 1970s have been referred to by Edginton et al. (2002) as the zenith of the movement. Great attention was paid to the further acquisition and development of parks and recreation resources. The Outdoor Recreation Resources Review Commission (ORRRC) drew national attention to recreation needs at all levels. Further developments for local, state, and federal resources were greatly enhanced by the passage of the Land and Water Conservation Fund Act in 1964. The 1960s were also a time of urban turmoil and riots following the assassinations of John Kennedy, Robert Ken-

Figure 2.14. War Camp Community Service Poster. *Source:* WWIPropaganda.com (2011)

Figure 2.15. Works Progress Administration Developed Swimming Pool, New York City, 1936. *Source:* NYCparks (n.d.)

Figure 2.16. Americans Outdoors. *Source:* President's Commission on Americans Outdoors (1987)

Figure 2.17. Commission for Accreditation of Park and Recreation Agencies logo. *Source:* NRPA (n.d.)

nedy, and especially Martin Luther King, Jr. The Kerner Commission report identified the lack of recreation as one of the main contributors to the riots. There were also tax revolts in the latter part of the 1970s, especially Proposition 13 in California, that encouraged parks and recreation systems to rethink their funding strategies.

In the 1980s and 1990s, the parks and recreation profession focused its energies on a benefits-based orientation and also adopted a program for accrediting local agencies. President Ronald Reagan's Commission on Outdoor Recreation Resources Reviews called for lighting a "prairie fire" at the local level to advance parks and recreation concerns: "Americans working together in their own communities will spark a renaissance of caring about our great outdoors" (See Figure 2.16). The Commission for Accreditation of Park and Recreation Agencies (CAPRA) was initiated in 1989 (See Figure 2.17). This accrediting body provides 10 basic categories of standards against which the effectiveness and efficiently of a parks and recreation system can be measured. As we have moved into the 21st century, significant changes in American society have occurred. People are now more place-bound, seeking community-focused leisure experiences; thus, the importance of community parks and recreation is bound to increase.

PROFESSIONAL SOCIETIES/ORGANIZATIONS

Several professional organizations, societies, and associations emerged as the parks and recreation movement developed. The first of these was the New England Association of Park Superintendents, which later became known as the American Institute of Park Executives (AIPE) in 1898. Initially this organization's membership was drawn from park superintendents, landscape architects and individuals supervising other large public horticultural areas. The memberships came from individuals practicing in Massachusetts, Rhode Island, and Connecticut. The organization was focused on (Doell & Fitzgerald, 1954):

The gathering and disseminating of facts and information with reference to public parks, gardens and other recreation grounds, facilities, and programs; to act with all people to make more abundant facilities for a more expressive life through recreation, and to engender a spirit of cooperation between all agencies related to our common cause. (p. 42)

APIE's official publication was known as *Parks & Recreation* and continues to be published to this day.

In 1906, the Playground Association of America was established with the endorsement of President Theodore Roosevelt. Luther Gulick was the first president, Jane Addams the second vice president, and Joseph Lee the third vice president of this organization. (See Figure 2.18) Joseph Lee became known as the "father of recreation" (See Figure 2.19). Later this organization changed its name to the Playground and Recreation Association of America in 1911. It later changed its name in 1935 to the National Recreation Association. This organization included citizens, professionals, and other interested parties who valued the advancement of the playground and recreation movement. The initial purpose of this organization was to (NRA, 1906),

> ...collect and distribute knowledge of and promote interest in playgrounds throughout the country. It shall also seek to further the establishment of playgrounds and athletic fields in all communities, and directed play in connection with the schools. It shall aim...to establish... a national Playground Museum and Library, which shall have models of every form of playground construction and apparatus, a library of all published books and articles relating to play, pictures of games and playgrounds throughout the world and an information department which shall furnish cities and towns with lecturers, pictures, articles, or advice on any phase of the work. (p. 30)

Figure 2.18. Luther H. Gulick, first president of the Playground Association of America. *Source:* National YMCA Hall of Fame, n.d.

In 1938, the Society of Recreation Workers of America was established. This group was comprised of recreation professionals from across the United States. In 1946, the name of the organization was changed to the American Recreation Society.

In 1965, the American Institute of Park Executives, the National Recreation Association, the American Recreation Society and several other professional organizations and associations came together to form the National Recreation and Park Association (NRPA). This merger consolidated the work of several organizations into a unified and concentrated effort to advance the recreation and park field. Today the organization continues to operate as a combined entity of laypersons and professionals. The mission of the organization is "To advance parks, recreation, and environmental conservation efforts that enhance the quality of life for all people." The vision of NRPA is to ensure that "Everyone will have easy access to parks and recreation opportunities in sustainable communities."

Figure 2.19. Joseph Lee, the "Father of Recreation" *Source: Play and Playground Encyclopedia,* n.d.

SUMMARY

The development of public parks and recreation emerged in the late 1800s early 1900s in response to the need for social reform. Conditions of this period found people in crowded slum environments with very poor sanitation and living conditions. Out of this emerged several social inventions, including playgrounds, parks, open spaces, settlement houses, and recreation centers. Two basic strategies addressed social and environmental problems. One approach was aimed at reforming city government, especially applying the principles of scientific management. This was reflected in the work of the New York Bureau of Municipal Research, which directed its efforts at reforming budgeting processes and establishing enabling legislation aimed at creating government entities to support parks and recreation services. The second approach was a more humanistic one and reflected in the crafting of programs and services focused on improving living conditions, care, and seeing the city as a home. This approach was more process driven and encouraged citizens to be involved in decision-making processes.

Several social developments were noteworthy. The first of these was the establishment of Central Park in New York City and the work of Fredrick Law Olmsted and Calvert Vaux in its design. Their work and influence spread throughout the United States very quickly, and their ideas for the creation of pastoral parks that created opportunity of reflection, contemplation, and linkage to nature were dominant themes to pervade park design for decades. Another large landscape park across the United States that also exemplified the influence of Olmsted was that of Golden Gate Park in San Francisco. In a short period of two decades, the park movement had spread from the East Coast to the West Coast. Parks as isolated entities were also being reviewed, and comprehensive systems of parks and open spaces were being proposed and implemented, the first of these being the Boston Metropolitan Park System. Again, this idea was followed by one in the Chicago metropolitan area where the Forest Preserves of Cook County were established to create an outer park belt around the city of Chicago.

Somewhat parallel to the development of the park movement was the development of the recreation movement, initially established in 1885 with the Boston Sand Gardens. This movement, which became focused on the crafting of playgrounds and playground programs, quickly gained favor throughout the United States. This was complemented by the establishment of field houses, public baths (swimming pools), playgrounds, and athletic fields in Chicago with the passage of a $5 million-dollar bond issue in 1903 by the South Side Park District. Hull House in Chicago also served as a model demonstration site, offering programs and facilities such as playgrounds for individuals living in challenging circumstances.

Several professional and civic organizations have emerged to advance parks and recreation services. The first of these was the American Institute of Park Executives, established in 1899, first known as the New England Association of Park Superintendents. Next was the National Recreation Association, founded in 1906 as the Playground Association of America, and later known as the Playground and Recreation Association of America in 1911. Its name was changed to the National Recreation Association in 1930. This group was a mixture of lay citizens and professionals. Following was the establishment of the Society of Recreation Workers of America in 1938. In 1965, these and other professional associations and societies merged to become the National Recreation and Park Association.

DISCUSSION QUESTIONS

1. Why is it important to study the history of the parks and recreation movement?
2. What factors led to the establishment of the parks and recreation movements in the United States?
3. What characterizes "Bureau Men"? What characterizes "Reform Women"?
4. Is the park movement separate from the recreation movement? In what ways have they been joined with one another?
5. How would one characterize the park movement in its early history when comparing large landscape parks of the Olmsted era with those of today?
6. In what ways did the evolution of metropolitan integrated park systems serve to advance the values of parks and green spaces?
7. What were the main developments in the rise of the park movement in the United States?
8. How did the play movement evolve into one focused on recreation?
9. In what way did the development of field houses and public baths in Chicago influence the continued evolution of parks and recreation in the United States?
10. What factors in more recent years influenced the development of parks and recreation in America?

REFERENCES

Biography.com. (2014). Jane Addams. Retrieved from http://www.biography.com/people/jane-addams-9176298

David Rumsey Map Collection. (n.d.). Retrieved from http://www.davidrumsey.com/luna/servlet/detail/RUMSEY~8~1~265404~5524792:Golden-Gate-Park,-San-Francisco,-Ca

Digital Commonwealth. (n.d.). Map of Boston and vicinity including the metropolitan park system [Map]. (1894). Retrieved from http://ark.digitalcommonwealth.org/ark:/50959/wd376714t

Doell, C. E., & Fitzgerald, G. B. (1954). *A brief history of parks and recreation in the United States.* Chicago, IL: Athletic Institute.

Edginton, C. R., & Chen, P. (2014). *Leisure as transformation.* Urbana, IL: Sagamore.

Edginton, C. R., DeGraaf, D. G., Dieser, R. B., & Edginton, S. R. (2002). *Leisure and life satisfaction foundation perspectives* (4th ed.). New York, NY: McGraw-Hill.

Grese, R. (1992). *Jens Jensen: Maker of natural parks and gardens.* Baltimore, MD: John Hopkins University Press.

Hall, L. (1995). *Olmsted's America: An "unpractical" man and his vision of civilization.* New York, NY: Little, Brown and Company.

LaGasse, A. B., & Cook, W. L. (1965). *History of parks and recreation.* Wheeling, WV: American Institute of Park Executives.

Miller, S. C. (2003). *Central Park, an American masterpiece.* New York, NY: H.N. Abrams.

Morgan, K. N. (1999). Charles Eliot: The man behind the monograph. In C. W. Eliot (Ed.), *Charles Eliot: Landscape architect* (Introduction to the 1999 edition). Amherst, MA: University of Massachusetts Press.

National Recreation and Park Association. (n.d.). CAPRA logo. Retrieved from http://bellasartesalliance.org/paf-2013/capra-logo/

National YMCA Hall of Fame. (n.d.). Pridenet. Retrieved from http://pridenet.springfield.edu/ics/ExtPages/YMCA/List_Inductees.aspx

NRA Board, April 13, 1906: Recreation, I (May 1907), 5, 12-13. The story of the growth of public recreation in Washington, yet to be told, is a chronicle of local and national agencies, both public and private, all working within one city.

NYC Parks. (n.d.). History of parks' swimming pools. New York City Department of Parks & Recreation. Retrieved from https://www.nycgovparks.org/about/history/pools

Perkins, D. H. (1905). *The Metropolitan Park System, Report of the Special Commission to the City of Chicago – 1904* (Chicago).

Photos of Old America. (n.d.). Ice-skating in Central Park-Dakota. Retrieved from http://www.photosofoldamerica.com/index.cfm/New_York_City_Parks_Landmarks-Iceskating_in_Central_Park_150.htm https://pgpedia.com/l/joseph-lee

Play and Playground Encyclopedia. (n.d.). Retrieved from https://pgpedia.com/l/joseph-lee

Playground and Recreation Association of America. (1909, 1926). *The normal course in play: Practical material for use in the training of playground and recreation workers.* New York, NY: A. S. Barnes and Company.

President's Commission on Americans Outdoors. (1987). *Americans outdoors: The legacy, the challenge, with case studies: The report of the President's Commission.* Washington, D.C.: Island Press.

Rainwater, C. E. (1922). *The play movement in the United States: A study of community recreation.* Chicago, IL: The University of Chicago Press.

Riis, J. (2004). *How the other half lives: Studies among the tenements of New York.* Whitefish, MT: Kessinger Publishing.

SFPix.com. (n.d.). Golden Gate Park in the beginning. Retrieved from http://www.sfpix.com/park/history/Hall_1870/index.html

Stivers, C. (2000). *Bureau men, settlement women: Constructing public administration in the progressive era.* Lawrence, KS: University Press of Kansas.

United States National Advisory Commission on Civil Disorders, & Kerner, O. (1968). *Report of the National Advisory Commission on Civil Disorders*, March 1, 1968. Washington, DC: U.S. Government Printing Office.

Vena, N. B. (2013). Preservation's loss: The statutory construction of forests in Cook County, IL. American Anthropological Association. Retrieved from http://ae.americananthro.org/preservations-loss-the-statutory-construction-of-forests-in-cook-county-i

Waugh, F. A. (1927). *Landscape architecture in North America, U.S., and Canada, in Gotham's History of Garden Art.* New York, NY: Cambridge University Press.

Women in the Progressive Era. (n.d.). Sources. Retrieved from https://www.nwhm.org/online-exhibits/progressiveera/sources.html

World War 1 Propaganda Posters. (n.d.). Retrieved from http://www.ww1propaganda.com/ww1-poster/spirit-war-camp-community-service-united-war-work-campaign

Young, T. (2004). *Building San Francisco's parks, 1850–1930.* Creating the North American Landscape Series. Baltimore, MD: Johns Hopkins University Press.

Chapter Three

Serving Diverse Communities and Populations

CHAPTER OBJECTIVES

- To recognize current and future cultural and diversity demographics and projections in the United States
- To comprehend primary and secondary dimensions of diversity
- To gain an appreciation of leisure constraint theory and how system-directed change can be implemented to prevent and overcome leisure constraints in the processing of serving diverse communities and populations
- To gain an understanding how parks and recreation agencies can partner with other community organizations to better serve diverse communities and populations
- To understand the multiple ways parks and recreational professionals can show their commitment to diversity

INTRODUCTION

America is becoming more diverse with each changing day. According to the U.S. Census Bureau's 2014 National Projections (Colby & Ortman, 2015), by 2044, more than half of all Americans are projected to belong to a minority group (any group other than non-Hispanic White alone) and by 2060, nearly one in five of the nation's total population is projected to be foreign born. Table 3.1 presents race projections in the United States from 2014 to 2060. What is clear is that race diversity will continue to increase, with bicultural races (two or more race populations) projected to be the fastest growing over the next 46 years. Between 2014 and 2060, the U.S. population is projected to increase from 319 million to 417 million, and in 2030, one in five Americans is predicted to be 65 or over (Colby & Ortman, 2015).

A Pew Research Center (2014) study on religious composition underscores a 1.2% increase among non-Christian faiths, with Judaism, Buddhism, Islam, and Hinduism collectively making up approximately 6% of the population in 2014 (70.6% of the U.S. population identified as Christian in 2014, down from 78.4% in 2007). According to the U.S. Census Bureau (Brault, 2012), approximately 18.7% of the civilian noninstitutionalized population, aged 15 or older, had a disability in 2010, with 12.6% having a severe disability. Furthermore, this government study reported that only 41.1% of adults with disabilities aged 21 to 64 were employed in 2010, and that 10.8% of adults with disabilities experience persistent poverty. The U.S. Census Bureau (DeNavas-Walt & Proctor, 2014), reported that

Table 3.1

Race Projections in the United States

Race	2014 Percentage	2060 Percentage
Asian	5.4	9.3
Hispanic	17	29
African American	13	14
Native Hawaiian/Pacific Islander	Less than 1%	Less than 1%
American Indian/Alaska Natives	1	1
Bicultural (two or more races)	2.5	6.2
Non-Hispanic White	62.2	43.6

(Colby & Ortman, 2015)

in 2013, the official poverty rate was 14.5% in the United States, with African-American and Hispanic Americans having the highest percentage of poverty when examining financial scarcity from a race composition perspective. Furthermore, the poverty rate for children was higher than the rates for American adults, hovering at 19.9% (DeNavas-Walt & Proctor, 2014).

The purpose of this chapter is two-fold. First, to describe how leisure constraints affect the leisure experience among people from diverse and marginalized cultures. Second, to explain how system-directed change in community parks and recreation, along with diversity training and a commitment to enhancing diversity services, can be used to prevent and overcome leisure constraints so that people from diverse and marginalized cultures can have positive leisure experiences.[1]

KEY TERMS AND CONCEPTS

Culture is defined as a learned system of beliefs, feelings, and rules for living in which groups of individuals organize their lives; the way people act and live their lives, which consists of shared assumptions, values, learned responses, and ways of being (Dieser, 2013). *Diversity* refers to the awareness and celebration of differences among people and encompasses both primary and secondary dimensions of individuals (Edginton, DeGraaf, Dieser, & Edginton, 2006). Primary dimensions are the obvious impressions upon meeting an individual and are extremely difficult to change. Examples of primary dimensions include gender, age, physical abilities/disabilities, sexual orientation, and ethnicity/race. Secondary dimensions reveal themselves after primary dimensions, and are generally learned, chosen, and, compared to primary dimensions, easier (but still difficult) to change. Examples of these are religion, economic status, education, geographic location, nationality, marital status, parental status, and occupation.

Cultural competence is defined as being able to work successfully with cultures other than your own by using a set of behaviors, attitudes, and policies that are fitting with that

---

[1]This chapter will speak less about serving people with physical or developmental disabilities as Chapter 16 on community-based therapeutic recreation will give voice toward inclusion of people with disabilities into community parks and recreation.

culture (Cross, Bazron, Dennis, & Isaacs, 1989). Differing authors (e.g., Morris, 2010; Peregoy & Dieser, 1997) have suggested that cross-cultural training is needed in order to develop cultural competencies, and such training is designed to increase an individual's understanding in three areas.

The first area is to gain awareness of one's personal values, biases, beliefs, attitudes, and assumptions related to multicultural experiences. In examining beliefs and attitudes, youth sport coaches, for example, can learn not to penalize a person who cannot practice or play on a certain religious day, even if it means missing many games or practices (e.g., someone who is Jewish may need to miss every Saturday practice or game due to religious beliefs).

Second, to gain knowledge about the history and cultural backgrounds of diverse communities and populations. Although readers need to be aware of the many within and between-group differences of cultural grouping, Table 3.2 presents broad-based behaviors differences between individualistic culture (e.g., White/Anglo-American) and collectivistic cultures (e.g., African-American, Asian-American, Mexican-American, and American-Indian populations). In individualistic cultures, the self or individual is more important than the group, and common cultural behaviors include asserting and expressing oneself. In collectivistic cultures, the group is more important than the self, and common cultural behaviors include adjusting oneself to fit into a group, attending to relationships, and expressing group desires (see Peregoy & Dieser, 1997 and Sue & Sue, 2007 for excellent overviews of the difference between individualistic and collectivistic cultures).

Third, to learn specific skills that will help leisure professionals work more effectively with culturally different people. Community parks and recreation agencies can have in-service trainings and have staff attend local, national, and international conferences related to diversity and cross-cultural competency or go on professional development leaves to learn how other parks and recreation agencies are inclusive of diversity. Table 3.3 presents a cross-cultural training framework in order to develop cultural competence.

Cultural competence means having a plan of action, or strategies, related to ensuring that people with diverse backgrounds are welcome in community parks and recreation settings. For example, the Department of Parks, Recreation and Culture of West Valley City (Utah) general plan (detailed document that describes what West Valley City expects to become) has an explicit aim to record cultural assets, a goal to enhance cross-cultural communication and information sharing, and an action plan of a cultural advisory board to engage in discussions between the city and disparate ethnic/cultural groups related to leisure services (see http://www.wvc-ut.gov/DocumentCenter/Home/View/1863). Furthermore, Dahl (2000) suggested that leisure agencies can complete or hire an outside agency to conduct cultural audits in order to make a park and recreation agency more competent related to serving diverse populations.

When it comes to serving communities and diverse populations, Schneider, Shinew, and Fernandez (2014) outlined how academic research in leisure constraints are ". . . particularly relevant to racial and ethnically diverse group" (p. 170) along with other dimensions of diversity. For example, all forms of prejudice (having predetermined thoughts that lead to unfair judgments), discrimination (the act of disqualifying people on the basis of their group membership) racisms (belief that some races or ethnic groups are inherently inferiors or superior) and stereotypes (oversimplified opinion or characteristic that is used to label people) are interpersonal constraint which can lead to feelings of discomfort and lower enjoyment or motivation of a leisure experience among people from ethnic minority backgrounds (Sharaievska, Stodolska, & Floyd, 2014).

Table 3.2

Life Features of Individualistic and Collectivistic Cultures

Life Features	Individualistic culture	Collectivistic culture
Social Distance	People keep a moderate distance People value their own space	People keep a close distance Close physical contact
Family	Nuclear families Marriage contract can be broken Father's surname usually used	Extended families Variety of family arrangements Use Father's and mothers surname
Age Orientation	Youth oriented	Elder oriented
Individuality	Individual shapes destiny Self-reliance is paramount Self-discipline is valued	Accept group sanctions Dependent on others (e.g., family) Humility is valued
Work	Money is a symbol of success Material possessions are important	Work for present needs/survival Care of other is important
Time	Governed by clock Future oriented	Governed by here and now People oriented (past and present)
Eye Contact	Eye contact shows respect	Indirect eye contact shows respect
Smiling	Shows pleasure and acceptance	Used to hide embarrassment
Noise	Silence is preferred	Noise is preferred and shows enthusiasm
Listening	Listen to one person at a time	Listen to many people all at once
Leisure	Self-focused Smaller spaces for nuclear family	Group-focused Larger spaces for extended family

Drawn from Morris (2010), Peregoy & Dieser (1997) and Sue & Sue (2007).

Table 3.3

Cross-Cultural Training to Develop Cultural Competence

Parks and Recreation Leader's Cultural Values and Biases

Attitudes and Beliefs

1. Recreation leaders must possess self-awareness and sensitivity to their own cultural heritage. Leaders must:
   - Identify cultures to which they belong
   - Challenge their attitudes and beliefs that do not support valuing differences
   - Understand the cultural heritage of recreation and leisure activity

Table 3.3 (cont.)

---

2. Recreation leaders must be aware of how their own cultural background and experiences influence their attitudes, values, and biases about psychological processes. Leaders must:
   - Identify the history of their culture
   - Articulate the beliefs of their own culture groups as they relate to differing cultures and the influence of those beliefs in their profession
3. Recreation leaders should recognize the limits of their multicultural competencies. Leaders must:
   - Recognize when and how their attitudes, beliefs, and values interfere with providing the best service to a client
   - Identify training that contributes to expertise in parks and recreation
   - Provide real examples of cultural situations in which they recognize their limitations and how to gain more cultural competencies
4. Recreation leaders must recognize that their own discomfort with differences between themselves and others (e.g., participants, co-workers) in terms of race, ethnicity, and culture. Leaders must:
   - Recognize their sources of comfort and discomfort
   - Identify differences
   - Communicate acceptance of and respect for differences

Knowledge
1. Recreation leaders must learn about their own racial and cultural heritage and how it personally and professionally affects their definitions and biases. Leaders must:
   - Have knowledge regarding their heritage
   - Recognize their family's and culture's perspectives of acceptable and unacceptable codes of conduct
   - Recognize their family's and culture's perspectives of recreation and leisure
2. Leaders must understand how oppression, racism, discrimination, and stereotyping affect them personally and in their work. Leaders must
   - Identify their identity development
   - Be able to define racism, prejudice, discrimination, and stereotype
3. Recreation leaders should understand their social impact on others. Leaders must:
   - Define their communication style and describe their verbal and nonverbal behaviors
   - Describe the behavioral impact of their communication styles on participants who are different from themselves
   - Provide an example of an incident in which communication broke down with a participant from a different culture

Table 3.3 (cont.)

Skills

1. Recreation leaders must seek educational, consultative, and training experiences that improve their understanding and effectiveness in working with culturally different populations. Leaders must:
    *   Be able to describe objectives of at least two professional development activities that pertain to diversity
    *   Develop professional relationships with professionals from differing cultural backgrounds
    *   Maintain an active referral list (e.g., social ethnic clubs)and engage in professional and personal growth activities pertaining to working with clients from different cultures
    *   Consult with other professionals regarding issues of culture
2. Leaders must constantly seek to understand themselves as racial and cultural beings and to develop a nonracist identity.

Parks and Recreation Leaders' Awareness of Clients' Worldview

Attitudes and Beliefs

1. Recreation leaders must be aware of their own negative and positive emotional reactions to other racial and ethnic groups. Leaders must:
    *   Identify their common emotional reactions about people different from themselves
    *   Identify how emotional reactions observed in themselves can influence effectiveness in parks and recreation services
    *   Be able to describe at least two examples of cultural conflict between themselves and culturally different clients
2. Recreation leaders must be aware of the stereotypes and preconceived notions that they may hold toward other racial and ethnic minority groups. Leaders must:
    *   Recognize their stereotyped reactions to people who are different from themselves
    *   Consciously attend to examples that contradict stereotypes
    *   Recognize assumptions made concerning different cultures

Knowledge

1. Recreation leaders must be knowledgeable about groups with whom they work. These leaders must be aware of the life experiences, cultural heritage, and historical backgrounds of the culturally different people. Leaders must:
    *   Be able to identify differences in nonverbal and verbal behavior of different cultural groups
    *   Be familiar with at least two models of minority identity development
    *   Understand the historical implications of contact with dominant society for various ethnic groups
    *   Be able to identify within-group differences of cultures

Table 3.3 (cont.)

2. Recreation leaders must know about sociopolitical influences that impinge on the life of people from racial and ethnic minorities. Leaders must:
    - Understand the implications of concepts such as internalized oppression, institutional racism, privilege, and the historical and current political climate regarding immigration, poverty, and welfare
    - Be able to explain the relationship between culture and power
    - Understand the unique position, constraints, and needs of those clients who experience oppression
    - Identify current issues that affect different cultures in legislation and social climate
    - Understand how documents and affirmative action legislation affect society's perceptions (both positive and negative) of different cultural groups

Skills

1. Recreation leaders must become familiar with research relevant to their discipline that affects racial and ethnic groups. Leaders must:
    - Be knowledgeable of recent research regarding relevant topics related to different cultural populations
    - Complete workshops, conferences, and in-service training regarding multicultural skills and knowledge
    - Be able to identify professional growth activities
2. Recreation leaders must become actively involved with members of minority groups outside of the work setting (e.g., community events, social functions). Leaders must:
    - Be able to identify at least five multicultural experiences in which they have participated in within the past 3 years
    - Actively plan experiences and activities that will contradict negative stereotypes and preconceived notions they may hold

Adapted from Peregoy & Dieser (1997)

LEISURE CONSTRAINT THEORY

The hierarchical model of leisure constraints, which is presented in Figure 3.1, suggests there are three types of constraints (Jackson, 2005). First, *intrapersonal constraints* refer to psychological factors that arise internal to the individual, such as personality, temperament, attitudes, and moods. For example, a woman who has body dissatisfaction (negative thoughts and feelings about her body), developed from a personal attitude can become less interested or not motivated to participate in aquatic leisure (see James, 2000).

Second, *interpersonal constraints* are those that arise out of interactions with other people, such as family, friends, community members, and other socialization agents, such as mass leisure and popular culture. All forms of discrimination are interpersonal constraints.[2] Gobster's (2002) study of urban parks in Chicago found that racial discrimination were highest among people who were African-American and concluded that discrimination can

---

[2]Readers are encouraged to see Sharaievksa, Stodolska, and Floyd (2014) for an excellent overview of the many forms of discrimination that can occur in leisure settings.

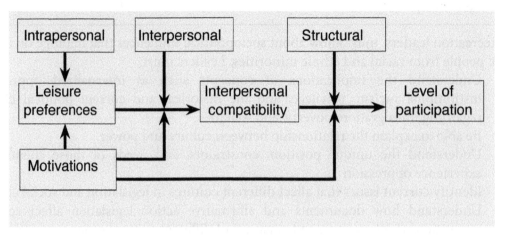

Figure 3.1. Hierarchical Model of Leisure Constraints. Source: Jackson (2004)

lead to lower participation of leisure and in severe cases can lead to anger and physical violence, which can ultimately lead to stoppage of leisure altogether. Dieser's (2003) study in therapeutic recreation reported that various clients from ethnic minority backgrounds with special needs did not feel comfortable participating in community parks and recreation settings with predominately White people due to past racial actions on the part of White people. Stodolska, Acevedo, and Shinew (2009) and Stodolska, Shinew, Acevedo, and Izenstark (2011) studies underscore that gang activity in Latino inner-city neighborhoods and parks was the major intrapersonal constraint among Latinos visiting community recreation areas. More specific, some of the parks in these Latino inner-city communities were described as "wastelands" awash with trash and graffiti-filled walls that were settings for drug trafficking, and Latino residents of lower socioeconomic status lacked the political clout to make needed changes relevant to community recreation (Stodolska et al., 2011). Likewise, sexual harassment comments and unwanted eye gazes (lookism) that women often experience in aquatic centers is another example of an interpersonal constraint.

Third, *structural constraints* refer to external conditions in the environment that inhibit participation in a leisure activity. Financial struggles that block an already existing desire to participate in community recreation are a structural constraint. Research on structural leisure constraints directed toward women (e.g., Henderson, Bialeschki, Shaw, & Freysinger, 1996) observed that poor street and parking lot lighting was a constraint that caused women to participate less in leisure due to safety issues.

Although the hierarchical model of leisure constraints presents intrapersonal, interpersonal, and structural constraints as three distinct areas, in everyday life there is considerable overlap between these three constraints and sometimes it is difficult to distinguish between them (Dieser, 2013). For example, James (2000) reported that body image/body dissatisfaction is a factor that limit some women to participate in aquatic leisure, such as going to a community swimming pool (in her study, James suggests that body image constraints accounted for 29% of young women not participating in aquatic leisure). This could be an intrapersonal constraint, in the sense that a healthy woman may have an attitude that her body is "ugly" and she might feel embarrassed being seen in a swimsuit. However, mass leisure[3]—such as female body image representations on television and popular magazines, where borderline anorexic women with health problems are viewed as attractive—can play a significant role in shaping female attitudes of body image. As such, this is an interpersonal constraint because an attitude that one's body is "ugly" (the intrapersonal constraint) arises out of interaction with other actors, namely the socialization effect of the media and mass leisure. If the swimming pool facility design is one where the female locker rooms are far away from the pool so that women have to walk long distances to get into the pool—what James (2000) described as walking through the gauntlet—this structural constraint can further augment body image embarrassment.

Crawford and Stodolska (2008) developed a more complex leisure constraints model that outlines how cultural beliefs play an essential role in leisure constraints. This model begins with basic or individual constraints, such as cost, transportation, or lack of equipment. Intermediate constraints reside within society, such as economic structures. Fundamental constraints, such as cultural attitudes or ethnic identity, can have a far-reaching influence that can prevent participation in leisure.[4] Figure 3.2 presents Crawford and Stodolska model of leisure constraints.

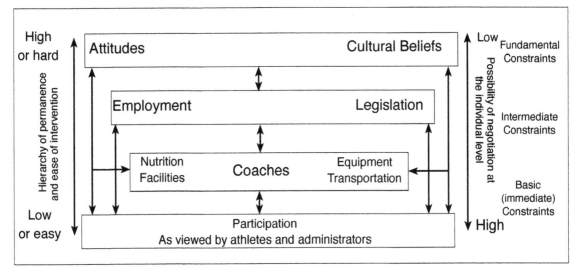

Figure 3.2. Crawford and Stodolska model of leisure constraints. Source: Crawford & Stodolska (2008)

PREVENTING AND OVERCOMING LEISURE CONSTRAINTS

System-directed change, also known as an ecological approach (see Bronfenbrenner, 1979, 2005), occurs when strategies are put forth by parks and recreation agencies to improve communities and environmental factors in order to provide inclusive services (Dieser, 2013). System-directed models examine how environmental factors, such as

---

[3]Mass leisure is defined as the everyday recreational activities of the majority of the populations such as T.V. or Internet watching, sports, popular magazines (Edginton et al., 2006).

[4]To learn more on how ethnic identity can influence leisure choices and behaviors see Dieser (1997, 2013).

neighborhoods, family, parks, recreation centers, or low living wages need to change in order to help people with behavioral change, such as participating in leisure services.

An important step parks and recreation professionals can take to ensure that people from diverse backgrounds have access to recreation is to make system-directed change specific to financial, transportation, and physical entrée to leisure settings (CAPRA, 2014; Schneider, Shinew, & Fernandez, 2014). In regard to financial entrée, there are many actions (system-change) that parks and recreation professionals can take. Parks and recreation agencies can offer sliding-scale fees in which recreation services have variable (lower) prices for products, services, or taxes based on a customer's ability to pay.

Taylor and Frisby's (2010) web-based study of leisure access policies suggests that most parks and recreation agencies give scant attention to such access policies and they are extremely difficult to find on agency websites. These authors suggest that offering sliding fees in a callous and insensitive manner can stigmatize people who are poor and prevent them from taking advantage of fee reductions. Using insulting names (e.g., charity policy), implementing a "prove-you-are-poor" verification system, and having people in the community write "character letters" on behalf of the poor can be stigmatizing because such approaches are based on an assumption that people who are poor are "cheats" (dishonest) and "less than," which can result in embarrassment and shame that can then cause people who are poor to not take advantages of sliding-scale fees.

Parks and recreation agencies can eliminate "character letters" and could use an honor system, based on professional judgment and observation, in assessing financial needs. Does a person who lives in an extremely poor inner city need to show his or her W2 income tax form to verify financial hardship? Could not verification of residence in an extremely poor area of a city suffice for a parks and recreation agency? If parks and recreation agencies need to verify income, professionals need to treat financially struggling people with the utmost respect and focus on welcoming them to use leisure services.

Parks and recreation agencies can create low-cost and free programming and then provide active and engaged electronic and physical outreach by finding people who are poor and invite them to participate in leisure services. An example of this type of outreach is the City of Edmonton Community Services' (Alberta, Canada) *Leisure Access Program and Priceless Fun Guide* (see Figure 3.3), which is specifically focused on helping people who have financial difficulties participate in leisure and has strong community connections to other human services agencies, such as mental health counseling, translators, and legal services. This 24-page document outlines a broad range of free and low-cost leisure services, such as free participation in ice skating, tobogganing/sledding areas, museums and arts galleries, fitness centers, historical sites, festivals and special events, summer day camps, art classes, and indoor swimming pools (see Figure 3.4 regarding free swimming).

In regard to transportation entrée, parks and recreation professionals can travel to lower socioeconomic neighborhoods and provide programs rather than have people who are poor travel to recreation facilities. For example, summer recreation-based baseball games, along with baseball equipment, can be transported and played in parks within lower socioeconomic communities or ice rinks can be created in neighborhood parks (with free skates being donated to families) also in poor neighborhoods. Project-based programming (Dieser & Fox, 2002) can be used in parks and recreation outreach in which professionals move away from "expert" to "explorer" and learn how to facilitate leisure in low-income neighborhoods by involving members who are from low-income communities and genuinely learn from

Figure 3.3. City of Edmonton Community Services (Alberta, Canada) *Leisure Access Program and Priceless Fun Guide*

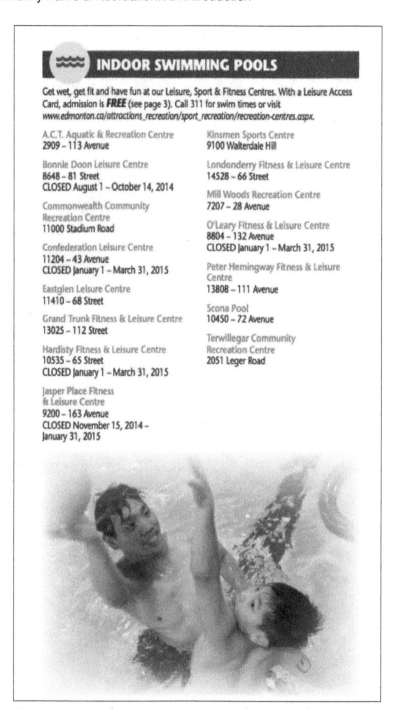

INDOOR SWIMMING POOLS

Get wet, get fit and have fun at our Leisure, Sport & Fitness Centres. With a Leisure Access Card, admission is *FREE* (see page 3). Call 311 for swim times or visit www.edmonton.ca/attractions_recreation/sport_recreation/recreation-centres.aspx.

A.C.T. Aquatic & Recreation Centre
2909 – 113 Avenue

Bonnie Doon Leisure Centre
8648 – 81 Street
CLOSED August 1 – October 14, 2014

Commonwealth Community
Recreation Centre
11000 Stadium Road

Confederation Leisure Centre
11204 – 43 Avenue
CLOSED January 1 – March 31, 2015

Eastglen Leisure Centre
11410 – 68 Street

Grand Trunk Fitness & Leisure Centre
13025 – 112 Street

Hardisty Fitness & Leisure Centre
10535 – 65 Street
CLOSED January 1 – March 31, 2015

Jasper Place Fitness
& Leisure Centre
9200 – 163 Avenue
CLOSED November 15, 2014 –
January 31, 2015

Kinsmen Sports Centre
9100 Walterdale Hill

Londonderry Fitness & Leisure Centre
14528 – 66 Street

Mill Woods Recreation Centre
7207 – 28 Avenue

O'Leary Fitness & Leisure Centre
8804 – 132 Avenue
CLOSED January 1 – March 31, 2015

Peter Hemingway Fitness & Leisure
Centre
13808 – 111 Avenue

Scona Pool
10450 – 72 Avenue

Terwillegar Community
Recreation Centre
2051 Leger Road

Figure 3.4. Indoor Swimming Pools, City of Edmonton Community Services *Leisure Access Program and Priceless Fun Guide*

them. Furthermore, community parks and recreation administration can partner with the transit authority (e.g., bus services) to ensure that city transit routes are linked to parks and recreation facilities and can advocate that people who are poor received free transit (e.g., bus passes). In 2012, the Helena (Montana) Department of Parks and Recreation collaborated with the public health department, public transit, and a nonprofit organization called Youth Connections (committed to creating safe spaces and partnerships for youth in Helena) to create a free trolley system to transport low-income youth to parks, trails, pools, and other recreation settings (Lehmann & Oehmke, 2012).

In regard to physical entrée, it is not uncommon for community parks and recreation settings, especially in inner-city and poor neighborhoods, to have physical deterioration and less access to attractive and well-maintained infrastructure (Schneider, Shinew, & Fernandez, 2014), with some parks being described as "wastelands" (see Stodolska et al., 2011). The Stodolska and Shinew (2010) study on leisure constraints that affect Latinos' participation in recreation underscored poorly maintained parks, with ". . . jogging trails full of potholes, dilapidated playground equipment, trash, lack of water fountains, and unsanitary restrooms" (p. 321). Stodolska and Shinew's (2014) suggestion to increase recreation participation among people who live in inner cities begins with ensuring safe, well-maintained, and welcoming recreation areas. Specifically related to Latino inner-city parks and recreation settings, Stodolska and Shinew further suggest that "Research has shown that providing large, family-friendly picnic areas with adequate access to parking, restrooms, water, and waste receptacles helps encourage use among Latinos" (p. 95).

The New York City (NYC) Department of Parks and Recreation has been committed to upgrading older parks and recreation facilities in order to prevent physical deterioration and to sustain attractive and well-maintained leisure infrastructure and settings. According to Salwen (2000), the NYC Department of Parks and Recreation has replaced or refurbished more than 378 parks and playgrounds. Nelson Playground in the Bronx had a 12-month, $1.17 million upgrade and expansion, and the Paerdegat Park in Brooklyn acquired an additional 3.5 acres of land in its 12-month reconstruction project. The NYC Department of Parks and Recreation website (2015) (see http://www.nycgovparks.org/planning-and-building/planning/neighborhood-development) outlines numerous upgrades of parks and recreation entities as part of the "Neighborhood Development Plan" that specifically focuses on increasing the quality of life of all New Yorkers. For example, the Hunter's Point South Park in Queens (completed in 2015) engaged in system-directed change by transformed a previously abandoned and postindustrial area (wasteland) full of crime, drug use, and prostitution into a dynamic site for recreation along the East River with a magnificent view of the Manhattan skyline. Hunter's Point South Park includes a central green, playground, waterside promenade, 13,000-square-foot pavilion housing comfort stations, concessions, café plaza, and a maintenance facility for NYC Parks (http://www.nycgovparks.org/parks/hunters-point-south-park/dailyplant/22981). Figure 3.5 shows Hunter Point before and after the creation of this park.

HOMELESS POPULATIONS

In the process of transforming physical deteriorating and dilapidated leisure spaces into safe, well-maintained, pro-social community parks and recreation areas leisure professionals will often have to deal with people who are homeless. A recent *New York Times* article (Foderaro, 2014) outlined the conflict that can occur between park participant and park professionals versus homeless people in various parks in New York City (e.g., Harlem River Park in Manhattan, Fort Greene Park in Brooklyn). A *Los Angeles Times* article (Holland, 2013) underscored how parks and recreation professionals have teamed up with the city

Figure 3.5. Hunter's Point South Waterfront Park (Queens, NYC) before and after the creation of Hunter's Point South Park. *Source:* NYC Parks, n.d.

police in an attempt to criminalize homelessness and arrest homeless people who loiter in parks (readers should note that most people loiter and relax in parks).

Although homeless people in parks present unique challenges, including used needles laying on park grounds if a homeless person is a drug user, simply teaming up with police to kick homeless people out of parks is a shortsighted solution that lacks critical thinking and ethical decision making (see Chapter 5 in this book related to problem solving, critical thinking, and ethical decision making related to recreation conflict). As LaPage (2007) highlighted, city parks have a long history of being a safe refuge for people who are homeless and should be a public place that creates hope for the homeless. Writing specifically to help leisure professionals understand homelessness, Mair and Trussell (2010) outlined that homelessness is a result of multiple factors, such as urbanization, socioeconomic forces, lack of social and city services, unemployment, mental illness, family break-up, disabilities, and substance addictions. According to the National Coalition for the Homeless (2009), 20% to 25% of the homeless population in the United States suffers from severe mental illness (compared to 6% of the general population), and mental illness, according to the National Coalition for the Homeless (2009), is the third largest cause of homelessness.

Instead of creating simplistic policies—such as arresting or thrusting homeless people out of parks—which is kicking the can down the street (as people who are homeless will then sleep and loiter in other areas of the community),[5] community parks and recreation agencies should develop creative solutions, partner with other agencies (e.g., social services, churches), and embark on social policy programming (see Chapter 12 of this book) to better not only members of their community but to also extend a hand of community fellowship and help to people who are homeless. Mair and Trussell (2010) summarize the importance of social responsibility that is needed by the parks and recreation professions related to the issue of homelessness:

> It must be said that turning the blame onto the individual who has made 'bad choices' pushes us toward what C. Wright Mills (1959) warned us about long ago: the separation of private troubles and public issues. When we turn away from issues such as homelessness by positioning it as a question of private troubles, we are nurturing the dismantling of our collective sense of responsibility for this public issue (p. 212).

Taylor (2014) highlighted numerous creative and partnership solutions that community parks and recreation agencies have facilitated related to the issue of homelessness in parks and in the broader community. A sampling of these approaches and initiatives are below.

- Every Thursday night, the Portland (Oregon) Park and Recreation department offers "Strike Night" underneath Burnside Bridge in Waterfront Park in which city park rangers interact with the homeless community and offer the following free services: hot meals, haircuts, shave, feet washing, and replacement of old shoes, clothes, and

---

[5]A recent article in the *Salt Lake Tribune* titled "Is 500 West Salt Lake City's new Pioneer Park?" by Christopher Smart reports that as police have kicked out homeless people from pioneer park they have simply walked approximately four miles east and are camping out on 500 West Commons. Police are acting circular by simply traveling to this different section of Salt Lake City and removing homeless people out of the West Commons (see http://www.sltrib.com/news/2762800-155/is-500-west-salt-lake-citys).

sleeping bags. Such programs develop trust so that people who are homeless will become interested in housing opportunities and mental health counseling as this parks and recreation agency partners with social service agencies to remedy some of the underlying issue of homelessness.

- The Columbus (Ohio) Recreation and Parks department works with the Dowd Education Center to provide homeless youth with outdoor education programs and opportunities to play in nature. This school parks and recreation partnership offers homeless families an academically focused after-school and summer program that includes activities such as rock climbing, archery, fort building, a night hike, campfires, and class learning about fossils and trees.

- Working in partnership to prevent and remedy homelessness, the Las Vegas (Nevada) Parks, Recreation and Neighborhood Services sit on the Southern Nevada Regional Planning Coalition Committee of Homelessness (partnering with a number of faith-based and nonprofit institutions) to develop numerous services, including the "Reconnecting Families to Home" program.

Another creative partnership related to parks and homelessness/poverty is Gladys Park and San Julian Park—often summed together as Skid Row Park—between the nonprofit SRO Housing Corporation (see http://www.srohousing.org/community-development) and the City of Los Angeles Department of Recreation and Parks.[6] The SRO Housing Corporation also owns apartment complexes adjacent to both parks for emergency, transitional, and permanent supportive housing (see http://www.srohousing.org/property-management). Since 1988, SRO Housing has managed San Julian and Gladys Park with ownership of the park residing with the City of Los Angeles' Department of Recreation and Parks. In order to serve homeless populations, the City of Los Angeles' Department of Recreation and Parks took over the management of Gladys Park (in 2013) and San Julian Park (in 2015). San Julian Park, which was once a trash-filled vacant lot, was transformed into a park by SRO Housing staff, and both parks have been used for multiple events related to helping people who are homeless/poor along with other community events (e.g., voter registration, food drives, hygiene kit distribution, and hosting an annual National Homeless Persons' Memorial Day and Tree Lighting Ceremony). This creative endeavor offers an array of recreation opportunities, including its "skid row 3-on-3 streetball league" (basketball), and a pathway to reduced and supportive housing.

COMMITMENT TO DIVERSITY

Community parks and recreation agencies can show their commitment to diverse communities and populations by adopting the I-Triad (invite, include, involve). Building on the academic labor of Chavez (2008), Long and Robertson (2010) have advocated a three-phase model for cultural inclusion. The first phase is to invite all people to use parks and recreation services and can be facilitated via (1) printing brochures and materials in different languages, (2) portraying diversity in photos and advertising, (3) advertising

---

[6]Beyond the website references to the nonprofit SRO Housing Corporation the additional information located in this paragraph about Gladys Park and San Julian Park came from e mail personal communication with Anita Nelson, Chief Executive Officer of SRO Housing Corporation, dated 7/10/2015.

through media that caters to specific populations such as Spanish-language newspapers, and (4) visiting and partnering with churches and social-ethnic clubs (see Figures 3.6 and 3.7 of photos of the Copernicus Center Polish American club[7] in Jefferson Park in Chicago and the Hungarian-Canadian Club in Lethbridge, Alberta (Canada). The second phase is to include a diverse array of people in parks and recreation services which can be facilitated via (1) providing multilingual public announcers and interpreters at events, (2) programming cultural activities or special events, and (3) conducting information-gathering activities both inside and outside your agency. The third phase is to involve a diverse group of people in the ongoing operations of a parks and recreation agency and can be facilitated via (1) hiring staff that are diverse (race, gender, sexual orientation, disability, nationality, religion), (2) recruiting a board of directors that are made up of a diverse groups of people, and (3) creating culturally focused advisory or task committees.[8]

Parks and recreational professionals can show their commitment to diversity in various ways. Below are a sampling of community parks and recreation examples that show a commitment to serving diverse communities and populations.

- Seattle (Washington) Parks and Recreation Department named over 20 buildings and parks in honor of African Americans such as Edwin T. Pratt Park, named after the slain Seattle civil rights leader and executive director of the Seattle Urban League, and Flo Ware Park, named after the central area activist dedicated to social change in education and health care (see http://www.seattle.gov/parks/history/BlackHistory.htm).
- The Miami-Dade County (Florida) Parks, Recreation and Open Spaces Women's Park is the first park dedicated to women in the United States created to honor all women, past, present, and future for their contributions to the betterment of the quality of life in Miami-Dade County (see http://www.miamidade.gov/parks/releases/2014-05-30-roxcy-bolton.asp).
- The City of Dearborn (Michigan) Recreation and Parks Department offers *halal*—a food that adheres to Muslim dietary restrictions—in recreation center snack bars and has a women-only exercise class for Muslim women (see DeLisle, 2004).
- The Parks and Recreation Department in Larchmont (New York) refrains from scheduling recreational sports on Saturday and Sunday mornings due to Jewish and Christian religious beliefs (see DeLisle, 2004).
- To prevent all bullying, but especially bullying of lesbian, gay, bisexual, and transgender youth, the Washington (DC) Department of Parks and Recreation became an active member of a Youth Bullying Prevention Task Force that influenced the Youth Bullying Prevention Act of 2012 (see http://dpr.dc.gov/bullyingprevention/taskforce).
- Inclusion of the Osaka Garden and Japanese history in Jackson Park within the Chicago Park District (see http://www.hydepark.org/parks/osaka2.htm).
- The City of Bloomington (Indiana) Parks and Recreation Department's normative registration forms have an inclusive service request section, a specific inclusion questionnaire, and a full-time inclusive recreation coordinator who can help

---

[7]The Taste of Polonia festival, which celebrates Polish culture and occurs in the Copernicus Center and Jefferson park, is the largest ethnic festival in Chicago, drawing crowds between 40,000 to 60,000 each year over the span of four days during the Labor Day weekend (http://copernicuscenter.org/about-us/).

[8]Parks and recreation agencies can use churches, nonprofit organizations, and social-ethnic clubs to create cultural advisory boards. See Chapter 16 in this book regarding how to create advisory boards related to inclusive practice.

Figure 3.6. Copernicus Center Polish American Club in Jefferson Park in Chicago. *Source:* Copernicus Center, n.d.

Figure 3.7. Hungarian-Canadian Club in Lethbridge, Alberta, Canada. *Source:* YouTube, 2012

participants with disabilities and can train parks and recreation staff toward inclusive practices. Furthermore, the Parks and Recreation Department has an eight-member inclusive recreation advisory council made up of people with disabilities, parents of children with disabilities, and professionals who work with people with disabilities (see https://bloomington.in.gov/inclusive).

SUMMARY

As noted by Floyd, Walker, Stodolska, and Shinew (2014), research related to diversity in leisure settings clearly suggests that people from diverse and marginalized cultures tend to have less positive leisure experiences. Relevant to future leisure services, "there is a long way to go" (p. 298) to better understanding and serving diverse communities and populations. This chapter began with posting current and future diversity demographics and projections in the United States. America will continue to become diverse in the future and if parks and recreation professionals and agencies have mission statements to be inclusive to all people, they need to understand how to serve diverse communities and populations.

To this end, leisure constraint theory and system directed approaches can aid the parks and recreation professional in serving people and communities from diverse cultural backgrounds. Parks and recreation agencies need to continue ongoing and in-service training related to diversity, and can initiate outreach and partnerships building with differing diversity-based organizations in their communities (e.g., churches, advocacy groups, ethnic clubs, nonprofit organizations) to better serve marginalized and even forgotten populations (e.g., homeless populations). Although Floyd and colleagues' mantra of "There is a long way to go" is relevant and should not be forgotten, this chapter provided numerous exceptional examples of parks and recreation departments' commitment to diversity.

DISCUSSION QUESTIONS

1. What conclusions can you draw about current and future cultural and diversity demographics and projections in the United States? Based on projections, speculate from a demographic perspective how the United States will be different in the next 10 to 50 years.

2. How might developing a cultural or diversity advisory board help to serve diverse communities and populations?

3. Explain various leisure constraints and describe how understanding this body of knowledge can assist parks and recreational professionals in serving diverse communities and populations. In additional, discuss how intrapersonal, interpersonal, and structural constraints can overlap related to issues of diversity.

4. Describe how system-directed change strategies can be used to prevent or overcome leisure constraints experienced by people from diverse backgrounds in relation to community parks and recreation.

5. Discuss the strengths and weaknesses of creative solutions and partnerships that parks and recreation agencies have facilitated related to the issue of homelessness in parks and in the broader community.

6. Explain the social responsibility role that parks and recreation agencies should play in their communities (and with social issues/problems) and explain the dangers when society tries to separate private troubles and public/societal issues.

7. Explain how a local community parks and recreation agency can use the "I-Triad" as a strategy to serve diverse communities and populations.

8. Describe broad-based behaviors differences between individualistic White-American culture and people from collectivistic cultures.

9. Identify various churches, nonprofit organizations, or social-ethnic clubs in your community that a local parks and recreation agencies can partner with in order to better serve people from such cultures. Further, attend an ethnic festival or special event and write a two-page reflection paper describing the experience and what you learned about this ethnic culture.

10. Describe how various community parks and recreation have demonstrated a commitment to diversity.

REFERENCES

Brault, M. W. (2012). Americans with Disabilities 2010: Household economic studies (Report No. P7131). Retrieved from http://www.census.gov/prod/2012pubs/p70-131.pdf

Bronfenbrenner, U. (1979). *The ecology of human development.* Cambridge, MA: Harvard University Press.

Bronfenbrenner, U. (2005). *Making human beings human.* Thousand Oaks, CA: Sage.

Chavez, D. (2008). Invite, include, involve! Racial groups, ethnic groups, and leisure. In T. M. Allison & I. E. Schneider (Eds.), *Diversity and the recreation profession: Organizational perspective* (rev. ed., pp. 223–232). State College, PA: Venture.

Colby, S. L., & Ortman, J. M. (2015). Projections of the size and composition of the U.S. Population: 2014 to 2060 (Report No. P25-1143). Retrieved from http://www.census.gov/content/dam/Census/library/publications/2015/demo/p2511pdf

Copernius Center. (n.d.). Retrieved from https://www.google.com/search?q=Joseph+Lee,+the+%E2%80%9CFather+of+Recreation%E2%80%9D&source=lnms&tbm=isch&sa=X&ved=0ahUKEwjOk5CUtsLTAhVp04MKHaa7CXwQ_AUIBygC&biw=1120&bih=637#tbm=isch&q=Copernicus+Center+Poli

Crawford, J., & Stodolska, M. (2008). Constraint experiences by elite athletes with disabilities in Kenya with implications for the development of a new hierarchical model of constraints at the societal level. *Journal of Leisure Research, 40,* 128–155.

Cross, T., Bazron, B., Dennis, K., & Isaacs, M. (1989). *Toward a culturally competent system of care* (Vol. I). Washington, DC: Georgetown University Child Development Center, CASSP Technical Assistance Center.

Dahl, R. F. (2000). Intercultural dynamics and organizational models for change. In M. Allison & I. E. Schneider, I. (Eds.), *Diversity and the recreation profession: Organizational perspectives* (pp. 225–234). State College, PA: Venture.

DeLisle, L. J. (2004). Respecting religious traditions in recreational programming. *Parks & Recreation, 39*(10), 74–82.

DeNavas-Walt, C., & Proctor, B. D. (2014). Income and poverty in the United States: 2013. (Report No P60-249). Retrieved from http://www.census.gov/content/dam/Census/library/publications/2014/demo/p60249.pdf

Dieser, R. (1997). Pluralistic leadership and program planning: Understanding minority/ethnic identity development. *Journal of Leisurability, 24*(3), 33–37.

Dieser, R. B. (2003). Understanding cross-ethnic interactions when using therapeutic recreation practice models in therapeutic recreation practice. *Therapeutic Recreation Journal, 37*(2), 175–189.

Dieser, R. B. (2013). *Leisure education: A person-centered, system-directed, social policy perspective.* Urbana, IL: Sagamore.

Dieser, R. B., & Fox, K. (2002). Cross-cultural therapeutic recreation: A project-based leisure education approach. *American Journal of Recreation Therapy, 1*(1), 21–24.

Edginton, C. R., DeGraaf, D. G., Dieser, R. B. & Edginton, S. (2006). *Leisure and life satisfaction: Foundational perspectives* (4th ed). Boston, MA: WCB McGraw-Hill.

Floyd, M. F., Walker, G. J., Stodolska M., & Shinew, K. J. (2014). Emerging issues. In M. Stodolska, K. J. Shinew, M. F. Floyd, & G. J. Walker (Eds.), *Race, ethnicity, and leisure: Perspectives on research, theory, and practice* (pp. 297–305). Champaign, IL: Human Kinetics.

Foderaro, L. W. (2014, Nov. 14). Tensions over park behavior as homelessness rises in New York City. *New York Times.* Retrieved http://www.nytimes.com/2014/11/15/nyregion/conflicts-in-new-york-city-parks-ashomeless-population-rises.html

Gobster, P. (2002). Managing urban parks for a racially and ethnically diverse clientele. *Leisure Sciences, 24,* 143–159.

Henderson, K. A., Bialeschki, M. D., Shaw, S. M., & Freysinger, V. J. (1996). *Both gains and gaps: Feminist perspectives on women's leisure.* State College, PA: Venture.

Holland, G. (2013, August 31). L.A.'s urban parks: For the homeless too? *Los Angeles Times.* Retrieved at http://articles.latimes.com/2013/aug/31/local/la-me-homeless-parks 20130901

Jackson, E. L. (2004). Leisure constraint research: Overview of a developing theme in leisure studies. In E. L. Jackson (Ed.), *Constraints to leisure* (pp. 3–19). State College, PA: Venture.

James, K. (2000). You can feel them looking at you: The experience of adolescent girls at swimming pools. *Journal of Leisure Research, 32*(2), 262–280.

LaPage, W. (2007). *Parks for life: Moving the goal posts, changing the rules, and expanding the field.* State College, PA: Venture.

Lehmann, E., & Oehmke, N. (2012). Public health at work: Case studies of successful programs at the local level. *Parks & Recreation, 47*(10), 47–48.

Long, T., & Robertson, T. (2010). Inclusion concepts, processes, and models. In Human Kinetics (Ed.), *Inclusive recreation: Programs and services for diverse populations* (pp. 61–78). Champaign, IL: Human Kinetics.

Mair, H., & Trussell, D. (2010). Restoring our collective obligations: Exploring opportunities for addressing homelessness and social housing. In H. Mair, S. M. Arai, & D. G. Reid (Eds.), *Decentering work: Critical perspectives on leisure, social policy, and human development* (pp. 203–228). Calgary, AB: University of Calgary Press.

Morris, P. V. (2010). Building cultural competencies. In Human Kinetics (Ed.), *Inclusive recreation: Programs and services for diverse populations* (pp. 39–60). Champaign, IL: Human Kinetics.

NYC Parks. (n.d.). Hunter's Point South Park. Retrieved from https://www.google.com/

Chapter Four

Benefits and Impacts of Parks and Recreation

CHAPTER OBJECTIVES

- To recognize the importance of repositioning parks and recreation to be viewed as a contributor to alleviating community and social problems
- To comprehend a multitude of benefits that results from community parks and recreation services
- To gain an appreciation of the transformation power that leisure services provides in community parks and recreation settings
- To understand how to optimize net benefits of parks and recreation services by awareness of the simultaneous negative and positive outcomes of leisure services
- To gain an understanding of how a 100-year partnership between the world-renowned Mayo Clinic and the City of Rochester (Minnesota) Parks and Recreation has provided many benefits to the community and transformed a city

INTRODUCTION

Over a half century ago, Butler (1959) argued that community parks and recreation leaders need to advocate that recreation is a fundamental human need. Today it has become more evident that the benefits of public parks and recreation services are numerous and varied. These benefits include personal (e.g., mental health, psychophysiological), social and cultural (e.g., community satisfaction, understanding diverse cultures), economic (e.g., decrease health care costs, increase local and regional economic growth), and environmental (e.g., increase air quality, protection of biodiversity and ecosystems). The National Recreation and Park Association (NRPA) has developed a national campaign focused on the theme that the benefits of parks and recreation are endless. There are many research-based studies attesting to the many social and personal benefits of leisure services (e.g., Compton, 2007, Driver, 2008a; Driver, Brown, & Peterson, 1991). Farrell and Lundegren (1991) advocated over 25 years ago that parks and recreation professionals need to spend time educating the general public about the benefits of leisure and more recently, Dieser (2013) outlined how leisure can combine with social policy in order to prevent and remedy social problems (e.g., obesity, crime).

One can think of a benefit as an advantage or value that one derives from their participation or involvement in a community parks and recreation program. Whereas

Edginton (2010) views benefits as goals, Driver (2008b) regards them as outcomes, and Tucker and Allen (2008) consider them, within a community parks and recreation setting, as measures of local government services. In a literal sense, community parks and recreation benefits can simultaneously be goals, outcomes, and measures of local government services. Community parks and recreation benefits often promote the well-being of an individual. They enable individuals to gain or add to their social, cultural, physical, spiritual, or perhaps even their economic well-being. A well-organized benefit structure not only offers advantages to individuals, but also provides value to a neighborhood or a community as a whole.

The purpose of this chapter is to explain the beneficial outcomes of community parks and recreation. In particular, community parks and recreation services provide economic, environmental, social, and personal benefits. To this end, Crompton (2007) suggested that the future viability of community parks and recreation agencies rests on the concept of repositioning so that community members, including key stakeholders, understand that community parks and recreation services *save* the community money (not cost money) and provide a plethora of beneficial outcomes. Crompton argues that community parks and recreation services need to be repositioned so that they are viewed to be a central contribution to alleviating the major problems in a community identified by taxpayers and decision makers.

THE TRANSFORMATIONAL INFLUENCE OF PARKS AND RECREATION

The term *transformation* has been used to underscore how parks and recreation services are an active change agent that can impact millions of people (Edginton & Chen, 2014). Different parts of this book outline how to reposition community parks and recreation services to underscore its transformational power. However, to explain how community parks and recreation are beneficial and transformational to communities and people, articulating the benefits of leisure is a beginning step.

Crompton's (1999) historical analysis of the consequences of tax revolts and tax reductions suggests that the parks and recreation profession is undervalued. That is, during difficult economic times, parks and recreation services are often the first government services that receive financial cuts. Five wasteful spending areas were identified by a representative in the 2008 Iowa House of Representatives, two were directly related to parks and recreation, and the third had connections to parks and public works. The first was $100,000 for the creation of a recreation center, and the second was $750,000 for the Principal Riverwalk (a parks and tourism development), both located in Des Moines (Iowa). The third item of wasteful spending was $120,000 on flower pots used to beautify the city.

The Principal Riverwalk, which was completed in 2013, is a recreational park district along the banks of the Des Moines River, which features a 1.2-mile recreational trail connecting the east and west sides of downtown via two pedestrian bridges with networks to many downtown venues, such as the Greater Des Moines Botanical Garden and Iowa Events Center. A landscaped public walk connects the riverfront amphitheater and several plazas, including an outdoor ice skating rink and summertime fountain plaza. Further, the Principal Riverwalk links to over 300 miles of Central Iowa trails. Beyond the health and community development benefits, the City of Des Moines gains over $1 million in tax receipts from a sample of tourism activities, many occurring in the Principal Riverwalk area.

The study (STEP/R2S, 2013) that provided the basis for the City of Des Moines Parks and Recreation 2014 report, delineated four factors of economic value of the public parks and recreation system, to include revenue (increased tax receipts from increased property values, and from parks and recreation-related tourism, at $2.1 million per year), wealth-increasing factors (increase in personal property values for homes located close to parks, and profits from tourism and businesses at $66,190,517 per year), cost savings for residents (direct use, health, and community cohesion value calculated at $21,399,331 per year), and cost savings for city government (storm water management and floodplain replacement value calculated at $2,181,642 per year).

The history of community parks and recreation can be viewed as a history of social and community well-being. As mentioned in different parts of this book, Jane Addams and the women at Hull House, for example, developed community recreation, youth programs, and community-based therapeutic recreation to remedy the social problems of poverty and discrimination (Dieser, 2005, 2008; Dieser, Harkema, Kowalski, Osuji, & Poppen, 2004). Crompton (2013, 2014) documented the health benefits rationale articulated by physicians and sanitarians in the mid- and late 19th century in the United States in support of community parks. In short, community parks were perceived to provide oxygenated oases that offered protection against miasmas—defined as noxious emanations carried into the air from urban squalor and filth. Miasmas were thought to spread disease, and parks would benefit air quality, thus controlling disease.

In the last two decades, the National Recreation and Park Association (NRPA) has developed an ideology related to communicate the benefits of community parks and recreation. Often this NRPA value is summarized in the motto, "The Benefits are Endless." Over 20 years ago, Rudick (1996) reported that close to 500 parks and recreation professionals had taken part in the Benefits of Parks and Recreation training program. Starting in the latter 1990s, and as part of the benefits are endless value, the National Recreation and Park Association partnered with the National Heart, Lung, and Blood Institute to create the Hearts N' Parks initiative to augment the health benefits of community parks and recreation.

According to the National Institutes of Health (2004), the Hearts N' Parks program is offered in over 50 parks and recreation departments (through 11 states) and is specifically focused on remedying the social problem of obesity. More recently, the National Recreation and Park Association has distributed a series of research publications that provide "scientific evidence" regarding the benefits of community parks and recreation. As one example, Godbey and Mowen (2010) published a 34-page document that summarizes research-based evidence of the benefits of physical activity provided by community parks and recreation services. Today, many community parks and recreation agencies use the benefits of parks and recreation framework in their marketing and programming (see Chapter 12 on benefits-based/outcome-focused programming and Figure 12.3 in Chapter 12 of the City of Columbia Parks and Recreation website that is based on the benefits are endless value).

There is a great deal of research-based evidence that community parks and recreation services provide psychological or mental health beneficial outcomes. Kleiber, Walker, and Mannell (2011), drawing from a psychological perspective, explain a number of research-based mental health benefits of leisure, which include community parks and recreation services. First, community parks and recreation services can be selected to satisfy unmet needs in other life domains. A person who belongs to a community recreation reading club can develop friendship that may be absent elsewhere in his or her life. Second, community parks and recreation services can increase personal growth or human development. Youth recreation-based sports can provide physical skill development and sitting in a quiet park to reflect about one's life can increase emotional development. Third, community parks and recreation services allow identity formation to develop. A person can be viewed as an "expert" as part of a park birding society or as a volunteer historical park interpreter. Fourth, community parks and recreation services influence health and wellness by facilitating coping behaviors in response to stressful life events. Being able to walk or bike on city trails or enroll in a high-impact aerobics class at a recreation facility are healthy ways to deal with stressful life events. Fifth, community parks and recreation can provide psychological hedonism, such as pleasure, relaxation, and fun. A family picnic in a park or a family running through a waterpark can be simultaneously pleasurable and relaxing. Table 4.1, adapted from the academic labor of Driver and Burns (1999), summarizes the multiple research-based benefits of parks and recreation experiences.

Table 4.1

Benefits of Community Parks and Recreation

I.   Personal Benefits
   1. Psychological
      a. Better mental health and health maintenance
         i.   Wellness
         ii. Stress management
         iii. Catharsis
         iv. Prevention of or reduced depression, anxiety, and anger
         v.   Positive change in moods and emotions
      b. Personal development and growth
         i.   Self-confidence
         ii. Improved cognitive and academic performance
         iii. Sense of control
         iv. Autonomy and independence
         v.   Leadership
      c. Personal appreciation and satisfaction
         i.   Sense of freedom
         ii. Self-actualization
         iii. Creative expression
         iv. Spirituality
         v.   Appreciation of nature
   2. Psychophysiological
      a. Cardiovascular benefits
      b. Reduce or prevent hypertension
      c. Decrease body fat and obesity
      d. Increase muscular strength
      e. Reduced consumption of alcohol and tobacco
      f. Reduced serum cholesterol and triglycerides
      g. Improved bone mass
      h. Improved functioning of immune system
      i. Respiratory benefits
      j. Increase life expectancy

Table 4.1 (cont.)

II. Social and Cultural Benefits
1.   Community satisfaction
2.   Cultural and historical awareness
3.   Ethnic identity
4.   Family bonding
5.   Understanding and tolerance for others
6.   Reduced social alienation
7.   Pride in the community and nation
8.   Social support
9.   Enhanced worldview
10. Prevention of social problems by youth-at risk

III. Economic Benefits
1.   Reduced health care costs
2.   Increased productivity at work
3.   Decreased job turnover
4.   Local and regional economic growth
5.   Contribution to national economic development

IV. Environmental Benefits
1.   Maintenance of physical facilities
2.   Husbandry and improved relationships with natural world
3.   Understanding human dependency on the natural world
4.   Development of an environmental ethic
5.   Environmental protection of biodiversity and ecosystems

Adapted from Driver & Burns (1999)

Social and public policy researchers outside of the parks and recreation profession have also provided research evidence regarding the benefits of parks and recreation. Robert Putnam, a distinguished professor of public policy at Harvard, was propelled toward international acclaim when he outlined the importance of "social capital" to community building and civic engagement (see Putnam, 2000). Putnam's (2015) most recent book, *Our Kids: The American Dream in Crisis,* which examines upward mobility and provides evidence that public policy changes over the last 40 years have been detrimental to children from poor neighborhoods, specifically identifies community recreation as beneficial for upward mobility for children from lower socioeconomic backgrounds.

In providing case studies, including changes in his hometown of Port Clinton (Ohio), Putnam outlines how the decline of community recreation centers and pools, along with no-cost recreation activities (social capital), has harmed youth and communities and argues how such programs are needed today to help youth flourish. Barton's (2011) extensive research syntheses related to social policy clearly outlines that risk factors related to crime and juvenile delinquency are neighborhoods and communities with physical deterioration, poverty, low resident attachment, and scant leisure services for the constructive use of free time and boredom. Barton underscores that communities and neighborhoods that are beautified—which is one role of community parks—and has leisure resources is a protective and promotion factor that prevents crime and juvenile delinquency.

Harnik and Welle (2009), writing for The Trust for Public Land, underscored the many community benefits of community parks and then converted various benefits (e.g., air quality) into economic values. For example, in Washington D.C., there are 4,839 acres of tree cover in the city's 7,999 acres of park land. Tree species include Japanese cherry, elms, and massive oak trees. Tree extract air pollution and Harnik and Welle calculated that 4,839 acres of tree cover removed 244 tons of combined pollution (e.g., carbon dioxide, nitrogen dioxide, sulfur dioxide, ozone, particulate matter) each year (note that this does not provide the many other benefits of trees, such as their aesthetic value). Based on the dollar values assigned to these pollutants, the savings amount to $1.13 million. Table 4.2 summaries the economic value of various beneficial outcomes of community parks.

Community parks and recreation programs can provide social justice benefits focused on helping people who are typically marginalized in society. As outlined in Chapter 3 of this book, there are numerous creative and partnership solutions that community parks and recreation agencies have facilitated related to helping people who are homeless. To

Table 4.2

Benefits of Community Parks Equated to Economic Values

Benefit	Cost Savings Per Year	Description
Health care savings	$19,871,863	Park exercise in Sacramento California (e.g., 116 basketball hoops, 78 soccer fields)
Decreasing air pollution	$1,130,000	Extraction of air pollution by trees located in parks in Washington D.C. (4,839 acres of tree cover in the cities 7,999 acres of park land)
Decreasing stormwater	$5,948,613	Reduction of water runoff that enters city sewer system due to parks in Philadelphia Pennsylvania (average of 43.29 inches of rain per year distributed through 10,334-acre park system)
Stimulating tourism	$40,033,031	Total park derived tourism spending San Diego California (e.g., visitations to beach parks and harbor parks, 1,200-acre Balboa Park)
Increase property values	$6,953,377	Residential properties with 500 feet of a park increase in Washington D.C.
Increase community cohesion	$8,600,385	Formal and informal actions of more than 100 "friends of parks" organization in Philadelphia Pennsylvania

(Harnik & Welle, 2009)

this end, the City of Portland (Oregon) Parks and Recreation provides over 50 community gardens, and in 2014 was able to donate 43,693 pounds of produce to 23 community partner agencies to combat Portland's high poverty rate (see https://www.portlandoregon.gov/parks/39846 and https://www.portlandoregon.gov/parks/65818). Figure 4.1 provides a picture of the Kennedy Community Garden program of the City of Portland Parks and Recreation. Likewise, the Seattle (Washington) Parks and Recreation Good Food program has partnered with 18 nonprofit and governmental organizations and has produced 18,000 pounds of food donated to food banks (see http://www.seattle.gov/parks/goodfood?).

Building on Edginton and Chen's (2014) leisure as transformational proposition, the town of Beattyville and the Lee County Tourism Commission (Kentucky) Woolly Worm Festival is an example of how an original small town festival to create community belonging and pride (benefits of leisure) can be a transformational in its influence to stimulate the economy by tourism. This fun community festival started in 1988 and has attracted as many as 110,000 visitors (see http://www.beattyville.org/tourism/feastivals-and-events/). Although the bulk of this festival is driven by Lee County Tourism Commission the small Beattyville parks system supports this unique community gathering. Figure 4.2 shows the 28th year anniversary (in 2015) of the Woolly Worm Festival.

Figure 4.1. Kennedy Community Garden program of the City of Portland (Oregon) Parks and Recreation *Source:* Lankford (2015)

Figure 4.2. Woolly Worm Festival in Beattyville and the Lee County (Kentucky). *Source:* YouTube (2008)

OPTIMIZING NET BENEFITS: CAN PARKS AND RECREATION SERVICES CAUSE HARM?

Sometimes parks and recreation professionals can be overzealous in articulating the benefits of community parks and recreation services and forget to pay attention to the negative outcomes that can also occur in parks and recreation settings. In Driver's pioneering work to articulate the benefits of parks and recreation services, he outlined that recreation can create negative impacts and that leisure professionals need to be aware of undesirable outcomes as they optimize net benefits (Driver & Burns, 1999). Over 35 years ago, Iso-Ahola (1980) explained how youth involved in youth baseball can develop learned helplessness (decreased mental health) when parents, coaches, and other players view winning as a supreme goal and then located team failure (losing) on less skilled players. In summarizing the potential damaging consequence that can occur in youth baseball, Iso-Ahola created a theoretical attributional model of learned helplessness and shared " . . . the present author has witnessed numerous coaches who get angry at players after losing, and condemn the player as unable. Such behavior puts the main blame for failure on individual players, who consequently are faced with dispositional attributes and perhaps helplessness" (p. 122). To this end, More (2002) stated

In some situations, competition and its associated achievement are obvious benefits. In other cultural contexts, however, they can be seen as antithetical to the development of cooperation and altruism. And for every child who leaves the youth sports field victorious, at least one other goes home in defeat. If we [community parks and recreation leaders] are anxious to accept credit for the benefits of recreation, shouldn't we also accept the blame for hurt feelings, broken bones, and other negative consequences that occur so often during participation . . .? (p. 68).

Dieser (2013) reminds us that greater attention should be directed toward the problematic aspects of leisure services because such awareness is the first step toward helping professionals optimize the net beneficial aspects of leisure by minimizing negative outcomes.

To help parks and recreation professionals optimize net benefits of leisure services by having an awareness of the simultaneous negative and positive outcomes of services, the example below, regarding golf courses and water usage, serves as an exemplar. It is paramount that parks and recreation professionals continue their education and be informed about advancements in the parks and recreation profession as a method to optimize net benefits. Figure 4.3 explains how golf course management can optimize net benefits by being aware of the negative outcome of the tremendous amount of water usage related to golfing and through management and technology can augment the benefits of golfing while decreasing the negative concerns.

Furthermore, an essential component to demonstrating the benefits of community parks and recreation is program evaluation (Edginton & O'Neill, 2010). Although different parts of this book explain evaluation, Chapter 12 explains evaluation as it relates to the broader concept of community parks and recreation program development. Tucker and Allen (2008), writing specifically for community parks and recreation, provided two examples of how evaluation was used in order to document and then market the benefits of leisure services. The first example is from the Catch Kid Club program from the City of Jackson (Ohio) Parks and Recreation department that was an after-school program to teach children aged 6-9 the importance of living a healthy lifestyle. This program used the FITNESSGRAM assessment and the perception factor assessment in a pre- and post-manner to document/evaluate that ". . . there was a tremendous shift in all six [health knowledge areas of] neighborhood resources, value on achievement, life-long fitness, physical health, knowledge of nutrition, dangers of tobacco." The second example is from the Club Carter Reach Our Kids Now Program from the City of Fort Lauderdale (Florida) Parks and Recreation that specifically targeted the prevention of juvenile delinquency among at-risk youth aged 10-18. This program also used a standardized test, called the Interpersonal Assessment Scale, to measure pro-social peer behavior upon enrollment and at different times during the program. It also used qualitative evaluation in having participants write in a community service log, used school progress reports, and had youth complete the Family Assessment Devise to measure family communications. By using these different evaluation techniques, this community parks and recreation program had evidence-based data that demonstrated that this program improved interactions with peers and adults, improved school attendance, improved family functioning, and had youth participate in community services.

It is common knowledge that golf courses use a tremendous amount of water. Although the game of golf is declining, it is still a popular American pastime with over 14,500 golf facilities throughout the United States (http://www.economist.com/blogs/economist-explains/2015/04/economist-explains-1), including many located in community parks and recreation departments. Writing right before the new millennium, Godbey (1997) outlined the ethical dilemma that in the year 2025, many American golf courses will continue to use massive amounts of water related to this popular recreation activity, yet it is projected that in this same year of 2025, over one billion people worldwide will be living in areas subject to extreme water scarcity. Over 15 years ago, Snow (2001), acting as the National Director of the United States Golf Association, remarked that the most important issue facing the future of golf is water use. Snow also outlined how golf courses throughout America, including those located within community parks and recreation, can decrease water usage by (1) introducing new grass varieties that use less water or can tolerate poor quality water, (2) using new technologies that improve the efficiency of irrigation system, (3) implementing "best management practices" in golf course maintenance that result in less water use, (4) fostering alternative water sources that reduce or eliminate the use of potable water, (5) creating golf course design concepts that minimize the area maintained with grasses that require considerable use of water, and (6) providing programs that educate golf course superintendents and other water users about opportunities for ongoing water conservation. In each of these areas, Snow presented application steps. Best management practices for water conservation, for example, include the following:

- Selecting low-water-use turfgrasses, groundcovers, shrubs, and trees for use on the course.
- Providing adequate levels of nutrients to the turf, including a balance of potassium and nitrogen, while avoiding excessive levels of nitrogen.
- Using mulches in shrub and flower beds to reduce water evaporation losses.
- Adjusting mowing heights to the ideal levels, depending on species and seasonal water use characteristics.
- Using soil cultivation techniques such as spiking, slicing, and core aerification to improve water infiltration and minimize runoff during irrigation or rainfall events.
- Improving drainage where needed to produce a healthier turf with better root systems that can draw moisture from a larger volume of soil.
- Limiting cart traffic to paths to minimize turf wear and limit soil compaction.
- Cycling irrigation sessions to ensure good infiltration and minimize runoff.
- Root pruning trees near critical turf areas to prevent tree root competition with the turf for moisture and nutrients.

For a more recent example of best management practices for water conservation on golf courses, see the academic research of Kopp, Johnson, Klotz, and Miller (2015) regarding how the use of water conservation practices reduced water-use efficiencies from 81% to 94% in a four year period on golf courses in Utah. By becoming aware of undesirable outcomes of leisure services, parks and recreation professionals can remedy the negative outcomes in order to optimize net benefits.

Figure 4.3. Case Example of How to Optimize Net Benefits through Golf Course Management

THE MAYO CLINIC/FOUNDATION AND ROCHESTER PARKS AND RECREATION:

A PARTNERSHIP CASE STUDY

There are many books and research-based articles that outline the pervasive benefits of community parks and recreation (e.g., Crompton, 2007; Driver, 2008a; Driver, Brown, Peterson, 1991). Harnik and Welle's (2009) publication for The Trust for Public Land provides research-based evidence of the value of city parks related to economic, environmental, social, and personal impacts, and Edginton and Chen (2014) outline how leisure services can transform people and communities. To this end, this section of the chapter provides a case study of a long and durable partnership between the internationally known Mayo Clinic and Rochester Parks and Recreation that transformed the City of Rochester (Minnesota).

The world-famous Mayo Clinic (and Mayo Foundation) and Rochester Parks and Recreation have a 100-plus-year partnership of benefiting and transforming the City of Rochester through parks and recreation development. Today, Rochester Parks and Recreation owns the Plummer House as a tourist and historical site—as Dr. Henry S. Plummer was hired at the Mayo Clinic in 1901 and also become a world-famous medical doctor (Berry & Seltman, 2008) (see http://www.rochestermn.gov/departments/parks-and-recreation/indoor-facilities/plummer-house)—and has many parks situated around the Mayo Clinic campus. For example, Central Park, which is located on the north side of the Mayo Clinic campus, is used by both patients and staff in many beneficial ways (e.g., solitude, lunch conversations, distraction from medical procedures, family space, child play area, historical interpretation) and administrators of Rochester Parks and Recreation are members of the Mayo Clinic/Foundation Destination Medical Community Planning Committee (Michael, Nigur, personal communication, 7/6/15). Destination medicine provides an integrated system of comprehensive care that addresses patients' medical problems in an efficient and time-condensed manner as a means to accommodate patients (and families) traveling from long distances (Berry & Seltman, 2008). In keeping with the original thinking of Dr. William Worrall Mayo, and his sons, Dr. William James Mayo and Dr. Charles Horace Mayo (see Clapesattle, 1969), parks and recreation services provide beneficial outcomes of enhancing the downtown area where the Mayo Clinic is located.

Most years, the Mayo Clinic is ranked as one of the best hospitals and medical campuses in the United States and the world. In 2014–2015, the *U.S. News and World Report* ranked the Mayo Clinic as the best hospital in the United States with eight specialties (e.g., neurology) ranked as number one in medicine (see http://newsnetwork.mayoclinic.org/discussion/mayo-clinic-earns-no-1-rank-in-the-nation-on-u-s-news-world-reports-honor-roll/). The Mayo Clinic was started in a collaborative fashion by Dr. William Worrall (W. W.) Mayo, his sons, William and Charles, other local physicians, and Mother Alfred Moes and the Sisters of Saint Francis after a ravaging tornado destroyed much of Rochester in 1883 (Clapesattle, 1969). Saint Marys Hospital opened on September 30, 1889, and today William James and Charlie Horace Mayo are known in medical history as two of the greatest American practitioners and surgeons (Berry & Seltman, 2008; Starr, 1982). The Mayo Clinic is the first and largest integrated nonprofit medical group practice in the world, employing 4,100 physicians/scientists and 53,600 allied health practitioners with more than 1 million patients seen each year with revenue exceeding $8.8 billion per year (Olsen & Dacy, 2014).

Historically, the Mayo doctors understood and advocated that community parks and recreation have tremendous social benefits for community building and city/town transformation. In fact, part of William James Mayo and Dr. Charles Horace Mayo's approach to attract well-trained and capable medical doctors to Rochester was to beautify the community, and part of their overall strategy was the development of parks (Clapesattle, 1969), and as such, these three doctors become great advocates for parks and recreation. Clapesattle (1969) outlined that after William Worrall Mayo was elected mayor in 1882, a battle was waged on numerous community projects, including a city park: "The park project was his special pet . . . [William Worrall Mayo proposed to] turn the flats along Bear Creek into a pretty lake whose shores could be made into a park" (p. 49). His park proposal eventually became a reality in 1904 after the Zumbro river in Rochester was dammed to furnish power to the city and was called the Bear Creek Project (Clapesattle, 1941).

Both William James and Charles Horace Mayo followed in their father's footprint in parks and recreation advocacy in an effort to transform the town/city of Rochester. Both brothers, along with A.C. Gooding, purchased a piece of property connected geographically to the Bear Creek Project. This property was eventually named Mayo Field, with the Mayo brothers and Gooding ultimately transferring the land in a conditional deed to the City of Rochester in 1904 and was completed in 1910. According to an internal Rochester Parks and Recreation document (n.d.), a portion of that agreement stated that the premise shall always be used for the playing of baseball, football, and any and all athletic work, games, sports, and exhibitions, permitting under the Laws of the State of Minnesota. It further allows the holding of legal gatherings and assemblages, for school, college, and agricultural fairs and exhibits, school athletics, for any and all educational, charitable, instructive, or entertaining purpose *and for purposes beneficial to the City of Rochester, Minnesota, and the residents thereof*. The February 1949 *Holiday Magazine* featured a picture of Mayo Clinic patients at a Sunday semipro baseball game at the Mayo Fields.[1] Today Mayo Field continues to exist and is the home of the Rochester Honkers Baseball Club (http://www. downtownrochestermn.com/go/mayo-field) of the Northwood League. The Mayo Field has benefited the City of Rochester in many ways (e.g., social bonding and cohesion through sports, pride in community).

Situated next to Mayo Field is Mayo Park, which is also connected geographically to the original Bear Creek Project. According to the *Rochester Post-Bulletin* (1984), in 1902 the Ladies of Rochester were advocating that a park be built in the Bear Creek Project (also known as the island) and city council was prepared to reject the development of the park because a landscape artist reported that "quicksand" in the area would make park construction too expensive to complete. In response to the city council, William James and Charles Horace Mayo donated $5,000 (and a John R. Cook donated $1,000), which caused the city council to agree to build Mayo Park. The Mayo Clinic and Mayo brothers/doctors ". . . always subscribed a large share of money required to support a band, which furnishes excellent music in the Mayo Park during the summer months" (Mayo Clinic Division of Publications, 1926 p. 136). According to an internal Rochester Parks and Recreation document (n.d.), one unique part of Mayo Park was the Leonard House, which was used as public housing for traveling people. Its physical closeness to the Mayo Clinic was important as patients (and possibly visiting medical doctors who wanted to observe and learn from

---

[1] *Holiday* magazine was an American travel magazine published from 1946 to 1977. The *Holiday* magazine archival site (https://holidaymag.wordpress.com/) does not have a copy of the February 1949 issue. The picture referenced in this chapter is located at the Historical Center of Olmsted County in the Mayo Park file.

the Mayo brothers) needed a place to stay when traveling to Rochester to visit the Mayo Clinic. Mayo Park helped sick people gain medical services and began to make Rochester a medical and travel destination, which contributed to the Mayo brothers becoming famous for their medical achievements.

In 1907, the Mayo brothers bought two blocks of land right next to St. Marys Hospital from the Rochester Water Works and presented it to the City of Rochester as a park, which eventually was named St. Marys Park (Mayo Clinic Division of Publications, 1926). Today, St. Marys Park is located right next to St. Marys Hospital[2] and falls under the operations of the Rochester Parks and Recreation Department.

In 1938, Charles Horace Mayo gave another major donation to the City of Rochester and the Rochester Park Board of somewhere between $150,000 to $175,000 to pay half of the construction cost of the Mayo Civic Auditorium (at a total cost of $300,000 to $350,000) located within the Mayo Park boundaries (*Rochester Post-Bulletin*, 1938). This auditorium, which today is the Mayo Civic Center (see http://www.mayociviccenter.com/),[3] originally had a seating capacity of 5,500 people and was designed for professional and amateur theatrical productions, educational motion pictures, conventions, and sporting events (e.g., basketball, indoor track). At the signing ceremony, Charles Horace Mayo spoke of an "urgent need" for the City of Rochester to gain "social and recreation" resources and now had an opportunity to rival the twin cities as the only other Minnesota city to have a large enough auditorium to host large conventions and sporting events (*Rochester Post-Bulletin*, 1938). Harold A. Thompson, president of the Rochester Park Board, also spoke at the donation signing ceremony and articulated that recreation was needed to solve community problems, and both Mayor Moore and Dr. D. C. Balfour pronounced that recreation was needed to help with youth development (*Rochester Post-Bulletin*, 1938). The beneficial outcomes of parks and recreation development were multivariate and included youth development, a greater ability to solve community problems, and it brought in large conventions that boosted economic prosperity and contributed to community pride. The benefits of community recreation were clearly known by Dr. William Worrall Mayo and his sons, and the consequence transformed the city of Rochester.

When Drs. William James and Charles Horace Mayo died within a few months of each other in 1939 (July 28 and May 26, respectfully), a statue of the two brothers and their father was installed at Mayo Park in 1952 (commissioned in 1943) by the Mayo Memorial Association working in collaboration with the Rochester Park Board. The statue has the brothers dressed in their surgeon gowns within an amphitheater that is symbolic of operating rooms of the Mayo Clinic on the East end and statue of their father on the West end (Mayo Memorial Associations, 1949). Figure 4.4 is an architectural drawing of Mayo Park in 1952. These statues remain at Mayo Park today and provide additional benefits related to community pride and history (see Chapter 12 in this book related to how parks can tell the historical story of a community).

---

[2]St. Marys Hospital is part of the Mayo Clinic Campus.

[3]Today the Mayo Civic Center is Southern Minnesota's premier destination for local, regional, national and international conventions, entertainment, social, and sporting opportunities. Serving as a vital economic generator for the region, Mayo Civic Center focuses on providing an exceptional experience by delivering world-class service and high-quality, versatile facilities. In 2015, ground was broken for a significant expansion that will add a 38,500 sq. ft. grand ballroom and 16 breakout rooms. Construction is expected to be complete in 2017 (see http://www.mayociviccenter.com/about-us).

Figure 4.4. An architectural drawing of the Mayo Park in 1952. The Mayo Memorial. Rochester, MN. *Source:* Mayo Memorial Associations (1949)

SUMMARY

There is a tremendous amount of evidence-based research that community parks and recreation provide multiple economic, environmental, social, and personal benefits. Beyond the body of knowledge of the benefits of community parks and recreation created by leisure academics, social and public policy researchers have also provided research evidence regarding the benefits of parks and recreation, including internationally known Harvard professor Robert Putnam. Using benefits and transformation propositions, community parks and recreation agencies need to repositioning themselves so that (1) community members, including key stakeholders, understand that community parks and recreation save the community money (not cost money) and (2) can be a paramount contributor to alleviating major problems in a community.

Community parks and recreation can be transformational, and the case example of the partnership between the world-famous Mayo Clinic/Foundation and Rochester Parks and Recreation demonstrates how a city can be transformed into a global identity with community parks and recreation playing an important role.

DISCUSSION QUESTIONS

1. Explain what a benefit is and how community parks and recreation benefits can simultaneously be goals, outcomes, and measures of local government services.
2. Do you agree with the view that the future viability of community parks and recreation agencies rests on the concept of repositioning? Explain your answer.
3. Interview a local community parks and recreation leader and ask him or her to share with you how parks and recreation service can help alleviate community, state, and even national social problems.
4. Explain how community parks and recreation services provide psychological or mental health beneficial outcomes.
5. Describe the multiple benefits of community parks and recreation.
6. List a variety of local, state, and national social problems (e.g., obesity). Describe how community parks and recreation can help remedy such social problems.
7. Articulate why it is important for community parks and recreation to be aware of the negative outcomes that can occur in parks and recreation settings in order to optimize net benefits.
8. Explain the role of evaluation in demonstrating the benefits of community parks and recreation services. Furthermore, explain how the Club Carter Reach Our Kids Now Program from the City of Fort Lauderdale Parks and Recreation used evaluation to demonstrate the benefits of this program.
9. Describe how and why Dr. William Worrall Mayo, and his sons, Dr. William James Mayo and Dr. Charles Horace Mayo, advocated for community parks and recreation.
10. How does the Rochester Parks and Recreation Department fit into the Mayo Clinic destination medicine strategy?

REFERENCES

Barton, W. H. (2011). Juvenile justice policies and programs. In J. J. Jenson & M. W. Fraser (Eds.), *Social policy for children and families: A risk and resilience perspective* (2nd ed., pp. 306–352). Los Angeles, CA: Sage.

Berry, L. L., & Seltman, K. D. (2008). *Management lessons from Mayo Clinic: Inside of the world's most admired service organizations.* New York, NY: McGraw Hill.

Butler, G. D. (1959). *Introduction to community recreation* (4th ed.). New York, NY: McGraw Hill.

Clapesattle, H. (1941). *The doctors Mayo.* Minneapolis, MN: University of Minnesota Press.

Clapesattle, H. (1969). *The doctors Mayo* (5th ed.). Rochester, MN: Mayo Foundation for Medical Education and Research.

Crompton, J. L. (1999). *Financing and acquiring park and recreation resources.* Champaign, IL: Human Kinetics.

Crompton, J. L. (2007). *Community benefits and repositioning: The keys to park and recreation's future viability.* Ashburn, VA: National Recreation and Park Association.

Crompton, J. L. (2013). The health rationale for urban parks in the nineteenth century in the USA. *World Leisure Journal, 55*(4), 333–346.

Crompton, J. L. (2014). Lessons from nineteenth-century advocacy in the USA for urban parks as antidotes for ill health. *World Leisure Journal, 56*(4), 267–280.

Dieser, R. B. (2005). Jane Addams and Hull House: Understanding the role of recreation and leisure in bridging cross-cultural differences in human service work. *Human Service Education, 25*(1), 53–63.

Dieser, R. B. (2008). History of therapeutic recreation: In T. Robertson & T. Long (Eds.), *Foundations of therapeutic recreation* (pp. 13–30). Champaign, IL: Human Kinetics.

Dieser, R. B. (2013). *Leisure education: A person-centered, system-directed, social policy perspective.* Urbana, IL: Sagamore.

Dieser, R. B., Harkema, R. P., Kowalski, C., Ijeoma, O., & Poppen, L. L. (2004). The portrait of a pioneer: A look back at 115 years of Jane Addams work at Hull-House, her legacy still lives on. *Parks & Recreation, 39*(9), 128–137.

Driver, B. L. (2008a). *Managing to optimize the beneficial outcomes of recreation.* State College, PA: Venture.

Driver, B. L. (2008b). Why outcome-focused management is needed. In B. L. Driver (Ed.), *Managing to optimize the beneficial outcomes of recreation* (pp. 1–17). State College, PA: Venture.

Driver, B. L., Brown, P. J., & Peterson, G. L. (1991). *Benefits of leisure.* State College, PA: Venture.

Driver, B. L., & Burns, D. H. (1999). Concepts and uses of the benefits approach to leisure. In E. L. Jackson & T. L. Burton (Eds.), *Leisure studies: Prospects for the twenty-first century* (pp. 349–369). State College, PA: Venture.

Edginton, C. R., & Chen, P. (2014). *Leisure as transformation.* Urbana, IL: Sagamore.

Edginton, C. R., & O'Neill, J. (2010). Program services and event management. In M. Moiseichik (Ed.), *Management of parks and recreation agencies* (pp. 155–192). Ashburn, VA: National Recreation and Park Association.

Farrell, P., & Lundegren, H. M. (1991). *The process of recreation programming: Theory and technique* (3rd ed.). State College, PA: Venture.

Godbey G. (1997). *Leisure and leisure services in the 21st century.* State College, PA: Venture.

Godbey G., & Mowen, A. (2010). *The benefits of physical activity provided by park and recreation services: The scientific evidence.* Ashburn, VA: National Recreation and Park Association.

Harnik, P., & Welle, B. (2009). *Measuring the economic value of a city park system.* Washington, D.C.: The Trust for Public Land.

Iso-Ahola, S. E. (1980). *The social psychology of leisure and recreation.* Dubuque, IA: Wm. C. Brown Company.

Kleiber, D. A., Walker, G. J., & Mannell, R. C. (2011). *A social psychology of leisure* (2nd ed.). State College, PA: Venture.

Kopp, K., Johnson, P. G., Klotz, E., & Miller, C. (2015, January). Water-use efficiency on golf courses in Utah. *Golf Course Magazine,* 114–117.

Mayo Memorial Associations. (1949). *The Mayo memorial.* Rochester, MN: Author.

More, T. A. (2002). "The parks are being loved to death" and other frauds and deceits in recreation management. *Journal of Leisure Research, 34,* 52–78.

National Institutes of Health. (2004). Hearts N' Parks program continues to help participants of all ages adopt heart-healthy behaviors. Retrieved from https://www.nhlbi.nih.gov/news/press-releases/2004/hearts-n-parks-program-continues-to-help-participants-of-all-ages-adopt-heart-healthy-behaviors

Olsen, K. D., & Dacy, M. D. (2014). Mayo Clinic: 150 years of serving humanity through hope and healing. *Mayo Clinic Proceedings Sesquicentennial Commemorative*, p. 11–22.

Putnam, R. D. (2000). *Bowling alone: The collapse and revival of American community.* New York, NY: Simon & Schuster.

Putnam, R. D. (2015). *Our kids: The American dream in crisis.* New York, NY: Simon & Schuster.

Rochester Parks and Recreation. (n.d). *Mayo Park.* Rochester MN: Author.

Rochester Post-Bulletin. (1938, February 5). Dr. C. H. Mayo gives auditorium to city.

Rochester Post-Bulletin. (1952, September 27). Mayo brothers' memory honored: Park shrine is dedicated at ceremony.

Rochester Post-Bulletin. (1984, June 15). Mayo Memorial Park has undergone many changes in 80 years.

Rudick, J. (1996). Parks and recreation: The benefits are endless. *Parks & Recreation, 31*(9), 143.

Snow, J. T. (2001). Water conservation on golf courses. In International Turf Producers Foundation (Ed.), *Water right: Conserving our water, preserving our environment* (pp. 48–51). Rolling Meadows, IL: International Turf Producers Foundation.

Spangler, K., & O'Sullivan, E. (2008). NRPA's health initiatives. In B. L. Driver (Ed.), *Managing to optimize the beneficial outcomes of recreation* (pp. 347–374). State College, PA: Venture.

Tucker, T. W., & Allen, L. R. (2008). Implementing OFM in municipal parks and recreation departments. In B. L. Driver (Ed.), *Managing to optimize the beneficial outcomes of recreation* (pp. 75–94). State College, PA: Venture.

Starr, P. (1982). *The social transformation of American medicine.* New York, NY: Basic Books.

STEP/R2S. (2013). Economic Impact of the Des Moines Park and Recreation Services. Retrieved from http://www.uni.edu/step/reports/economic_impacts_des_moines_parks.pdf

YouTube. (2008). Woolly Worm Festival. Retrieved from https://www.youtube.com/watch?v=-xfrY_XBNAg

Chapter Five

Organizational and Administrative Practices

CHAPTER OBJECTIVES

- To develop an appreciation and awareness of various administrative processes and procedures
- To understand the forms used in establishing municipal government
- To understand forms used in establishing county government
- To understand ways used structuring parks and recreation systems at the local level of government
- To examine examples from the field related to the above mentioned topics
- To develop an appreciation and awareness of various administrative processes and procedures

INTRODUCTION

The organization and administration of parks and/or recreation systems is the focus of this chapter. One can think of the administrator of a parks and recreation department as the individual who is in charge of the day-to-day operations of the organization. Administrators often provide oversight and direction to the work of organization employees. Administrators also work to organize the efforts of the organization. This can be a complex and demanding task as it may involve synchronizing the work of individuals, groups, community leaders, and other organizations. Administrators lead, manage, and support others. They provide overall leadership in the provision of programs, services, areas, and facilities.

As the symbolic face of the organization, administrators are often responsible for interpreting its vision and mission to the public and to individuals in decision-making roles who have the ability to influence the organization's research base. Such individuals also often provide inspiration to a community's members, providing them with a sense of hope that their quality of life, health, and wellness and the environment may be improved dramatically through the provision of parks and/or recreation services. This same sense of inspiration is also carried on within the parks and recreation organization, as the manager must work to inspire his/her employees to greater levels of achievement. Parks and recreation administrators work with and through people to achieve organizational goals often linking to both the internal and external environment to archive the organization's vision and mission.

This chapter is organized to present information regarding various administrative process and procedures. Topics discussed include (1) rallying the community to the vision/mission; (2) decision-making; (3) problem solving; (4) balancing support and control; (5) connecting staff to the community; (6) developing effective administrative practices and policies; (7) conflict resolution; (8) managing up, managing down; (9) practicing acceptance, compassion, and forgiveness; and (10) removing barriers. This is followed by a discussion of the ways in which municipal/county services are organized, including forms of municipal and county government. Structuring the parks and recreation system is the next topic revealed in the chapter. There are several ways of organizing parks and/or recreation systems, including (1) combined parks and recreation departments; (2) separate parks departments; (3) separate recreation departments; (4) community services, arts, and culture, leisure and tourism; and (5) school-sponsored programs. Last, the roles and functions of positions in parks and/or recreation systems are presented.

ORGANIZATIONAL AND ADMINISTRATIVE PROCESS AND PROCEDURES

There are numerous organizational and administrative practices that must be addressed by parks and recreation organizations and their staffs. Such practices enable an organization and its staff to carry out actions to provide meaningful and relevant services for the public. When such practices are held in high esteem, they are often referred to as *best practice* or processes that have consistently demonstrated superior results when when compared with other less successful practices that are not supported by evidence. Following is a discussion of various important organizational and administrative processes and procedures.

Rallying the Community to the Vision/Mission

A central administrative practice in community parks and recreation agencies is the need to rally the community to the vision of the organization. Vision can be thought of as the "power of forward thinking" (Edginton, Hudson, Lankford, & Larsen, 2015, p. 52). Visions are dynamic, inspiring, and encouraging of the best efforts of individuals and promote action. A mission statement often builds on the vision statement and further helps to identify the aims of the organization. Vision and mission statements should be clearly articulated to the public on every possible occasion.

It is important for these same statements to be first believed and internalized by the staff. Without such a commitment to the vision and mission of the organization, it is difficult to propel the work of the agency forward. Vision and mission statements often require a commitment of the heart. In other words, they require individuals to believe in the work of the organization. Successful organizations are often ones that operate not only with their heads but with their hearts. Passion and commitment to the ideals of the organization are important for any public parks and recreation department's success.

Decision-Making

Parks and recreation administrators, supervisors, and direct service providers are engaged in ongoing decision-making on a daily basis. As Edginton et al. (2015) have noted, the decision-making process may be informed by rational or irrational thinking. Further, they note that decision-making is often the end product of a creative process and offer "The extent to which…[decision-making]… is rationally driven or driven by creative thought.

Is never constant and is related to the type and range of planning and decision-making processes by a particular agency (p.160). Decision -aking must keep the participants of the organization in mind at all times and keep their welfare as their major focus. Bureaucratic organizations often become focused on their own processes rather than ensuring that they have a participant-focused orientation.

The myriad decisions made on a day-to-day and sometimes moment-to-moment basis usually are small ones with minor consequences. Such decisions must be made rapidly in order to ensure the continuous flow of the work of the organization. These types of decisions are like purchasing toothpaste at the supermarket. One does not give a great deal of thought to such purchasing decisions as choices will be based on previous experiences and the purchasing customs within the organization. On the other hand, there are also larger decisions with enormous implications that require in-depth examination and thoughtful consideration. Good decision-making requires that there is communication up and down the chain of command. Further, it is important for individuals to understand the consequences and relevance of their decision making. Often, key parties are not involved in the decision-making process and do not feel that their views have been heard and understood.

Problem Solving

Many organizations operate from the perspective that they're responsible for solving problems not creating them. Parks and recreation personnel are going to be presented with problems that require solutions. Some will be simple; others will be more complex. Edginton et al. have suggested that problem solving is a distinct and deliberate process (p. 158). Whatever the problem may be, there are three basic steps that can be employed to solve a problem. They are the following:

1. **Defining the problem.** If one seeks to solve a problem, one first must be able to define it. There are times when our own processes prevent us from clearly defining the problem at hand. This involves gaining and understanding of the symptoms of the problem.
2. **Developing alternatives.** There are many ways to solve problems, and the next step in the process is one of generating alternative strategies. Following the identification of alternative strategies, one must evaluate potential solutions and select alternatives. This can be done in terms of risk and the certainty of outcomes.
3. **Implementing and evaluating solutions.** The final step in the process is the implementation and evaluation of solutions. In any situation, there are costs associated with implementing solutions to problems. These must be evaluated and plans revised to promote the most optimal outcome.

Problem solving often requires the use of one's creative energies. Defining the problem and understanding its complexity and consequences requires a great deal of energy on the part of staff. When problems are simple, solutions are easy to find. However, with greater complexity, there are more factors that have to be taken into consideration to resolve a given problem.

Balancing Support and Control

We all want to support our staff, yet at the same time, there is a need to exercise a degree of control and influence over the work of our employees. The millennial generation values engaging in worthwhile work and being able to operate with high degrees of freedom. This

21st century perspective of the workplace by millennials requires different concepts of support and control. From an administrative perspective, parks and recreation personnel must be able to provide degrees of freedom in the work environment while at the same time crafting ways of holding individuals accountable for their actions. This is a delicate administrative balancing act—providing individuals with support, yet at the same time exercising degrees of control within the work environment.

There is no easy way of addressing this issue other than to be aware of the fact that changing dynamics in the work environment require new and different strategies and administrative approaches. Over 30 years ago, Peters and Waterman (1982) authored the groundbreaking book, *In Search of Excellence*. They suggested that managers offer "loose and tight couplings" in working with their employees. In other words, in some situations, a great flexibility would be offered to an individual, but in others they would be subject to greater control. Another concept that may come into play in the balance of support and control is the idea of "task-relevant maturity" (Hersey & Blanchard, 1977). This idea suggests that the greater the maturity relative to preforming a task that an individual has, the more freedom they can be given.

Connecting Staff to the Community

Often, the perception of administrative staff is that they operate at a distance from the participants and staff whom they serve. We believe that administrative staff should reach out to the community and engage them. This is important for several reasons. First, if administrators are to understand and be empathetic to the participants whom they serve, they must have direct contact. Second, to understand the problems of the community, one must operate within the community. Third, to gain an appreciation of the ways in which ones staff impact upon participants one must observe them as they are engaged in the delivery of services. This hands on approach to administration is one that requires a commitment of time, energy and willingness to engage.

Connection to the community can take form in many ways. Administrators and staff can take an active role in community groups. They can serve as members of such organizations as the Rotary Club, Kiwanis, Lions, Elks, Shriners, and other fraternal-type organizations. They can be evident at and participate in community events such as 5K runs, festivals, parades, charity events, and other activities where their presence makes them available to the public. Further, parks and recreation administrators can take an active role in organizing and participating in community forums, town hall meetings, and other similar type eactivities. All of these place the parks and recreation administrator and his or her staff in the public's eye.

Developing Effective Administrative Practices and Polices

Parks and recreation administrators play a key role in assisting policy-making boards and commissions in evaluating and further developing policies. In addition, it is the role and responsibility of the parks and recreation staff to effectively apply policies in a way in which they are fair and supportive to all. Policies provide general guidelines to steer human actions and behavior. As such, polices can be interpreted and are often humanized in such a way as to support the needs of individuals. Of course this is a delicate balancing process to ensure that individual interests are represented while at the same time protecting the integrity and intent of policy statements.

In proposing new policies or modifications to policies, the parks and recreation administrator should engage all relevant stakeholders in the process. This means not only drawing citizens into the process, but also staff members who can provide insight into their development. Often, it is important to get individuals who are in the field and closest to the action for comment regarding policy development and review. Successful policies are ones that are perceived by individuals as enabling behaviors, although policies do in fact inhibit and regulate routine behaviors. When developing new policies, it is important to spell out why compliance is necessary and useful to the community. Policies should not be viewed as monoliths that cannot be changed or modified but rather, living breathing guidelines that incorporate degrees of flexibility.

Conflict Resolution

It has been suggested in some circles that conflict is natural between individuals and within organizations. Certainly, while conflict may be avoidable, it does in fact exist. We can think of conflict as a disagreement, dispute, or clash between individuals, groups, and/ or organizations. Conflict can be harmful to an organization in that it creates dissension and often promotes hard feelings and disagreements that are difficult to untangle. When dealing with conflict, one should consider a four-step process. First, it is often necessary to diffuse the tension. This may involve actually having the conflicting parties separate for a short period of time so that they may reflect. Second, in dealing with conflict it is important to separate emotion from fact. Often conflict is emotionally laden without due consideration to the facts, giving rise to the tension. Third, would be to deconstruct or analyze the problem to determine or expose hidden factors that may have influenced the conflict. Last, mediation aimed at finding solutions and resolutions to the conflict with an eye toward creating a win-win environment should be undertaken.

There are several strategies or ways to go about engaging in conflict resolution. These include (1) problem-solving techniques, (2) ethical decision-making, and (3) critical thinking. Problem solving often involves a sequential logical approach to identifying a problem and locating solutions to a problem. Ethical decision-making involves resolving conflicts based upon the value systems and standards of community parks and recreation systems. Critical thinking is a method to evaluate information in the act of problem solving (See Figure 5.1).

Manage Up, Manage Down

Administrators, those in senior managerial-leadership positions or in mid-level supervisory positions, occupy roles that require them to communicate both up and down the chain of command. In others words, information and efforts to influence senior as well as subordinate staff constitute an up-and-down process. Effective administrators must master this challenge to be successful.

Interestingly, successful administrators spend more time with their peer group and superiors than their subordinates. Why is this the case? Administrators are often confronted with similar problems, challenges, and concerns at the same time. The synergy that comes from shared thinking and action between and among colleagues is very powerful. Further, the process of influencing one's superior to pave the way for a new initiative or garnering additional resources may draw on the experiences of others.

At a surface level, most students of the parks and recreation profession might think that recreational conflict involves disagreement among patrons, such as a verbal or physical altercation during an intramural basketball game. Recreation conflict is inevitable and has many dimensions. Recreation conflict can include community groups upset that a Nativity scene has been set up in a public park during the holiday/Christmas season or parents may become upset and demand that their child have a different youth leader, if a parks and recreation youth worker has body piercings and "sleeve" tattoos on both arms and hands.

Recreational conflict can occur within a parks and recreation organizations, such as administrators having different views related to a vision statement, how to go about completing a community needs assessment, or how to accommodate people with disabilities. Recreational conflict about parks and recreation programs can occur in city council meetings. For example, OgleCountynews.com reported (see http://www.oglecountynews.com/2015/04/21/swimsuit-rules-spark-debate-in-polo/ac4dq3f/) that swimsuit attire for lifeguards at the Polo City Pool (Illinois) sparked conflict and a lively discussion at a city council meeting related to the topic of one-piece versus two-piece swimsuits, along with "sports bra-type tops" related to women who are well-endowed. Alderman Troy Boothe argued with Park and Recreation Committee members that one-piece swimsuits are more likely to stay in place when rescuing a distressed swimmer and can discourage flirting and distraction, while giving lifeguards a more official, authoritative appearance. Critical thinking, problem-solving techniques, and ethical decision making are tools that can help parks and recreation professionals prevent and remedy such recreational conflicts. Paul and Elder (2012) suggest that critical thinking questions should focus on six areas:

- **Clarity.** To make easier to understand; to be precise, specific, or exact
- **Accuracy.** Free from errors, mistakes, or distortions
- **Relevance.** A close logical relationship with the matter or problem under consideration
- **Breadth.** Exploring alternative perspectives, ideas, solutions; going beyond the first or most obvious answer
- **Depth.** Wrestling with the complexity of an issue or problem
- **Logical.** Reflective about logical structures related to problem solving, such as assumptions, data collection, missing information, theories, claims, or implications

Arnold, Heyne, and Busser (2005) provide a 7-step problem-solving framework for the profession of parks and recreation, which includes (1) search for problems or potential problems, (2) identify problems, (3) understand the problem, (4) generate solutions, (5) analyze alternatives, (6) implement change strategies, and (7) evaluate and monitor. They also suggest problem-solving techniques such as brainstorming, nominal group technique, focus groups, role playing, mathematical modeling, fishbone diagram, decision trees, and literature or systematic reviews of both research and professional articles dedicated to the problem at hand. McLean and Yoder (2005) have outlined a three-stage ethical decision-making model of (1) identifying moral problems, (2) deciding what is praiseworthy and blameworthy, and (3) choosing a moral action plan.

Figure 5.1. Conflict and Problem Solving

Although one's subordinates need care and support, one could argue that if the administrator is spending extensive time with his/her staff, it may be that he or she is not getting work accomplished in a satisfactory fashion. If an individual is not performing effectively, then there may be a serious problem with one's training, job skills, attitude, or motivation. A careful analysis of the needs of subordinates needs to be undertaken in order to determine the ways in which one's supervisory actions can best be applied. It may be that too much time with one's subordinates also challenges the need for greater freedom in one's job. People just do not desire to be oversupervised.

Practice Acceptance, Compassion, and Forgiveness

Mayo Clinic renowned physician Dr. Amit Sood (2013) has developed a model to enable individuals to engage in stress-free living. Selected principles of this model can be useful in administrative practices. Three principles provide a backbone for administrative action. These include (1) acceptance, (2) compassion, and (3) forgiveness. These principles can assist individuals in dealing with challenges not only in their work life but also in their personal lives. Such principles, if acted upon, can promote greater individual and community well-being and happiness.

Acceptance implies that as an administrator one is willing to reach out to individuals and embrace them for who they are, their uniqueness, regardless of their race, ethnicity, sexual orientation, or lifestyle. Compassion suggests that individuals will make mistakes in the work environment. Recognizing the imperfection in human beings and enabling them to experience failure without drastic consequences is a way of viewing the process of compassion. We all have imperfections in our lives, and it is difficult for any one individual to be perfect day in and day out. Forgiveness suggests that as people make mistakes in the environment, they will be forgiven for their transgressions. It is difficult at times to forgive others for personal slights, imperfections in their personalities, and/or not meeting the highest work standards. However, if we are to recognize that people are fallible and that people make mistakes, as Sood (2013) notes, it is "a gift that provides gift and freedom to all" (p. 47).

Remove Barriers

Administrators are responsible for ensuring that the parks and recreation department achieves its vision, mission, goals, and objectives. In achieving such ends, there are often barriers that emerge that hinder individuals and community members. Such barriers may include the lack of will to proceed as a result of psychological perceptions that individuals and community members have that their efforts will be for naught. Barriers can be numerous and at times perceived as being difficult to overcome including (1) lack of community support, (2) lack of leadership, (3) inability to distill focus and generate interest in some type of development, (4) lack of fiscal resources, (5) lack of qualified and competent personnel, (6) and others. All of these barriers to the success of individuals and community members can be overcome. The role of parks and recreation administrators is that of assisting individuals and community members and to address such barriers and developing strategies to address such challenges.

In the work environment itself, there are also barriers that may prevent individuals from successfully accomplishing their work assignments. Conflicts with other employees, lack of resources, limited training, lack of knowledge of job requirements, and even perhaps the need for greater recognition and encouragement can all be barriers that prevent individuals from success in the work environment. All of these can and should be addressed by parks and recreation administrators. Part of the responsibility of individuals in administrative roles is to gain an understanding of what barriers prevent individuals from operating at an optimal level of performance. This requires communication, dialogue, and problem-solving to find solutions to addressing such barriers.

WAYS OF ENABLING MUNICIPAL/COUNTY SERVICES

In this section of the book, a discussion of the ways municipal parks and recreation services are enabled will be presented. Municipalities and county governments enable through their charter the various ways in which parks and recreation services can be organized, including their powers, functions, and procedures. At the county level, the structure of government is specified in state constitutions and statues. Like municipal forms of government, counties can also enact a charter that is approved by their electorate which is tailor-made to their needs. Chapter 1 includes a discussion of recreation and parks operating as a special purpose district (see Chapter 1, p. 15).

Forms of Municipal Government

There are several forms of municipal government. These include the council-manager, mayor-council, town meeting, and representative town meeting. The *council manager* form of municipal government is one wherein an elected city-council oversees the general administration of the city. The city council's major responsibilities include establishing policy, setting the budget, and hiring a professional city manager. Over 55% of all municipalities use this form of organization. Usually, the mayor is drawn on a rotating basis from the city council.

The next form of municipal government is known as the *mayor-council.* In this approach to municipal government, the mayor is separately elected and operates on a full-time, paid basis. The role of the mayor is an administrative one with budgetary responsibilities. In this situation, the mayor could have either weak or strong powers. Mayors with strong powers have great executive authority and are involved in the appointments of key administrative staff members. The weak mayor form of government finds the council more powerful and the mayor not serving in the role of the chief executive officer of the city. Often, separate administrative boards and conditions provide oversight to various city functions and services including parks and recreation. In the United States, 34% of the municipalities employ this form of government.

The *commission* form of government is one where individual commissioners are elected by the citizenry. Organized into a small governing board, a commission will be responsible for supervising one specific type of public service such as parks and recreation. Commissions are led by a chairperson and operate with both legislative and executive powers. Although the commission is the oldest form of government in the United States, it is employed in less than 1% of communities.

Town meetings are still practiced in communities across the United States wherein voters meet to elect officials and determine policies. This form of municipal government is practiced in 5% of communities across the United States. The last form of government employed in the United States is known as the *representative town meeting.* In this form of government, citizens elect individuals to represent them at town meetings. Such individuals are known as selectmen. They are responsible for carrying out policy decisions. Again, this form of government is not widely practiced within the United States, with less than 1% of communities utilizing this form of services.

Forms of County Government

Nearly every state in the United States uses the county form of government. Today there are over 3,000 counties that are in existence ranging in population from less than 50 residents to nearly 10 million individuals. Although county government has focused its activities on property task assessment, record keeping, road maintenance, administration of elections, and public welfare, counties also provide parks and recreation services. There are three basic forms of county government. They are (1) commission, (2) commissioner/administrator, and (3) council-executive.

The *commission* form of county government has elected commissioners or a board of supervisors with legislative powers to enact policies. In addition, this form of government provides executive opportunities for the appointment of staff and oversight to their professional endeavors. Often, the commissioners or board of supervisors appoints a senior administrator who in turn has the authority to formulate budgets and present them to the commission for their approval. The senior administrator would also be responsible for the hiring and firing of department heads.

The next form of county government organizations is known as *commissioner/administrator*. This form of county government is similar to the commission form of government; however, the administrator is provided with greater powers in the execution of the budget and staffing for the county government. In this type of organization, strong political leadership is combined with the managerial experience of the senior manager.

The last form of county government is known as the *council-executive*. In this approach to governance in counties, there is a separation of powers. The senior administrative officer has the authority to veto ordinances and policies enacted by the county board. In addition, this individual is responsible for the hiring and firing of department heads.

STRUCTURING THE PARKS AND RECREATION SYSTEM

There are a number of ways in which parks and/or recreation systems are organized across the United States. These include (1) combined parks and recreation departments; (2) separate parks departments; (3) separate recreation departments; (4) community services, arts, culture, leisure, and tourism; and (5) school-sponsored programs. Generally speaking, from a historical perspective, park services were separated from recreation services until the early 1950s. However, in more recent years, parks and recreation services have been combined and also have involved other administrative units of government combined into their operations.

Combined Parks and Recreation Departments

This approach to providing service is the most common form of organization for parks and recreation services at the municipal and county levels. In this approach to service delivery, parks, grounds, areas, and related facilities are combined with other recreation and leisure programs and services. These combined services are under the jurisdiction of one administrator who provides oversight and direction to the combined unit's operations. Figure 5.2 is an organizational chart for the Westerville, Ohio Parks and Recreation Department. As one can see, in viewing this organizational chart, there is a parks and recreation director who provides oversight to the overall department. From a functional standpoint, there are four divisions, including (1) parks and recreation development division, (2) support services division, (3) parks and facilities maintenance division, and (4) recreation services operations division.

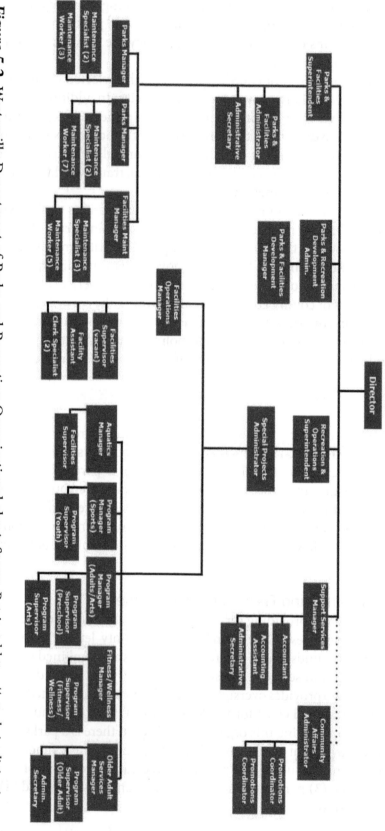

Figure 5.2. Westerville Department of Parks and Recreation Organizational chart. *Source:* Retrieved https://otterbein.digication.com/aaron_mcphersons_case_study/Needs_Assessment

Separate Parks Department

Separate parks departments focus their attention toward the management of parks, forest, grounds, and natural resources. The reporting structure for such a department may vary depending upon the nature of the organization of the municipal and or county government. However, separate parks departments in contemporary times often come under the jurisdiction of parks commissions. Figure 5.3 is an example of an organizational chart from the East Bay (California) Regional Park District. As one can see in viewing this organizational chart, it is quite complex. It reflects many divisions focused on the management of the districts, parks and natural resources.

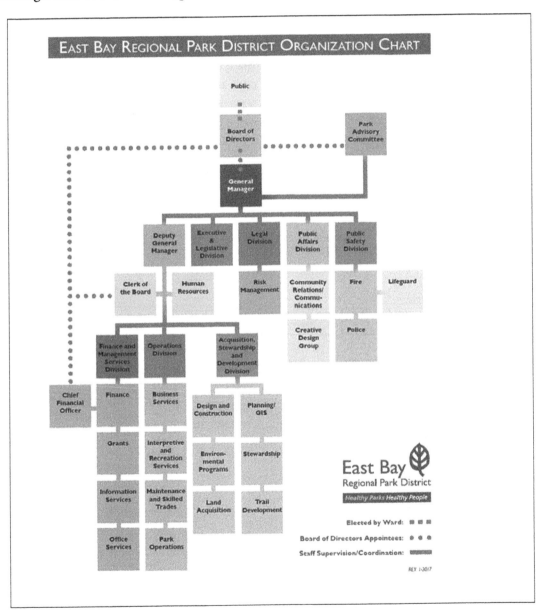

Figure 5.3. East Bay Regional Park District. *Source:* Retrieved from http://www.ebparks.org/about/orgchart

Separate Department of Recreation

Still another form of organization is the separate department or division of recreation. Again, depending on the form of municipal government, the reporting structure from the senior administrator would be from a board or a city manager/administrator. Separate recreation departments focus their attention toward the promotion and provision of recreation and leisure services. Such departments trace their historical heritage to the early years of the movement when departments of recreation were focused on the provision of playground programs, often during the summer months.

Community Services, Arts and Culture, Leisure and Tourism

Increasingly across the United States, administrative units are being combined for a variety of reasons including cost efficiency. It's not unusual to see recreation services aligned with other community services, libraries, museums, the arts, cultural programs as well as tourism. All of these programs have at their core the leisure experience and therefore have similar connections, administrative challenges and opportunities. Figure 5.4 is an organization chart from the city of Cedar Falls, Iowa, which recently reorganized its services to promote greater efficiency in the way in which its administrative units were aligned. In addition to creating a department of public safety combing police and fire, the city created

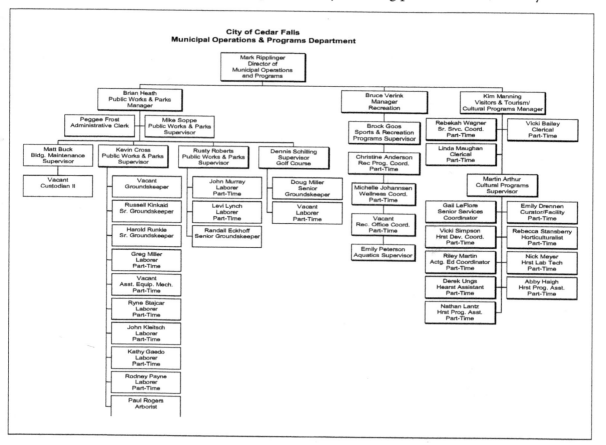

Figure 5.4. Municipal Operations and Program Department organizational chart, Cedar Falls, Iowa. *Source:* M. Ripplinger, personal communication, June 9, 2015

a department of municipal operations and programs. This combination of administrative units includes traditional parks and recreation services as well as including the visitor and tourism bureau and cultural programs such as the Hearst Center for the Arts. Another example of a combined administrative unit is that drawn from Fresno, California. This department combines parks, after-school, recreation, and community services. See Figure 5.5.

Figure 5.5. Fresno, California Parks, After School, Recreation and Community Services. *Source:* Retrieved from http://www.fresno.gov/DiscoverFresno/ParksRecreationandCommunityServices/default.htm

School-Sponsored Programs

In a selected number of states, recreation services are a part of the school system and/or are offered as joint effort between other local subdivisions of government and the school system. Such programs are often linked to the adult educational services of a school system. The joint use of resources between a community and/or nongovernmental organizations is a cost saving activity. The state of Wisconsin has employed this form of organization to provide recreation services for many years.

ROLES AND FUNCTIONS

The James City County (Virginia) operates 1,500 acres of park land and shoreline along the James and Chickahominy rivers. The parks and recreation department operates many services including aquatics programs, arts, before- and after-school care, camps, senior citizens programs, fitness/aerobics, health/wellness, programs aimed at the disabled, outdoor services, sports and athletics, and teens. Faculties includes recreation centers, community gardens, and a facility known as Legacy Hall, available to individuals, civic and community groups for such events as weddings, banquets, and meetings. To staff and operate these facilities and the programs contained within, the parks and recreation department has crafted 60 position descriptions (See Table 5.1). Although some of these are filled by one individual, many have multiple staff members fulfilling roles. Thus, the complexity of the organization from an organizational and administrative position is significant.

Most administrative schemes are layered within the bureaucratic structure of a local jurisdiction of government. Figure 5.6 is a model that presents levels of responsibility and authority within public parks and recreation. At the top of the pyramid are policy-making units. Such bodies can include city council, separate parks and recreation boards, or even individuals who have been elected or appointed as commissioners. Following the policy-making units include the professional staff of the organization; at the very top are those occupying senior administrative positions. In general these individuals are responsible for ensuring the success of the organization, including its financial transparency and stability. Following this are positions referred to as middle management. This category is somewhat broad as it may include individuals who provide oversight to entire divisions such as a parks division or recreation divisions or individuals in a supervisory role who may be responsible for a program area or a geographic region within the community. Last but not least are those individuals involved in recreation service delivery. This reflects individuals who are involved in actually delivering the services to individuals in the community. It could involve individuals who are engaged in park maintenance or who are serving as recreation leaders or instructors. This group of people is often the front line of the organization and its bottom line. They are often engaging on a day-to-day basis with community members in the implementation of programs and services and the maintenance of areas and facilities.

As noted above, from a staffing perspective, at the apex of an organizational structure will be the senior administrator of the organization. Titles frequently used include parks and recreation director, parks and recreation superintendent, and/or general manager. The person in this role would provide general oversight to the development of the parks and recreation department including planning, coordinating, evaluating, and directing the work of the professional staff. Depending on the way in which the municipal government is organized the individual in this position would report to a mayor, city/community services

Table 5.1

Parks and Recreation Position Titles

Account Clerk	Park Supervisor
Account Clerk Senior	Parks and Recreation Business Analyst
Aquatic Coordinator	Parks and Recreation Director
Administrative Services Coordinator Senior	Parks Superintendent
Assistant Recreation Supervisor	Planner (Parks/Greenways)
Budget Management Specialist	Planner I Senior (Parks/Greenways)
Communications Specialist II	Planner II Senior (Parks/Greenways)
Community Centers Administrator	Recreation Administrator
Customer Assistant	Recreation Leader I
Customer Assistant - Facilities	Recreation Leader I (Therapeutic)
Customer Service Coordinator	Recreation Operations Coordinator - Recreation Services
Deputy Director of Parks and Recreation	Recreation Operations Coordinator - Parks
Field Supervisor	Recreation Operations Coordinator - Community Facilities
Fiscal Specialist	Recreation Operations Coordinator - Youth Services
Fitness Attendant	
Fitness Trainer I	Recreation Program Coordinator
Fitness Trainer II	Recreation Program Specialist
Fitness Trainer Senior	Recreation Program Specialist - Fitness
Information Systems Technician	Recreation Program Specialist - Recreation Services
Instructor I (Recreation Services)	Recreation Supervisor
Instructor II (Recreation Services)	Seasonal Bus Driver
Instructor III (Recreation Services)	Seasonal Leak Park Attendant - Upper Co. Park
Lead Lifeguard	Seasonal Lifeguard
Lead Park Attendant	Secretary
Lifeguard I	Secretary (Recreation Services)
Office Assistant	Senior Park Attendant - Chickahominy Riverfront Park Office
Park Attendant I	Senior Customer Assistant - Community Centers
Park Coordinator	Senior Office Assistant
Park Ranger	Senior Recreation Program Coordinator
Park Ranger Lead	Volunteer and Resource Coordinator

Source: James City/County (Virginia) Parks and Recreation

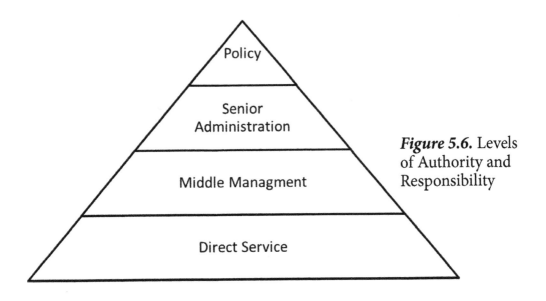

Figure 5.6. Levels of Authority and Responsibility

manager or a parks and recreation board. Figure 5.7 is an example of a job description for the City of Boaz, Alabama parks and recreation director. This job description is comprehensive in detailing specific functions as well as the qualifications.

JOB DESCRIPTION
CITY OF BOAZ, ALABAMA

JOB TITLE: DIRECTIOR OF PARKS & RECREATION   **CODE: 300**

JOB DEFINITION

This position involves professional administrative and technical work in the direction of the activities in the Parks and Recreation Department of the City of Boaz. The employee is responsible for developing, administrating, and supervising a comprehensive citywide recreational program, including the maintenance of a wide variety of recreational areas, facilities, and equipment. In addition, the employee exercises general supervision over the maintenance, beatification and improvement of parks and public grounds. The employee must exercise independent judgement and ingenuity in accomplishing program objectives and interpreting the needs and desires of the public. Work is performed under the general supervision of the Mayor. The position is classified as **EXEMPT**.

ESSENTIAL FUNCTIONS

< Insure the safety of assigned personnel.
< Organize and direct activities and use of public recreational facilities including playgrounds, swimming pools, nature park, athletic fields, and community recreational facilities.
< Exercise supervision over technical and supervisory personnel responsible for the care and maintenance and beautification of park areas and other public grounds.
< Plan and develop recreational programs and activities for the community, evaluate the effectiveness of programs and recommend improvements.
< Explain recreational programs and needs to public as necessary and exercise liaison with other City departments for assistance with Parks & Recreation programs.
< Organize and direct comprehensive athletic, recreational, and sport programs for all age groups and genders.
< Evaluate job performance of all subordinate personnel.
< Select and assign recreational personnel; supervise training of assigned employees; and participate in maintenance of buildings, grounds, and equipment.
< Participate in delivering a variety of recreational programs; provide technical knowledge in organizing programs; arbitrate disputes and complaints.
< Coordinate the City program with other community recreational activities and assist representatives of other groups in developing and extending recreational programs.
< Prepare budget estimates for Parks and Recreation Department and direct the expenditure of funds.
< Perform related work as assigned or required.

KNOWLEDGE, SKILLS, AND ABILITIES

< Extensive knowledge of the objectives of public recreation, including a thorough understanding of activities with make up a community recreational program.
< Extensive knowledge of the facilities and equipment needed in a broad recreational program and of the proper arrangement of recreational areas.
< Thorough knowledge of a wide variety of recreational activities, the associated equipment and necessary safety requirements.
< Considerable knowledge of human behavior, psychology, and mental hygiene as applied to varied groups participating in recreational activities.
< Considerable knowledge of the methods, equipment and materials used in parks and ground maintenance.
< Considerable knowledge of the established rules which govern organized youth activities.
< Ability to plan, organize, coordinate and direct the activities and personnel involved in well-rounded recreational program.
< Ability to establish and maintain effective working relationships with employees, City officials, other City departments, social organizations, and the general public.
< Ability to effectively explain the policies of the department to the employees and the public.
< Ability to communicate clearly and concisely, both orally and in writing.

QUALIFICATIONS

Any combination of training and experience equivalent to extensive experience of a progressively responsible nature in organized recreational activities, including considerable experience in a supervisory capacity. Graduation from an accredited College or University with a degree in Recreation Administration or related field is preferred.

Figure 5.7. Adapted from Park and Recreation Director, Job Description. Boaz (Alabama). *Source:* Retrieved from http://www.cityofboaz.org/admin/pdf/job_descriptions_april_2013.pdf

Major mid-level management positions in community parks and recreation departments are far ranging depending on the organizational structure of the unit. In some respects, the structure can be as simple as containing two major units, first a parks division and second a recreation division. On the other hand, structures can be somewhat complex, including divisions focused on tourism, arts, museums, golf courses, and others as separate units. Figure 5.8 is the position description for the position of park superintendent for the City of Palm Coast (Florida); as one can see, this position is clearly identified as a middle management one with reporting responsibilities to the recreation and parks director. Responsibilities include planning, organizing, and managing community parks and grounds operations. A parallel position would be that of recreation superintendent. Such a position might involve the responsibility for providing oversight of the planning, development, implementation, and evaluation of community-wide recreation programs and services. For example, the City of Escondido's recreation superintendent is responsible for overseeing, developing, and implementing city-wide recreation programs. This position calls for

> Under administrative direction, oversees, supervises, and coordinates the activities and operations of the Recreation Division within the Community Services Department; develops and implements City-wide recreation programs; coordinates assigned activities with other divisions, outside agencies, and the general public; and provides highly responsible and complex staff assistance to the Assistant Director of Community Services. (City of Escondido, n.d.)

Further, other mid-level management positions can best be described as supervisory ones. One occupying a role as a supervisor is usually responsible for a unit of operation within the broader parks and recreation system. For example, there are numerous program areas that involve individuals serving in supervisory capacities such as sports/athletics, youth, arts and culture, outdoor recreation/education, fitness and wellness, and others. Further, individuals may be assigned as supervisors to a facility or area. A number of areas and facilities often have supervisors assigned in order to assure that they are operated effectively and efficiently. In terms of park management, positions with titles such as park supervisor, park attendant, park foreman, and others can be thought of as supervisory roles. Figure 5.9 is a job description for a recreation supervisor for the city of Eagle Pass, Texas. In reviewing this position statement, one can see that the individual occupying this role would be involved in planning, creating, coordinating, and supervising parks and recreation activities. This particular position is involved in scheduling, coordinating, developing, and evaluating activities for special events and programs such as tournaments, sport leagues, and senior and youth programs. This position also involves supervising part-time and seasonal employees and assisting these individuals in maintaining areas and facilities in proper functioning condition.

CLASSIFICATION DESCRIPTION

TITLE: PARK SUPERINTENDENT   **JOB CODE: 16 (Exempt)**

GENERAL DESCRIPTION OF DUTIES

Under general direction, the purpose of the position is to perform responsible administrative and professional work planning, organization and management of community parks and grounds operations. Employees in this classification perform at middle management, and are responsible for ensuring safe, quality parks and facilities are made accessible to the general public. Position has considerable responsibility in recommending and overseeing the upkeep, upgrade, construction and/or renovation of parks facilities, as needed. Employee works with a high degree of independence and initiative, however, confers with the Recreation and Parks Director on matters involving unusual administrative problems.

SPECIFIC DUTIES AND RESPONSIBILITIES

The list of essential functions, as outlined herein, is intended to be representative of the tasks performed within this classification. It is not necessarily descriptive of any one position in the class. The omission of an essential function does not preclude management from assigning duties not listed herein if such functions are a logical assignment to the position.

- Assists in the planning, organization and implementation of parks and facilities goals and objectives; assists in the formulation of division policies and procedures.

- Plans, prioritizes, and implements parks maintenance, repair and development activities; coordinates renovation, construction and development projects.

- Directs, supervises, evaluates and schedules assigned parks and grounds crew personnel and supervisory staff.

- Manages assigned parks and facilities and ensures the safety and cleanliness of parks equipment; inspects park grounds and facilities and submits recommendations on the upkeep, upgrade, construction and/or renovation of parks.

- Participates in the development and implementation of city-wide special events.

- Performs public relations functions between the city, community and various civic agencies and groups.

- Performs administrative and accounting duties, e.g., purchases new equipment, materials and supplies, generates and submits reports and documentation; researches special projects and issues; assists with grant preparation; maintains receipts and budgetary expenditures.

Figure 5.8. Park Superintendent Job Description adapted from the City of Palm Coast Florida. *Source:* Retrieved from http://docs.palmcoastgov.com/departments/hr/position-descriptions/Park%20Superintendent.pdf

- Serves as project supervisor for parks projects and monitors facilities improvements and consults with contractors to ensure safety, cost effectiveness, aesthetics and compliance with City policies.

- Researches and evaluates existing facilities and park grounds to ensure the safety, general welfare and enjoyment of the general public.

- Performs related duties as directed.

MINIMUM TRAINING AND EXPERIENCE

High School Diploma or GED; supplemented by (7) years progressively responsible experience in public parks and facilities work, to include four (4) years within a lead capacity; or an equivalent combination of education, training, and experience.

LICENSES, CERTIFICATIONS OR REGISTRATIONS

Must possess and maintain a valid Florida Class B Commercial Driver's License.

KNOWLEDGE, SKILLS AND ABILITIES

- Ability to understand, follow, coordinate and direct written and oral instructions

- Ability to effectively supervise a staff comprised of entry and journey level employees engaged in carrying out departmental functions.

- Considerable knowledge of the principles and practices of parks and grounds maintenance programming development, and administration.

- Considerable knowledge of pertinent Federal, State and local rules, regulations, ordinances, and other regulatory standards applicable to the work.

- Considerable knowledge of parks and facilities development and maintenance for a public government agency.

- Ability to clearly communicate information both verbally and in writing.

- Ability to operate basic office equipment, e.g., computer terminals, printers, copy machines, telephone systems, facsimile machines.

- Ability to read, update and maintain various records and files; ability to utilize standard software applications, e.g., word processors, database software, spreadsheet applications.

- Ability to establish and maintain effective working relationships with employees, division and department heads, public/private sector contacts, and County administration.

- Ability to organize work, establish priorities, meet established deadlines, and follow up on assignments with a minimum of direction.

PHYSICAL REQUIREMENTS

- While performing the essential functions of this job the employee is frequently required to stand, walk, sit; use hands to finger, handle, or feel; talk or hear; and lift and/or move up to 30 pounds.

- In responding to critical incidents, the incumbent may be exposed to fire, fumes or airborne particles, toxic or caustic substances, excessive noise, temperature extremes, and dampness/humidity. The incumbent may be exposed to possible bodily injury from falling from high, exposed places; and moving mechanical parts of equipment, tools, and machinery.

Figure 5.8. (cont.)

Eagle Pass, Texas

Job Description
Job Code: 9301

RECREATION SUPERVISOR

DEFINITION:

Under general direction, plans, creates, coordinates, supervises, and participates in City's parks and recreational activities.

ESSENTIAL FUNCTIONS:

(Essential functions, as defined under the Americans with Disabilities Act, may include the following tasks, knowledge, skills and other characteristics. This list of tasks is ILLUSTRATIVE ONLY, and is not a comprehensive listing of all functions and tasks performed by positions in this class).

TASKS:

Oversees and provides technical guidance regarding City's recreational activities; plans and coordinates work assignments and schedules, coordinates and develops activities for special events and programs such as tournaments, sport leagues, senior and youth programs and activities; responds to citizens inquiries and complaints related to programs, special events, services or facilities.

Supervises recreational activities and employees daily; picks up and delivers necessary equipment and supplies to worksites, events, and programs; sets up, monitors and tears downs equipment and supplies necessary for special events and programs; inventories and maintains all sporting equipment and supplies; directs and assists staff in maintaining all recreational fields and centers in proper working order.

Within the recreation program unit, supervises and recommends regular and temporary staff to be hired; conducts performance evaluations, provides direction to subordinate staff in the supervision of seasonal employees; establishes and communicates goals and operational standards for public service. Responds to citizens' inquiries and complaints related to programs, special events and services. Monitors annual budget and maintains unit expenses. Assists in promoting and marketing recreation programs and special events, communicating with all local media outlets.

Instructs/trains personnel in proper maintenance, operation, and safety procedures related to specific job tasks or special projects; ensures all safety policies and procedures are followed in the operation of equipment and materials; schedules, assigns and evaluates employee performance; maintains equipment in safe working order; schedules equipment for regular preventative maintenance, may perform related work as required.

Figure 5.9. Adapted from Recreation Supervisor Position Description Eagle Pass, Texas. *Source:* Retrieved from http://www.eaglepasstx.us/users/0004/docs/HR/Jobs%20 2013/2013.eagle9301recsprv.pdf

```
Eagle Pass, Texas                                    Job Description
                                                     Job Code: 9301

                       RECREATION SUPERVISOR

KNOWLEDGE, SKILLS AND OTHER CHARACTERISTICS:

Knowledge of City's governmental organization, policies and procedures.
Knowledge of federal, state and city rules, regulations, policies, procedures, codes and
ordinances related to parks and community recreational programs.
Knowledge of supervisory principles and practices.
Knowledge of recreational sports fields maintenance.
Knowledge of variety of sports rules and regulations.
Knowledge of adult and youth recreational programs.
Knowledge of machinery, equipment and tools necessary for the maintenance of recreational fields
and facilities.
Skill in loading, unloading and transporting equipment, materials and supplies up to 25 pounds.
Skill in the use of proper health and safety precautions when operating or working with power tools,
cleaning, and maintenance materials and supplies.
Skill working in temperature and weather extremes.
Skill in supervising, evaluating, training and motivating employees.
Skill in creating, planning, prioritizing, and managing a diverse number of public recreational
facilities and recreational programs.
Skill in oral and written communications.
Skill in utilizing public relations techniques in responding to inquiries and complaints.
Skill in establishing cooperative work relationships with those contacted in the course of work.


QUALIFICATIONS:

High school diploma or GED, valid driver's license, satisfactory motor vehicle record; and any
combination of education and/or experience equivalent to four years recreation specialist work.

Depending on the needs of the City, some incumbents in this class must be able to demonstrate
fluency in both Spanish and English as a condition of employment.
```

Figure 5.9. (cont.)

There are many direct service roles found in community parks and recreation departments. The individuals occupying such positions are in fact the mainstay of such systems. Some positions are full time, whereas the majority of positions, especially in the recreation area, are part-time seasonal jobs. In the park maintenance area, titles for direct service workers often include park maintenance workers/laborers, groundskeepers, and others, as well as positions associated with the trades such as carpenters, plumbers, painters, electricians, and mechanics. Table 5.2 provides a list of seasonal and part-time jobs available with the Saint Paul, Minnesota parks and recreation department. Many job titles are reflected in this table, including lifeguard, pool supervisor, senior pool attendant, recreation leader, refectory attendant, ski instructor, golf ranger, parks and recreation worker, parks and recreation assistant, sport official, and water safety instructor. Without these individuals it would be very difficult for community parks and recreation officials to provide a full range of programs and services in a cost-effective fashion.

Table 5.2

List of Seasonal and Part-Time Jobs

Job Title	Position Descriptions
Life Guard (June–August)	• Maintains order in and around a beach or pool • Supervises swimmers • Administers first aid and CPR • Assists with aquatic lessons • Must be certified
Pool Supervisor (May–September)	• Supervises the operation of a public pool or beach • Supervises staff
Senior Pool Attendant (June–August)	• Performs lifeguard duties • Assists in supervising the operation of a public pool
Swimming Pool Supervisor (May–September)	• Performs and supervises the work involved in operating a public swimming pool
Recreation Leader (Year-round, part-time)	• Organizes, leads, and monitors recreational activities at a recreation center for all age and ability groups • Assists in scheduling and supervising the use of building space and fields • Maintains an orderly, friendly, and safe environment • May also be assigned to work with S'more Fun
Refectory Attendant (April–October)	• Performs food service and/or sales work • Prepares, sells, and serves short order meals, refreshments, and beverages • Sells tickets and merchandise • Rents golf, ski, or aquatics equipment
Ski Instructor (November–March)	• Teaches basic skiing concepts
Golf Ranger (April–October)	• Assists golfers • Enforces rules and regulations at one of our four municipal golf courses
Park Worker 1 (April–October)	• Temporary • Assisting in the maintenance of park grounds and buildings • Performs routine labor in a park or other public grounds • Performs related tasks as assigned
Parks and Recreation Worker (Temporary)	• Assists with leading and monitoring recreation activities during the summer at recreation centers, day camps, and S'more Fun • Teaches specialized activities such as painting, gymnastics, or ceramics to youth or adults

Table 5.2 (cont.)

Parks and Recreation Assistant (golf courses (March–November), pools (June–September), Midway Stadium (April–September), ski centers (winter), and recreation centers (year-round))	• Assists with maintenance, stocking, and clerking • Monitors activities at recreation facilities and parks
Sport Official (Year-round, part-time)	• Officiates various youth and/or adult sports throughout Saint Paul, including a choice of football, soccer, volleyball, basketball, broomball, hockey, softball, and baseball
Water Safety Instructor (WSI) (June–August)	• Teaches swimming lessons and water safety at the City's pools.
Right Track	Right Track is designed for youth 14-21 who are interested in career exploration and summer employment. The jobs created through Right Track provide needed community services during the summer months with worksites scattered throughout the City. Qualified candidates for this program will have the opportunity to work in a variety of industries.

Source: Saint Paul Minnesota Parks and Recreation Department, Retrieved from https://www.stpaul.gov/news/parks-recreation-jobs

A mainstay of many public parks and recreation departments is the involvement of volunteers. A volunteer is an individual who is willing to give of himself or herself without financial remuneration. Many individuals care deeply about their communities and wish to contribute to their well-being and prosperity. This can be done by serving as a volunteer. Edginton, Hudson, Dieser, and Edginton (2004) have suggested that there are three types of general areas within which volunteers serve in a parks and recreation system: administrative, program related, and service oriented. A number of community parks and recreation systems operate the volunteer program for their entire community. The city of Milpitas, California, operates a volunteer's partner program that involves opportunities for individuals with the park system (See Figure 5.10). Colorado Springs, Colorado provides opportunities to serve as volunteer coaches and officials. This community advertises the program as a "rewarding way to spend time with your kids and their friends while helping them to learn sports skills from soccer, t-ball to football." Their philosophy is one of "athletes first, winning second." Figure 5.11 is a job description for a volunteer for the city of Bloomington, Indiana's parks and recreation department to serve as a parks ambassador. This position involves reporting safety and maintenance concerns to parks officials.

Volunteer Program
Application & Information
Please print all information clearly in ink.

MILPITAS VOLUNTEER PARTNERS

Completion of the volunteer program application does not guarantee placement or engagement as a City of Milpitas volunteer program participant. Qualified volunteer applicants are considered without regard to race, color, religion, sex, national origin, age, marital status, non-job related medical condition or disability. **Return to: Milpitas Recreation Services, Attn: Volunteer Coordinator, 457 E. Calaveras Blvd, Milpitas, CA 95035.** For more information please call (408) 586-3210.

Choose one: ☐ Miss   ☐ Ms.   ☐ Mrs.   ☐ Mr.   *I prefer to be called by the name:* _____

Full Name: _____   Date of Birth (m/d/y): _____

Address: _____   City: _____ Zip Code: _____

Daytime Phone: (_____)_____   Evening Phone: (_____)_____

Email Address: _____   Driver's License No.:_____

Emergency Contact Name: _____   Relationship: _____

Address: _____   City: _____ Zip Code: _____

Daytime Phone: (_____)_____   Evening Phone: (_____)_____

Availability & Assignment Request

How often would you like to volunteer? _____

Please list times and days you are available to volunteer:

	Monday	Tuesday	Wednesday	Thursday	Friday	Saturday	Sunday
Times available:	_____	_____	_____	_____	_____	_____	_____

Check all areas of interest:

☐ Community Development   ☐ Administrative Services   ☐ Financial Services   ☐ Fire Department

☐ Youth/Teen Programs   ☐ Police Department   ☐ Public Works   ☐ Recreation

☐ Senior Citizens Programs   ☐ Special Events   ☐ Cultural Arts   ☐ Sports/Fitness

☐ Foreign Language/Translating   ☐ Environment/Recycling   ☐ Planning/Engineering   ☐ Clerical Support

☐ Print Shop/Mail Processing   ☐ Reception/Greeter   ☐ Education/Training   ☐ Marketing/Promotions

☐ Park Clean-up/Graffiti   ☐ Other: _____

Volunteer assignment preference (optional): _____

Have you ever been convicted of a felony or misdemeanor (not including traffic citations)?   ☐ Yes   ☐ No
If "yes", please explain. A "yes" answer to this question is not an automatic bar to acceptance into the MVP Program.

_____

DO NOT SIGN THIS DOCUMENT BEFORE YOU READ IT AS IT CONTAINS A WAIVER AND RELEASE OF LIABILITY TO WHICH YOU WILL BE BOUND
I hereby give Milpitas Volunteer Services permission to request and obtain data pertinent to my volunteering at City of Milpitas programs for the individual named herein, and the California State Department of Justice if necessary. I also release from all liability or responsibility all persons and institutions supplying information. I certify that all statements made in this application are true and correct to the best of my knowledge, and I agree and understand that if I am accepted into the Milpitas Volunteer Partners program, any false statements may result in my dismissal.

I the undersigned do hereby agree to allow the individual named herein to participate in the Milpitas Volunteer Partners program and I further agree to indemnify and hold the City of Milpitas, its employees and contractors, harmless from and against any and all liability for any injury which may be suffered by the aforementioned individual arising out of or in any way connected with his/her participation in this program. I also agree to grant full permission to the City of Milpitas to use my name and any photographs, videographs, motion pictures or recordings for any publicity and promotion purposes without obligation or liability to me. *I ACKNOWLEDGE THAT I HAVE CAREFULLY READ THIS WAIVER AND RELEASE AND I FULLY UNDERSTAND THAT, BY SIGNING BELOW, I AM WAIVING ANY RIGHT THAT I MAY HAVE TO BRING A LEGAL ACTION OR TO ASSERT A CLAIM AGAINST THE CITY OF MILPITAS FOR NEGLIGENCE.*

Signature of Applicant: _____   **Date:** _____

Signature of Parent/Legal Guardian (if under 18): _____   **Date:** _____

Print Name of Parent/Legal Guardian: _____

Figure 5.10. City of Milpitas Volunteer Partners Program. *Source:* Retrieved from https://www.ci.milpitas.ca.gov/resident/volunteer.asp

CITY OF BLOOMINGTON
parks and recreation

Volunteer Job Description
City of Bloomington
Parks and Recreation

Position: Park Ambassador
Department: Operations
Job Category: Volunteer
Program Supervisor: Barb Dunbar, dunbarb@bloomington.in.gov, (812) 349-3498

Incumbents serve as assistants to the Operations Division with responsibilities for reporting safety and maintenance related deficiencies to park officials for follow-up action.

Duties:

1. Visit park at least once per week to assess the overall condition.
2. Report unusual or suspicious activity taking place in the park.
3. Complete one-page Observation Report on park condition and park activity once per month and submit it to program supervisor.
4. Organize one park beautification work day and schedule with volunteer coordinator a minimum of once per year.

Training:

1. Ambassadors are required to attend a volunteer orientation prior to park assignment.
2. Ambassadors may be asked to attend follow-up training related to safety standards and/or community issues.

Job Requirements:

1. Ability to take directions from program supervisor.
2. Ability to communicate with co-workers, other volunteers and members of the general public in a courteous, tactful, and professional manner.
3. Willingness to commit to volunteer experience which includes at least one day per week along with park maintenance projects at least one day per year.
4. Ability to track and report volunteer hours to the program supervisor by the last day of the month.
5. Willingness to commit to the program for at least one year.
6. Good oral and written communication skills.
7. Volunteers must be at least 18 years of age.

Difficulty of Work:

Some lifting, ability to hike for long periods of time, and ability to be in the elements is required.

Figure 5.11. City of Bloomington Parks and Recreation (Indiana), Volunteer job description. *Source: Retrieved from* https://bloomington.in.gov/media/media/application/pdf/8134.pdf

SUMMARY

There are a number of administrative process and procedures that have been discussed in this chapter, including the importance of (1) rallying the community to the vision/mission; (2) decision making; (3) problem solving; (4) balancing support and control; (5)

connecting staff to the community; (6) developing effective administrative practices and policies; (7) conflict resolution; (8) managing up, managing down; (9) practicing acceptance, compassion, and forgiveness; and (10) removing barriers. Further, organizational forms of municipal and county government have been presented. Municipal government can be organized in several different ways, including the council-manager, mayor-council, town meeting, and representative town meeting. County government can be organized in three basic forms: (1) commission, (2) commissioner/administrator, and (3) council-executive.

There are a number of ways in which parks and /or recreation systems can be organized. These include (1) combined parks and recreation departments; (2) separate parks departments; (3) separate recreation departments; (4) community services, arts and culture, leisure and tourism; and (5) school-sponsored programs. There are numerous roles that are found in parks and/or recreation systems. In general they can be divided into several layers and often are organized bureaucratically into a pyramid scheme. At the top of the pyramid is the senior administrator of the unit, often identified as the parks and recreation director, parks and recreation superintendent, or general manager. The next layer can be defined as middle management and includes individuals who direct major divisions and/ or individuals under their direction who operate in a supervisory capacity. Below this level are individuals who are involved in direct service delivery, including the area of recreation leaders, instructors, attendants, and so on. On the park side of an organizational structure are individuals with titles such as park worker, laborers, or persons who are involved in the trades.

DISCUSSION QUESTIONS

1. What is meant by rallying the community to the mission/vision of a parks and recreation agency?
2. Discuss a process that may be used for addressing conflict within a parks and recreation organization or within a community as a whole.
3. Outline and describe the problem-solving process.
4. What are the challenges in balancing support and control within a parks and recreation organization?
5. Why is it important for parks and recreation administrators to connect with their community? What are some of the ways that parks and recreation administrators can reach out and engage community members?
6. What does "managing up, managing down" imply?
7. Compare and contrast various forms of municipal government.
8. Compare and contrast various forms of county government.
9. What are the ways in which parks and/or recreation departments can be structured?
10. What are the major staffing roles and functions of community parks and recreation departments?

REFERENCES

Arnold, M. L., Heyne, L. A., & Busser, J. A. (2005). *Problem solving: Tools and techniques for the parks and recreation administrator*. Urbana, IL: Sagamore.

City of Escondido. (n.d.). Job description, Recreation Superintendent. Retrieved from https://www.escondido.org/recreation-superintendent.aspx

Edginton, C. R., Hudson, S. D., Dieser, R. B., & Edginton, S. R. (2004). *Leisure programming: A service-centered and benefits approach* (4th ed.). Boston, MA: WCB/McGraw-Hill.

Edginton, C. R., Lankford, S. V., Hudson, S. D., & Larsen, D. (2015). *Managing recreation, parks and leisure services: An introduction* (4th ed.) Urbana, IL: Sagamore.

Hersey, P., & Blanchard, K. H. (1977). *Management of organizational behavior: Utilizing human resources* (3rd ed.). Upper Saddle River, NJ: Prentice Hall.

McLean, D. J., & Yoder, D. G. (2005). *Issues in recreation and leisure: Ethical decision making.* Champaign, IL: Human Kinetics.

Paul, R., & Elder, L. (2012). *Critical thinking: Tools for taking charge of your learning and your life.* Boston, MA: Pearson.

Peters, T. J., Waterman, R. H., & Jones, I. (1982). *In search of excellence: Lessons from America's best-run companies.* New York, NY: Warner Books.

Sood, A. (2013). *The Mayo Clinic guide to stress-free living.* Rochester, MN: Mayo Foundation for Medical Education and Research, Da Capo Press.

Chapter Six

Planning for Parks and Recreation

CHAPTER OBJECTIVES

- To understand the role of comprehensive planning, master planning, and site planning for parks and recreation
- To appreciate the role of planning as an important phase of parks and recreation organization operations
- To provide insight into the challenges and difficulties of planning
- To review the roles and responsibilities of the planner
- To understand that planning guides land acquisition, facility development, and management, policy, fiscal management, personnel management, and citizen engagement

INTRODUCTION

Community parks and recreation agencies are involved with long-range planning in general and in more specific ways such as site master plans. This brief overview of planning, acquisition, development, and the implementation process involved, will introduce an important phase of parks and recreation agency operations. Planning is a widely used process that cannot be defined narrowly. Planning not only plays into land acquisition and classification, but it is also inherent in areas covered in this book such as facilities, policy, budgeting, personnel management, and civic engagement and involvement. As a framework for addressing problems, planning is a major factor in maintenance and safety, environmental concerns, preventing vandalism, and visitor conflicts.

Successful parks and recreation agencies invest in and rely on comprehensive community plans, parks and recreation master plans, and strategic plans to promote organizational effectiveness. Parks and recreation professionals must become informed about planning in order to manage their facilities, resources, and services effectively. Of particular importance is the notion that agencies must link community values, needs, and priorities with organizational goals, policies, and plans. The planning function provides a means to make these important linkages in a systematic, equitable and effective manner.

This chapter addresses comprehensive and master planning for community parks and recreations agencies. Example processes are explained, as well as the roles and responsibilities of planners. Characteristics of effective parks and recreation planning are presented. No matter whether the parks and recreation agency is engaged in internal strategic planning, or in the development of a community-wide recreation element as part of the community comprehensive plan, there are key and fundamental practices necessary in carrying out effective plans. The first part of the chapter defines and provides examples of the various forms of planning, planning processes, and critical considerations for success. The second part addresses the tools available to acquire park lands in a community.

IMPORTANCE OF PLANNING

There are many definitions of planning. Planning has been defined as an activity concerned with the systematic collection, analysis, organization, and processing of technical information to facilitate decision making. Planning is the process of preparing in advance and in a systematic fashion, recommendations for policies and courses of action to achieve accepted objectives. It is important to note that the process of planning helps solve community parks and recreation problems, not the plan itself. The process allows stakeholders to discuss issues and come to some sense of agreement or understanding. The plan itself is a static document; the process is dynamic. Harper (2009) notes that planning is a "systematic process leading to the achievement of desired objectives. In this context, planning can be seen as a problem-solving process using relevant information and applying critical thinking to realistic options and alternatives."

Harnik (2003) notes that a plan is more than an "intention." Rather it is a document built upon a process, demonstrating a path of achievement, and expressing a final outcome. Plans lay out a logical process to further develop the parks and open space systems. Therefore, in order to serve the public and save critical park open-space systems, it is crucial that parks officials embark on a well-structured and process-oriented parks and recreation planning effort to serve the needs of future generations. Community parks and recreation agencies make critical decisions concerning the following:

- Ways to preserve significant natural and cultural resources for public enjoyment
- Competing demands for limited resources
- Priorities for using available funds and staff
- Varied and conflicting local interests and views of what is most important, affordable and necessary

The City of Boulder (2014) parks and recreation master plan notes the following benefits for the plan. Interestingly, the list suggests the plan guides an extensive and wide-ranging management decision-making processes:

- Ensure the public health, welfare, and safety of the community
- Assess the current state of the parks and recreation system
- Guide the development of the parks and recreation system within a community
- Provide a foundation for financial security of the department
- Develop a tool for rational decision-making
- Engage the public in discussing issues and developing solutions
- Coordinate the various functions of the department and other municipal agencies
- Create feasible actions to translate the strategic concepts of the plan into actual implementation

It is imperative that parks and recreation managers and their staff become more involved in local development efforts. Schanuel (2005) reports that urban planning for parks and recreation leads to increased value for the community in terms of economic development. However, the general public, decision makers, and some planners are unaware of the economic, social, community, and environmental benefits of parks and open space. Many times, opposition to more parks and open space note the ongoing maintenance as a liability. Yet, studies have shown the benefits and return on investment in communities who have place a priority on adequate parks and open space acreage to serve the needs of the community.

COMPREHENSIVE COMMUNITY PLANS, GENERAL PLANS, AND PARKS AND RECREATION MASTER PLANS

The following section describes the relationships of the recreation system and plan to local planning and development activities. The city general plan (or sometimes referred to as the comprehensive plan, master plan, or development plan) is a statement of development policies in the form of a text, maps, and diagrams explaining objectives, standards, growth issues, environmental concerns, and alternative development proposals. The plan is an attempt at presenting the ideal physical arrangement of the built environment. The general plan consists of a number of related elements. The comprehensive plan usually contains the following elements:

1. Background of the processes used to develop the plan, citizen input processes, and methods for amending and updating the plan in the future.
2. Goals, objectives, standards, vision, and value statements that clarify the intent, scope, breadth, and depth of the plan. Implementation tools may be discussed and any ordinances pertinent to the plan.
3. Existing conditions, to include the following:
   a. Environmental and natural resource areas (opportunities and constraints)
   b. Historical and cultural resources (opportunities and constraints)
   c. Economic and social conditions
   d. Legal, jurisdictional, and other conditions
4. Elements (sections or chapters that are considered sub-sections of the overall plan) of the plan may include, but are not limited to the following, based on state guidelines and legal requirements:
   a. Land use element indicating types and locations of allowed uses (typically residential, commercial, light and heavy industrial, open space, sensitive lands such as wetlands, etc.)
   b. Housing element describing condition of existing stock, needs for further housing by type (single family, multi-family etc.)
   c. Transportation to include highways, roads, streets, connectors, mass transit, and bicycle lanes, etc.
   d. Open space element to include delineation of river and wildlife corridors, wetlands, view sheds, and other areas that need to be acquired and managed

    e.   Parks and recreation to identify existing and proposed parks, facilities, sports fields, open space, trails, etc. It should be noted that recreation is often addressed in open space and the parks and recreation master plan is a separate document.

    f.   Economic development or renewal provides a plan for the central business district, commercial corridors, and industrial parks

    g.   Capital improvements or financial plan for improvements and infrastructure

The comprehensive plan is the guide for all other community plans. Therefore, as with all city or county parks and recreation master plans, the comprehensive plan is based on the overall policy direction from the community or county comprehensive plan. The comprehensive plan outlines core values and guidance to achieve sustainability, intergovernmental cooperation, organized urban development, expansion of utilities services, and other initiatives. For example, the Boulder Park and Recreation Master Plan (2014) is considered a key implementation strategy under the city's primary planning document, the 2010 Boulder Valley Comprehensive Plan (BVCP). According to the BVCP, Boulder's parks and recreation programs are tangible ways to shape neighborhoods and to move the community toward the vision of becoming one of the most sustainable and livable communities in the world. Community members, local organizations, and city governments are collaborating to produce plans to inform and guide that evolution and thus pursue the best future possible.

PARKS AND RECREATION ELEMENTS TO COMPREHENSIVE PLANS

Parks and recreation services and issues within a community-wide comprehensive plan are usually addressed in what is called the "recreation element" of the comprehensive plan. For the purposes of this section, "element" is interchangeable with "plan." It is important to note that terminology in one setting is not the same in another setting. For example, comprehensive plans or city plans, may also be known as master plans (although parks and recreation agencies sometimes refer this to a design plan for a park), development plans, the general plan, or simply the city (or county) plan. Of particular interest to parks and recreation agencies is that no matter what it is called, the content and process and subsequent decision-making procedures have a significant impact on the parks and recreation system in the community.

The recreation element, in particular, is more directly related to the land use, circulation, housing, and open space elements. The purpose for the development of the recreation element of the comprehensive city plan is to help provide for both present and projected recreation needs. It is designed as a guide for future planning decisions and actions. This recreation element contains findings based on community surveys, policies that address citizen needs and concerns, and an implementation program to put these policies into effect. These policies are aimed at fulfilling the overall objective of the element or plan.

In order to help address present and projected needs, the parks and recreation element provides information to support the environmental, social, and economic significance of recreation, parks, and tourism at the community level. A recreation element to the general plan must be explicit in stating how parks and recreation are tied to economic development, community livability, and positive social change. The remainder of the element addresses issues such as improving recreational facilities and resources in the area. Recreational standards, which are designed to determine deficiencies rather than the adequacy of the recreational outlets available, are also identified. Figure 6.1 depicts the relationship to the city comprehensive plan and the park plans.

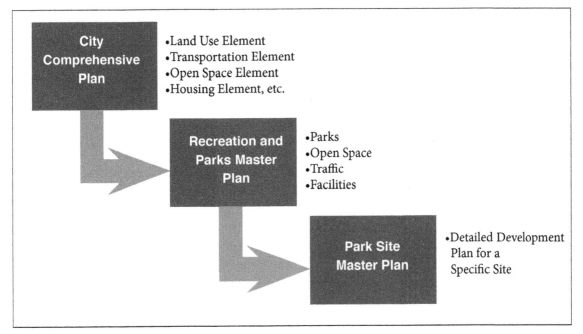

Figure 6.1. Relationship of City Comprehensive Plans to Park and Recreation Plans

Importantly, the recreation element/plan should be coordinated with the other elements in the plan, such as housing, neighborhood plans, transportation, education, health, tourism, and economic development. For example, the El Dorado County (California) General Plan (El Dorado County, 2015) states:

...within this General Plan, preferred locations for parks are also addressed in the Land Use Element. The use of open space for recreational activities is also discussed in the Conservation and Open Space Element. In the Land Use Element, scenic and cultural resources and scenic roadways are discussed. Bikeways are also discussed in the Circulation Element of this General Plan.

The Eldorado Plan presents the Parks and Recreation Element as:

(1) acquisition and development of regional, community, and neighborhood parks; (2) provision of a trail system; (3) conservation and promotion of waterways for recreation; (4) coordination with other recreation providers; (5) securement of funding; and (6) provision of opportunities to increase tourism.

California only requires an open space element to the General Plan. However, many communities use it to identify recreation development. The recreation element to the general plan is an "optional element." Oregon uses "goals" instead of elements. Goal 8 in

Oregon is the equivalent of an element. Oregon's comprehensive land use planning system requires jurisdictions to address recreation needs through what is legislated (OAR 660-015-0000(8) as "Oregon's Statewide Planning Goals & Guidelines - GOAL 8: RECREATIONAL NEEDS (LCDC, 2015). The goal is to "satisfy the recreational needs of the citizens of the state and visitors and, where appropriate, to provide for the siting of necessary recreational facilities including destination resorts." The requirements for governmental agencies is to coordinate with local and regional plans to meet the needs through coordination with private enterprise, in appropriate proportions to the community, and in such quantity, quality and location to meet the recreation requirements of the community.

PARKS AND RECREATION MASTER PLANS

Another type of plan is parks and recreation master plans (sometimes also referenced as parks and recreation comprehensive plans) at the community, county, or district-wide level, which defines what the department does, for whom they do provide services, and how the department functions. These plans are also based on the city or county comprehensive plan. Most planners recommend that the master plan is updated every five years. However, that is rarely the case due to work load and elected officials lack of support. The ideal master plan should have the following elements (Harnik, 2003):

- Inventory of natural, recreational, historical and cultural resources
- Needs analysis
- Analysis of connectivity and gaps in services, areas and facilities, and open space
- Analysis of the agency's ability to carry out its mandate
- Implementation strategy (with dates), including a description of other parks and recreation providers' roles
- Budget for both capital and operating expenses
- Mechanism for annual reviews and evaluation

The following provides two interesting examples of master plans that are well developed yet quite different in their organization and scope. The City of Boulder Department of Parks and Recreation Master Plan (2014), for example, addresses factors such as the following:

- Community health and wellness
- Financial sustainability
- Youth engagement and activity
- Taking care of what we have
- Building community and relationships
- Organizational readiness

In contrast, the Mecklenburg County Park and Recreation 10-Year Master Plan (2012) addressed components such as the following:

- Community and stakeholder information
- Community needs survey data
- Green printing process

- Facility and parks standards
- Natural areas plan
- Greenways plan
- Recreation program plan
- Capital improvement plan
- Demand analysis for sports fields
- Sports tourism plan

One can see that the Mecklenburg plan consists of conservation and stewardship, parks and greenways, and recreation programs and facilities. The city of Boulder plan suggests factors such as social capital, health and engagement, and organizational effectiveness. Importantly, the type of plan, the focus of the plan, and benefits cited should reflect local needs and issues. No one template for a plan will fit all communities. The important factor is that the process and content of the plan reflect the community, its needs and desires and is feasible.

Well-developed and implemented parks and recreation plans enhance the government's ability to foresee and respond to changes in service needs and desires, potential acquisitions, and potential opportunities for service improvement. What follows is a review of eight critical elements that should be reflected in parks and recreation, general plan recreation elements, and master plans. Table 6.1 provides an overview of critical elements for planning parks and recreation systems (modified from Edginton, Lankford, Hudson, & Knowles-Lankford & Lankford, 1995; Larsen, 2013; Lankford, 1989).

STRATEGIC PLANNING

This section describes the process for strategic planning. Parks and recreation organizations engage in strategic planning to focus internal efforts for the efficient delivery of services. One should note that some organizations title their parks and recreation comprehensive or master plans as "strategic master plans." The following information addresses strategic planning from the internal perspective. This process is of particular importance to managers in addressing the internal and external environmental influences that affect the way in which the organization functions and prospers. The strategic plan expresses the values of the community and how the organization operationalizes programs based on those values. Figure 6.2 depicts this process.

Essentially, strategic management planning is:

1. A process for identifying internal and external strengths and weaknesses of an organization.
2. A process for identifying future trends, opportunities, and problems, both internally and externally.
3. A process for identifying a means to innovate and create opportunities in management and service provision.
4. A process for decision-making using those staff who are closest to problems, opportunities, participants, and facilities.
5. A process for organizing tasks, and setting priorities, goals, and objectives.

Table 6.1

Critical Elements of Park and Recreation Planning

Critical Elements	Description
Plans should be based on local values	Values, vision, and position statements (from the point of view of the users) should be developed with regard to ecological conditions, social issues and conditions, outdoor or environmental education values, economic needs and conditions, aesthetic issues, and finally political constraints and realities. A value-driven process helps recreation professionals identify needs and values in order to create this vision of sustainable, livable, and healthy communities.
Plans should reflect local approaches to problem solving	Knowing community values is the basis for developing responsive solutions to problem solving and policy development. Recreation, parks, and leisure service policies and problem-solving solutions will most likely fail without due consideration of local values and needs (Lankford, 1994). Park and recreation standards are useful reference tools and guides; however, programs and solutions should reflect local expectations, needs, differences, values, and standards.
Plans should reflect broad public participation	When citizens are involved in developing a parks and recreation plan or strategy, they are much more likely to be committed to implementing the plan and supporting the recreation, parks, and leisure service agency's efforts (Harper, 1993; Lankford, 1994). People can be involved through committees, workshops, public hearings, informal reviews of plans, and neighborhood councils. Citizen involvement can be defined as the opportunity for all citizens of the community to have access to all stages of the planning process—from gathering data to final plan adoption—and to have the opportunity of having their views made known to decision makers prior to the actual decisions being adopted.
Plans require data on recreation use, needs and constraints	Both the perceptions of citizens and empirical data should be used to describe the current local situation and to project a vision of the future for the park and recreation system. Myths regarding recreation may be dispelled by quality data. However, deeply held convictions may not be affected by contrary evidence, no matter how accurate the data. In these instances, convictions and their consequences must be dealt with as realities in the planning process, in spite of other evidence to the contrary. A mix of data-collection techniques is required and will prove most beneficial to the recreation planner. Community surveys (either mail or telephone, or a combination) are effective in collecting important quantitative and qualitative recreation and park information. Qualitative research methods such as observation studies and case studies are also important and are complementary to survey data collection methods. Basic to the development of any park and recreation plan is the quantity and quality of information on which decisions can be based.
Plan alternatives and recommendations should be clearly defined	Park and recreation plans help communities make rational, informed choices regarding service delivery. Meaningful alternatives may involve a range in cost, timing, doing nothing, doing a little, or doing a lot. Sometimes it may be beneficial to present conservative to radical alternatives in response to situations in order to demonstrate to decision makers and the community the range of options and the extent or seriousness of the situation.

Table 6.1 (cont.)

Plans and issues should be clearly articulated	Technical reports with an abundance of data, tables, graphs, charts, economic models, and such are helpful for planners and managers, but they are of little practical value for the layperson. Decision makers have little time to read lengthy documents and usually prefer executive summaries, which highlight key findings and recommendations. An effective park and recreation plan and technical report should be well-organized with a clear and simple format. The agency should (a) keep factual information separate from analysis and opinion, (b) use an easy-to-read format to organize the presentation of information, (c) use the same basic format for all future park and recreation plans and documents, with some minor adaptations when necessary, and finally, (d) keep the narrative to a minimum when presenting factual information.
Plans must reflect leadership and commitment	Plans must identify positions and divisions within the park and recreation agency that will be responsible for implementing and monitoring portions of the plan. Schedules for phased implementation, criteria for evaluating the plan's success, and identification of responsible positions and divisions within the agency should be detailed in the plan. Commitment to promoting staff and citizen involvement in decision making concerning future recreation, parks services should be established in the plan.
Plans must be practical, realistic, and appropriate for the agency and community	Citizens, parks and recreation staff, and decision-making bodies should be receptive to the proposals and plan recommendations. The proposals have to be politically feasible in the context of the local political environment. Plans must address needs identified. If the implementing strategies and recommendations in the plan are not realistic, they are of little or no use to the community.

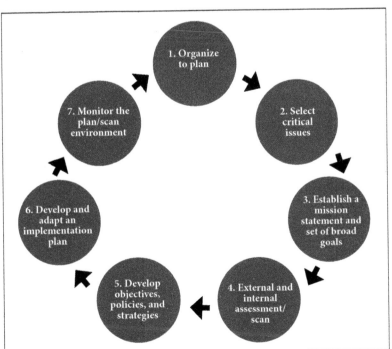

Figure 6.2. The Strategic Planning Process

For example, the City of Portland Parks and Recreation Strategic Plan 2012–2015 (City of Portland, 2015) is titled Healthy Parks, Healthy Portland. The plan contains goals, objectives, and strategies that address improvements in service delivery for health, recreation, and access and equity. Also included are strategic initiatives for managing and improving assets with a focus on trails, asset management, and sustainability. Importantly, the strategic planning process begins with communication and dialogue with the community.

There are seven basic distinct steps in the strategic management planning process. It should be noted that there are many variations of this process in the literature and in management planning practice. For more specifics on this topic, refer to McLean, Bannon, and Gray (1999). However, the following seven steps provide the basis for strategic planning within recreation, parks, and leisure organizations.

Step 1. Organize, Scan, or Scope out the Environment

Establish objectives, definitions, and expectations of the planning effort. Establish time frame for the project, focus of the planning effort, and area to be covered by the plan (geographic or departmental). Identify future important trends and determine external environmental factors that will affect these trends. Getting organized to plan will include some or all of the following:

- Get support from decision makers, managers, and staff
- Define expectations (your intentions and desires)
- Select a planning team (staff and community members)
- Define how long the process will take

Step 2. Select Critical Issues or Opportunities

Using the information in step 1, choose the most critical or important issues to resolve or address. The list of issues should be prioritized based on resources, staffing, strengths and weaknesses, realistic time frames, and the political (internal and external) environment.

Step 3. Establish a Mission Statement and a Set of Broad Goals

This step establishes the direction for strategy development to keep the organization on track during the planning program. The mission statement should be a marriage of external demands and internal limitations, a combination of dreams and reality. Mission formulation should answer the following questions:

- What does the organization do?
- For whom?
- How does the organization serve?
- Goals should clarify the agency mission and what the organization hopes to aspire.

Step 4. External and Internal Assessment

Identify forces outside and inside the Metropolitan Statistical Area (MSA) affecting change and achievement of mission or goals. The MSA should conduct a situational analysis consisting of the following:

- External constraints and opportunities
- Who or what is impacting your organization and how

- Internal strengths and weaknesses
- Get input for the entire organization (i.e., conduct an employee survey)

Step 5. Develop Objectives, Policies, and Strategies

Using the information from the above step, develop action-oriented statements with respect to each strength and weakness identified and how action will be achieved. Objectives should be specific, measurable, and lead to the attainment of goals. Policies should express values of the recreation services and programs, and define why they exist. Strategies should include assumptions and targets for achievement.

Step 6. Develop and Adopt an Implementation Plan

This step identifies timetables, responsibilities, budgets, resources, and so on for carrying out the actions identified above. Action plans should identify who does what, when, and how within specified time increments. Action plans might address communication, facilities, programs, finances, and resources.

Step 7. Monitor the Plan and Scan the Environment

This step is merely a monitoring of plan accomplishments. It is critical that the strategies adopted are working or carried out. When the environment changes, the organization should be prepared to adjust strategies and update the plan. This monitoring system sets up controls for review of action plans and objectives, strategies, and so on using the expertise of all staff. Basically, this step is the evaluation phase of the planning program.

ROLES AND RESPONSIBILITIES OF THE PARKS AND RECREATION PLANNER

Due to the complexity of community parks and recreation planning and the several skills necessary to comprehend the planning of land use, planners come from many disciplines. They could be landscape architects, civil engineers, urban planners, geographers, or graduates of one of several planning programs now offered in Canada and the United States that address park management. Some planning tasks are handled by planners who are staff employees, while others are consultants. However, the most effective plans are produced with a team approach. Here the planner has access to expertise from foresters, soil specialists, historians, geographers, and archaeologists (i.e., persons from disciplines pertinent to the site in question, including the park manager and maintenance personnel).

Planners are not decision makers; the agency director, park board, or park commission has that responsibility. However, in their deliberations, these decision makers must rely on the planners' presentation of the situation, on those alternatives the planners have chosen to prepare, and on the planners' expertise. It is imperative, therefore, that planners provide data that is accurate and fairly analyzed. It is also imperative that these data were developed from extensive and exhaustive citizen participation.

Planning is traditionally thought of as the development of several possible futures or alternatives and the alternative courses toward a selected, preferred future. However, in this more conventional view, planning does not adequately address the process of transferring thought into reality. The planned reality and the reality that results from the plan, are quite different. As with decision making, the process of planning can be viewed as a sequence in time in which the direction of action informed through planning is continually adjusted based on the new realities that the action reveals. For example, Cornia (2002) noted that the plan to save Hanauma Bay in Hawaii was highly controversial and subject to much debate on the intent of the plan and the reality of the situation. There were varied and conflicting views by stakeholders.

Quality parks and recreation plans can help agencies serve the needs of their community, now and in the future, by assessing current and possible future recreation and park needs, and comparing those needs to current and possible future deficiencies in the system. In order to save critical parks and open space systems, it is imperative that parks and recreation officials embark on a well-structured and process-oriented planning effort to serve the needs of future generations. As we envision the future of public parks and recreation and the relationship to community development, agencies need to look further to the next generation (Knowles-Lankford, 1993; Lankford, Lankford, & Wheeler, 2011).

Understanding the context of planning in one's own community lies in the process itself. If the process directly involves the public in creating the solution, then it must be a reflection of the public interest or, as stated above, societal values. This appears to be a developing trend of the future. The call for public participation in the planning process is frequent. The tone of that call has been shifting to meaningful public participation in the planning process. Although the methods continue to evolve, the relationship between the planner and the planned for must be mutually responsive. It is through this process that the agency, decision makers, and the public are able to know more about the values that must be served in providing parks and recreation services (Edginton, Lankford, Hudson, & Larsen, 2015; Knowles-Lankford & Lankford, 1995). This approach allows planners and managers to know more about the world of the problem and perhaps identify the interrelationships among the worlds of many problems in an aim for the brilliant solution.

Recreation planners know how to produce plans and studies about parks, recreation, and open space systems. The problem, however, is how to produce a plan that can or will be accepted and carried out by the community. Although no single planning approach can guarantee implementation, the local planners, with the assistance of the interested citizens of the community, can develop a process that will ensure that the results, at a minimum, will be taken seriously by the decision makers and the community. Well-developed parks and recreation planning processes and plans improve community public relations (Lankford, 1994; Lankford, Lankford, & Wheeler, 2011).

How can community parks and recreation agencies enhance the chances that their plans will be implemented? First, the agency must involve citizens, decision makers, business leaders, and parks and recreation professionals at the beginning and throughout the planning process. Webler, Tuler, and Tanguay (2004) report that planners must find the best or most appropriate means of civic engagement and participation. Second, the agency must develop recreation plans that are focused on the serious concerns of citizens and community leaders, and on issues and opportunities confronting the parks and recreation system. Third, the agency should use the recreation planner's technical knowledge and skills to help citizens, other recreation, parks, and leisure professionals (staff and managers), and decision makers better understand the issues and opportunities and the alternative methods for dealing with the issues identified. Finally, the assumptions, values, attitudes, language, and specific concerns of the people who will use the services and the people who will implement the plan must be built into the plan from the beginning of the process. A number of observations have been made with regard to planning and working to enhance community access to the planning process:

1. Use surveys to identify issues and concerns of residents.
2. Use the Nominal Group Technique (NGT) to refine process.
3. Help citizens and the decision-making body be visionary with regard to the desired results.
4. Use public balloting for designs and plans when possible.
5. Listen to residents; if they feel they are listened to, they tend to support change.
6. Provide as many means as possible for public access to the planning and decision-making process.
7. Be prepared to provide training sessions for citizens.
8. Ensure an atmosphere that encourages citizens to speak freely.
9. Be precise about what is meant by citizen participation, how it works, and what voice citizens have.
10. Total congruency of opinion may not be possible, but a fair, effective, and accessible planning process that includes participation and representation of the public is possible.

A great deal of effort on the part of the parks and recreation agency is needed in order to solicit input on development proposals that identify and respond to the public interest in the context of contemporary values and issues. Recreation, parks, and leisure services plan development and adoption should reflect shared responsibility of citizens, elected officials, and professional staff. Oftentimes, planners and developers assume, conveniently so, that the public interest is defined by the decision-making body and various commissions. An effective citizen participation program may be defined as one that enhances the legitimacy of the planning process and acceptability of the decisions and recommendations, and that improves decision making.

Planners and Determination of Need

Planners must anticipate the needs of the public from a process that engages the public, and determine potentially suitable areas for parks and open space and their optimum capacities. They frequently must estimate costs for development and operations. This must be a continuing function that considers the total recreation requirements of their level of planning responsibility (city, county, region, state).

Information on inventory, classification, and use limits for current and projected parks must be gathered. Objectives are set in light of this information, and a program must be outlined for systematic accomplishment of the objectives. Planners assist in the development of a needs assessment in the community. These needs assessments utilize multiple methods of data collection, to include mail, intercept and electronic surveys, community workshops and meetings, observations, and interviews.

Planners also have established mechanisms to help in determining need. In the United States, each state must have on file a Statewide Comprehensive Outdoor Recreation and Open Space Plan (SCORP), which provides the basic data for recreational acquisition and development by state and local agencies. The section of this chapter entitled "Land Acquisition" addresses the various methods by which an agency can acquire such lands.

Canada also has collected appropriate data for broadly based recreational planning, which began with the Canadian Outdoor Recreation Demand Study. Provinces have conducted similar studies and have produced provincial models of the Canada Land Inventory. Data from these studies helped establish system processes that continue to identify and provide a diversity of recreation experiences for Canadian citizens.

THE PLANNING PROCESS

The standard planning phases are described here. These are by no means the only processes available to the planner and manager, but these steps address key aspects of planning.

Identifying Goals and Objectives

As guides to specific action, goals state a desired end. Objectives must state an overall purpose, consider the implications of action to achieve that purpose, and identify a specific target and course of action to reach that target. These objectives should be measurable.

Data Collection

This step is a complex set of requirements in terms of user data, surveys, observations, public input, analysis of needs, constraints, and opportunities. Pertinent data must be compiled on use and users, present and potential, and on the characteristics of the resource base. Significant efforts are made via survey research to document recreational needs in a community.

Analysis of Data

Examination of all data and their prospective interrelationships occur during this phase. This should be a consultative process with experts in such disciplines as ecology, economics, soils, transportation planning, and forestry, to name only a few. In addition, the analysis of data should include citizen interpretation of the findings. Planners compile data and then work with citizens and special interest groups to interpret the findings. A reasonable understanding of the resource, the user, and the possible management strategies and patterns can be gained from these data for the development of the management plan.

Alternatives and Planning Choices

Several different courses of action should be delineated in the planning document. The planner's creativity, specialized knowledge, and citizen perspectives should find expression here, always guided by the objectives and channeled by economic restraints. The different possibilities must be sufficiently developed in this synthesis so the decision makers can determine the advantages and disadvantages of each course of action and judge how well each might fulfill the objectives. Their choice of a plan, of a modification of a plan, or of a combination of plans is the final step in the synthesis phase.

Adoption of a Plan

The selected plan must be elaborated upon. This includes the environmental impact statement and sometimes a social impact statement required by the jurisdiction in which the proposed park will lie. On occasion, a cost-benefit analysis will accompany the plan. The plan document should provide an accurate base map indicating existing conditions on the land as well as all proposed changes. These include boundaries, access and other roads, utilities, previous use, existing and proposed developments, vegetative cover, open space, unusual features, and soil types. Facilities should be located precisely enough so that no substantial facility relocations should be necessary for the preparation of the more detailed site plans. There should be a written narrative report explaining what is in the plan and the justification for these elements. At certain stages of the procedure, there must be an opportunity for both public and agency feedback.

Implementation

Consideration of developmental phases, to include acquisition, capital investment projects, and environmental impacts are central to this task.

Evaluation and Revision

This process should be operating during all phases of planning, but must be formally instituted at this point. Do the plan's results meet the stated objectives? Periodic review of monitoring results and attention to feedback from independent sources should enable evaluation and guide revision. Unfortunately, this step is rarely completed due to a lack of legal mandates, budget, or staffing issues. Major updates to plan occur as a result of a lack of regular evaluation and monitoring of the plan and implementing measures.

The City of Boulder Park and Recreation Master Plan (2014) process is depicted in Figure 6.3. Their plan consisted of three phases:

- Research (including significant fact finding via public input processes)
- Assessment (determining needs and service levels, core programs, and funding priorities)
- Action (recommendations, actions, funding, and strategies for implementation)

In contrast is the City of Waterloo, Iowa park and recreation master plan process (Figure 6.4). This process had seven distinct steps, with multiple tasks. The process also has an approval and organizational phase of the plan, a data collection and analysis phase, and an extensive reporting phase.

SUMMARY

Few decisions made in parks systems are more long lasting or obvious than those made in planning, acquisition, or development. It should be clear that many planning and acquisitions systems are in place to develop parks for use by the public. If mistakes are made, they seldom go away or lend themselves to easy solutions. All three of these phases require masterful orchestration of many processes. These processes are vulnerable to change and political exigencies. The appearance of a park complete with facilities ready to serve the public represents the culmination of a long and complex process.

This chapter discussed the relationships between decision making and planning. It is of particular importance to note that managers make decisions that affect the organization in both short- and long-term perspectives. They need information to make those decisions. Managers also need to use planning processes and subsequent plans to provide the necessary structure in order to make relevant, timely, and educated decisions. It was noted that many times the process of planning is more important than the actual plan produced. It is the interaction of staff, management, citizens, and decision makers that makes planning useful in managing parks and recreation organizations.

The chapter highlighted a critical path method that can be used in comprehensive, master, or site planning situations. In addition, eight essential elements of effective community recreation planning were identified. These elements should be prevalent within

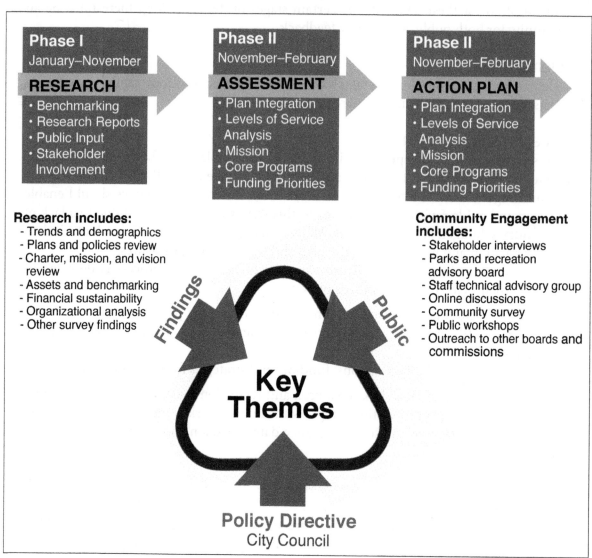

Figure 6.3. Boulder Park and Recreation Master Plan Process

any planning procedure or process. It was stressed that citizen involvement is necessary and of the utmost importance in planning for parks and recreation organizations.

Linkages were made between recreation planning and land use, transportation, open space, and housing at the community level. It is important that the community parks and recreation professionals become involved in local development issues and projects. It is equally important that community parks and recreation professionals educate the decision makers on the value of recreation in the context of comprehensive community planning.

DISCUSSION QUESTIONS

1. Define comprehensive planning.
2. What is a parks and recreation master plan?
3. How can strategic planning help to make organizations effective?

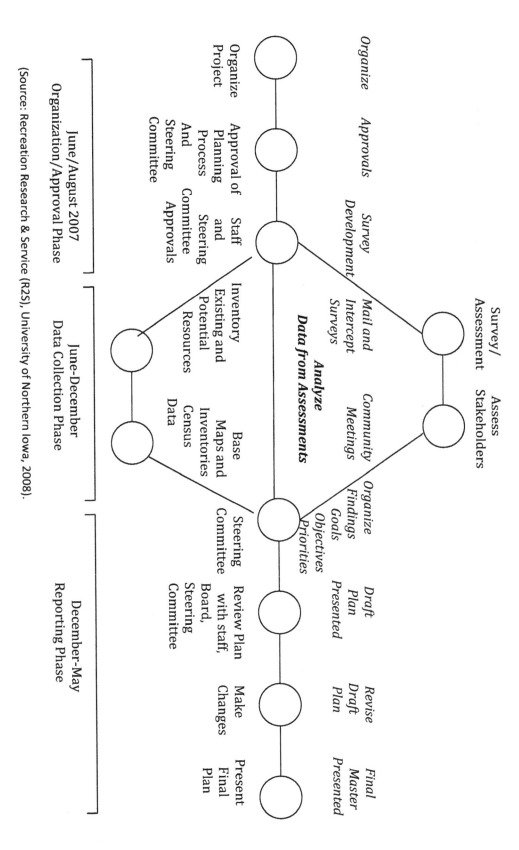

Critical Path for Developing the Park and Recreation Master Plan Waterloo, Iowa

Figure 6.4. City of Waterloo, Iowa Park and Recreation Master Plan Process

(Source: Recreation Research & Service (R2S), University of Northern Iowa, 2008).

4. How can planning enhance the effectiveness of decision making?
5. What are some factors recreation planners need to be aware of?
6. List and discuss the essential elements of any planning project or effort.
7. Identify elements in your local master plan that are related to the essential elements of planning.
8. Describe the steps in the planning process presented in this book.
9. Describe and then review and discuss a local recreation master plan.
10. Describe the differences between Goal 8 in Oregon and the recreation element in California.

REFERENCES

City of Bellevue. (2010). Bellevue parks and open space system plan. Parks and community services. Retrieved from www.bellevuewa.gov/parks-community-services.htm

City of Boulder. (2014). Parks and recreation master plan. Retrieved from https://bouldercolorado.gov/pages/parks-recreation-master-plan.

Cornia, K. (2002). Helping Hanauma? Depends on who's talking. *Parks & Recreation, 37*(5), 80–83.

East Bay Regional Park District. (n.d.). Acquisition. Retrieved from http://www.ebparks.org/planning.

Edginton, C. R., Lankford, S., Hudson, S., & Larsen, D. (2013). *Managing recreation, parks, and leisure Services: An introduction* (4th ed.). Urbana, IL: Sagamore.

El Dorado County. (2015). El Dorado County Parks and Recreation Element. Retrieved from https://www.edcgov.us/.../9_parks-recreation.aspx

Harnik, P. (2003). The excellent city park system. San Francisco: The Trust for Public Land. Retrieved from https://www.tpl.org/sites/default/files/cloud.tpl.org/pubs/ccpe_excellentcityparks_2006.pdf

Harper, J. (2009). *Planning for recreation and parks facilities: Predesign process, principles, and strategies.* State College, PA: Venture Publishing.

Knowles-Lankford, J. (1993). The role of parks and recreation in sustainable community development. *Journal of the World Leisure and Recreation Association, 35*(2), 13–17.

Knowles-Lankford, J., & Lankford, S. (1995). Our professional responsibility for a preferred future. *World Leisure and Recreation Association Journal, 36*(4), 40–44.

Lankford, S. (1994). Attitudes and perceptions toward tourism and rural regional development. *Journal of Travel Research, 32*(3), 35–43.

Lankford, S., Lankford, J., & Wheeler, D. (2011). *An introduction to park management* (3rd ed.). Urbana, IL: Sagamore.

LCDC. (2015). Oregon's statewide planning goals and guidelines. Retrieved from http://www.oregon.gov/LCD/docs/goals/goal8.pdf

Mecklenburg County. (2012). Mecklenburg County Parks and recreation master plan. Retrieved from http://charmeck.org/mecklenburg/county/ParkandRec/Parks/ParkPlanning/Pages/10YrPlan.aspx

Schanuel, S. (2005). The economics of urban park planning. *Parks & Recreation, 40*(8), 64–184.

Webler, T., Tuler, S., & Tanguay, J. (2004). Competing perspectives on public participation in national park service planning: The Boston Harbor Islands national park area. *Journal of Park and Recreation Administration, 22*(3), 99–113.

Chapter Seven

Social Marketing

CHAPTER OBJECTIVES

- To gain an understanding of the origins of social marketing
- To understand the impact of exchange theory and target market segmentation on social marketing
- To gain an awareness of how the Four Ps of marketing, as well as partnerships, influence marketing and promotion strategies
- To glimpse into various examples of traditional and digital marketing and promotional strategies by community-based parks and recreation agencies
- To delve into the importance of public relations in promotional campaigns for parks and recreation programs and services

INTRODUCTION

The concept of social marketing was first introduced in the early 1970s, stressing the need to design, implement, and effectively manage programs calculated to influence the acceptance of social ideas (Kotler & Zaltman, 1971). The concept has continued to expand in scope, encompassing multiple disciplines and fields, including parks and recreation, health promotion, physical education, youth development, community engagement, and natural environment protection (Andreason, 2004; Colquitt, Alfonso, & Walker, 2014; Kotler, Roberto, & Lee, 2002; McKenzie-Mohr & Smith, 1999; Stead, Gordon, Angus, & McDermott, 2007). As community-based parks and recreation agencies work toward improving the quality of life for citizens, social marketing is in the "front seat" of the parks and recreation vehicle, inclusive of the promotional channels for discussing socially acceptable ideas. Successful social marketing campaigns include knowing the needs and desires of the participants so well that the programs and services offered by the community parks and recreation agency pre-sell themselves.

Social marketing incorporates traditional marketing concepts, such as the Four "Ps" of marketing (product, price, place, promotion) and exchange theory, to "sell" prosocial behaviors to specific niche, or target, audiences (Colquitt et al., 2014, Edginton, Hudson, Lankford, & Larsen, 2015). Social marketing also includes a fifth P, partners. Partnerships between community-based organizations trying to promote prosocial behaviors should include community-based parks and recreation agencies. The public parks and recreation agency, in many communities, is the hub of activity; it is where prosocial behaviors (i.e., physical activity, intergenerational relationship building) occur on a regular basis throughout the year. A parks and recreation agency is the "cornerstone" of the community, and the place where participatory benefits to citizens outweigh the costs of involvement.

In this chapter, multiple topics related to social marketing will be covered. First, a brief historical discussion of social marketing will be explored. The tenets of exchange theory, target market identification and segmentation, and the connection with social marketing will be investigated. A discussion of the traditional Four "Ps" of marketing, as well as how partnerships can work as the fifth P associated with social marketing will follow. Examples of traditional as well as digital marketing and promotional strategies for programs and services will be included. The chapter will conclude by highlighting the influence of public relations on social marketing.

WHAT IS SOCIAL MARKETING?

In 1952, G.D. Wiebe, a noted research psychologist, asked the question, "Why can't you sell brotherhood like you sell soap?" The purpose of his question was to explore whether commodity marketing techniques could be applied to social objectives. This question planted the seed for the concept of social marketing. During the middle part of the 20th century, while numerous social causes were gaining a foothold in the United States, there were few discussions about how to market these social causes to specific audiences. Social marketing was seen as a promising framework or plan for implementing social change—it was an idea. It was not until 1971, with Kotler and Zaltman's seminal work on social marketing, that the concept was solidified.

Using communications, mass media, and psychological research, Kotler and Zaltman (1971) outlined the required conditions for effective social marketing: (a) monopolization by the media, (b) canalization, (c) supplementation, (d) force, (e) direction, (f) mechanism, (g) adequacy and compatibility, and (h) distance (Lazarsfeld & Merton, 1949; Wiebe, 1952). Monopolization by the media is highlighted by a singular direction of promotional advertising; there is an absence of counterpropaganda or advertising refuting the social cause. Canalization includes building on an already existing supportive attitude among target audience members for the promotional campaign. Supplementation includes mass promotional campaigning, but also face-to-face interaction with citizens by representatives of the social objective or goal being marketed. Force addresses the intensity of a person toward achieving a goal. Direction highlights how or where a person might go to accomplish his or her goal. The mechanism is the existence of an agency that enables a person to accomplish a goal. Adequacy and compatibility deals with the effectiveness of the agency in helping a person meet his or her goals. Last, distance is the analysis by a person of the energy and cost for achieving a goal. These eight conditions became the bedrock for the development of social marketing.

Once these conditions were presented, the social marketer's task was analogous to a puzzle—how to get the all of the pieces to fit together, providing support and drive for a social cause. McCarthy (1968) discussed this puzzle in marketing and referred to the essential pieces as the Four Ps of Marketing—Product, Price, Place, and Promotion. But in order to move forward with a marketing strategy that involved the Four Ps, it is important to recognize the catalyst associated with effective marketing—exchange theory.

EXCHANGE THEORY

Edginton and Williams (1978) noted that an integral component of marketing involves exchange theory. Two conditions must be present for an effective exchange to occur: (a) two or more parties are present, and (b) each party involved has something that might be valued by another party (Howard & Crompton, 1980). The exchange that occurs within parks and recreation involves users buying an expectation of benefits, not programs or services (Howard & Crompton, 1980). Some of the benefits to users that are experienced when participating in a program or service include social interaction with others, skill development, increased levels of self-confidence, or excitement. As Resnick and Siegel (2013) point out, the potential benefits from participation in parks and recreation programs and services outweigh the cost of involvement due to the improved quality of life. As administrators ponder what programs and services to provide, the following questions should be considered:

- What core values do the programs or services address?
- What are immediate, tangible benefits from participation?
- Are the benefits from participation clear to the target market?

These three questions are central to the concept of social marketing. Program participants are looking for abstract as well as concrete benefits from involvement. For example, do the recreation programs or services highlight improvement in health and wellness that is tangible (e.g., weight loss or increased cardiovascular fitness)? Does program involvement teach good sportsmanship (e.g., respecting the opponent, whether winning or losing occurs)? Providing clear, tangible benefits that can be readily obtained from program participation will lead individuals to place greater value on program involvement. Simpson and Vuchinich (2000) explain that the fluctuating value associated with benefits is due to the temporal proximity of cost to benefit. Simply put, the sooner a participant benefits from participation and the sacrifices associated with it, the better. Smaller benefits can be valued higher than larger benefits due to when the participant obtains the benefit from program participation. As Bickel and Marsh (2000) stated, the current environment and culture encourages "shortened temporal horizons"—promotion that places greater value on immediate benefits over long-term outcomes.

The "calling" of community-based recreation agencies is to highlight the importance of immediate AND long-term benefits, and both categories of benefits can be found in the agency's programs and services. The debate that participants may experience, choosing between a "larger later benefit" and a "smaller sooner benefit," is remedied by the potpourri of programs offered by parks and recreation agencies. Whether the time frame of a program is seasonal or year-long, a one-time offering or an ongoing opportunity, there can be numerous short and long-term benefits. Providing what people indicate they want from parks and recreation agencies will garner support from the individuals who are a part of the programs. In exchange, participants provide financial support to parks and recreation agencies via tax dollars, fees, charges, travel costs, and spending time participating in programs and services.

REPOSITIONING COMMUNITY PARKS AND RECREATION AGENCIES

Shrinking tax revenue within the public parks and recreation field since the 1970s has led to many agencies redeveloping their marketing strategy in relationship to the general public (Kaczynski & Crompton, 2004). The revised strategy includes highlighting the public benefits to all constituents; this stance can be used to influence tax allocations as well as fee-based participation. This is done through effective marketing campaigns that place the public parks and recreation agency at the forefront of individuals' thoughts regarding participation in services. A key to carrying out this repositioning strategy is "agencies need to empirically identify priority issues in a community and stakeholders' perceptions of strengths and weaknesses of parks and recreation services in addressing those issues" (p. 1).

Repositioning the public parks and recreation agency within the community can be a challenge. Administrators should avoid looking at what to do to the service or activity to make it appealing, and instead look at how the service or activity is perceived by the potential user (Kaczynski & Crompton, 2004). This is done by learning what qualities or attributes of community parks and recreation services are important to the public. Tools and locales exist that can help administrators learn what the public thinks; examples include distribution of surveys, open forums or city council meetings, and face-to-face interaction.

The current financial state of community parks and recreation agencies has led to the inclusion of fee-based programs as vital sources of revenue. When considering repositioning a community parks and recreation agency in the minds of the public, the agency itself must be viewed in relationship to other public, private, and nonprofit competitors (Kaczynski & Crompton, 2004). Due to the excessive amount of marketing materials and information that may bombard potential users, it is important for a community parks and recreation agency to explore branding. Branding involves developing marketing tools that distinguish the public parks and recreation agency from other organizations that offer similar services (Nolan, 2014). As Kaczynski and Crompton highlight, "brands are ranked based on attributes (e.g., price, quality, etc.) relevant to the buying decision" (p. 5). Branding can help potential users filter through information and make decisions to participate in the fee-based services of a public parks and recreation agency. The creation of a brand and the selected priorities that a community parks and recreation agency is trying to convey to the public may take years to develop and prove challenging to organizations that have not experienced this type of marketing strategy. The byproduct of this work, though, is the planting of the public parks and recreation agency as a vital contributor to the community, and an organization that provides quality services that are worth fees for participation.

WHAT IS A TARGET MARKET IN THE RECREATION FIELD?

Different users of parks and recreation programs are often described as leisure target markets (Edginton & Williams, 1978). A market is a group of people who have certain needs and are willing to be a part of the exchange process. Markets are differentiated in a number of ways, including (a) population size, (b) geographic location, (c) demographic characteristics (e.g., gender, ethnicity), and (d) psychosocial characteristics (e.g., risk-taking level). Using questionnaires, census data, and participatory trends in programs and services are just a few methods to enhance community-based parks and recreation agencies' ability to meet the needs of their users via programs and services.

There are three basic strategies used to identify target markets (Edginton et al., 2015). The first strategy is undifferentiated marketing. *Undifferentiated marketing* means the same marketing approach is developed and implemented with all potential users. A community-based recreation manager uses an undifferentiated marketing approach after analyzing the different target markets and realizing that the common needs of the target markets outweigh their individual needs. At times, this approach is often misused—it is implemented due to the lack of time spent by the agency assessing the target markets. Sound analysis by administrators will show that not all target markets can be serviced in the same way. *Differentiated marketing* includes tailoring a marketing strategy for each target market. A major benefit to differentiated marketing is that the agency can adapt services and programs to the wants of each population group. A major drawback is that differentiated marketing can be costly from a time and monetary standpoint to the agency. The ideal of matching certain benefits to certain target markets' needs is an effective way to involve participants. *Concentrated marketing* is a strategic combination of undifferentiated and differentiated marketing. Using concentrated marketing allows a parks and recreation agency to focus on one target market for a certain event, program, or service. Developing a promotional and pricing strategy that targets a specific market is more cost effective than trying to tap into each target market specifically. But, since a community-based recreation agency is a public, government organization, there still needs to exist a general promotional campaign for all citizens.

Not all target markets want the same services from a parks and recreation agency, so how do community parks and recreation agencies differentiate among population groups and the services that can be provided? Recreation and leisure service administrators break down the larger target markets into smaller segments (Edginton et al., 2015). These smaller segments allow managers to design and implement more satisfying programs and services. The target market segments are developed using three criteria: (a) size, (b) measurability, and (c) accessibility. The size of the segment (whether large or small) will help in consideration of whether a program is worth creating. For example, if there are not enough potential users for a program, then it may not be cost-effective for a leisure services agency to expend financial resources (e.g., hire staff, purchase equipment) in order to facilitate the program. Measurability involves collecting information regarding the user population and quantifying the potential target market; this helps articulate the size of the market segment. Accessibility includes making sure that if a market segment exists and there is the potential for user involvement, does the community-based recreation agency have the tools to communicate with that segment? Creative and unique marketing campaigns may need to be developed in order to access specific market segments.

Identifying target markets and potential segments of parks and recreation users can be a time-consuming, tedious process. Community-based parks and recreation managers may need to enlist staff and volunteers to help collect information in order to make beneficial decisions that positively impact all groups involved. Once the information is gathered associated with parks and recreation target markets, administrators may put together an effective marketing strategy to maximize the exchange process at their agency.

THE FOUR Ps of MARKETING

Constructing a successful marketing strategy includes the four Ps of marketing—product, price, place, and promotion (Edginton & Williams, 1978; Howard & Crompton,

1980). These factors are interrelated and should be discussed concurrently when forging a strategy (McCarthy & Shapiro, 1975).

Product

The product is the services or programs offered to the public to satisfy a need (Edginton et al., 2015). In the parks and recreation field, there is a difference in marketing products and marketing programs or services. In the early part of the 21st century, some marketing experts argued that experiences will become the prime "product" of recreation; we are seeing this prediction come to fruition. As Poria, Butler, and Airey (2003, p. 239) pointed out, this movement toward marketing and promoting experiences "challenges the perception that all those who visit a place come only to 'gaze', be educated or to enjoy themselves. For some, it is argued this is an emotional experience, that people come to 'feel' rather than to 'gaze.'"

Community parks and recreation programs and services are not stagnant; there is an "ebb and flow" to the design, implementation, social marketing campaign, and participant population (Kotler, 1982). The product life cycle embodies this fluctuation in the life of a program or service. There are five stages associated with the product life cycle: (a) introduction, (b) growth, (c) maturation, (d) saturation, and (e) decline. The introduction stage involves generating acceptance and interest in a new program or service. Positive customer relations are a hallmark of the introduction stage, going so far at times as to offer special promotions or discounts for introductory participant involvement. The growth stage occurs when there is satisfaction with the new program or service. Early participant involvement and excitement associated with the new program will attract other participants. The goal of the social marketing campaign at this stage is sustainability. The maturation stage is indicative of slower enrollment rates; although new participants may still sign up, the rate is slower than the first two stages. The maturation stage is also when competing programs or services are introduced, especially in the commercial sector. The shift in the social marketing campaign is now on influencing the preference of participants for community parks and recreation programs and services. The saturation stage includes a leveling-off of participation rates; no new participants are signing up for the program. Reliance is on repeat participants, and the public parks and recreation agency must decide whether to revamp the program or service or let it decline. Unless strong reasons exist to retain the program, it can be costly to carry a weak or low revenue-generating program or service under the community parks and recreation umbrella of offerings. In the decline stage, community parks and recreation administrators must decide between revitalization, petrification, or death to a program or service. Considerations associated with these three options may include changing when the program is offered (e.g., day, time), expenses associated with allowing the program to continue or actively dropping it from the list of offerings, or allowing low or nonexistent enrollment to lead to removal of the program.

Marketing researchers highlighted a number of logistical items for consideration when marketing programs or services in the community recreation field: (a) people, (b) process, (c) physical evidence, (d) public image, (e) peripherals, (f) political impact, and (g) perInfo.Com (Ipson, Mahoney, & Addams, 2005; O'Sullivan & Spangler, 1998). People are the foundation for marketing services. Community recreation administrators should be concerned with how participants interact with staff members, how participants interact with the area or facility where the program or service occurs, and how participants interact with each other. These three interactions impact participants' levels of satisfaction with a program or service.

The process includes the procedures, such as registration intake or payment policies, that enhance or detract from the participant-minded approach to programs and services. Attention to detail is crucially important in the discussion of process—scripting what staff members say when they answer the phone or making sure the registration procedures are clear and streamlined on the agency's website illustrate a level of care and concern for potential users.

The physical evidence associated with marketing includes items such as the presentation of the facilities (e.g., the cleanliness of the building, organization of the supplies for each activity) and staff members' attire. These components of marketing communicate the importance of professionalism to current and potential participants in programs.

Public image involves effective and "catchy" representation design—for a community recreation agency, items such as logos and slogans describing the organization and the relationship with the community should be eye-catching and pique participants' interest (O'Sullivan, 1991). For example, the City of Fresno PARCS (Parks, After School, Recreation and Community Services) is an eye-catching acronym describing the programs and services offered in Fresno (http://www.fresno.gov/DiscoverFresno/ParksRecreationandCommunityServices/default.htm). Steering clear of questionable or polarizing designs should be considered, since the parks and recreation agency is a place for the general public.

Peripherals are the "added value" that help a participant discern between two similar programs. For community recreation managers, marketing programs and services requires innovation and imagination to "wow" the customer. This is done by addressing consumer needs, meeting their expectations during participation, and helping create lasting memories through active user engagement. Meeting expectations and the creation of memories add value to a service; they also create a personal connection with the participant.

The political impact of a parks and recreation agency should be measured against the representation as a government-based organization. Although administration and staff members may feel strongly regarding a specific economic, social, or technological factor, it is important to "take a step back" and consider how personal opinion may influence work done at the community recreation agency. The agency is a beacon for all people; it may represent many things for the general public—a safe haven, comfort zone, or place of pure enjoyment. Personal goals and ambitions that detrimentally impact the organization's mission may drive users and potential participants away from programs and services.

Lastly, PerInfo.Com stands for personalization, information, and communication (O'Sullivan & Spangler, 1998). Communicating with current and potential users about their needs in relationship to a particular program or service is integral to the promotional campaign. Relaying the importance of each individual's experience in a personalized manner will hopefully spark further involvement in programs and services.

Programmatically, there are a number of areas that serve as domains for programs and services offered by community recreation agencies: (a) arts and crafts; (b) performing arts; (c) hobbies; (d) sports, games, and athletics; (e) outdoor recreation; (f) social recreation; (g) volunteer services; (h) travel and tourism; and (i) literary activities (Edginton & Williams, 1978). The activities generated in one or more the program areas deliver leisure benefits to the target markets. Each program or service has a "shelf life," or time frame for optimal impact; continually reviewing programs and services allows parks and recreation agencies to effectively meet the needs expressed by citizens.

Including the target market in program or service development greatly increases the chance of programmatic success (Resnick & Siegel, 2013). A community parks and recreation agency can gather input through investigatory research (i.e., survey or questionnaire distribution), but a target market advisory group may benefit the agency in multiple ways as well. First, the advisory group could suggest ideas for program or service form, distribution, pricing, and promotion. An advisory group could also serve as "champions of the cause," spurring and encouraging other citizens to be involved in what the parks and recreation agency is offering.

Price

Price represents what a user is willing to spend in order to gain the benefits associated with participation in a program or service (Edginton et al., 2015; Howard & Crompton, 1980). Every program and service also has a variety of costs associated with the price: (a) time cost, (b) opportunity cost, (c) psychic cost, and (d) social cost. Time cost includes travel to and from the program, as well as participation in the program. Opportunity cost is the benefit value from participating in one program as opposed to an alternative program. Giving up an opportunity to participate in one program to participate in a parks and recreation program provides a beneficial opportunity to an individual, but at a cost to the person. Psychic cost addresses the emotional, mental, and psychological "expenditures." Examples of psychic costs associated with program participation include the anxiety associated with trying something new or fear of failure. Social cost includes sacrificing or giving up old ideas, values, or patterns of behavior and replacing them with what is learned through participation in a program or service.

Community-based recreation administrators should consider multiple objectives when contemplating pricing for a program or service (Edginton et al., 2015). Not all objectives are easily teased out, and conflict may arise when deciding what price to charge for participation. If a program is priced too high, it may drive potential participants away; too low of a price and participants may perceive the program is not valuable. It is a balancing act that requires regular analysis of pricing and discussion of whether to adjust the price of participation, or proceed with the same price.

The pricing objectives to consider when reflecting on charges for users include the following: (a) efficient use of all financial resources, (b) fairness or equitableness, (c) maximizing participation, (d) rationing, (e) positive user attitudes, and (f) commercial sector encouragement (Howard & Crompton, 1980). Efficient usage of all financial resources includes recognizing that charging a fee can be a source of revenue for an agency, including funding and starting new programs or services. Charging a user fee can ease financial pressure within the community-based recreation organization in two ways. First, the more users in a program, the more revenue can be generated by user fees. An indirect result of a user fee may be participant attrition from the program; this reduces program expenditures because there are few people involved.

Fairness and equitableness in charging user fees absolves those individuals who do not frequent parks and recreation agencies, programs, and services from paying for others. Although all citizens do support the development of community-based recreation agencies via taxes, it is equitable that more frequent users should be paying more for government services, such as public recreation.

Maximizing participation involves developing a pricing strategy that encourages high numbers of a target market to participate in the program or service. Setting a low price provides "visibility" to a new program and helps build momentum for program participation. Although the low price associated with the new program may lead to little or no revenue generation, it can serve as a conduit, exposing users to other programs within the parks and recreation agency.

Rationing gives community-based recreation managers insight into which programs or services are most desired by users. This pricing objective may also be used to manage participant usage. Participants who have a strong desire to be involved in a program or service will pay the cost associated with usage. Conversely, for those individuals who have a casual interest in the program, the price may discourage their participation. The result is a manageable group of people who are vested in the benefits associated with the program and will get the most out of their participation.

As Howard and Crompton (1980) pointed out in their discussion of rationing, there is a dilemma associated with usage rates and satisfaction of the experience. There is not a positive correlation between high usage rates and enjoyment via participation; just because there are a lot of people involved in a program does not mean every person is satisfied or enjoying the experience. Malekoff (2015) suggests that ratios between staff and participants are a significant factor in program and service design. For example, in youth programs, the higher the ratio of children to staff, the lower the direct contact between individual children and staff. Reducing the opportunity to interact one-on-one with a child can detrimentally impact skill development, the growth of self-confidence, or refinement of social skills. "Packing them in" to programs is a consideration that should be weighed by administrators; this approach does not always lead to positive results for participants.

Rationing may also be used to manage participant attendance and usage during operational hours. Charging a different price during "peak" hours for parks and recreation services may help regulate the attendance, therefore reducing overcrowding and accommodating all participants when there are a limited number of areas or facilities for recreation. Using rationing in this way influences participants to actively choose certain times or areas for recreating, increasing the benefit from involvement in a program or service.

Positive user attitudes allude to the relationship between the quality of the participatory experience and the price associated with it. People are wary or skeptical of a program that is free; there is a belief that if participation is free, then the program is not worth it. If there is a fee charged for participation, the expectation is the quality of the program will be higher since a participant is paying for it. Participants are more dedicated to attending since they are paying, and the overall care and concern for equipment or supplies associated with the program or service will be higher than a free program.

Lastly, commercial sector encouragement can aid in reducing the challenge associated with managing large numbers of participants. If a community-based parks and recreation agency and a private company offer similar programs, and the fees are comparable, there may be a better balance in attendance between the two agencies, thus assisting in crowd management. If the community-based parks and recreation agency charges significantly less than the private company, there may be usage issues, overcrowding, and management quandaries that administration will have to address during the program.

The price of participation in a community parks and recreation program or service should be related to the target market, and may vary due to economic inequalities among users of a target market. There are various types of pricing that can be employed when constructing programs and services: (a) multiple-unit, (b) full-line, (c) leader, (d) penetration, and (e) skimming. Multiple-unit pricing involves discounts or reduced fees if users buy in quantity; this often pertains to entry fees, registration fees, or season passes. The Breckenridge, Colorado Recreation Department offers multiple-unit pricing for daily usage. A single adult day pass is $15, and a single youth day pass is $7.50. There is also a family (2 adults/2 youth) day pass for $38, and a family 6-pack (2 adults/4 youth) day pass for $50. The family day pass purchase is a savings of nearly $8, or the cost of one youth, and the family 6-pack day pass purchase is a savings of $10. The benefit for the participant is purchasing in bulk, or quantity. Full-line pricing refers to variance of the price of participation based upon the type of service provided. The variance in service may include equipment, challenge of the activity, length of time for the activity, and instructional method(s). The South Kingstown, Rhode Island Parks and Recreation Department offers multiple options for their nature camps and classes, with prices fluctuating due to length of time (e.g., half or full day, one day or multiple days) and the activities that children can engage in at camp. Leader pricing involves a set cost for initial entry into the program or service, and then additional costs for ancillary activities or additional equipment paid directly to the instructor of the program. To participate in the League City, Texas Parks and Recreation Department's Summer Karate Program, the registration cost is $50. An ancillary cost, paid directly to the karate instructor, is $30 for the uniform. Penetration pricing is setting a lower cost at the inception of a new program or service to build a user audience. Administrators gradually increase the price once the target market has been captured and participation is on a regular basis. Lastly, skimming involves systematic reduction of a price for program participation in order to reach individual in lower income brackets who are a part of the target market. In conjunction with skimming is a pricing strategy known as a sliding scale. A sliding scale is a variance in the program participation fees for potential users, from the onset of participation, based upon their income brackets. A hybrid method of this pricing strategy is employed by the Mesa, Arizona Parks, Recreation and Commercial Facilities Department through fee assistance. An example of how fee assistance is carried out is illustrated in Figure 7.1.

Place

Place, or distribution, deals with the availability and accessibility of parks and recreation programs or services to target markets (Edginton et al., 2015; Edginton & Williams, 1978; Howard & Crompton, 1980). There are four major areas of consideration when developing an effective distribution system for programs and services: (a) the level and quality of customer service, (b) the number and location of facilities or branches, (c) the facility or space design, and (d) third party usage.

The level and quality of customer service involves balancing convenience for the participants' involvement with the financial cost to the agency. Considering the number and location of facilities or branches may help in reducing costs associated with program operation (i.e., staffing). The decision to go with one central location, or multiple locations, for programs and services also impacts the cost associated with participant involvement. The facility design will exude a certain aura or attitude, impacting participants' expectations and behavior toward a parks and recreation agency. Dilapidated, rundown facilities that are eyesores to the community may invite vandalism and other antisocial behavior. Conversely, paying attention to details inside and outside of facilities and usage areas (e.g., athletic

Mesa Parks, Recreation and Commercial Facilities Department
2017 Fee Assistance Application

What Is Fee Assistance?

Mesa Parks, Recreation and Commercial Facilities Department offers Fee Assistance to **Mesa Residents Only.** The program is designed to provide residents in Mesa an opportunity to participate in quality recreation programs that they may not be able to afford without assistance. Eligibility for the program is determined by completing an application and supplying the correct documentation prior to registering for programs.

What Kind of Documentation Is Needed?

Each household is required to submit **one** of the following:

- A copy of current Eligibility Notification Letter from Mesa Public Schools Food Service Department Free or Reduced Lunch Program
- **Or**
- A copy of any of the below Government Assistance verification documents: Unemployment Verification, Nutrition Assistance Verification, WIC Assistance verification, AHCCCS Verification

Please send or bring in a copy of these documents, as they will not be returned.... **Do Not Send Original Documents**

What Are The Steps to Apply?

Complete a Fee Assistance Program Application and provide the correct documentation.
Mail to:

   Mesa Parks & Recreation
   PO Box 1466, MS - 7010
   F/A Application
   Mesa, AZ 85211
   Phone: 480-644-2352
In Person at:
   200 S. Center St.
   Building #1
   Mesa, AZ 85210

Will My Submitted Information Be Kept Confidential?

All information submitted for the purposes of Fee Assistance eligibility is confidential and is not shared with program staff.

When Will I Know I Am Accepted?

Eligibility will be verified and a letter or e-mail will be sent to you within 14 business days. If you are accepted into the program, your family members will be eligible for a 50% discount of approved program registration fees for up to 5 programs per calendar year.

What Programs Can I Use It For?

The discount given from the Fee Assistance Program can be used for the following programs: Summer Boredom Busters, Safe Kids, Youth Sports Programs, Swim Lessons, Competitive Swim Teams, Diving Teams, Synchro Swim Teams, Water Polo Teams, Adaptive Programs, Jefferson and Webster Sports Zones, novice level Youth Tennis Lessons.
Fee assistance is not allowed in combination with any other discount offered by Mesa Parks, Recreation and Commercial

How Long Can I Use the Discount?

Applications will be accepted in December and are effective for the calendar year. January 1, 2016 - December 31, 2016. **You must reapply every calendar year.**

Payment Information

If accepted into the Fee Assistance program you will be expected to pay the discounted fee at time of purchase. If for any reason your account becomes delinquent, you must pay the outstanding balance on the account, as well as any service fees that apply, prior to registering for a future program (discounted or full price).

Contact Us If You Have Questions?

Mesa Parks, Recreation and Commercial Facilities
200 S Center St, Bldg 1,
Mesa, AZ 85210
Phone 480-644-2352
Email : parksrecinfo@mesaaz.gov

How Do I Contact Mesa Public Schools Food Service?

Eligibility Notification Letters that verify your child participates in the Free or Reduced Lunch Program can be requested by calling the Food Service Department at 480-472-0918

** Food Service cannot fax or send letters directly to Parks, Recreation and Commercial Facilities Department.

Figure 7.1. Fee Assistance as a Pricing Strategy for Program Participation

fields, outdoor green spaces) communicates a concern for user satisfaction, as well as staff performance. Finally, third party usage is an alternative option when considering distribution of programs and services. Considering who to work with, how the collaboration will impact the parks and recreation agency's image, and the terms of the third party agreement are all important factors when deliberating whether a third party should be involved.

Promotion

Promotion involves communication between the parks and recreation agency and target markets (Edginton et al., 2015; Edginton & Williams, 1978; Howard & Crompton, 1980). In the latter decades of the 20th century, the main consideration when discussing promotion was the distance between parks and recreation agencies and the potential users regarding information sharing. In today's society, the aforementioned distance between parks and recreation agencies and target markets is "virtually" absent due to the Internet. The Internet allows users instant accessibility to program and service information (e.g., location, times, availability), and has created avenues affiliated with the four traditional forms of promotion: personal sales, publicity, advertising, and incentive-based sales. For example, the Massillon, Ohio Parks and Recreation Department offers Internet-only coupons for participation in its personal training and fitness classes (https://www.groupon.com/deals/city-of-massillon-parks-recreation-department). A few of the benefits of digital accessibility to recreation programs and services are that individuals can register for programs and services at any time or day, and the community parks and recreation agency can distribute environmentally friendly marketing materials (e.g., online brochures and forms).

Personal selling involves the face-to-face interaction parks and recreation staff members, as well as current program and services users, have with members of the public. Publicity is unpaid, nonpersonal communication about the parks and recreation agency and programs and services offered to the public. The agency is not the sponsor; usually publicity is generated by various media outlets, and those media outlets control what is communicated to the public. Advertising is paid, nonpersonal communication to the public, and the parks and recreation agency is the sponsor of the advertising. The agency has the ability to design and craft the advertising campaign since it is the sponsor. Lastly, incentive-based sales such as coupons, groupons, and discounted admission fees, are used to connect with target markets and allow potential users an opportunity to participate in a program or service without experiencing the full financial cost. Although most incentive-based sales are one-time opportunities, the participatory experience communicates what is offered by the parks and recreation agency.

Sales promotion has been a staple of social marketing for decades; this type of promotion involves distribution of items intended to persuade individuals into participating in community parks and recreation programs and services. Examples of sales promotion items include (a) pencils, (b) notepads, (c) buttons, (d) t-shirts, (e) toys, (f) hats or caps, (g) water bottles, (h) luggage tags, (i) keychains, (j) stickers and decals, (k) postcards, and (l) patches. These items are usually emblazoned with the logo, emblem, or tagline of the public parks and recreation agency, and serve as "triggers" for potential participants when they are deciding on participating in a program or service.

There are a number of media tools that can be used as a part of a successful promotional effort by a parks and recreation agency (Edginton & Williams, 1978). Annual reports, billboards, brochures, displays, fliers, newspapers, patches, posters, stickers, and t-shirts are just a few of the tangible, concrete options that can be created and distributed to promote parks and recreation programs and services within a community. Radio and television "spots" can be used for public service announcements (PSAs) and advertising commercials. With the advent of the digital age, the Internet and social media have become major vehicles as well for promoting programs and services.

As mentioned earlier, the Internet (and social media) has created avenues for instantaneous information gathering by reducing the "virtual" distance between parks and recreation agencies and potential target markets. Personal sales and word-of-mouth communication are still hallmarks of promotion, but a parks and recreation agency can increase the potential clientele by creating Internet and social media outlets for promotion. Nearly all public parks and recreation departments have accounts with social media outlets such as Facebook, Twitter, Youtube, Pinterest, Instagram, and Snapchat. These outlets allow users to see what is happening with the agency's programs and services—in some cases, instantaneously—by "following" them. For example, Facebook is an integral tool of promotion for public parks and recreation agencies; the Oshkosh, Wisconsin Recreation Department has created a Facebook account that outlines their programs, highlights fund-

Figure 7.2. City of Santa Ana, California Parks and Recreation Department website– lower portion (social media outlets)

raising ventures, and provides recognition to individuals who support community endeavors (https://www.facebook.com/pages/Oshkosh-Recreation-Department/420598041413830). The Boston, Massachusetts Parks and Recreation Department has created an Instagram account housing photos of participants involved in the programs and services (https://instagram.com/bostonparksdept/). The City of Santa Ana, California Parks and Recreation Department invites all participants to stay connected via all the major social media outlets, as indicated by the icons on the bottom right corner of their general website (see Figure 7.2).

A fifth P, partners, has emerged as an integral discussion point when outlining a marketing strategy (Colquitt et al., 2014). Parks and recreation agencies should consider the impact of individuals and organizations surrounding target markets when promoting a program or service. For example, if a recreation department is marketing summer sports leagues for youth, a good partner in the promotional campaign would be local school district. Distributing fliers or brochures about the summer sports leagues at the end of the school year for children to take home is an excellent way to collaborate with an organization that has a significant impact on children's lives.

PUBLIC RELATIONS AND SOCIAL MARKETING

For a community parks and recreation agency to move forward with a marketing strategy, each staff member should be aware of his or her role in the campaign. The organizational process of communicating each component of the marketing strategy is called public relations (Kotler, 1980). Public relations involves the cultivation of a community parks and recreation agency's image. The goal of public relations, from a parks and recreation agency's perspective, is to create programs and services that positively impact the quality of life for citizens within the community. In return, citizens will hopefully feel good about the work of the parks and recreation agency and realize that the organization is vital to the well-being and success of the community. As Edginton et al. (2015, p. 260) noted,

> Public relations efforts are directed toward engendering good will toward the organization and establishing an understanding of its operations. Public relations efforts seek to develop a positive rapport with the public served by establishing management policies and practices conducive to the public interest and well-being.

A great way to attract new users to a community parks and recreation agency is to cultivate good community relations. Positive interactions by staff with potential customers, whether it is a face-to-face conversation in a public setting such as a grocery store, or over the phone at the administration building, will shape the public image of the community parks and recreation agency. Public relations is a communicative tool used with organization representatives to discuss large and small items affiliated with the agency.

SUMMARY

As mentioned at the beginning of the chapter, social marketing includes the design and implementation of programs associated with social causes—the ideas or behaviors that impact a community. Developing programs and services that reinforce improving the quality of life for citizens in a community is the social cause that all community-based recreation administrators and staff work toward. These programs are unique and work toward attracting various target markets who are interested in benefitting from participation.

The marketing and promotional strategy associated with each program or service that is offered can vary. Not all target markets have the same desires and dreams, but all want to gain something from participation. Administrators and staff members of a parks and recreation agency who spend the time researching and gathering information about potential target markets tend to be successful and achieve solid program participation rates once the programs are offered. Maintaining effective programs and services involves communicating with participants, gauging costs and fees, and continually reviewing if the program design is meeting the needs of the participants. While short-term benefits from participation may be the prevailing goal for individuals in programs, relaying the importance of long-term benefits that impact one's quality of life is a goal of parks and recreation agencies.

The digital revolution that has globally impacted society can be used by parks and recreation agencies to instantaneously connect with citizens, enhancing social marketing campaigns associated with programs and services. These connections are a unique way to continue to spread goodwill and cultivate a positive public image of the parks and recreation agency. Partnering digital promotion with the other traditional forms of marketing allows community-based parks and recreation administrators to spread the organization's mission to all citizens; this is social marketing in the 21st century within the community parks and recreation environment.

DISCUSSION QUESTIONS

1. What is the definition of social marketing?
2. What are the four "Ps" of marketing?
3. What are examples of benefits that users receive from participation in public parks and recreation programs?
4. What is the definition of target market?
5. What are the three strategies used to identify a target market?
6. Outline the various stages associated with the product life cycle.
7. What are two types of pricing when constructing public parks and recreation programs?
8. What are the four types of promotion?
9. How has the Internet and social media impacted promotion?
10. What are the various components of the public relations process?

REFERENCES

Bickel, W. K., & Marsch, L. A. (2000). The tyranny of small decisions: Origins, outcomes, and proposed solutions. In W. K. Bickel & R. W. Vuchinich (Eds.), *Reframing health behavior change with behavioral economics* (p. 355). Mahwah, NJ: Lawrence Erlbaum.

Boston Parks and Recreation Department. (2015, August 14). BostonParksDept. [Photo Album]. Retrieved from https://instagram.com/bostonparksdept/

City of Fresno, California. (n.d.). Parks, after school, recreation, and community services. Retrieved from http://www.fresno.gov/DiscoverFresno/ParksRecreationandCommunityServices/default.htm

City of Mesa, Arizona. (2015). Mesa Parks, Recreation and Commercial Facilities Department 2015 Fee Assistance Application.

Colquitt, G., Alfonso, M. L., & Walker, A. (2014). Becoming a physical activity champion: Empowerment through social marketing. *Strategies: A Journal for Physical and Sport Educators, 27*, 38–41.

Edginton, C. R., Hudson, S. D., Lankford, S. V., & Larsen, D. (2015). *Managing recreation, parks, and leisure services: An introduction* (4th ed.). Champaign, IL: Sagamore.

Edginton, C. R., & Williams, J. G. (1978). *Product management of leisure service organizations: A behavioral approach.* New York, NY: Wiley & Sons.

Howard, D. R., & Crompton, J. L. (1980). *Financing, managing and marketing parks and recreation resources.* Dubuque, IA: William C. Brown Co. Publishers.

Ipson, N., Mahoney, E., & Adams, J. (2005). Public relations, marketing, and customer service in management of parks and recreation agencies (2nd ed.). In B. Van Der Smissen, M. Moiseichik, V. Hartenburg (Eds.), *Management of park and recreation agencies* (pp. 403–487). Ashburn, VA: National Recreation and Park Association.

Kotler, P. (1980). *Principles of marketing* (2nd ed.). Englewood Cliffs, NJ: Prentice-Hall.

Kotler, P. (1982). *Marketing for nonprofit organizations* (2nd ed.). Englewood Cliffs, NJ: Prentice-Hall.

Kotler, P., Roberto, N., & Lee, N. (2002). *Social marketing: Improving the quality of life* (2nd ed.). Thousand Oaks, CA: Sage.

Kotler P., & Zaltman, G. (1971). Social marketing: An approach to planned social change. *Journal of Marketing, 35*, 3–12.

Lazarsfeld, P. F., & Merton, R. K. (1949). Mass communication, popular taste, and organized social action. In W. Schramm (Ed.), *Mass communications* (pp. 459–480). Champaign-Urbana, IL: University of Illinois Press.

League City, Texas. (n.d.). Beyond the Oaks: League City Parks, Recreation and Helen Hall Library summer activities guide–Summer 2015. Retrieved from http://leaguecity.com/DocumentCenter/View/12756

Malekoff, A. (2015). *Group work with adolescents* (3rd ed.). New York, NY: Guilford.

Massillon, Ohio Parks & Recreation Department. (2015). Fitness services at city of Massillon Parks & Recreation Department (Up to 61% off). Three options available. Retrieved from https://www.groupon.com/deals/city-of-massillon-parks-recreation-department

McCarthy, J. E. (1968). *Basic marketing: A managerial approach* (3rd ed., pp. 31–33). Homewood, IL: Richard D. Irwin, Inc.

McCarthy, J. E., & Shapiro, S. J. (1975). *Basic marketing.* Georgetown, Ontario, Canada: Irwin-Dorsey.

McKenzie-Mohr, D., & Smith, W. (1999). *Fostering sustainable behavior: An introduction to community-based social marketing.* Gabriola Island, BC: New Society Publishers.

Oshkosh Recreation Department. (n.d.) In Facebook. Retrieved from https://www.facebook.com/pages/Oshkosh-Recreation-Department/420598041413830

O'Sullivan, E. L. (1991). *Marketing for parks, recreation, and leisure.* State College, PA: Venture Publishing.

O'Sullivan, E. L., & Spangler, K. J. (1998). *Experience marketing, strategies for the new millennium.* State College, PA: Venture Publishing.

Poria, Y., Butler, R., & Airey, D. (2003). The core of heritage tourism. *Annals of Tourism Research, 30*, 238–254.

Resnick, E. A., & Siegel, M. (2013). *Marketing public health: Strategies to promote social change* (3rd ed.). Burlington, MA: Jones & Bartlett Learning.

Sergeant, A. (1999). *Marketing management for nonprofit organizations.* New York, NY: Oxford University Press.

Simpson, C. A., & Vuchinich, R. E. (2000). Reliability of a measure of temporal discounting. *The Psychological Record, 50*(1), 3.

South Kingstown, Rhode Island. (2015). South Kingstown Parks & Recreation: Where tradition meets adventure – summer brochure 2015. Retrieved from http://www.southkingstownri.com/files/Summer%2015%20Website.pdf.

Stead, M., Gordon, R., Angus, K., & McDermott, L. (2007). A systematic review of social marketing effectiveness. *Health Education, 107*, 126–191.

Town of Breckenridge. (n.d.). Breckenridge, Colorado recreation center daily admission rates, passes, & memberships. Retrieved from http://www.townofbreckenridge.com/index.aspx?page=1075.

Wiebe, G. D. (1952). Merchandising commodities and citizenship on television. *Public Opinion Quarterly, 15*(4), 679–691.

Chapter Eight

Budgeting and Financial Management for Parks and Recreation

CHAPTER OBJECTIVES

- To explore the various forms of revenue that support public parks and recreation agencies
- To outline different categories of expenditures associated with day-to-day operations and improvements
- To investigate the steps included in the budget cycle, inclusive of the process and types of budgets that can be used by administrators in the field
- To discuss future trends in budgeting that can impact the operations of public parks and recreation agencies
- To highlight the various budgets that are used by public parks and recreation agencies

INTRODUCTION

Nationwide, public parks and recreation agencies provide programs and services for people to build healthy lifestyles within their communities. Programmatic opportunities range from individual to group-oriented activities, natural to manmade settings, and novice to expert skill levels. At the center of functionality with all community parks and recreation programs and services is the economics of the situation. Simply put, each administrator must ask the following questions when considering programs and services for the community: (a) how will the program be funded, (b) what will the budget look like, and (c) is the cost worth it.

The current personal spending trends show that the population as a whole in the United States has spent nearly three times as much money on recreation since the early 1990s (U.S. Census, 2010a). In 1990, the total personal recreation expenditures were roughly

$315 billion; in 2009, that figure jumped to $897 billion (U.S. Census, 2010a). A few of the recreation expenditures in this category included sports equipment and services, parks and recreation memberships, museum entrance fees, and travel tours. Government spending trends show that 3% to 7% of public spending goes to parks and recreation; unfortunately, in some cases the percentage is less than 1% (U.S. Census, 2010b). When viewing a select number of the largest counties in the United States, the amount spent by these types of community government entities can be as high as $319 million (U.S. Census, 2010b). While this dollar amount may seem like a significant amount of money spent on recreation, it is actually one of the lowest dollar figures associated with general government expenditures in the United States (U.S. Census, 2010b).

The aforementioned statistics refocus on the three questions administrators must ask when considering a parks and recreation program or service. As Kaczynski and Crompton (2006) pointed out, public parks and recreation managers will better position their agency in the community by examining spending patterns within their own "backyard." Using these statistics in support of fiscal resources and development of the community parks and recreation budget is one small step in the larger vision of financial stability and success.

This chapter will delve into a number of items associated with budgeting for community parks and recreation agencies. A discussion of revenue and expenditures associated with public parks and recreation agencies will be included. Following this discussion, various budgets used within the parks and recreation field will be outlined.

SOURCES OF REVENUE

Bartram (2014) highlights that public parks and recreation is probably the most complicated government service; this is due to how many different types of programs are provided. The umbrella of services provided by agencies has grown to include Baby Boomer and senior programs and services, before and after-school activities for kids, hosting concerts and movies, and overnight travel trips. These offerings often involve partnerships with other governmental entities, and public parks and recreation administrators regularly need to justify funding and support to lawmakers and politicians.

The complexity of what community recreation agencies do has been an ongoing point of discussion among political representatives for years (Lovell & Snook, 2011). The interpretations are that parks and recreation areas, facilities and services allow individuals to "reconnect with nature, reflect on life, and relax from the daily rigors our lives" (p. 24). These comments are a small part of what is done in the field. While these statements may be true, there is much more that public parks and recreation organizations do for individuals and communities. Unfortunately, this political sentiment has led to public parks and recreation agencies "feeling the pain" of government cutbacks in revenue.

In the midst of this thinking regarding community parks and recreation, administrators persevere and lead staff members in the development of high-quality programs and services. Revenue generation is a significant factor in development and sustainability, and one that can "make or break" the longevity of a program or service. Revenue is income that comes into the public parks and recreation agency to financially support various programs and services. Outlined below are forms of revenue that support public parks and recreation.

Taxes

Most of the revenue used to support public parks and recreation efforts are from property taxes, specifically real property taxes (Edginton & Williams, 1978). Real property tax dollars are associated with assets such as homes, land, industry, and commercially based businesses within the governmental jurisdiction. Any additions or improvements to existing buildings also fall under real property taxes. Real property taxes are determined by finding out the assessed value of property, or the taxable worth. A local tax assessor's role is identifying the assessed value of all property in a specific area. In most government jurisdictions, the assessed value of property is a percentage of the full value of the property, referred to as the rollback value.

Once the assessed value is determined, it is multiplied by the tax rate. Tax rates are established by local government authorities and are subject to fluctuation depending on the needs of a community. Real property tax dollars are a part of the general operating fund for a government entity; each portion of the local government operations—such as public parks and recreation—receive a percentage of the general operating fund. This portion of funding supports the work done by the public parks and recreation organization. An example of how to calculate real property taxes is outlined in Figure 8.1. There are other minor taxes that also fund community recreation operations; those taxes include a sales tax and special product or service taxes. The collection and allocation of these tax dollars is similar to the distribution of real property taxes.

Step 1. Finding the assessed value if full value of property is $100,000.

Assessed ratio value X Full Value of the Property = Assessed Value
54.4% X $100,000 = $54,000

Step 2. Finding the property taxes paid for the fiscal year 2015.

Tax Rate X Assessed Value = Property Taxes Paid

.3207 X $54,400 = $1,744.60

Figure 8.1. Calculating real property taxes, Cedar Falls, Iowa Fiscal Year 2015.

Fees and Charges

Participants involved in programs and services may pay a fee or incur a charge for involvement; these fees and charges are used as revenue to offset program operations and expenses. Users of programs and services are asked to pay for the cost of specialized activities since there is a direct benefit to the user. For example, the New York City Department of Parks and Recreation requires all individuals who play tennis to purchase a permit for usage of the courts; the permit is good for the entire tennis season (http://www.nycgovparks.org/facility/tennis/rules). The permit charge goes to facilitation, staffing, and maintenance of the multiple tennis courts under the supervision of the parks and recreation department.

There are different types of fees and charges associated with public parks and recreation programs and services. Entrance fees are charged when a person enters a park or recreational area; parking fees also fall under entrance fees. The areas are usually defined and identifiable within the public parks and recreation supervision, but not always enclosed, since many parks and recreational areas are outdoors. There may be additional charges or fees for subsequent ancillary services once the participant is admitted.

Admission fees are charged to participants when they enter the recreational building or structure. These locations are usually enclosed and offer exhibits, shows, ceremonies, performances, demonstrations, or involve special equipment. Entry and exit of the facility are regulated by staff members, and user attendance is usually kept on a daily basis.

Rental fees are payments made to a public parks and recreation agency for exclusive usage of an area or facility. The renters are able to use the facility or area, as well as all ancillary services associated with the rental, yet still follow all policies and procedures associated with usage. Rental fees provide private usage for individuals or groups.

User fees are charges for using a facility or area or participation in an activity. Participants who pay a user fee are usually enjoying the recreational experience simultaneously with other users. These fees are charged at driving ranges, campsites, sports fields, swimming pools, ice rinks, and golf courses (Landes, 2012).

Sales revenues are funds generated from operating stores, concessions, restaurants, or from the sale of parks and recreation-related merchandise (e.g., t-shirts, towels, and sporting equipment). With gift store sales, there are two different categories of items sold that can generate revenue (Landes, 2012). The first category includes items that relate to the community recreation area or facility and can be used by participants for recreation purposes. Examples of this category would include water bottles, sunscreen, and trail guides. The second category includes souvenirs; these are often gifts or keepsakes that remind people of their visit. A key point with souvenirs is to include the public parks and recreation logo, emblem, or tagline on the merchandise. For sales revenue to be generated, ownership of the item must pass from the public parks and recreation agency to the user.

License and permit fees are written acknowledgments providing consent to participants, allowing them to engage in a lawful act in accordance with the public parks and recreation user policies. Usually license and permit fees involve written permission as well, which is documented and kept on file at the community recreation agency. The privilege extended to participants via license and permit fees does not traditionally include occupying space or property.

Special service fees are charges made for extraordinary programs, services, or leadership not commonplace within the routine operations of the community recreation agency. Normally, special service fees are unusual in character or unique in request. The City of Tuscon Parks and Recreation Department categorizes private lessons (e.g., swimming) and staffing for special events as special service fees (City of Tuscon Parks and Recreation Department, n.d.).

Grants

State and federal grants are a common source of revenue for public parks and recreation agencies. When a public parks and recreation agency solicits grant funding from a state or federal granting agency, the goal is to alleviate a specific issue, problem, or concern within the community (Crompton, 1999). The City of Twentynine Palms, California Park and Recreation Department coordinates the Community Development Block Grant (CDBG) programs. The CDBG program grants funds that can be used to acquire, construct, and rehabilitate recreation areas and facilities, and/or develop recreational programs within a community (Howard & Crompton, 1980). The services provided for the City of Twentynine Palms, through the Park and Recreation Department, facilitate the growth of the community's parks, while still preserving the character and uniqueness of the environment). There are a number of granting agencies that exist; some examples include Lowe's Charitable and Educational Foundation, Miracle's Grants for America's Children, and the National Park Service Land and Water Conservation Fund.

A caveat exists if public parks and recreation agencies are going to pursue grant funding as a source of revenue for programs or services. Grant funds tend to be for a limited timeframe and usually dissipate when the issue, problem, or concern has been rectified. This means that if programs and services are going to continue after the grant funding is removed, then the agency needs to have a plan for sustainability in association with other sources of revenue.

Donations

It is common for public parks and recreation agencies to accept donations, in some cases as a gift from a donor, as a form of revenue. Parks and recreation administrators can set up a special account for donations. These accounts allow individuals to donate money for the purchase of specialized items. For example, the City of Boston, Massachusetts Parks and Recreation Department has developed a Tree and Bench Donation Program (http://www.cityofboston.gov/Parks/donate.asp). This type of program is facilitated through a special donor account created within the City's Parks and Recreation Department budget (Figure 8.2).

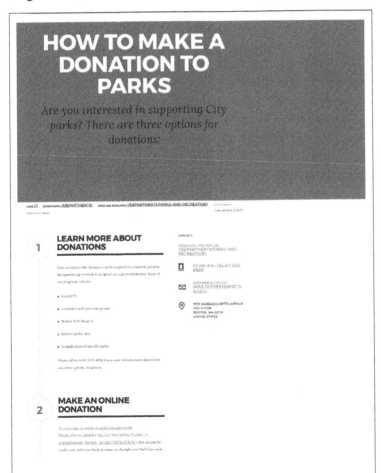

Figure 8.2. Tree and Bench Donation Program, Boston (MA) Parks & Recreation Department

Administrators can take the action one step further and aid in the creation of a foundation to foster growth within the parks and recreation jurisdiction. The foundation is housed outside of the public parks and recreation agency and managed by private citizens. There are a number of financial advantages to establishing parks and recreation foundations (Sellers, Gladwell, & Pope, 1999). A foundation is not under the governmental umbrella that encompasses the parks and recreation agency; therefore, donations can be tax deductible to the donor. Foundations are able to act without all of the political and bureaucratic obstacles, and foundations are good public relations tools when affiliated with the community recreation agency.

Bonds and Bond Programs

Bond programs and the issuance of bonds are the main source of revenue for funding capital improvements that are done within public parks and recreation organizations (Edginton & Williams, 1978). A bond is defined as "a promise by the borrower...to pay back the lender...a specific amount of money with interest within a specific period of time" (Crompton, 1999, p. 32). Procedures for bond programs are usually established by state laws; these laws govern items such as the timeline for a bond program and the voting percentages for passing a bond. Two major types of bonds exist that are used in government bonding are (a) general obligation bonds and (b) revenue bonds (Edginton & Williams, 1978).

General obligation bonds. General obligation bonds are guaranteed and backed by the local municipality regarding repayment. The municipality guarantees to pay out of its general operating budget a certain amount of money on an annual basis for the privilege of borrowing the money. This agreement allows the municipality to acquire millions of dollars expediently for the purchase of land or construction of capital facilities that it could not otherwise do. In order to move forward with general obligation bonds as a revenue source, voter approval needs to occur within the community. The reason for voter approval is that the main source of repayment for general obligation bonds is property tax dollars. To gain voter approval, the municipality needs to provide voters with the following items: (a) a vested interest in the citizens' needs, (b) no increase in taxes in conjunction with the project, (c) confidence in the sponsoring agency, (d) clarity regarding the bond issue, and (e) good timing regarding proposal of the project (Edginton & Williams, 1978).

A good example of strategic general obligation bond program has occurred in Albuquerque, New Mexico. In 2013, the City of Albuquerque, as a part of the Capital Improvement Plan for the community, employed general obligation bonds as a revenue source (https://www.cabq.gov/municipaldevelopment/programs/2013-go-bond-program-and-2013-2022-decade-plan/capital-program-by-bond-purpose/bond-questions). Over $10 million in general obligation bonds were issued for renovations and improvements to parks, shooting ranges, and swimming pools; acquisition of land; and mapping, research, and redesign of existing parks and recreation areas. In this instance, the municipality that will support repayment is the City of Albuquerque.

Revenue bonds. Revenue bonds are not backed by the local municipality; rather, repayment usually comes from revenue that is accrued through the capital project supported by the bond program (Crompton, 1999). Revenue bonds are often used to finance facilities such as golf courses and swimming pools. The Parks, Recreation, and Culture Service Area associated with the city of Portland, Oregon, used revenue bonds in association with the golf program. The Golf Revenue Bond Redemption Fund was paid out by net revenues of the Golf program (https://www.portlandoregon.gov/cbo/article/163139). A fundamental tenet when considering usage of revenue bonds is whether the capital project can generate enough revenue for operating costs and the retirement of the debt associated with the bond (Howard & Crompton, 1980). Before taking the step of issuing revenue bonds, most public parks and recreation agencies in conjunction with the local municipality will conduct a feasibility study to see how much potential revenue will be generated by the capital project.

There are a few items to consider when debating the usage of revenue bonds. First, due to the riskiness associated with repayment, revenue bonds tend to be more challenging to sell to investors than general obligation bonds. Second, elements outside of management's control, such as inclement weather conditions, can impact participants' usage, therefore affecting generation of revenue. For example, if a public waterpark is not able to be open regularly due to poor weather, this will impact entrance fees as a source of revenue to repay the bond debt. Third, revenue bonds do not require voter approval as do general obligation bonds. This is due to the fact that tax dollars would be used as a form of repayment with a general obligation bond, and citizens need to approve the usage of their money is this fashion. While no voting approval may seem like a benefit when considering revenue bonds, it can be "fool's gold." A public park and recreation agency can borrow more money than it is able to repay, putting the agency in a financial quandary and hurting the operations of the organization as a whole. Lastly, the interest rates associated with repayment of revenue bonds is higher than general obligation bonds due to the method of repayment. Investors feel safer when the municipality is able to pledge the backing of its general operating fund as a source of repayment (if needed), since it is a dedicated and stable source of revenue.

EXPENDITURES

The costs associated with parks and recreation program design and implementation are called *expenditures*. Although there are many examples of costs associated with programs and services, there are two main categories of expenditures: (a) operating expenditures and (b) capital expenditures (Edginton, Hudson, & Lankford, 2001).

Operating expenditures. Operating expenditures are regularly occurring costs associated with personnel, materials, supplies, and services. Community parks and recreation agencies usually have a bulk of their operating expenditures tied up in personnel services due to the large number of full-time, part-time, temporary, and seasonal personnel and staff. Care should be paid to the influx of revenue; if this drops or begins to decrease, operating expenditures are usually the first items to be cut from the budget. As cuts are made, a number of intangible factors associated with personnel may be impacted, such as a commitment to the public parks and recreation agency, enthusiasm for work, and effective leadership.

Capital expenditures. Capital expenditures are costs associated with large, financially significant projects; these endeavors are referred to as capital projects (e.g., land acquisition, new building construction). There may be immediate costs, such as construction of temporary locker rooms in a public parks and recreation facility if the permanent locker rooms are part of a large-scale renovation project. There also may be long-term costs; if the large-scale renovation project involves expansion of the facility to provide additional programs, those programs will need staff members and the new portion of the facility will incur regular maintenance. This is why many administrators forecast and engage in their budgeting process several years into the future.

Public parks and recreation administrators may address operating and capital expenditures in different ways. Operating expenditures are analogous to daily expenses a person may have (e.g., food or clothing). These personal costs are usually paid off by one's salary income, and do not require borrowing money to do so. For the public parks and recreation administrator, operating expenditures are usually taken care of via the operating fund. Capital expenditures, on the other hand, would be analogous to an individual purchasing a large-scale item, such as a house or a car. Most people may not be able to purchase a home or car without borrowing money from a lending institution, such as a bank or credit union. The repayment would be over a specific amount of years, with interest. For a public parks and recreation agency, capital projects may require funds that exceed the operating revenue for the organization. This leads to the agency borrowing money in some fashion, and repaying the debt, plus interest, to the lending institution over a specific period of time. Whether it is one's personal budget or an operating budget for a community parks and recreation agency, prudence should be taken when planning for operating and capital expenditures.

BUDGET TYPES

There are certain commonalities that exist within the budgeting process of public parks and recreation agencies. Parks and recreation agencies are a part of a local government; all parts of the government are required by law to balance their budgets; this means that expenditures, or money spent on the operations of the public parks and recreation agency, should not exceed revenue generated (Howard & Crompton, 1980). Two scenarios should occur if the budget is properly managed: (a) the revenue and expenditures equal out, or (b) a surplus of revenue exists after expenditures have been addressed. The primary question all community parks and recreation administrators should ponder when considering financing programs, services and overall operations of their agency is "How much money is available?" As Wildavsky pointed out, the budgeting process then becomes a maintenance activity (1975), with the goal of making sure administrators manage expenditures effectively and "carry out policies within acceptable boundaries" (p. 115).

The Budget Cycle

The budget cycle involves months of preparation, consultation, and reviews in order to formally adopt the plan for each fiscal year (Crompton, 1999). A fiscal year can start any time during a calendar year and should end with the settling of financial accounts associated with the public parks and recreation agency. It is common to see a fiscal year for a public parks and recreation agency run from July 1 to June 30 of the subsequent year.

Public parks and recreation agencies often project the budget a number of years into the future (Edginton & Williams, 1978). This planning allows agencies to determine the types of commitments needed for the organization and be able to secure revenue for those commitments. Multiple-year projected budgeting allows administrators to plan for certain trends, such as inflation or shifting programmatic needs.

The budget process includes four main phases: (a) preparation, (b) design, (c) presentation, and (d) implementation. The budget preparation phase includes formal documentation on when the budget will be submitted, in what form, and any other procedures deemed integral to the process. Part of the preparation phase includes gathering ideas associated with the public parks and recreation agency's operations from various constituent groups. This can be done in-house via staff meetings and through public forums.

The budget design phase includes the budget message, budget summary, budget narrative, and budget detail. The budget message highlights existing programs or ideas for new programs. The budget summary lists major categories of the budget, such as expenditures (e.g., personnel services, materials) and revenue (e.g., grants, fees). The budget narrative focuses on each program and provides a deeper description than the general comments found in the budget message. Finally, the budget detail specifically outlines all of the public parks and recreation agency's expenditures and revenue. This is done with more detail than the budget summary.

The budget presentation phase includes formal presentations to the city manager or elected officials and the governing board which makes funding decisions. The presentation provides a summary of what the budget includes, inclusive of any new programs or services. Public parks and recreation agencies that have a history of running high-quality programs use this as a tool in soliciting revenue.

The final phase, budget implementation, includes adoption of the budget by the governing board after the presentation. A resolution is a legal binding document that provides the funds for the public parks and recreation agency's operations. If any needs arise to secure more funds for the overall operations after the resolution has been passed, a formal request needs to be submitted to the governing board. This formality is in place to secure proper management of funds for each area of the public parks and recreation agency. After implementation of the budget and at the end of the fiscal year, an outside firm does a budget audit to verify public funds were managed in a honest manner and with integrity.

The City of Portland, Oregon's Parks and Recreation Department has an extensive budgeting process (https://www.portlandoregon.gov/parks/66061). There are budget packages for one-time expenditures, recommendations by the City Council, value statements highlighting the goals the City of Portland is trying to achieve with public parks and recreation, and guidance from the mayor, to name just a few of the budgetary components. Since the Portland Parks and Recreation Department is a government agency, there are also presentation meetings for the general public to attend to ask questions associated with the budgeting process (https://www.portlandoregon.gov/parks/article/472706). These items are just a few of the many tools used to construct the budget that are taken into account by the Budget Advisory Committee, or BAC. Once the BAC decides what needs to be prioritized, those projects are included in the recommended budget (https://www.portlandoregon.gov/parks/article/480175).

Line-Item Budgeting

There are several types of budgets that may be used within the public parks and recreation setting. The oldest and most common form of budgeting used by public parks and recreation agencies is the line-item budget, with origins dating back to the early 20th century. The Progressive Era was occurring in the United States, and specifically in New York City; this was the flashpoint for the evolution of government budgeting, morphing economic management into a better system of policies and procedures (Stivers, 2000). This desire for better fiscal control and financial accountability led to the creation of line-item budgets. These budgets are simple, effective tools that allow public parks and recreation administrators the control and flexibility associated with managing the operations of their agency.

Line-item budgets allow government representatives to analyze the financial transactions of a public parks and recreation agency (Edginton, Hudson, & Lankford, 2001). All revenues and expenditures are listed as categories, or lines, within the budget. Each line describes the classification and the amount of money spent on that classification. Typical classifications of public parks and recreation services include (a) personnel services, (b) contractual services, (c) supplies, (d) materials, (e) current charges, (f) current obligations, (g) properties, and (h) debt payment.

The City of New Haven, Connecticut Department of Parks, Recreation and Trees provides uses line-item budgets for many programs and services (Figure 8.3). Various programmatic areas of the Department have line items based on the aforementioned classifications. A second example from Culver City, California's Parks, Recreation and Community Services Department highlights a larger community's usage of a line-item budget (http://www.culvercity.org/Home/ShowDocument?id=632). Multiple programs associated with the Department, including summer camps, aquatics, enrichment, seniors, youth mentoring and community excursions, are delineated in the budget for public viewing.

The focus of using a line-item budget format is on allocating funds (Crompton, 1999). One drawback is the difficulty drawing a connection between expenditures and program results or benefits. The costs for particular programs are spread out and not articulated specifically within each line-item. This stylistic attribute of line-item budgeting is why many administrators use this form of budgeting. It is easier to understand and beneficial when needing to consider budget reductions. It is easier to reduce concrete funds than to debate the abstract value or need of a program (Wildavsky, 1986).

Program Budgeting

With program budgeting, analysis is focused primarily on the outputs of the public parks and recreation agency. A program under this budget structure is a specific group of activities designed to meet a certain goal. A program budget could reflect a major program area, such as athletics, or a specific program within a major area, such as softball. Evaluation of the budget is focused on the costs of the programs.

The major steps associated with developing a program budget involve identifying each program the public parks and recreation agency provides and then determining the costs associated with each program. The budget philosophy of the agency may also include indirect costs, such as utilities, proportioned out to each program's costs on a percentage basis.

Program budgets provide more information on the cost effectiveness of programs, services, and activities by matching program objectives to the expenditures. This information also helps public parks and recreation administrators determine the costs and benefits to the programs that are offered. The Mason City Recreation and Golf Department's Softball program budget is outlined in Figure 8.4. Each component of the softball program has been illustrated in terms of current costs, year-to-date (YTD) costs, projected yearly costs, and the percentage of expenditures that have been met at that point. This example highlights the detailed nature associated with program budgeting.

Performance Budgeting

Program budgeting is the forerunner to performance budgeting; with performance budgeting, work done within the public parks and recreation agency is broken down into detailed subunits to determine the specific costs. Functional and objective classifications are divided so that the administration can understand the cost of each program offered by the

REVENUES	
Ice Time Sales	
Ice Rental - Resident	4,000
Ice Rental – Non-resident	90,000
Ice Rental – New Haven Public Schools	3,000
Public Skating/Admissions	
Public Skating - Youth	29,000
Public Skating - Adults	25,000
Special Groups	21,000
Programs	
Learn to Skate	19,000
Pro Shop	1,000
Parties	5,000
Vending	3,000
Total Revenues	**200,000**
Reserve (accrued excess of revenue over expenditures through 01/01/13)	10,000
Total Revenues and Reserves	**210,000**
ADMINISTRATIVE EXPENSES	
Management Fee	35,000
Salaries	55,000
Payroll Expenses	18,000
Workers Compensation	2,500
OPERATING EXPENSES	
Insurance	10,000
Start Up Costs Ice Making, Ice Painting, Equipment Start-up	15,000
Office Supplies	1,000
Rink Supplies	5,000
Rental Equipment	2,500
Maintenance Repairs	5,000
Marketing	4,000
CAPITAL ALLOCATION	
Sewage Pump Repair	20,000
Sub-Total Expenses	**173,000**
Revenue Sharing (.30 percent of net)	9,000
Total Expenses	**182,000**
ANTICIPATED BALANCE, 2014 SEASON	**28,000**

Figure 8.3. Ralph Walker Skating Rink Budget, New Haven Connecticut Department of Parks, Recreation & Trees Line Item Budget (FY 2013-2014).

public parks and recreation agency. Performance budgeting is a common form of budgeting when users pay for the cost of a given activity. Calculating all expenditures and knowing the overall cost for program will provide insight on the amount of money to charge to cover the program expenses.

A few key features associated with performance budgeting include using the classification system that is often seen in line-item budgeting. Additionally, the information gathered through the performance budgeting process, and the formal procedures in doing so, are

CITY OF MASON CITY
REVENUES WITH COMPARISON TO BUDGET
FOR 2 MONTHS ENDING AUGUST 31, 2015

YOUTH SOUTHBALL COMPLEX

	Current	YTD	BUDGET AMOUNT	VARIANCE	% OF BUDGET
SPECIAL ASSESSMENT					
535.0550.9017 SPECIAL ASSESSMENT	$558.00	$2,188.00	$23,600.00	$21,412.00	9.27%
TOTAL SPECIAL ASSESSMENT	$558.00	$2,188.00	$23,600.00	$21,412.00	9.27%
COMMISSION ON CONCESSIONS					
535.0700.7003 COMMISSION ON CONCESSIONS	$0.00	$652.00	$0.00	($652.00)	100.00%
TOTAL COMMISSION ON CONCESSIONS	$0.00	$652.00	$0.00	($652.00)	100.00%
CONCESSION TAXABLE					
535.0700.7018 CONCESSION TAXABLE	$0.00	$5,579.90	$13,500.00	$7,920.10	41.33%
TOTAL CONCESSION TAXABLE	$0.00	$5,579.90	$13,500.00	$7,920.10	41.33%
TOTAL FUND REVENUES	$558.00	$8,419.90	$37,100.00	$28,680.10	22.70%
PROFESSIONAL SERVICES					
535.4401.2740 PROFESSIONAL SERVICES	$1,591.00	$1,623.00	$2,500.00	$877.00	64.92%
TOTAL PROFESSIONAL SERVICES	$1,591.00	$1,623.00	$2,500.00	$877.00	64.92%
OTHER SUPPLIES					
535.4401.3035 OTHER SUPPLIES	$2,303.94	$3,315.66	$12,000.00	$8,684.34	27.63%
TOTAL OTHER SUPPLIES	$2,303.94	$3,315.66	$12,000.00	$8,684.34	27.63%
SITE IMPROVEMENTS					
535.4401.4644 SITE IMPROVEMENTS	$900.00	$900.00	$2,000.00	$1,100.00	45.00%
TOTAL SITE IMPROVEMENTS	$900.00	$900.00	$2,000.00	$1,100.00	45.00%
BALL DIAMONDS					
535.4401.4830 BALL DIAMONDS	$0.00	$490.00	$5,500.00	$5,010.00	8.91%
TOTAL BALL DIAMONDS	$0.00	$490.00	$5,500.00	$5,010.00	8.91%
BUILDING INSURANCE F & EC					
535.4414.2170 BUILDING INSURANCE F & EC	$0.00	$0.00	$600.00	$600.00	0.00%
TOTAL BUILDING INSURANCE F & EC	$0.00	$0.00	$600.00	$600.00	0.00%
SALES TAX					
535.4414.2540 SALES TAX	$365.04	$785.40	$1,500.00	$714.60	52.36%
TOTAL SALES TAX	$365.04	$785.40	$1,500.00	$714.60	52.36%
CONCESSION SUPPLIES					
535.4414.3135 CONCESSION SUPPLIES	$6.32	$2,924.06	$13,000.00	$10,075.94	22.49%
TOTAL CONCESSION SUPPLIES	$6.32	$2,924.06	$13,000.00	$10,075.94	22.49%
BALL DIAMONDS					
535.5675.4830 BALL DIAMONDS	$0.00	$0.00	$0.00	$0.00	100.00%
TOTAL BALL DIAMONDS	$0.00	$0.00	$0.00	$0.00	100.00%
TOTAL FUND EXPENDITURES	$5,166.30	$10,038.12	$37,100.00	$27,061.88	27.06%
NET REVENUES OVER EXPENDITURES	($4,608.30)	($1,618.22)	$0.00	$1,618.22	100.00%

Figure 8.4. Mason City, Iowa Softball Program Budget, Fiscal Year 2015

valuable to the upper administrators and governing board that appropriate funds for the public parks and recreation agency. Finally, using performance budgeting encourages decisions to be made in consideration of expenditures and program costs.

Zero-Based Budgeting

Zero-based budgeting (ZBB) is a process, with roots in private business, which has been used in the public parks and recreation field since the early 1970s. Traditionally, the steps of determining annual budget adjustments within an organization is accomplished by adding projected costs of new programs, as well as inflation, to the organization's base budget for the previous year. When these steps are taken, the public parks and recreation agency does not need to justify the previous year's appropriations. Zero-based budgeting requires a different approach to budgeting.

Usage of a zero-based budgeting process requires the organization to justify the total request for funding from a zero base level. This means that each fiscal year, each community parks and recreation program or service (inclusive of revenue and expenditures) is evaluated for funding as if it were being considered a part of the operations budget for the first time. Using this approach to budgeting requires careful evaluation of programs and services to make sure they are a part of the public parks and recreation agency's goals and that they are being managed effectively.

Zero-based budgeting also challenges the public parks and recreation agency to determine which programs and services to prioritize and fund within the fiscal year. This challenge encourages staff members and administrators to create and maintain high-quality programs and services for the community. If too many programs and services are "boiler plated," meaning they are just redone and there are little to no fresh, new ideas or thoughts that are a part of the programming, the result is insufficient in meeting the needs of the community.

The process associated with zero-based budgeting involves four main steps: (a) identification of decision-making units within an organization, (b) development and analysis of the decision-making packages within the decision-making units, (c) analysis and evaluation of all alternatives within the decision-making packages, and (d) preparation of an operational budget. Decision-making units are groups of individuals within the public parks and recreation agency that have the authority and responsibility for controlling financial resources, programs, and services. These units may be led by supervisors, managers, or division heads (e.g., superintendent of recreation); their role is to provide information to the group of people who will make budgetary decisions.

The decision-making package is the key component of the zero-based budgeting process; it is a document that outlines what is needed financially for each program or service. The decision-making package is used to evaluate whether or not to approve the program or service for funding. The following information is usually included in a decision-making package: (a) purpose and objective(s) of the program, (b) what is the proposed program and what will participants do as a part of the program, (c) what are the costs and benefits of the program, (d) staff members' responsibilities and performance measures or evaluations, and (e) alternative means of accomplishing the objectives of the program.

The management group that evaluates all decision-making packages considers all alternatives associated with program implementation due to the limited amount of funds allocated to the public parks and recreation agency. Evaluation of all decision-making packages and alternatives will also aid in justification of funding for each program. During the analysis and evaluation process, each decision-making package is rank ordered based on the benefit to the public parks and recreation agency. This systematic process allows management to make rational decisions for funding based upon a high volume of information produced by the decision-making units.

Once the decision-making packages and possible alternatives associated with program implementation are selected, an operational budget is put together. The actual budget may incorporate a classification system, similar to the one used in line-item budgeting. The design of the budget is the final step in the zero-based budgeting process; this process helps public parks and recreation administrators outline costs and benefits to programs and services, maintain effective offerings, and ensure organizational efficiency.

For the fiscal year of 2013–2014, the government for the City of Dallas, Texas, used a zero-based budgeting process to determine the allocation of funds for key focus areas (http://www.dallascityhall.com/Budget/proposed1314/FY14-ProposedBudgetBook.pdf). One of the key focus areas is Culture, Arts, and Recreation (Key Focus Area 4). As outlined in the decision-making package, "Dallas citizens and visitors enjoy and experience the benefits of vibrant, innovative, and diverse cultural, arts and recreational opportunities." Each program included in the decision-making package for this key focus area includes common elements: (a) description of the program or service, (b) sources of funds, (c) performance measures, (d) performance measure status, (e) service target benchmark, and (f) major budget items. These elements are integral as the city's governing body convenes to decide on the upcoming fiscal year's budget.

Capital Budgeting

The purpose of capital budgeting is to focus on long-term physical improvements within the public parks and recreation scope of management (Crompton, 1999). The efforts to raise the money to support these projects are called capital campaigns. Capital budgeting is connected to one-time expenditures that generally have a life expectancy of over 10 years. These expenditures, as discussed earlier in the chapter, include repair or replacement of existing facilities, and development of new facilities. Capital budgets are created independently of operating budgets, since the source of revenue for capital projects is often wholly separate from the operating revenue of a public parks and recreation agency.

The Grand Forks, North Dakota Parks and Recreation Foundation began a capital campaign in 2012 to develop new ice skating rinks and arenas, due to the critical shortage of indoor ice for youth hockey and figure skating programs (http://gfparksfoundation.org/wp-content/uploads/sites/8/2012/07/Presentation-Packet-Case-Statement-Addendums.pdf). The capital budget for the project includes the following items: (a) sources of revenue, such as naming rights to facilities and donor gift clubs, (b) arena operating costs (based upon comparable arenas), (c) arena income, and (d) arena expenses. This project, and the affiliated budget, is a separate item from the Grand Forks Parks and Recreation District operating budget due to the scope and magnitude of the work, inclusive of the financial needs.

The capital budget outlines the annual capital expenditures, and is part of plan that covers a 5- to 6-year time period. This plan is called a Capital Improvement Program (CIP), and highlights capital projects that will be undertaken during the time period, as well as the fiscal strategy for funding the projects. Once the local governing body of a community approves the CIP, the budget is the document that authorizes projects to be done each fiscal year. Figure 8.5. displays the CIP associated with parks, open spaces, trails, and recreation for the city of Durango, Colorado.

Project	Description	Funding Source	Estimated Total Cost	Priority
SMART 160 East Trail	Construct SMART 160 East Trail	2005 1/4 Cent Tax	8,400,000	High
SMART 160 West Trail	Construct SMART 160 West Trail	2005 1/4 Cent Tax	10,000,000	High
Camino del Rio At-Grade Crossing	Camino at-grade crossing at 12th St.	2005 1/4 Cent Tax	200,000	High
Natural Lands Preservation	Acquisition of natural lands	2005 1/4 Cent Tax	14,500,000	High
POST Planning & Maintenance	Planning, design & maintenance	2005 1/4 Cent Tax	1,924,418	High
Improvements	infrastructure, etc.	2005 1/4 Cent Tax	2,000,000	High
FLC Softball Fields	Upgrade restroom and lights	2005 1/4 Cent Tax	1,092,000	High
FLC Multi Use Fields	Construct new multi use fields	2005 1/4 Cent Tax	3,750,000	High
Durango Boating Park	Develop boating park for RICD	2005 1/4 Cent Tax	1,100,000	High
Community Park	Multi use fields in Three Springs	2005 1/4 Cent Tax	24,400,000	High
Chapman Ski Hill	Upgrade lifts, lighting and parking	2005 1/4 Cent Tax	1,450,000	High
Cundiff Park	Develop neighborhood park	2005 1/4 Cent Tax	2,400,000	Medium
BMX at ALP	Develop BMX track at ALP site	2005 1/4 Cent Tax	1,045,000	Medium
Holly Park	Develop neighborhood park	2005 1/4 Cent Tax	600,000	Medium
Camino del Rio Underpass	Underpass to link ART to downtown	2005 1/4 Cent Tax	3,000,000	Medium
Santa Rita to Goeglein Trail	Goeglein Trail	2005 1/4 Cent Tax	3,000,000	Medium
Hillcrest Trail	Construct trail around Golf Course	2005 1/4 Cent Tax	1,300,000	Medium
Santa Rita Park Volleyball Courts	Upgrade sand volleyball courts	2005 1/4 Cent Tax	100,000	Medium
33rd Street River Access	Improve 33rd Street River Access	2005 1/4 Cent Tax	350,000	Medium
FLC Tennis Courts	Remove & replace tennis courts	2005 1/4 Cent Tax	350,000	Medium
Year round ice rink	Year round ice rink, second ice rink	2005 1/4 Cent Tax	10,000,000	Low
CBD Park Plaza	Develop new park in the CBD	2005 1/4 Cent Tax	1,560,000	Low
SUBTOTAL			**$ 92,521,418**	
32nd Street Ped/Bike Bridge	ART Bike/Ped Improvements at 32nd Street	1999 1/2 Cent Tax	300,000	High
Memorial Park Trail	Construct ART 29th St. to 32nd St.	1999 1/2 Cent Tax	556,000	High
32nd Street to Iron Horse Trail	Construct ART north to Iron Horse	1999 1/2 Cent Tax	3,000,000	High
ART Greenway Acquisition	Acquire greenway Animas River Trail	1999 1/2 Cent Tax	6,250,000	High
ART Rebuild	Rebuild sections of Animas River Trail	1999 1/2 Cent Tax	5,055,000	High
Whitewater Park Trail	Rebuild and realign trail for boating park	1999 1/2 Cent Tax	1,100,000	High
32nd Street Underpass	ART Underpass at 32nd Street	1999 1/2 Cent Tax	1,000,000	High
ART connect to SMART 160	ART connect to SMART 160 trail	1999 1/2 Cent Tax	3,200,000	Medium
Junction Creek to CRC Trail	Trail under Main Ave. to Rec Center	1999 1/2 Cent Tax	3,200,000	Low
4th Street to Whitewater Park	Bridge over Hwy 550/160	1999 1/2 Cent Tax	3,000,000	Low
CBD Park Trail	Construct CBD Park trail	1999 1/2 Cent Tax	800,000	Low
SUBTOTAL			**$ 27,461,000**	
Cemetery Office/Shop	Upgrade Park office & shop at cemetery	General Fund	1,258,500	High
Recreation Center Third Gym	Relocate gymnastics to Rec Center	General Fund	1,930,000	Medium
Cemetery Roads Overlay	Overlay roads at Cemetery	General Fund	150,000	Medium
Grandview Recreation Center	New Recreation Center in Grandview	General Fund	45,100,000	Low
SUBTOTAL			**$ 48,438,500**	
GRAND TOTAL			**$ 168,420,918**	

Figure 8.5. CIP for Parks, Open Spaces, Trails, and Recreation, Durango, Colorado

It is important to review the capital budget after the completion of each project outlined in the CIP. There may be important items that came up in the planning process that can streamline the capital budgeting process for future projects in the CIP. The review should include (a) analyzing proposed financial resource consumption versus actual financial resource consumption, (b) comparing actual outcome measures of the project versus projected outcome measures, and (c) investigating the adherence to the public parks and recreation agency's mission, goals, and objectives (Crompton, 1999).

One of the largest counties in the United States, Clark County (Nevada), has a Capital Improvement Program for 2013-2017 (http://www.clarkcountynv.gov/Depts/finance/budget/Documents/Capital%20Improvement%20Program%202013-2017.pdf). A main area of the Capital Improvement Program is Parks and Recreation. The Department of Parks and Recreation is responsible for developing and maintaining the public parks and open recreation areas, special recreation use facilities, fine art galleries, senior centers, a museum and multiple sports fields—all within Clark County. All major programs and projects outlined in the Parks and Recreation section of the Capital Improvement Program report highlight proposed work, revenue sources, and impacts on the operating budget. This information is vital for the long-term development of Clark County and evaluated each year to make sure the proposed work, revenue, and expenditures are accurate within the Capital Improvement Program.

FINANCIAL TRENDS

As community parks and recreation forges ahead into the 21st century, there are vital questions lingering about the economics of the field. Professionals in the field are engaging in tireless efforts to demonstrate parks and recreation is a powerful force for a local community's growth, and that it is important that public parks and recreation agencies continue to receive financial support that is warranted from the local government. Yet, there are areas of concern that public parks and recreation administrators should be aware of as they make financial plans for their organizations.

Equitable Funding

The National Recreation and Park Association's three strategic pillars—conservation, health and wellness, and social equity—are important and valuable statements of how vital community parks and recreation is for society (Dolesh, 2014). The definition of social equity in this sense includes equal access for all current and future participants to the full range of opportunities provided by a community parks and recreation agency. Equal funding for every public parks and recreation agency is not realistic, but alternative funding sources can be provided for community parks and recreation agencies so that all people can still benefit. The social benefits that are derived from public parks and recreation programs can be significant, but what is trending are threats to these benefits and the agencies that provide them, especially to communities where residents are poor, minorities, or underrepresented.

There are a couple steps that can be taken to reducing the disparity with public parks and recreation funding. One step is to recognize the importance of private funding in the larger financial picture of public parks and recreation. Private funding, such as donations and foundation contributions, are integral sources of revenue, but there should still be an influx of public funding as well. The belief held by government entities that once private funding comes in for parks and recreation agencies, the public funding should be reduced is a misnomer. Private funding is a method of enhancing the overall revenue base for a community parks and recreation agency, yet public funding should still be a primary funding stream for public parks and recreation.

A second step is an ongoing point of emphasis—to reinforce the point that parks and recreation is an essential service to the public and not just a luxury. Emphasizing the economic, social, physical, emotional, and psychological benefits of participating in public parks and recreation programs and services for individuals is important, but also stressing the benefits (i.e., economic and environmental) to the community is crucial. Public parks and recreation should be viewed in the same category as public transportation and public schools—essential components of a community's infrastructure.

Changing Climate Patterns

In recent decades, reasonably stable national weather patterns have led to predictable facility designs, construction materials, and program design and implementation. Recently, though, fluctuating temperature changes and unpredictable weather patterns are affecting recreational activities. Dunnington (2011) pointed out that in the state of Vermont, the number of snow-covered days is decreasing and the water level in lakes is rising. Both of these environmental factors impact public park and recreation agencies' programs. Less snow means fewer winter activities, such as snowshoeing and cross-country skiing, and rising lakes limit shoreline and beach access and opportunities for waterfront activities. A reduction in these activities translates to a reduction in revenue that can be generated for parks and recreation.

Traditionally, local governments have been able to designate funds for adequate support of public parks and recreation programs and services, as well as budget for maintenance and upkeep of recreational facilities and structures. Changing climate patterns may require allocating funds for the aforementioned items but also for initiatives to enhance the well-being of the public parks and recreation agency. For example, funding vulnerability assessments that identify outdoor parks and recreation areas that are most vulnerable to climate change impacts is a step to help in the long-range budgeting and planning for the agency. Expanding certain public parks and recreation programs and services to facilitate the "new" or longer season is a way to offset the lost revenue from other "shortened" seasonal programming.

Community parks and outdoor recreation areas can also help offset the environmental impact of climate change. The Los Angeles County Department of Parks and Recreation is developing plans for six communities in Los Angeles County to help deter the impact of changing weather patterns in the area (http://losangeles.urbdezine.com/2014/07/29/parks-and-climate-change-the-l-a-county-story/). Funded through a grant program, the County explains that expanding the community's parks and outdoor recreation areas will improve air and water quality, protect natural resources, and reduce greenhouse gas emissions. Instead of burdening the local government for more funding via taxes, the Department of Parks and Recreation is accessing alternative revenue sources to financially support significant steps that can be taken to reduce the detrimental effects of climate change.

SUMMARY

As we continue to move forward into the 21st century, public parks and recreation will remain an important oasis in each community. Financing and budgeting for all the activities that take place under the auspices of the public parks and recreation organization can be a daunting task, especially if the prevailing notion regarding government revenue and operations "is to do more with less." This should be looked at as a challenge that can be dealt with; there are a number of alternative revenue sources available for public parks and recreation agencies that can greatly enhance the work done within the community.

As administrators dive into the budgetary process, it is important to recognize that developing a budget is a complex process. There are a number of groups, including community members, advisory committees, and staff members, who can be engaged and provide valuable insight during the process. Their input can provide the credibility needed to validate budget decisions regarding daily operations and capital projects.

When considering all the parts that go into budgeting for public parks and recreation, the most important part is still the administration leading the agency. Being able to gather revenue, manage expenditures, and be an active part of the budget planning process are essential job functions of management. In the end, the budget and financial system of the public parks and recreation agency are only as valuable as the programs and services provided to the public. This is because the final vote on how much financial support an agency receives is in taxpayers' hands.

DISCUSSION QUESTIONS

1. Describe two different sources of revenue for public parks and recreation agencies.
2. What is the primary source of revenue for public parks and recreation agencies?
3. Using the community where you live, calculate the amount of real property taxes paid for property values of $50,000, $150,000, and $200,000.
4. What are the differences between general obligation bonds and revenue bonds?
5. How is a capital budget different than an operational budget for a public parks and recreation agency?
6. Describe how the general public is involved in the budget cycle.
7. What is a Capital Improvement Program, or CIP?
8. How do program budgeting and performance budgeting differ?
9. Describe the process associated with zero-based budgeting.
10. What are the two main categories of expenditures associated with public parks and recreation budgeting?

REFERENCES

Bartram, S. (2014). Learning curve. *Parks & Recreation, 49*(7), 38–43.

City of Albuquerque (n.d.). 2013 GO bond summary. Retrieved from https://www.cabq. gov/municipaldevelopment/programs/2013-go-bond-program-and-2013-2022-decade-plan/capital-program-by-bond-purpose/bond-questions.

City of Boston. (2014). Donate to Boston's parks. Retrieved from http://www.cityofboston. gov/Parks/donate.asp.

City of Clarksville, Tennessee Parks & Recreation. (2014). User fees policy: Fees and revenue plan. Retrieved from http://www.cityofclarksville.com/modules/showdocument. aspx?documentid=4466

City of Dallas. (n.d.). City of Dallas – Annual budget for fiscal year 2013-2014. Retrieved from http://www.dallascityhall.com/Budget/proposed1314/FY14-ProposedBudgetBook. pdf

City of Durango, Colorado. (n.d.). Parks, open spaces, trails, and recreation master plan 2010-2019. Retrieved from http://www.durangogov.org/DocumentCenter/View/184

City of New Haven. (n.d.). Parks and recreation. Retrieved from http://cityofnewhaven. com/Mayor/pdfs/Without%20Contacts/2.6%20Parks%20and%20Recreation.pdf.

City of Tuscon Parks and Recreation Department. (n.d.). Revenue and pricing policy. Retrieved from https://www.tucsonaz.gov/files/parks/docs/PR_pricing_policy.pdf.

City of Twentynine Palms. (2011). Parks and recreation department – Community development. Retrieved from http://www.ci.twentynine-palms.ca.us/Community_ Developmt.25.0.html

Clark County Nevada. (n.d.). Capital Improvement Program. Retrieved from http://www.clarkcountynv.gov/Depts/finance/budget/Documents/Capital%20Improvement%20Program%202013-2017.pdf

Crompton, J. L. (1999). *Financing and acquiring park and recreation resources.* Champaign, IL: Human Kinetics.

Culver City. (2014). Culver City proposed budget: Fiscal year 2013-2014. Retrieved from http://www.culvercity.org/Home/ShowDocument?id=632

Dolesh, R. J. (2014). Equity in the Big Apple. *Parks & Recreation, 48*(8), 50–53.

Dunnington, G. (2011). *The potential impacts of climate change on recreation in Vermont.* Climate Change Adaptation White Paper Series. Climate Team: Vermont Agency of Natural Resources.

Edginton, C. R., Hudson, S. D., & Lankford, S. V. (2001). *Managing recreation, parks, and leisure services: An introduction.* Urbana, IL: Sagamore.

Edginton, C. R., & Williams, J. G. (1978). *Productive management of leisure service organizations.* New York, NY: John Wiley & Sons.

Godbey, G., & Rui, S. (2015). *Finding leisure in China.* State College, PA: Venture.

Grand Forks Parks & Recreation Foundation. (2012). Legends and heroes: Securing their future. Capital campaign: A case for support. Retrieved from http://gfparksfoundation.org/wp-content/uploads/sites/8/2012/07/Presentation-Packet-Case-Statement-Addendums.pdf

Howard, D. R., & Crompton, J. L. (1980). *Financing, managing, and marketing recreation and park resources.* Dubuque, IA: Wm. Brown.

Kaczynski, A. T., & Crompton, J. L. (2006). Financing priorities in local governments: Where do park and recreation services rank? *Journal of Park and Recreation Administration, 24*(1), 84–103.

Landes, S. E. (2012). *Financing municipal parks and recreation: A resource guide for recreation, parks, and conservation* (2nd ed.). Pennsylvania Department of Conservation and Natural Resources, Bureau of Recreation and Conservation in partnership with Pennsylvania Recreation and Park Society, Inc.

Lovell, T., & Snook, J. (2011). Game changing math. *Parks & Recreation, 45*(6), 24–26.

New York City Department of Parks and Recreation (n.d.). Tennis courts. Retrieved from http://www.nycgovparks.org/facility/tennis/rules

Portland, Oregon. (n.d.). Golf revenue bond redemption fund. Retrieved from https://www.portlandoregon.gov/cbo/article/163139

Sellers, J., Gladwell, N., & Pope, M., (1999). Financial management. In B. Van der Smissen, M. Moiseichik, V. Hartenburg, & L. Twardzik (Eds.), *Management of park and recreation agencies* (pp. 485–526). Arlington, VA: National park and recreation association.

Stivers, C. (2000). *Bureau men, settlement women: Constructing public administration in the Progressive Era.* Lawrence, KS: University of Kansas Press.

UrbDeZine Los Angeles. (2014, July 29). Parks and climate change: The L.A. County story. Retrieved from http://losangeles.urbdezine.com/2014/07/29/parks-and-climate-change-the-l-a-county-story/

U.S. Census. (2010a). Table 460: County Governments – Expenditures and debt for largest counties: 2006. Retrieved from http://www.census.gov/compendia/statab/2012/tables/12s0460.pdf.

U.S. Census. (2010b). Table 1233: Personal consumption expenditures for recreation: 1990 to 2009. Retrieved from http://www.census.gov/compendia/statab/2012/tables/12s1233.pdf.

Wildavsky, A. (1975). *Budgeting: A comparative theory of budgeting processes.* Boston, MA: Little, Brown and Co.

Wildavsky, A. (1986). *Budgeting: A comparative theory of budgeting processes* (2nd ed.). New Brunswick, NJ: Transaction.

Chapter Nine

Boards and Commissions

CHAPTER OBJECTIVES

- To gain an understanding of the different types of parks and recreation boards and commissions
- To gain knowledge of the reasons why it is necessary to have a board or commission
- To understand the relationship between boards, commissions, and policy-making
- To gain an appreciation of the role of board members
- To understand the way in which parks and recreation boards are structured

INTRODUCTION

Citizens have played a strong role in advocating for the advancement of the parks and recreation movement. Individuals and groups acting as activists have for 150 years provided great inspiration and enthusiasm for the provision of parks and recreation. One only has to review the development of organized societies and organizations such as the National Parks and Recreation Association offer witness to the fusion of citizen activities with the professional work of individuals in communities. Laypeople have generously contributed their time, financial resources, and creative ideas to ensuring high-quality parks and recreation systems.

A major way in which citizens have contributed to parks and recreation have been their participation as members of boards of directors and commissions. Such bodies have played a critical role in "gaining public trust, fostering partnerships, and securing necessary funds, which allow their organizations to thrive" (NRPA, 2007, p. 7). Further, such bodies have contributed to making parks and recreation agencies accountable to the community. Certainly, high-profile community members bring credibility, trust, and a heightened level of visibility to the work of an organization. By contributing their ideas and insights, parks and recreation organizations are able to move forward in a positive and productive fashion.

This chapter focuses on the general topics of boards and commissions. The first section of the chapter discusses different types of boards and commissions, including (1) independent policy-making boards, (2) semi-independent policy-making boards, (3) advisory boards, and (4) commissions. This is followed by a discussion of why do we have boards and commissions? It is evident that there are numerous reasons for such governing entities not the least is the need for protecting the integrity and promoting the transparency of the organization. In addition, a discussion will be included regarding boards, commission, and policy-making. Following this topic is a discussion of the role of a parks and recreation board member and/or commissioner. In addition, information regarding structuring the board is included as well as board committees, the role of the board chair, and problem areas between the board and the staff. Last, information regarding establishing a board meeting agenda is included.

TYPES OF BOARDS AND COMMISSIONS

One can think of a parks and recreation board or commission as the oversight body that is involved in establishing general policy or in the case of a commission, the organization's daily operations. Such parks and recreation boards and/or commissions may be appointed by city/governing boards or be elected by the general public. There are several types of parks and recreation boards and/or commissions. These are discussed in the following sections.

Independent Policy-Making Board

These types of boards are responsible for developing policies that enable an organization to carry out its basic functions. Boards are established by an authority it receives from state statutes. They are responsible for establishing the overall direction of the organization as reflected in its vision and mission statements, appointing the parks and recreation director of the organization, approving budgets, and crafting policy to guide the work of the organization. Figure 9.1 outlines the primary functions for the Winnetka (Illinois) Park District. As one can see reviewing this document the board's established policy through majority vote at its duly called and authorized Park Board meetings.

Winnetka Park District
Primary Function of the Board

The Park Board's major function is to establish policy through the majority vote at duly called and authorized Park Board meetings. Through its policy-making functions, the Board determines fiscal procedures, personnel matters, operational procedures, fees and charges, land dispositions, and facility development. Specifically included in the above items are the following:

A. To provide for the levy of taxes pursuant to the authority granted by State Statute. Such levies shall provide for the various operational concerns by fund so that sufficient revenue is generated to provide for quality parks and recreation activities.

B. Decide upon the proper use of funds generated by revenue-producing facilities after operational needs are satisfied and enact periodic adjustments in the operational policies of said revenue-producing facilities to ensure proper and meaningful controls for the benefit of the entire District and not just the revenue-producing facility itself.

Figure 9.1. Primary functions of the park board, Winnetka, Illinois. Retrieved from http://www.winpark.org/park-board-information/functions-of-the-board.aspx

C. The Board shall employ an Executive Director as the District's chief executive officer, upon whom the Board places its reliance and authority for the judicious administration of the day-to-day operation of the Park District. The Director of Parks and Recreation shall be charged with executing the Board's policy, enforcing its rules and regulations, and acting as an advisor to the Board by preparing or causing to be prepared written reports for the Board which recommend a course of action.

D. The Board shall adopt and periodically review a set of rules and regulations affecting all full-time, part-time, and seasonal personnel in a document known as "Personnel Policies of the Winnetka Park District."

E. The Board shall continually monitor the operational procedures of the Park District and make additions or alterations to said procedures at duly called and authorized Board meetings. The individual Board members shall keep themselves informed of the activities and functions of the District by observation, comments from its citizenry, and reports presented by the staff of the Park District. The Board shall act decisively on issues brought before it, in the best interest of the District as a whole. Park Board members should make decisions involving the welfare of the community as a whole based on study and evidence rather than on feelings, prejudices, personal opinions, or other similar subjective factors. Such judgment requires mutual considerations of varying points of view before final action is taken. Park Board members should accept the principle of Board unity and the subordination of personal interests by accepting and supporting majority decisions of the Board and identifying themselves with Board policies and actions.

F. The Board shall be responsible for establishing the operational philosophy of recreation programming for the Park District and setting fees and charges, to be approved at a duly authorized and attended Board meeting.

G. The Board shall recognize that land acquisition is of primary importance to the provision of leisure services and the proposition that open space, which is judiciously placed, produces benefits for active and passive use. Accordingly, the Board shall draw up and continually update a land acquisition plan, supported by a set of land acquisition criteria which will assist in evaluating various parcels. Cooperative ventures with local, county, state, regional, and national levels of government should be recognized as important and integral processes toward the orderly acquisition of parcels which otherwise may be too costly for one agency to purchase. Various state and federal land grant programs should be viewed as a vehicle for financial assistance. Such grants must be reviewed carefully for their dependencies and provisos, which may be considered unreasonable or perhaps too restrictive.

H. The Board shall direct itself to the establishment and continual care of a well-rounded and broadly based park system, recognizing the diverse needs and interests of the District's constituency.

Figure 9.1. (cont.).

Semi-Independent Policy-Making Board

Semi-independent policy-making boards have the ability and authority to make policies but are responsible to another city or county unit for their decision-making authority and budget. For example, a city council could appoint a semi-independent policy-making board with full decision-making powers, except that it would be dependent on that body for its budget. In this way, some control is maintained. An example of a semi-independent policy-making unit is that of the The Lafayette (Indiana) Board of Parks and Recreation, which is a policy-making authority for the Lafayette Park and Recreation Department. "The Board is bipartisan and comprised of four members appointed by the Mayor to serve staggered four-year terms. The Lafayette Parks and Recreation Department and its Board operate under the provision of the 'Indiana Parks and Recreation Law' (IC36-10-3) in accordance with City Ordinance."

Advisory Boards

Advisory boards provide advice and council to a higher authority (see Figure 9.2). They do not make policy but rather review policies and make recommendations to other policy-making units such as a city council. They provide advice to the director or the elected executive. With careful selection, such an advisory board can provide a community-level sounding board for the department and can broaden the basis of public support for the agency's endeavors. Advisory boards can also help alleviate the stigma of insensitivity that is attached to many government agencies that have little or no input from the public they serve. There must be adequate recognition for the services and accomplishments of the group or for outstanding board members. Ongoing advisory boards provide the necessary public involvement to ensure that the taxpayers' needs are being met or are at least considered. The administrative authority of the agency still rests in the hands of the elected officials, but the advisory board can serve as a buffer for repercussions from decisions made by the agency, thus freeing the agency administrator from various outside pressures (See Figure 9.3).

An example of a recreation and park's advisory board is that drawn from the city of Charlottesville, North Carolina. This advisory group serves to provide council to the Charlottesville City Council and is the liaison between that body and the parks and recreation department and the citizens of the community. "The Advisory Board shall consult with and advise said bodies in matters affecting parks and recreation promotion, marketing, membership, programming, planning, and other leisure services related aspects of the Parks and Recreation program, and to input its long-range planning for resources for capital projects for rehabilitation, design and/or development for indoor/outdoor recreation." The Advisory Board consists of nine members: seven citizens, one school representative, and one member of the Planning Commission. Figure 9.4 provides terms for the organization for the parks and recreation advisory board for Baker (Oregon) City Parks and Recreation. Figure 9.5 provides a partial presentation of the bylaws for the city of San Diego Park and Recreation Board.

Carol Lilly
Member, Board of Commission
Cedar Falls (Iowa) Park & Recreation Department

Carol Lilly is a member of the Cedar Falls (Iowa) Parks & Recreation Commission, an advisory body to the city council. The role of the commission is one of viewing policy, rules, regulations, ordinances, and budgets relating to city parks, playgrounds, recreational centers, golf courses, and cemeteries. The Parks and Recreation Commission consist of seven members who serve 3-year terms.

Currently serving as the Executive Director, Community Main Street for Cedar Falls, Iowa, Lilly pursued a position on the commission because she wanted to contribute to the community in an area which she felt she could provide a unique perspective. Quality-of-life amenities overseen by public entities are often an important part of a community's identity and have an indirect effect on its economic vitality. Her vision of the downtown district includes both private and public spaces that can be referred to as a downtown streetscape, which is an urban park. Public spaces are important, according to Lilly to the entire community. She notes that "A community that balances on all three elements—parks/public space, recreational facilities and programing, and cultural services and programming—improve the quality of life for all types of citizens. Citizen engagement helps create a sense of place and serves as method to develop community pride."

The city of Cedar Falls has an extensive number of areas, facilities, and programs, including a recreation center, aquatics complex, golf course, beach house, band shelter, playgrounds, camping grounds, boat ramps, picnic/shelter areas, softball/baseball diamonds, climbing wall, basketball court, tennis/pickle ball courts, dog park, handicap fishing dock, multi-use synthetic turf field, skate park, museums, art center, disc golf course, nature preserve, ice skating rink, and an extensive number of trails. The city maintains over 40 parks, the earliest dating to 1853. The commission focuses attention to long-range planning and the programming of parks and recreation services, areas, and facilities.

Lilly notes that a community is made up of citizens with a variety of interests and values. Providing opportunities for the public to engage in activities of interest contributes to the overall good of the community's economic health. In today's world, when people are advancing in their careers or changing jobs, the amenities a community offers are an important part of workforce recruitment process. In my experience, parks, recreation, and cultural services are key to workforce recruitment and development. Her greatest satisfaction in serving as a member of the Parks & Recreation Commission is spending time at the parks or on the trails and seeing so many people enjoying the space. Says Lilly, "Large projects are always exciting, and I look forward to an expansion of the recreation center and the addition of a whitewater park on the Cedar River, but seeing the everyday use of our public facilities is rewarding to me."

Figure 9.2. Carol Lilly, Cedar Falls (Iowa) Parks & Recreation Commissioner

To advise Golden City Council and staff on how to best provide safe and comprehensive parks and recreation facilities, programs, and services on behalf of all current and future residents of the City of Golden. In order to increase community involvement, a Parks and Recreation Advisory Board was created in 1982. Board members are appointed by City Council and represent Golden citizens. The Parks and Recreation Advisory Board, consisting of seven members and one alternate which serve four-year terms, makes suggestions about policies and procedures, fees and charges, acceptance of park land, design of parks, and other projects relating to the Parks and Recreation Department.

Board Advisory Duties

- The operation of all Divisions of the Parks and Recreation Department.
- Grant application efforts for specifically designated projects.
- Establishing department policy relating to fee structures and facilities usage and design. The Board shall provide a forum for citizen input regarding Parks and Recreation.

The Board shall prepare a prioritized comprehensive Capital Improvement Plan that focuses on a 1- to 5-year program. The Board shall revise this program and priorities as required each fiscal year to reflect current citizen priorities and needs. The Board shall coordinate the long range plans of the City of Golden and the larger Metropolitan area with the Capital Improvements Plan and Parks Master Plan to include:

- Trails shall be coordinated with the Colorado State Trail System and the Jefferson County Trail System.
- The Board shall review and provide advice to the Planning Commission for PUD applications.
- The Board shall periodically update Parks Master Plan as needed.

Figure 9.3. Citizen Advisory Board, City of Golden Colorado. Retrieved from http://www.cityofgolden.net/government/boards-commissions/parks-recreation-advisory-board/

Government ▸ Boards & Commissions ▸ Parks and Recreation Board

PARKS AND RECREATIONS ADVISORY BOARD

Overview

The Baker City Parks and Recreation Advisory Board exists to promote and preserve parks and open spaces which are safe, provide beauty, enhance recreational experiences and are accessible to all members of the community. The Baker City Parks and Recreation Advisory Board shall permanently preserve, protect, maintain, improve, and enhance its natural resources, parkland, and recreational opportunities for current and future generations.

The Parks and Recreation Advisory Board was created to represent the community regarding matters related to our local parks. Here are some of the board's duties:

- To advise the initiation, planning, design, and to recommend a system of parks, facilities, etc., that will accommodate the public's need for parks and recreation activities.
- To assess at all times the safety and security of site locations and physical facility standards.
- To assist with the preparation and development of rules and regulations by which parks and recreation programs may operate.
- To monitor and evaluate the effectiveness of park and recreation programs.
- To advise and recommend ways and means by which parks and recreation programs may be improved or strengthened.
- To support new parks, programs, and activities as public need may dictate.
- To adopt bylaws and other rules of procedure to achieve its purposes and functions.
- To assist with the adjudication of complaints, disputes or other grievances from the public arising out of parks and recreation activities.
- To perform other duties and responsibilities as may be conferred by the Baker City Council from time to time.

Figure 9.4. Baker City (Oregon) Park and Recreation Advisory Board. Retrieved from http://www.bakercity.com/government/boards-a-commissions/parks-and-recreation-board

San Diego Park and Recreation Board
Bylaws

ARTICLE I-NAME

The name of this advisory committee shall be the San Diego Park and Recreation Board (Board).

ARTICLE II-PURPOSE

It is the purpose and intent of the City Council to establish a policy advisory board on matters relating to the acquisition, development, maintenance and operation of parks, beaches and recreation property and facilities and that the Board will, along with other duties, perform the functions of the former Park and Recreation Commission and the former Mission Bay Commission. Effective July 1, 2009, the Park and Recreation Board shall also fulfill the role of the San Diego Regional Parks Improvement Fund Oversight Committee as described in City Charter Section 55.2.

The Board is subject to the Ralph M. Brown Act of the State of California and shall conduct its meetings in accordance with the provisions thereof. The City of San Diego shall provide necessary administrative support to the Board as shall be consistent with the Board's purposes, as set forth in City Charter 55.2.

ARTICLE III-DUTIES AND RESPONSIBILITIES

The powers and duties of the Park and Recreation Board shall be as follows:

(a) Advise the City Council through the City of San Diego Mayor on public policy matters relating to the acquisition, development, maintenance and operation of parks, beaches, playgrounds and recreational activities in the City of San Diego.

(b) Periodically review the recreational program of the City in relation to the needs and desires of the citizens.

(c) Coordinate the work of such committees as may be established towards the end of developing integrated and balanced policy recommendations.

(d) Conduct such investigations, studies and hearings which, in the judgment of the Board, will aid in effectuating its general purposes.

(e) Pursuant City of San Diego Municipal Code 26.30, the San Diego Park and Recreation Board serves as the San Diego Regional Park Improvement Oversight Committee.

ARTICLE IV-MEMBERSHIP

Section 1. Number

The Board shall consist of eleven (11) members as outlined in the City of San Diego Municipal Code 26.30 (b) Park and Recreation Board.

Section 2. Appointment and Terms

(a) The members shall be appointed by the Mayor, based on nominations from City Council Members, and confirmed by the City Council.

(b) The members shall serve two (2) year terms and each member shall serve until his successor is duly appointed and qualified. The members shall be appointed in such a manner that the terms of not more than six (6) members shall expire in any year. The expiration date shall be March 1.

Section 3. Qualifications

Each of the members of the Board shall possess expertise, or demonstrated experience or knowledge, in one or more of the following areas: auditing, finance or municipal finance, general business, planning, biology or environmental science, resource management or protection, wildlife management or protection, construction management, recreation management or planning.

Section 4. Ethics-Conflict of Interest

By accepting appointment to the Board, each member agrees to comply with the City of San Diego's Conflict of Interest Code.

Figure 9.5. Park and Recreation Board Bylaws, San Diego, California. Retrieved from http://www.sandiego.gov/parkandrecboard/pdf/prbbylaws.pdf

Commission

This form of government is one of the basic forms of municipal government in the United States. Commissions are usually made up of elected governing commissioners who are responsible for various aspects of the operations of parks and recreation services. Commissions usually are made up of five to seven individuals with one person designated to serve as the chair of the commission. The commission form of government blends together both legislative and executive functions into a single unit. The city of Philadelphia, Pennsylvania Parks and Recreation Commission includes 15 members. Of these individuals, nine are appointed by the mayor from nominations by the City Council and six who serve as an ex officio fashion including other individuals of the City Council and various commissions. Figure 9.6 presents a position description for a parks and recreation commission member for the City of Delano, Minnesota. This commission serves as an advisory capacity to the City Council with a responsibility to study, investigate, and make recommendations regarding short- and long-term park planning and systems management.

WHY DO WE HAVE A BOARD OR COMMISSION?

There are numerous reasons why parks and recreation boards and commissions exist. Certainly, they serve as a vehicle that links the citizenry to its governmental services. That linkage or connections is an important one, but not the only reason why parks and recreation boards and commissions exist. Some of the more important reasons are discussed here.

Integrity and Transparency

Parks and recreation boards and commissions ensure the integrity and transparency of the unit's operations. Such integrity and transparency is important in today's political climate where government actions are often called into question. The parks and recreation board or commission is accountable for ensuring that not only are its actions conducted with great integrity and transparency, but also those of the professional staff.

Legality

Various forms of enabling legislation require a parks and recreation department or district to establish a board to provide oversight to its programs and services. For example, the state of Oregon statutes require the establishment of a parks and recreation board to enable the organization of services. The parks and recreation government code for establishing parks and recreation districts in the state of Texas is very specific in terms of spelling out responsibilities including that a board shall be composed of seven appointed members and that board members will serve overlapping terms.

Vision and Mission Statements

Parks and recreation boards and commissions are involved in the establishment and review of an organization's vision and mission statements. Their responsibility includes reviewing such statements and ensuring that the organization remains vision and mission-driven in terms of its programs and services. Visions are powerful statements that when acted upon, can successfully drive the work of the entire organization.

The Park and Recreation Commission is an advisory commission to the Delano City Council. It is charged with the responsibility to study, investigate, and make recommendations regarding short and long-term park planning and systems management. This includes, but is no limited to, acquisition, development, construction, maintenance, and operation of City parks and playgrounds; coordination of recreational programming; preservation of natural resources; promotion of environmental awareness; and such other matter as may be referred to it by the City Council.

Commission Logistics

Membership: 7 Commissioners, appointed to rotating 3-year terms by the City Council
1 City Council member, non-voting liaison
City staff, as assigned

Meetings: Monthly, last Wednesday of the month, 5:00pm, City Hall
Special meetings, as needed and determined by the Commission and/or City Council

Commissioner Profile

The City of Delano seeks interested persons from the Delano community to serve on this Commission. Appointed Commissioners are required to meet the following criteria:

1. Reside in Delano, or own commercial/business property and operate a business within the City

2. Serve in accordance with the City's Code of Ethics and Values Statements (attached)

The City of Delano provides all applicants to the opportunity to present their skills, talents, and interest in serving for all vacant positions on this Commission. The City of Delano has an interest in providing a diverse membership on the Park and Recreation Commission. Commission members with the following skills and experiences are desirable:

- Background in recreational programming or park planning
- Experience with parks or recreation programs in other communities
- Interest in promoting healthy community lifestyles
- Interest in recreational programming for all ages
- Interest in community park and trail systems
- Interest in natural resource preservation
- An active sport or leisure participant who would like to share their experience and knowledge
- Knowledge of real estate acquisition, development

Figure 9.6. Position Description Park and Recreation Commission Member, Delano, Minnesota. Retrieved from http://www.delano.mn.us/Commission_Description/Park_and_Recreation_Commission.pdf

Establishing and Recommending Policies

A major responsibility of any policy-making board is to establish and provide oversight to the organization's policies. Policy-making is a challenging process because it has numerous implications. As policies are implemented and evaluated, a cycle for review should be established that enables the board to determine their effectiveness. It is interesting to note how many policies exist in organizations that no longer have merit, but continue to exist because of the lack of an ongoing review process.

Financial Resources

Organizations must have adequate resources in order to operate in an effective and successful fashion. Parks and recreation boards and commissions play a critical role in ensuring that there is a financial base in place to enable not only the management of current programs, services, areas, and facilities, but also the upgrading and enhancement of various resources for the future. The mismanagement of fiscal resources can jeopardize the standing of a parks and recreation department in any community. The public standing of a parks and recreation department or its credibility in the community can be severely limited if the organization is viewed as one that misappropriates or misuses its funds.

Connection/Engagement to the Community

A very important role of any parks and recreation board is its connection to the citizenry to the community. The board is in fact an important conduit for communication and information between the citizens of the community and the professional staff. As such, parks and recreation boards often serve as representatives of the community, interpreting needs, interests, and attitudes regarding parks and recreation services. In this case, the board often acts as a sounding board between the community and a parks and recreation organization.

Professional Staffing

It is the responsibility of any parks and recreation board or commission to ensure that there are competent, capable, professional staff in place. This requires the hiring of an effective parks and recreation director/superintendent and/or general manager who can provide visionary, managerial leadership to the organization. It also requires the board to ensure that there are defined roles as in job descriptions, a fair and effective compensation plan, and a means for supervision and evaluation. It does not mean that the board engages in the administration of the program, but rather ensures that the tools are in place for the effective operation of the organization.

Strategic Planning

Board members are responsible for developing plans that enable the organization to have the necessary resources in place for the future. This includes land acquisition, facility development, staff and board development, fiscal resource management, and other important functions. Such plans must be updated annually and require the board's attention on an ongoing basis to determine the extent to which they have been acted upon.

Building of Cooperative Relationships

Board and commission members can play a critical role in the building of cooperative and collaborative relationships with other community boards. By extending the work of the parks and recreation board and/or commission externally into the community, board members are enable to gain greater sensitivity and awareness regarding their role and that of others in the community. The importance of inner-agency relationships cannot be diminished and nurtured.

Developing the Board

Like the professional staff, it is important for parks and recreation board or commission members to seek opportunities for their development and that of the board as a whole.

There are numerous responsibilities that must be address by the board and not everyone will have the expertise necessary to examine and review critical issues. Therefore, it is important for the board to develop ways to enhance its own abilities, capabilities, knowledge, and skill sets. A board development program might examine such topics as strategic planning, master planning, board/staff relations, developing a team approach, responsibilities to one's community, and the board members' basic responsibilities.

Accountability and Evaluation

There are numerous responsibilities to ensure that the organization is evaluated effectively and accountability maintained to fall to parks and recreation boards or commissions. Boards and commissions are often required to meet monthly if not more often to review reports, make decisions, and in general determine the status of the organization and its effectiveness.

BOARD, COMMISSION, AND POLICY-MAKING

A universal factor of the work of boards and commissions is that of policy-making. Even advisory boards review policies that are passed to a higher legislative body. Therefore, one could argue that policy-making is central to the efforts of boards and commissions. One can think of a policy as the parks and recreation organization's formal and informal guidelines. Such guidelines influence human behavior in multiple ways, as follows:

- **Enabling behavior.** Policies serve to enable organizations and individuals to pursue goals or ends that would not be possible without them. For example, policies enable organizations to hire staff, levy taxes, build facilities, develop areas, and manage various operations.
- **Regulating behavior.** Many policies are regulatory in nature; that is, they regulate routine behaviors. For example, a stoplight regulates routine traffic behavior. In recreation, parks, and leisure service organizations, control points in buildings regulate the flow of participants in and out in a systematic fashion.
- **Inhibiting behavior.** Policies also inhibit behaviors. For example, access to a park may be limited to a certain time frame so as to ensure that there is proper supervision when people are in the park. Many rules and regulations that are established by recreation, parks, and leisure service organizations often inhibit behaviors that help maintain the safety of individuals (Edginton, Hudson, Lankford, & Larsen, 2015, p. 56–57).

The formal policy statements of a parks and recreation organization are often embedded in written documents that offer direction to the organization's employees and participants. Informal policies are manifested in the norms, customs, and rituals found within an organization. Both the formal and informal policies have tremendous impact on the organization. Informal policies sometimes displace the formal ones and create challenges to the parks and recreation agency.

Policies can be viewed as existing on a continuum. At one end of the continuum are what is known as *major policies*. These types of policies are general statements that reflect the ends or aims of the organization. At the other end of the continuum are *procedures, plans, and rules*. These are very definitive statements that outline the step-by-step procedures for various operational aspects of the organization. The process of policy-making involves three steps: (1) formulation, (2) implementation, and (3) evaluation (p. 59). Formulation is the process of developing a policy in relationship to the overall vision and mission of the parks and recreation agency. Many questions have to be considered when formulating policy. Is the policy realistic? Can it be achieved? Will it influence the desired behavior of individuals? Second is the process of implementation. Basically, policy implementation is one of putting the policy into action. Last, policy evaluation is focused on determining the extent in which the policy has achieved its intentions.

In the development of policies, certain factors must be emphasized in order for policy development to be successful. First, policies must be aligned with the vision and mission of the organization. Second, policies cannot be ambiguous or contradict another policy. Third, policies must be flexible and adaptable. Forth, policy must easily distinguish major policies from rules and procedures. Policies must be in writing and the policy process should be understood by employees and others. Last, policies must include elements of control in order to be successful.

Many factors may impact on the policy-making process. However, a most "…important component in the process of policy-making in the public sector is to involve the public being served" (p. 62). Obviously, it is important to engage all of the individuals who will be affected by a policy, not only the public but also the employees of an organization. Edginton et al. suggest that "participation in the policy process may make objective and rational planning difficult" (p. 62). Further, these authors argue that political biases may also influence the policy-making process. However, there are numerous ways to involve the citizenry to gain input in the policy formulation and evaluation process. Some of these include (1) use of citizen advisory groups, (2) task forces, (3) focus groups, (4) social media, (5) polls and surveys, (6) public meetings and hearings, (7) community forums, (8) written submissions, (9) plebiscites, and (10) use of the media.

THE ROLE OF A BOARD MEMBER

What exactly does a board member do? The duties of a board member are numerous and broad in scope (see Figure 9.7).

However, three specific standards of conduct must be observed by each and every board member. The first is known as "duty of care." In other words, each board member must exercise responsible and prudent care on having decisions on behalf of the organization. The second is known as "duty of loyalty." This item suggests that individuals should not benefit personally from their efforts as a board member. Last, is the "duty of obedience." This duty suggests that a board member must be committed to the organization's vision and mission. Further, they must operate in a fashion consistent with the precepts of the organization.

- **Represent the broader community constituency and not narrow special interest.** As a board member, each individual has a responsibility of representing all of the members of a community, not just a select few.
- **Avoid conflicts of interest.** Individuals should avoid situations where they may benefit directly or indirectly financially from decision-making activities. (See Figure 9.8, Code of Ethics)
- **Open and transparent meetings and transactions.** Open meeting laws require that the public have access to decision-making processes except in the case where personnel concerns are being discussed. Final decisions regarding staffing are rendered publicly.

- **Provide leadership.** Board members must provide leadership advancing parks and recreation concerns serving as a steward for natural and environmental resources and ensuring that there are programs and services for all ages and ability levels.
- **Comply with local, state, and federal laws.** As a legally empowered representative of a municipal body of government, it is essential that board members comply with all local, state, and federal laws, statutes, and regulations.
- **Work through the parks and recreation director/superintendent/general manager.** Board members are not involved in the administration of the program. They are involved in setting policies which impact on the administration of the organization. They should work through the director/superintendent/general manager and not directly with the staff unless authorized.
- **Trust and respect fellow board members.** Respect for one another's board colleague members is important. People will have differences of opinion, but if you respect an individual because of his or her worth and trust the person's ability to offer the best opinions and judgments, processes and decision-making will move forward in a collaborative fashion.
- **Attend and be prepared for board meetings.** Board members need to be prepared for meetings. This sometimes means study and investigation in advance of the actual meeting. Board members should not dodge issues at meetings, but rather should be prepared to address concerns in a forthright manner.
- **Hire responsible, professional staff.** One of the most important roles of a board member is to hire the best possible staff that can be retained.
- **Hold professional staff accountable.** Professional staff should be held accountable for their responsibilities and actions by the board of directors.
- **Make sure the board and professional staff work in a collaborative fashion.** The board and professional staff should work as a team. Board members should trust and respect the professional staff.
- **Board members' relationship with other board members.** Board members should take responsibility for one another. At times, this may involve stepping back on an issue or offering insights that another board member does not have. As a board, all members are responsible for each other.
- **Promotion of the agency.** Board members should be involved in the promotion of the parks and recreation department's programs and services. At times this means the board member will be responsible for representing the organization at various activities, events, and other functions.
- **Knowledge of the parks and recreation field.** Board members should have a working knowledge of the parks and recreation field and its importance in the community. Further, board members should be able to interpret the values and benefits of parks and recreation when called upon.
- **Encourage citizen participation.** Board members should work to encourage participation. They should create avenues for the expression of community needs, interests, and attitudes toward various parks and recreation concerns.

Millie Keith
Member Board of Commissioners
Freeport (Illinois) Park District

Millie Keith serves as a member of the Board of Commissioners for the Freeport (Illinois) Park District. Retired for 15 years, the Freeport Park District has been a very important part of her life. Over the years, Keith has enjoyed taking her sons, grandchildren, and now great-grandchildren to the parks to play and teach them about nature. She pursued a position on the Board of Commissioners initially in 1993 and felt that it would be very challenging process as a newly elected commissioner to learn the responsibilities, policies, and procedures of the volunteer position.

Established in 1911, The Freeport (Illinois) Park District is the 12th oldest park district in the state of Illinois. In 1996 the state recognized it as a "Signature Park District." The park district manages more than 800 acres of owned and leased land that it operates and maintains. Areas and facilities include 10 parks, an aquatic center, golf course and driving range, nature preserve, antique carousel, 18-hole miniature golf course, boat rental operations, historical museum, skate park, and tournament-quality ball field complexes. Recreation and leisure programs include youth and adult athletics, adult special interests activities, aquatic services, trips and tours, martial arts, special recreation, youth development programs and cultural art activities.

As is the case with other park districts in the state of Illinois, as a legal entity, the board of commissioners includes five individuals who are responsible for providing oversight to the organization. This includes setting policy as well as being responsible for the fiscal affairs of the district. The functions and purpose of the park district include acquiring, protecting, restoring, restocking, developing and interpreting a well-balanced system of areas with scenic, ecological, recreational and historic values for the inspiration, education, use, and enjoyment by the public.

Keith has an extensive record of work with the Iowa Association of Park Districts, including serving as a member of many committees including public relations, honors and resolutions, membership, joint conference committee, and the ambassador committee.

She notes that "for families who locate in Freeport, their first impressions are the wonderful parks and programs offered to the community." She further offers that "... parks are common gathering places where people socialize, experience nature, enjoy family, exercise, and participate in sports, relax, and unwind." She reports that is has been an honor to "have served as a Park Board Commissioner for three terms (18 years). I am proud of the tradition and being involved with one of the finest park systems in the state."

Figure 9.7. Millie Keith, Freeport (Illinois) Park District Member Board of Commissioners

CODE OF ETHICS: BOARDS, COMMISSIONS, AND TASK FORCES

SECTION 204.01 Delano City Code

Open Meeting Law and Data Practices Act. All meetings and matter of any City board, commission, or task force shall be subject to the Minnesota Open Meeting Law and the Minnesota Government Data Practices Act.

Conflict of Interest. No member of any City board, commission, or task force may vote on a matter in which the member has a direct or indirect financial interest or other substantial interest.

Vacancies and Removal of Members. Except as otherwise noted, a member's position shall become vacant upon the occurrence of any of the following:

1. The death of a member.
2. A determination by the Council that the member's physical or mental disability renders the member incapable of service.
3. The member's resignation in writing.
4. A member's absence from 3 consecutive meetings, unless excused by action of the Council.
5. Termination of a member's qualifications (residence/business ownership).

Removal from Office. A member may be removed (with the exception of the Delano Water, Light, and Power Commission):

1. Upon petition of a board, commission or task force. The board, commission, or task force by a three-fifths vote of its members, may petition to the Council to remove any member when it believes the best interests of the City would be served thereby. The removal of the member is not accomplished unless and until the Council passes a motion removing the member.
2. By the Council. The Council shall have the authority, in its discretion, to remove any member without a petition from the board, commission, or task force.

Term Limit: The term of a member's appointment to any City board, commission, or task force shall be 3 years. A member's appointment to any City board, commission, or task force shall be limited to 2 full consecutive terms. An existing member of a City board, commission, or task force whose term is set to expire must apply for re-appointment to his or her position and be considered with any applicants for the position. The term limit imposed by this Subdivision shall not apply if there are no eligible applicants to fill a member's position that is set to expire or if the Council, upon a majority vote, re-appoints the member whose position is set to expire for 1 additional term.

Figure 9.8. Code of Ethics, Delano, Minnesota. Retrieved from http://www.delano.mn.us/Commission_Description/Park_and_Recreation_Commission.pdf

Figure 9.9 is an example of a board commissioner's job description from Bismarck, North Dakota Park and Recreation District. As one can see viewing this job description, the major function of the commissioner is to "preserves, protect the value of constituent/stakeholder investment in the Bismarck Parks and Recreation District." Job description calls for individual board members operating in a timely and professional manner.

Board Member Job Description
Bismarck Parks and Recreation District

Job Title: Commissioner of Bismarck Park and Recreation District

Major Function: In a timely and professional manner, to preserve, protect and increase the value of constituent/ stakeholder investment in the Bismarck Parks and Recreation District.

BOARD DUTIES & RESPONSIBILITIES:
To comply with all local, state and federal regulations as they apply to the Park District
To elect leadership
To set Vision, Mission and Core Values, using them to form policy, goals, planning strategy
To hire Executive Director
To receive and execute portfolio and committee responsibilities as assigned by the Board
To set and distribute rewards
To direct management through District
To visit with and represent constituent/stakeholder
To attend meetings and be prepared before meeting
To review financial information and understand and evaluate
To set overall direction and approve all plans and goals for the Park District
To participate in preparation and approval of budget
To evaluate District's performance, and specifically that of the Executive Director
To represent the Park District

BOARD RELATIONSHIPS:
To hire Executive Director and manage that position
To communicate with each other and constituent/stakeholder
To communicate with staff through Executive Director

BOARD AUTHORITY:
Authority to vote on any and all issues before the Board
Right to be informed and participate appropriately
Authority to commit financial resources of the Park District
Authority to execute all duties and responsibilities of the elected office of Park Commissioner
Authority to hire, evaluate and terminate the Executive Director

BOARD QUALIFICATIONS:
Reside within the boundaries of the District
Must be 18 years of age

Figure **9.9.** Board Member Job Description, Bismarck, North Dakota. Retrieved from http://bisparks.org/wp-content/uploads/2013/03/1-Board-Member-Job-Description.pdf

STRUCTURING THE PARKS AND RECREATION BOARD

Depending upon a given state's statutes, legislative or advisory decision-making responsibilities will be vested with a duly elected or appointed board of directors or commission. Such boards or commissions often involve odd numbers of individuals, five to seven or more people who have been given the authority to make policy decisions or recommendations regarding parks and recreation services. In addition, representatives can be drawn from other areas within municipal government to provide expertise where necessary. Often a representative of the city's planning commission, public works, or other body will provide representatives to the park and recreation board. This usually occurs to ensure that there is a good mix of expertise available to address the work of the agency.

Again, depending on state statutes, the officers of the board of directors may include several positions, such as (1) directors; (2) president, chair, presiding officer; (3) vice chairperson; and (4) recording secretary. Often the chairperson and the vice chairperson will be elected by the board as a whole and the recording secretary would be appointed by the board. Below is an organizational description of these types of positions from the Central Oregon Parks and Recreation District. Positions and brief job descriptions include the following:

- **Directors.** An individual who serves as a director is involved in decision-making focusing on the establishment of legislative policy. The directors establish policies and procedures to operate the district in accordance with Oregon Revised State Statutes.
- **Chairperson.** The chairperson is the individual who conducts the formal meetings of the board. His or her responsibility involves establishing the agenda, presiding over board meetings, and establishing committee assignments. The chairperson shall have a one-year appointment.
- **Vice-chairperson.** The vice-chairperson assumes the responsibilities of the chair in his or her absence or when requested by the chairperson. When this occurs, the vice-chairperson shall be fully vested with the powers of the chairperson. The vice-chairperson shall have a one-year appointment.
- **Recording secretary.** The recording secretary maintains accurate records of the official proceedings and decisions of the board. The recording secretary's role has been assigned to the administrative services coordinator.

Board Committees

To assist in the formulation and development of policy as well as policy recommendations, board of directors often create committees to manage their work. Committees are made up of smaller numbers of a board of directors and take time to study issues in greater detail. They bring a level of focus to concerns and problems that allow for a greater investigation. In addition, committee work can bring a greater level of intensity to the work of an organization inspiring greater in-depth insights into issues and problems as well as opportunities for development.

There are two types of committees found operating in parks and recreation boards. The first are known as standing committees. These are permanent, ongoing committees that extend over time. The second are ad hoc or temporary committees. These types of committees are usually advisory in nature and established to make recommendations regarding specific issues. Two types of standing committees seem to be prevalent within parks and recreation systems—budget and finance and strategic planning. Ad hoc committees usually emerge around current challenges and are established to encourage citizen involvement to help in identifying solutions to problems.

The Role of the Board Chair

The chairman of any board of directors is essential to its successful operation. The chair leads the board and sets the tone for the organization and the board's operations. In particular, the chairman of the board must develop trust between and among board members. Overseeing the policy-making function, the chair of the board has significant influence on the establishment of the agenda, priorities, and the way in which the board of directors spends its time and energy. The chair of the board must work with board members but at the same time assess their strengths and weaknesses and evaluate their contributions to the work of the organization.

In addition, the board chair must work closely and sometimes directly with the parks and recreation director/superintendent/general manager. Clearly defined roles and responsibilities are important in this regard so that there is an understanding of the authority vested in various positions. Some issues will be items for the board of directions whereas others will be matters for the organization itself. The chairman of the board working collaboratively with the parks and recreation director/superintendent/general manager will need to work in a way as to ensure that board policies are addressed and that strategic planning activities are undertaken. The chairman of the board will want to work closely with committee chairs and members to also ensure that their functions are addressed and reported on in a timely manner.

Board of Directors and Staff Problem Areas

There are several areas that can emerge between a board of directors and its professional staff. Many of these types of problems can be avoided with proper ongoing communication and dialogue. Some of the more common problem areas include the following:

- **Providing accurate and updated information to the board of directors.** In order for a board of directors to operate effectively and efficiently, they must have necessary information on what is transpiring within the parks and recreation agency and what are the reasons for the various developments.
- **Inaccurate media presentations.** It is important to speak with one voice especially to the media. This is especially the case when speaking on matters where final decisions have not yet occurred. One can only think of land acquisition and the difficulties surrounding the acquiring of lands and the costs associated with such acquisitions.
- **Following the chain of command.** For both the board and the professional staff, it is important to follow the chain of command. Lack of attention to this matter can be very disruptive to an organization.
- **Functions of committees**. It is important for committees to understand their role and have written guidelines for their activities. At times, committees step out of their role and project an image that is inconsistent with their mandate.
- **The board is the decision-maker.** Only the board as a whole can make decisions, not individual board members. Individuals members have no power, only the board as a

whole.

- **Compromise.** In the heat of decision-making, board members can often establish a position from which is difficult to retract. Efforts should be made to keep the board together as much as possible to enable them to explore compromises- at times, individuals are pushed so far out that it is difficult to move back toward a more centralized position.

Establishing a Meeting Agenda

When conducting board meetings, there should be an agenda prepared in advance and circulated to the board of directors before the regularly scheduled board meetings take place. Some of the items that are regularly featured on an agenda in a board meeting include the following: (1) call to order, (2) call the roll, (3) recognize visitors, (4) approve the agenda, (5) review previous meeting minutes, (6) report on good news, (7) present the director's report, (8) present committee reports, (9) conduct unfinished business, (10) call for new business, (11) announcements, (12) public comments, and (13) adjournment (NRPA, 2007, p. 15). Figure 9.10 is an example of an agenda for a regular meeting of the Des Moines (Iowa) Parks and Recreation Board. A smoothly run board meeting will often provide a timed agenda so that individual items may be addressed without delay. Such an organized agenda also provides meaningful ways to incorporate citizen dialogue in the decision-making processes.

PARKS AND RECREATION FOUNDATION BOARDS

It is not unusual for parks and recreation agencies to establish a separate foundation for the principal purposes of receiving funds, donations, and other contributions, including areas and facilities that can be used to advance the work of the organization. Such foundations are established as a nonprofit organization or a charitable trust. Section 501 of the Internal Revenue Service exempts such nonprofit foundations from taxes and requires them to meet certain regulations.

Parks and recreation foundations are governed by a board of directors. Their functions and roles are similar to that of board or commission members; that is to ensure the integrity and transparency of the work of the organization to engage in planning, to manage financial resources, and to align its vision and mission statement with worthwhile projects and initiatives.

An example of a parks and recreation foundation is that of Whatcom Parks and Recreation Foundation of Bellingham, Washington. The goal of this foundation is to "empower individuals and community groups to claim stewardship of their local parks, trails, and the vast recreation opportunities available to us in Whatcom County" (Whatcom Parks and Recreation Foundation, 2015). The foundation works to raise funds and receive charitable foundations to assist in the improvement of a park or related project. As a 501(c)3 tax-exempt organization, the Whatcom Parks and Recreation Foundation works to receive cash, materials, and real property and can operate in ways not necessarily open to government agencies. The foundation's work is highly complementary to government parks and recreation agencies.

Still another example of a parks and recreation foundation is that of the Burlingame (California) Parks and Recreation Foundation. This foundation was established to "enhance the life of all residents in Burlingame and the surrounding communities by working with

---

REGULAR MEETING
DES MOINES PARK AND RECREATION BOARD MEETING
5:00 p.m., May 26, 2015
City Council Chambers, City Hall
<u>AGENDA</u>

I.   ROLL CALL

II. APPROVAL OF AGENDA AS PRESENTED AND/OR AMENDED

III. DISCUSSION AGENDA

<u>MINUTES</u>

Minutes of April 28, 2015 Park and Recreation Board Meeting

REPORT OF PARK AND RECREATION DIRECTOR
- Earth Day Trash Bash
- Fishing signs
- Did You Know – Pioneer
- Jen's Secret Assignment
- Nature Trails
- Library Partnership

<u>BOARD ACTION</u>

A. Trails and Greenways Committee Appointment

B. Citizen Cemetery Advisory Committee Appointment

C. Citizen Golf Committee Appointments

<u>RECEIVE AND FILE</u>

D. Allen Park Community Garden Presentation

E. Slate of Officers

Report of Chair of Board and Committees
- Urban Conservation
- Citizen Golf Advisory committee
- Citizen Cemetery Advisory committee
- Trails and Greenways

<u>ADJOURNMENT</u>

Helping Des Moines Live Well, Play Hard and Protect the Earth

The City of Des Moines is pleased to provide accommodations to individuals or groups with disabilities and encourages participation in City government. Please notify us at least three business days in advance at 515-283-4209, should special accommodations be required. Assistive Listening Devices are available for meetings in the Council Chambers.

Figure 9.10. Sample Board Meeting Agenda, Des Moines, Iowa Park and Recreation Board Meeting. Retrieved from https://www.dmgov.org/Government/Boards/ParkandRecreationBoard/Agenda/ParkBoardMay2015agenda.pdf

our city staff to facilitate volunteer opportunities, provide community outreach for parks and recreation, and raise funds to support our local programs, facilities, and services" (Burlingame Park And Recreation Foundation in Burlingame, 2015).

The primary mission of this foundation is to raise funds that provide assistance to individuals so that they may enroll in parks and recreation programs as well as provide necessary equipment, repairs, and capital improvements. The board of directors of the foundation consists of the president, vice president, secretary, treasurer, and four additional individuals. These individuals are tasked with the responsibility of establishing priorities and the accompanied fiduciary activities associated.

SUMMARY

From a historical perspective, citizens have played a strong role in advancing parks and recreation services at the municipal level. Dating back to the formulation of the Playground Association of America, founded in 1906, the forerunner of today's National Recreation and Park Association, there has always been a strong tie between citizens involved as parks and recreation activists and professionals. Many prominent individuals have served as members of boards and commissions, lending their credibility to gain public trust, build partnerships, and secure funding to enable parks and recreation agencies to thrive and prosper.

A board or commission can be thought of as the oversight body whose main role and function is that of policy formulation, implementation, and evaluation. There are four types of boards or commissions. The first is known as the independent policy-making board. Receiving its authority from state statutes, these types of boards carry out the work of the organization on an independent basis with the ability to make policy, levy taxes, acquire land, and provide programs and services. The second type of entity is known as the semi-independent policy-making board. In this arrangement, the board operates independently but may have its budget established and controlled by a city council. The third type of board is known as advisory. Advisory boards provide advice and council to a higher authority. They do not make policy but recommend and review policies impacting the area of parks and recreation. Last is the commission form of government. The commission form of government involves the election or appointment of governing commissioners with the responsibility for both legislative and administrative functions.

There are numerous reasons why parks and recreation boards exist. Among these are the following: (1) to ensure the integrity and transparency of the organization, (2) to satisfy legal requirements found in state statutes, (3) to develop vision and mission statements, (4) to establish and recommend policy statements, (5) to secure financial resources, (6) to engage the community, (7) to ensure competent, professional staffing, (8) to engage in strategic planning, (9) to build cooperative relationships, (10) to assist in the development of the board, and (11) to promote accountability and evaluation of the work of the organization. With regard to the work of boards and commissions and policy-making, such units of government are involved in the formulation, implementation, and evaluation of policies. Board members engage in various duties that are broad in scope. Some of these duties include (1) representing the broader community constituency and not narrow special interest; (2) avoiding conflicts of interest; (3) having open and transparent meetings and transactions; (4) providing leadership; (5) complying with local, state, and federal laws;

(6) working through the parks and recreation director/superintendent/general manager; (7) trusting and respecting fellow board members; (8) attending and being prepared for board meetings; (9) hiring responsible, professional staff; (10) holding professional staff accountable; (11) making sure the board and professional staff work in a collaborative fashion; (12) maintaining relationships with other board members; (13) promoting the agency; (14) having knowledge of the parks and recreation field; and (15) encouraging citizen participation.

Depending upon a given state's statutes, legislative or advisory decision-making responsibilities will be vested with a duly elected or appointed board of directors or commission. Such boards or commissions often involve odd numbers of individuals, five to seven or more people who have been given the authority to make policy decisions or recommendations regarding parks and recreation services. Again, depending on state statutes, the officers of the board of directors may include several positions such as (1) directors; (2) president, chair, presiding officer; (3) vice chairperson; and (4) recording secretary. Some of the challenges that may emerge between the board of directors and its professional staff include the following: (1) providing accurate and updated information to the board of directors, (2) Inaccurate media presentations, (3) Following the chain of command, (4) Understanding the functions of committees, (5) Supporting the fact that the board as a whole is the decision-maker, and (6) Learning to compromise.

DISCUSSION QUESTIONS

1. Discuss the partnership and collaborative efforts between citizens and professionals used to advance the parks and recreation movement.
2. Describe the features of independent policy-making boards.
3. Describe the features of semi-independent policy-making boards.
4. Describe the features of advisory boards.
5. Describe the features of commissions.
6. Why do we have policy-making boards or commissions?
7. What is the relationship between boards and commissions and policy-making?
8. Discuss the role of board members.
9. Discuss the ways in which parks and recreation boards are structured.
10. Attend a parks and recreation board meeting and prepare a two- to three-page reflection paper describing the agenda and decision-making processes.

REFERENCES

Burlingame Park And Recreation Foundation in Burlingame, CA. (2015). We appreciate your help two ways to donate. Retrieved from http://www.supportburlingameparks.org/

City of Golden. (2015). Park and recreation board guidelines. Retrieved from http://www.cityofgolden.net/government/boards-commissions/parks-recreation-advisory-board/

Edginton, C. R., Hudson, S. D., Lankford, S. V., & Larsen, D. (2015). *Managing recreation, parks, and leisure services: An introduction* (4th ed.). Urbana, IL: Sagamore.

Freeport Park District. (n.d.). An ordinance setting forth the rules and regulations governing the use of the park sites of the district. Retrieved from http://freeportparkdistrict.org/

wp-content/uploads/2014/12/Freeport-Park-District-General-Use-Regulations.pdf

National Recreation and Park Association. (2007) NRPA advisory board member resource guide. Retrieved from https://krpa.wildapricot.org/Resources/Documents/Static%20 Web%20Page/Advisory%20Board%20Member%20Resource%20Guide-1.PDF

Whatcom Parks and Recreation Foundation. (2015). Donate shop for parks. Retrieved from http://wprfoundation.org/

Chapter Ten

Engaging the Community

CHAPTER OBJECTIVES

- To gain an understanding of citizen engagement in parks and recreation management by performing tasks under agency supervision, by participating in decision making through information input and/or by belonging to a special interest group
- To understand that within a parks and recreation organization, decision makers must obtain input from stakeholders. This input can come from within the agency, from other agencies, and from private citizens or groups of citizens.
- To gain awareness of how citizens provide assistance in the decision-making process and play an important role in the implementation of decisions
- To develop an understanding of the ways in which parks and recreation organizations can engage the public
- To gain an understanding of the ways in which citizens may be engaged on an individual and group basis

INTRODUCTION

Successful parks and recreation management is based on meaningful and collaborative citizen involvement. Importantly, parks and recreation professionals need to recognize the effort to engage the citizens is to broaden the bases of public support for the parks and recreation organization. Citizens can be involved in parks management by performing tasks under agency supervision, by participating in decision making through planning teams and providing input, or by belonging to a special interest group. It is important to note that there are differences between the personal assistance offered by individual volunteers and members of special interest groups, and those involved in an advisory role for plan and policy making. No matter the intent and level of involvement, these groups are considered stakeholders who have interests in the management, planning, funding, and maintenance of parks and recreation services. It should be noted that when speaking of citizen participation in parks and recreation, particular emphasis is placed on the users (citizens who use the parks) as opposed to the broader public. While it is important to involve the general public, it is especially essential to involve the users (Grybovych, 2011).

In some organizations, a few individuals or small groups make major decisions without soliciting ideas and input from several sources; however, within a parks and recreation organization, the person(s) responsible for decision-making must obtain advice from stakeholders. This can come from within the agency, from other agencies, and from private citizens or groups of citizens. Dennis (2001) notes that two major obstacles to quality citizen involvement: (1) a lack of commitment to the effort from the parks and recreation organization and (2) underrepresentation of all publics, interests, and value. The first obstacle occurs when the organization merely meets laws and regulations that guide public involvement. The second obstacle is most problematic for the organization. Plans, policies, and future direction are misguided without adequate and meaningful citizen engagement.

Citizen engagement and involvement in parks and recreation service delivery has been recognized as of critical importance to the organization and community. Specifically, the National Recreation and Park Association (2007; 2008) emphasizes open public participation as one communication strategy that has proven to be successful, and encourages citizen participation in parks and recreation agency events, programs, and services, as well as volunteering and advocacy. Furthermore, the American Planning Association (2002) notes that citizen participation in parks and recreation is an essential ingredient of creating successful open spaces, and that by understanding community benefits of parks, decision makers can develop constituencies that can sustain their park systems over time.

A number of topics are explored in this chapter. The first portion of the chapter addresses citizen involvement for planning, plan making, and policy formulation using a number of models that are based on social planning and community development. These models have formed the foundation of citizen engagement practices for planning and policy making at the community level. Pertinent information with regard to social capital, deliberative democracy, and a spectrum of involvement and engagement are presented. Where feasible, examples from practice in community parks and recreation are presented. The second portion of this chapter recognizes differences by type of stakeholder, and clarifies them through the framework of volunteerism. The individual and various groups are addressed, and are followed by a separate discussion of special interest groups and how they can positively influence parks and recreation practice.

FOUNDATIONS OF CIVIC ENGAGEMENT

Citizens provide assistance in the decision-making process and play an important role in the implementation of decisions. They inform the agency about special needs, generate feedback about facilities and programs planned or provided by the agency, and reflect public opinion concerning the agency itself. Correct handling of public input can assist continued growth of the parks and recreation agency and its services, help resist infringement by other departments, and aid in avoiding crippling reduction during times of limited financial resources. Citizen participation in parks and recreation has two primary benefits, according to Grybovych (2011). First, it allows the broader public to directly involve constituencies in the design, planning, and management of parks and other natural resources that create informed and engaged residents that feel better connected to their communities. Second, community participation provides residents with a venue for engagement, provides a sense of place, and enhances community and individual well-being. As one can see in Figure 10.1, the process of citizen involvement informs the plans, the management, and the programming of our parks (adapted from Lankford, Lankford, & Wheeler, 2011).

Figure 10.1. Community Engagement and the Park and Recreation Planning System

There are numerous issues related to mobilizing the citizens of a community parks and recreation planning and policy making. Today, members of a community are less engaged in civic affairs. Planners find it increasingly difficult to encourage involvement from community members that represent the diverse spectrum of interests in the community. In addition to establishing the involvement in civic affairs, the length of the planning process and time commitment often impede long-term involvement. Putnam (2001) in *Bowling Alone* identified problems of society as primarily having individuals insulated from one another, and therefore preventing meaningful interactions, which has resulted in a loss of social capital. The lack of social capital has created less interest and involvement in civic-related and community service activities. Putnam notes that there is a need for greater opportunities for bonding and social bridging. Unfortunately, many communities today lack the opportunities to engage in meaningful and purposeful activities, and much communication and engagement is being replaced primarily now through technology. However, communities continue to explore ways to engage the public. After some initial unsuccessful efforts to grab attention, the city achieved success by piggybacking on neighborhood events, such as picnics, and mixing in some fun with the community plan outreach. A particularly successful mobile workshop was combined with a Moonlight Movie night event that was cross-promoted with the community plan outreach effort (MRSC, 2015).

Engström, Mattsson, Järleborg, and Hallqvist (2008) provide a model to represent two dimensions and two aspects of social capital. Importantly, a community must provide the structural system to engage the public (structural) but also find means to ensure the public trusts the political system (cognitive) (Figure 10.2). Efforts must be made equalize power relationships. We know that when the public feels it has access to the decision-making process and that it can help influence local decisions, it is more supportive of plans and policies (Lankford & Howard, 1993). Therefore, engaging citizens and building trust and trust relationships enhance our ability to address difficult problems in our community.

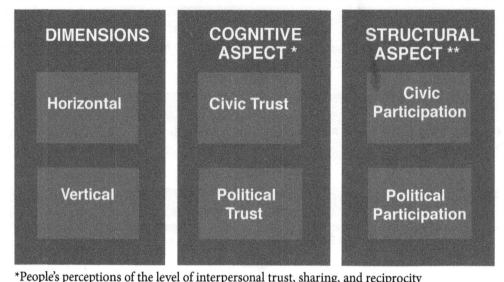

Figure 10.2. Dimensions of Social Capital

Perhaps an answer to the dilemma of a lack of civic engagement lies in the philosophy of the community leaders and public policy. The notion of deliberative democracy, which is not new but is noteworthy for this discussion. Deliberative democracy as noted by Grybovych and Hafermann (2010) offers a way of engaging citizens in deciding upon the matters that directly affect their lives and by doing so fosters the creation of livable communities characterized by community cohesion, exiting norms of trust and reciprocity, civic engagement, and participatory governance. Weeks (2000; 2003) noted the characteristics and philosophy of deliberative democracy include the following the following:

- Broad and representative public participation
- Informed public judgment
- Deliberate public participation
- Highly credible and methodologically sound outcomes and results

The goals of citizen engagement are to revitalize civic culture, improve public discourse, and generate the political will to take action. Grybovych and Hafermann (2010) suggest that embracing deliberative democracy sets high standards for community planning processes and provides important guidance for designing and implementing processes that would ensure meaningful citizen involvement in tourism planning and development. The importance here is planning that encourages civic engagement will strengthen social capital, which will enhance social sustainability. In communities where public controversy over plans is highly charged, little progress is made in implementing and realizing those plans. Where civic engagement is high, issues discussed and some effort made to recognized concerns and mitigate impacts, significant progress is realized. In practice, the application of the principles of deliberative democracy remains an ideal to strive for, this ideal is often constrained by the issues of power, inequality of resources, and legal and policy regulations among others (Grybovych, 2008).

The level, extent, and procedures for citizen engagement are critical to the success of any public agency. Arnstein (1969) published the now-famous *Ladder of Citizen Participation* (see Figure 10. 3), where she noted, "there is a critical difference between going through the empty ritual of participation and having the real power needed to affect the outcome of the process" (p. 216). Arnstein (1969) offered an analogy of a ladder with nonparticipation on the bottom, tokenism in the middle, and citizen power on top of the ladder as a prerequisite for genuine citizen participation. Importantly, Arnstein (1969) regarded the modern dominant approach of "consultations" with public as tokenism and dismissed it as conferring little real power of participants. The dilemma facing public agencies is how and by what means do we engage the citizenry. Legal requirements can be met by the simple nonparticipatory and tokenism strategies like public hearings whereby citizens can have a "comment period" to make their concerns known. An agency can "inform" and "consult" and meet legal requirements or think they have the guidance and endorsement of the community. The decision makers can then move forward with how they see fit. The problem of ignoring the higher levels of citizen engagement using partnerships, delegation of responsibility and control does not solve problems that are deeply embedded in a community. The problems will continue to arise unless genuine efforts are made to move citizens and interest groups to higher levels of participation.

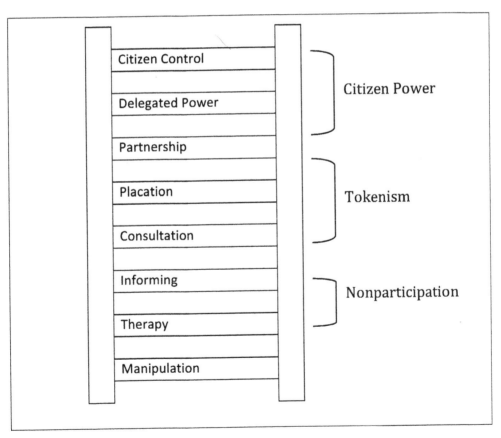

Figure 10.3. Ladder of Citizen Participation. *Source:* Arnstein (1969)

Friedmann (1987), nearly 20 years later, extended Arnstein's argument by proposing a distinction between two competing traditions of planning: planning as societal guidance, and planning as societal transformation (see Table 10.1). Friedmann (1987) offered four theories explaining the major approaches to planning, and advocated the need to "turn both scientific and planning inquiries into a dialogic process between the agency/planner and the participant/community, who typically proceeds on the basis of unarticulated, tacit knowing" (p. 415). He claimed that only recentering political power in civil society will help resolve crisis and lead to acceptable policy and planning processes.

Table 10.1

Classification of the Politics of Planning Theory (Friedmann, 1987)

Knowledge to action	Conservative	Radical
In societal guidance	Policy analysis	Social reform
In societal transformation	Social learning	Social mobilization

Community Participation and Planning in Practice

The City of Portland, Oregon, has developed a toolkit for engaging the public (City of Portland, 2006). The spectrum of involvement (note similarities between Arnstein and Friedmann) includes informing the citizenry, consulting, involving the citizens in deliberations, collaborating with the citizens, and finally deciding together (city agencies and citizens) the final recommendations. This level of engagement helps create a certain type of city with a high level of quality of life, in part due to the enhancement of social capital, as noted earlier. Another example includes the community of Renton, Washington. They completed a comprehensive plan which included the parks and recreation master plan. The following community engagement efforts were made for this plan (Table 10.2).

Table 10.2

Example of Community Engagement Methods

Techniques

Facilitated Meetings – Nominal Group Methods
Public Meeting Presentations by Planning Teams
Telephone Interviews
Mail Surveys
Intercept Surveys
Structured Interviews
Design Workshop
Radio, TV, Newspaper, and Public Displays of Reports, Plans, and Designs

The Bend Metro Park District (BMPD) in Oregon provides another illustration of the role of community engagement in parks and recreation management. BMPRD is committed to involving residents in the planning and development process by the following:

- Conducting periodic community interest and opinion surveys that help guide long-range planning and development efforts.
- Hosting project meetings to invite residents to share their desires and concerns regarding the development of smaller parks in their neighborhoods.
- Hosting community-wide meetings to gain citizen input concerning the design and development of larger parks projects.
- Staying in touch with the community through presentations to neighborhood associations, service clubs, professional and business associations, schools, and various other organizations.

When citizens are sharing their experiences, it is useful to set some guidelines to ensure authenticity of participatory initiatives. Specifically, parks and recreation agencies might consider the following:

- Becoming a part of their communities by building trust with the participants and citizens
- Speaking and writing in a clear language that their participants and citizens understand
- Developing an agency response system to engage participants and citizens (webpages, online surveys, feedback to concerns)
- Operating in a transparent manner and engage participants and citizens early, often and after projects start and end
- Use of technology and social media enables instant feedback from the participants, volunteers, citizens and other constituents

VOLUNTEER ENGAGEMENT

In addition to engaging citizens in policy and planning, volunteers also play a valuable role within parks and recreation systems. Volunteers can be individuals, special interest groups, and those willing to serve on advisory and policy-making boards and commissions. Parks and recreation programs rely on volunteers to help create successful programs. Zahra and McGehee (2013, p. 40) noted "the presence of the volunteers often results in increased participation in programs. These volunteers also had an effect on financial, human-built, and bonding social capital." Although difficult to measure, strong social capital operating within a community has an economic value. Effective social networks can reduce crime or the need for expanded social and health services. This shows that volunteers not only help to make the program run smoothly, but they also help to encourage participation from other community members.

Reasons for volunteering include a desire to serve, a need to learn about one's community, a desire for recognition, or a wish to share interest and knowledge with others. Businesses frequently encourage employees to volunteer their services in community work, thus providing incentive for citizen involvement. Often these volunteers formalize their efforts into a group called Friends of the Park. For example, the Hanauma Bay Nature Preserve Marine Park in Honolulu, Hawaii, is supported by volunteers aptly named Friends of Hanauma Bay. The Friends of Hanauma Bay volunteer for environmental education programs, parking and visitor services, and also support the management team in lobbying for support for policies and funding of the Preserve. (See http://www.friendsofhanaumabay.org/index.html for more information and for how they have organized a very effective program).

Involvement can be as passive as responding to a questionnaire or as active as offering to help and making a definite commitment. Some citizens who wish to be involved will contact the agency; others need to be sought. However they present themselves, volunteers are needed and should be welcomed, whether by the director of the agency, a park manager, or an employee at some other level within the parks agency. Volunteer assistance in various aspects of park management is becoming more important as budget cuts have decreased park staffing. Perhaps it might become necessary to have certain sections of linear parks maintained in this way (See Figures 5.10 and 5.11).

How and where should volunteers be found? How should needs be presented so that potential volunteers are attracted? How do we identify the ones who are willing to serve as individuals? How do we identify those who want to serve only within a group? The first thing that should be done in order to answer these four questions is to compile two lists.

1. List the job/function/service areas in which the parks and recreation agency needs help. Needed personnel could include instructors, office workers, research aides, or people to oversee such special time-consuming projects as the creation of a historical garden or the preparation of a living history costume event.

2. List individuals and groups who want to aid the parks and recreation agency. Contact retirement organizations, conservation organizations, recreation groups, churches, service/fraternal groups, and college outdoor recreation and parks management classes. Also consider contacting the National Center for Volunteer Action and the Volunteer Services of the American Association for Retired People.

Once these two lists have been prepared, match the first list to the second and contact the volunteers. Perhaps a key volunteer can be found to accomplish this organizational work and assist in running the volunteer program. As an example, in Renton, Washington, the Department of Park and Recreation programs offer a large variety of volunteer opportunities, ranging from one-time events to ongoing year-round or seasonal programs. Opportunities listed include youth athletics, special events, adopt a park program, recreation programs, Renton River Days, 4th of July, and trail and park ranger programs. The recruitment notice on the website (https://rentonwa.gov/working/default.aspx?id=7346) states, "Our volunteers have the opportunity to make a difference in our community while meeting new people and becoming familiar with programs and a park system that renew and refresh all who participate. You can help by joining volunteer groups that spread bark, pick up litter, pull weeds, and plant flowers. Volunteers assist with youth athletic events, special events, cultural arts programs and more." It is obvious that the presence of these opportunities in communities enhances social capital by providing bridging and bonding opportunities for citizens. In addition, the parks and recreation department gains labor and political and community support.

Types of Volunteers

The following are the types of ways in which the parks and recreation agency can engage the citizens and participants in a community.

The individual volunteer. Individual volunteer involvement presents far greater opportunities and advantages to the community parks and recreation organization than do groups. Individual volunteers are able to perform some of the same services as employees and cost the agency comparatively nothing. They can be used on a regular basis from daily to once per week. Such people can be utilized at the agency headquarters in general services, as a consultant, or for special needs. An example might be a retired business executive aiding in budget preparation. Volunteers can assist at individual parks as well. Most park managers would have no difficulty utilizing volunteers in a variety of functions, such as clerical and organizational work, special interpretive service, or sign preparation and repair.

"Friends" groups. As noted earlier about the Friends of Hanauma Bay, the friends group is one that should be given consideration especially during times of monetary or political difficulties. Friends often start by their own initiative to assist an agency with a particular need. Sometimes they continue in the role of "friends of the park," while at other times the organization may terminate, such as when the promotion of a bond issue is over. Sometimes the organization will actually become a bona fide partner with the government entity, whereby the government provides the area and facility and perhaps the major maintenance while the friends raise funds, provide minor maintenance, and operate the facility. For example, Stone Mountain Park near Atlanta, Georgia, which is a self-supporting park created by the state, and developed and operated by a committee appointed by the state. See http://www.stonemountainpark.org/ for more details.

Docents. To be a docent, volunteers take a course conducted by the agency to ready them for working with park visitors in a teaching or guiding capacity. The creation of a docent program should be considered for certain types of areas and for certain types of activities, particularly ongoing indoor programs. For example, in certain museums, there are excellent programs where people learn to become tour guides for the museum. An excellent example is the East Bay Regional Park District in Oakland, California. The following is an excerpt from their website (http://www.ebparks.org/getinvolved/volunteer/docent):

Something truly special happens when you share yourself with others ...

For over 30 years, the East Bay Regional Park District has provided opportunities for members of the public to do just that—share their love of nature or their passion for history by becoming docents.

Remember the first time you positively identified a red-tailed hawk? Or how excited you were when you first saw a butterfly chrysalis? These are life-changing moments for many of us. If you become a docent, you could be the one to share these moments with other park visitors!

If you have a passion for learning and sharing, a love for nature or history, and would like to share your passion with like-minded people who share your enthusiasm for encouraging stewardship in the parks, then you will find a visitor center that can help you become an East Bay Regional Park District docent. New docent training programs will be offered this winter at most of the visitor centers, so call a Visitor Center today and find out how you can get involved.

Groups Working With Parks and Recreation Agencies

There are numerous types of groups that work with parks and recreation agencies to advance their areas, facilities, programs, and services. Some of these are discussed here.

General interest groups. These groups are usually broad in scope and purpose, and will offer assistance even if they do not benefit directly. Service clubs fit this category. Scouts or other youth groups who do benefit directly may build trails for the experience and public service entailed, as well as for individual recognition within their groups. Also, volunteer search and rescue groups have proven extremely helpful to recreation agencies at all levels.

Special interest groups. Agencies must find ways both to give these groups access to information they request, and to incorporate these requests into the decision-making and planning process. If agencies do not keep communications open and practice good relations, they run the risk of having their policies and practices criticized and perhaps distorted in the media, or debated piecemeal at hostile public meetings. In addition, the need for developing and managing our parks and resources in a sustainable manner calls for extensive and meaningful citizen involvement.

Often, a group will favor the agency position on one issue and oppose it on another. For example, a group interested in the preservation of a natural area might join with a group desiring land for mountain biking. If successful in securing the area, the two groups might move to opposite sides when the question becomes "Should mountain biking be allowed?" These special interest groups may often be found among the ranks of volunteers helping individually or as a group within a park agency. ATV or horseback groups work with park managers to provide access and facilities and to create goodwill for their groups, both with the agency and with the general public. For other organizations, their main sphere of operations is in policy formulation, and they are usually well represented at public meetings and hearings, often by salaried personnel.

The Colorado Parks & Recreation Association created two special interest groups in 2014: the Marketing and Special Events Group and the Youth Professionals Group. The Marketing and Special Events Group is responsible for providing special events within the parks. The Young Professionals Group is for individuals with less than five years of experience in the field. These groups are still new enough that the full benefits for members and the parks and recreation association have not been identified.

Carrboro, North Carolina, created two special interest groups for volunteers; the Carrboro Park Project and the Carrboro Elementary Park Project. The Carrboro Park Project has helped to fund-raise for a number of park additions within the community. Each project has been volunteer driven to provide support for the parks and recreation department. The Carrboro Elementary School Park Project is a group of dedicated parents associated with the PTA. The focus is to renovate and improve the school grounds.

Citizens committees. Often parks and recreation departments will establish committees for a variety of purposes. Such committees may have a broad base of focus or may be dedicated to an individual area of interest.

There are many types of advisory committees. They are operated in various ways and for many purposes. They often give advice to the director or the elected executive. They may be specialists in a particular subject or represent a geographical area. Sometimes a committee for a specific purpose will be appointed by a park manager to function at that park or facility only, but advisory committees are usually appointed by the director. They can provide constructive support to a parks and recreation agency if used properly and if provided sufficient supportive assistance. These types of committees can provide effective input to the organization and broaden its base of public support.

Advisory committees require liaison and other departmental supportive services involving considerable staff time. If the advisory committee is to be an effective group, the projects or programs must have a real purpose and need. The act of establishing such an advisory committee represents a commitment on the part of the department for involvement in that service and in that program. The committee findings and the recommendations must be carefully considered and used in making decisions if the agency is to establish and maintain an image of integrity and credibility with the public. This does not mean that all recommendations must be accepted and acted on. There are basically two types of advisory boards: terminal and ongoing.

Advisory committees may deal with a specific subject matter or with a definite goal: either a specific problem that needs resolving or a general subject for a stated period of time. It is important that these committees end their term of service cleanly at the appropriate time. It is oftentimes easier to keep the interest of a terminal committee, as they usually are composed of people who are interested in the particular subject matter or they would not have been willing to serve in the first place. Since they know there is an end to the task or project, they tend to feel a sense of urgency and a need for accomplishment.

Governing bodies. As discussed in Chapter 9, there are several types of governing bodies, including policy-making boards, semi-independent policy boards, advisory boards, and commissions. Each of these types of governance structures draws its legal mandate from state statutes or charters. Participation in these bodies represent an additional avenue of community engagement and involvement. These types of governing structures are appointed by city council or county supervisors, or elected by the citizens of a particular geographical area, such as a parks and recreation district. Such governing bodies may have the right of hiring and dismissing the parks and recreation agency director. It is generally accepted that citizens are assured of a broader interest in their needs through such types of governing units, whose membership often provides a wide range of experience as well as representation of the total geographic area. Those citizens who are interested in parks and recreation matters are able to express their opinions to a board member who lives close to their location. The staggered appointment of board members usually provides that a majority of the board will survive a change in the appointing authority, thus decreasing the potential for partisan political maneuvering. For the board to be properly involved, the parks and recreation agency director should regularly communicate with the chairman, and, to a lesser degree, with the total board. The board should be actively involved in the decision-making process even when the director is the one to make the decision.

EVALUATION AND RECOGNITION OF VOLUNTEERS

The evaluation and recognition of volunteers is an important function for any parks and recreation agency. Volunteers often provide a critical base of manpower and support to a parks and recreation agencies programs and services. Thus, the evaluation of volunteers is important to make sure that excellent individuals are retained by the organization and furthermore recognized and acknowledged for their good work.

Evaluation of Volunteers

Volunteers should be evaluated in the same way that paid employees are, impartially and on an ongoing basis. If workers, volunteer or paid, are informed of desirable and undesirable qualities and performances at set intervals over the duration of the job, they have the chance to eliminate weak points and strengthen good ones. If volunteers undergo a firm, fair evaluation, they feel useful and know they are being taken seriously. If a volunteer fails to improve, thus becoming a detriment of the program, then that person can and should be dismissed as any paid employee would be. It is important to note that volunteers are sometimes working with an agency to gain experience for future paid employment. Therefore, these volunteers need feedback in order to improve their performances.

A report at the time the volunteer leaves the agency is done much in the same way as the evaluation, but with a different goal. Its goal is to provide a record of the volunteer's job experience that can be used as a reference for rehire or for the benefit of future employers. Evaluations of the supervisor and the staff by the volunteers is in use in some agencies. The intent of such an evaluation is to gain an understanding of the needs and wants of volunteers, to make sure their suggestions are under consideration, and to obtain an outsider's view of operations to which the volunteer has been exposed.

Recognition of Volunteers

Evaluation will bring light to certain individuals who have done outstanding work and will offer the agency or manager an opportunity to give such people recognitions and thanks. Recognition can take many forms. Special volunteer banquets can be held annually or even more frequently. Volunteers can be provided with certificates of appreciation signed by an important person, such as the head of that level of government or a representative from the legislative branch. British Columbia Provincial Parks provides deserving volunteers with a certificate of appreciation along with volunteer recognition pins. The local newspaper and other news media might do special articles on volunteers. Volunteer workers can also be recognized for their contributions at meetings of the legislative body of the appropriate level of government.

In summary, managing volunteers and support groups takes staff and agency time and supervision. However, the payoff in building trust and relationships in the community provide long-lasting support for the work of the parks and recreation agency. The California State Parks has developed a *Volunteer In the Park Program Guidelines*. This guide is designed to recruit, manage and supervise volunteers, and gives advice on how to evaluate and recognize the volunteers (See http://www.parks.ca.gov/pages/735/files/vipp%20 guidelines%202003.pdf for more information).

SUMMARY

There is no replacement for the goodwill of the community, and the interaction with volunteers, citizens, and community groups. Citizen engagement, if properly managed, will help inform the agency of policy and planning options that meet the needs of the community. Establishing formal means of civic engagement strengthens social capital and provides a foundation of support for the efforts of the parks and recreation agency. Agencies must expand beyond the legal mandate of public hearings and create opportunities for significant citizen engagement that includes collaboration and partnerships in delivering public recreation services.

Volunteers provide important help during times of stringent budgeting; they are invaluable. Creative thinking involving both citizen and agency personnel on the subject of volunteer assistance is now more important than ever. Volunteers also play a role to increase social capital within communities. Social capital can help to promote social connections and trust among neighborhood residents. The higher levels of social capital can be attributed to participation with others in public spaces (Baur & Tynon, 2010). When the levels of social capital are increased, this can lead to an increase in quality of life for residents within the community. Positive social capital is a must for communities, because it helps residents feel as if they are true members of the community. This leads to the residents beginning to take pride and ownership in how things take place in the community. Social capital can be increased within a community. This can be done through creating common spaces for interactions among community members. "The networks that overlap each other reinforce the sense of reciprocal obligation and extend the boundaries of empathy" (Putnam, 2003, p. 291).

Parks and recreation organizations must be responsive to public opinion from beyond the volunteer ranks, and they should be legitimately active in forming that opinion. Involving citizens is the best way of both serving their needs and addressing inequities in the parks and recreation service delivery system. Involving citizens also is a principle of sustainable park management. The richer the citizen involvement is for parks and recreation management, the more likelihood that plans and programs are responsive to needs and address diverse viewpoints and problem-solving strategies.

DISCUSSION QUESTIONS

1. How can citizens contribute to the work being done by a parks and recreation organization?
2. Why should a parks and recreation organizations request volunteers complete an application?
3. Why are public meetings and hearings necessary for a parks and recreation organization?
4. What are ways that citizens play an important role in the decision-making process of parks and recreation organizations?
5. In crafting a civic engagement process, what should the parks and recreation agency be aware of to ensure adequate involvement?
6. Discuss Arnstein's ladder of participation. What has your experience been with an agency or bureaucracy?
7. Review Friedmann's model of participation. How is your community engaged in that process?
8. In what ways can citizen engagement strengthen recreation programs in the community?
9. In what ways can citizen engagement strengthen park planning and parks in the community?
10. What are some difficulties in managing civic engagement?

REFERENCES

Arnstein, S. R. (July, 1969). A ladder of citizen participation. *Journal of the American Institute of Planners, 35*(4), 216–224.

Baur, J. W. R., & Tynon, J. F. (2010) Small-scale urban nature parks: Why should we care? *Leisure Sciences: An Interdisciplinary Journal, 32*(2), 195–200. doi: 10.1080/01490400903547245. http://dx.doi.org/10.1080/01490400903547245

Bend Metro Park and Recreation District. (n.d.). Citizen involvement. Retrieved from http://www.bendparksandrec.org/Planning__Development/

California State Parks. (2003). Volunteer in parks program guidelines. Retrieved from http://www.parks.ca.gov/pages/735/files/vipp%20guidelines%202003.pdf

Carrboro Parks and Recreation. (2014). Volunteer opportunities with Carrboro recreation parks. Retrieved from http://www.carrbororec.org/RecVolunteers.htm#6

City of Portland, Oregon. (2006). Public involvement toolkit. Retrieved from http://www.portlandonline.com/shared/cfm/image.cfm?id=137141

Colorado Parks and Recreation Association. (2014). Interest groups. Retrieved from http://www.cpra-web.org/?page=InterestGroups

Dennis, S. (2001). *Natural resources and the informed citizen.* Urbana, IL: Sagamore.

East Bay Regional Park District. (2015). Getting involved. Retrieved from http://www.ebparks.org/getinvolved/volunteer/docent

Engström, K., Mattsson, F., Järleborg, A., & Hallqvist, J. (2008). Contextual social capital as a risk factor for poor self-rated health: A multilevel analysis. *Social Science and Medicine, 66*(11), 2268–2280.

Friedmann, J. (1987). *Planning in the public domain: From knowledge to action.* Princeton, NJ: Princeton University Press.

Friends of Hanauma Bay. (2015). About us. Retrieved from http://www.friendsofhanaumabay.org/aboutus/

Grybovych, O. (2008). *Deliberative democratic practices in tourism planning: Toward a model of participatory community tourism planning.* (Doctoral Dissertation, University of Northern Iowa, 2008). ProQuest Dissertations and Theses. (UMI No. AAT 3321006).

Grybovych, O., & Haftermann, D. (2010). Sustainable practices of community tourism planning: Lessons from a remote community. *Community Development, 41*(3), 354–369.

MRSC. (2015). Creating inclusive communities. Retrieved from http://mrsc.org/Home/Explore-Topics/Governance/Citizen-Participation-and-Engagement/Effective-Communication-and-Public-Participation/Communication-and-Citizen-Participation-Techniques.aspx

National Parks and Conservation Association. (2017). Retrieved from http://www.parks.ca.gov/pages/735/files/vipp%20guidelines%202003.pdf

National Recreation and Park Association. (2002). Independent citizen board member resource guide. Retrieved from http://www.nrpa.org/uploadedFiles/Connect_and_Share/The_NRPA_Network_%28Socnet_Function%29/Independent%20Citizen%20Board%20Member%20Resource%20Guide.pdf

National Recreation and Park Association. (2007). NRPA advisory board member resource guide. Retrieved from https://krpa.wildapricot.org/Resources/Documents/Static%20Web%20Page/Advisory%20Board%20Member%20Resource%20Guide-1.PDF

Oregon's Citizen Involvement Advisory Committee. (2008). Putting the people in planning: A primer on public participation in planning. Retrieved from http://www.oregon.gov/LCD/docs/publications/putting_the_people_in_planning.pdf

Putnam, R. D. (2001). *Bowling alone: The collapse and revival of the American community.* New York, NY: Simon and Schuster.

Putnam, R., Feldstein, L. M., & Cohen, D. (2003) *Better together: Restoring the American community.* New York, NY: Simon and Schuster.

Stone Mountain Memorial Association. (2017). About. Retrieved from http://www.stonemountainpark.org/

Zahra, A., & McGehee, N. G. (2013) Volunteer tourism: A host community capital perspective. *Annals of Tourism Research, 42,* 22–45. Retrieved from http://dx.doi.org/10.1016/j.annals.2013.01.008

Chapter Eleven

Acquisition of Parks and Open Space

CHAPTER OBJECTIVES

- To gain an awareness of the need for park, land, and open space acquisition
- To gain an awareness of the need for building partnerships in the land acquisition process
- To understand the means by which parks and recreation agencies can acquire parkland and open space
- To become aware of how the acquisition process is related to planning and management of public parks and recreation systems
- To gain insight into how various agencies have developed parks and open space acquisition programs

INTRODUCTION

Community parks and recreation agencies who have approved and up-to-date plans are positioned to acquire parks and open space within the community. In addition, these plans can and do inform city planners, decision makers, residents, and developers of the intention to expand the tools used to expand parks and open space. Planning documents and processes help implement a land acquisition and classification system.

Planning, mapping, and identification of critical lands, resources, and habitats are essential building blocks for parks and recreation acquisition programs. For example, Fort Collins Colorado plans have been used in the regulatory review process and have played a key role in setting priorities for the open space acquisition program (Duerksen & Snyder, 2005). Acquisition programs across the country have helped prioritize facilities and parklands; enabled the development of walking, biking, and multiuse trails; and created opportunities for greenways within communities.

A variety of tools are used for a comprehensive acquisition program. Regulations are required for development, as are dedicated funding sources such as sales taxes and impact fee programs. This chapter identifies parkland and open space acquisition programs and the role of partnerships with nonprofits. Also discussed are the common tools available to the park and recreation agency, to include long-term funding programs, land dedication and impact fee systems, purchase of development rights, and land use regulatory measures.

NEED FOR PARKLAND AND OPEN SPACE ACQUISITION

Implementation strategies for parks and recreation master plans more often than not address land acquisition programs for expanding the parks and open space systems. It is critical that parks and recreation agencies inventory the natural and historical resources and have a plan to management them sustainably (Harnik, 2003).

Parks and recreation agencies are under increasing pressure to acquire enough lands and contiguous parcels for greenways due to development pressures. In some communities, other uses for the land may preempt recreational use if a well-planned program of acquisition is not employed to secure suitable land. There are six important factors adding to the recreational space problem:

1.   More and more residents are using parklands more frequently.
2.   There is far less open space owned by private citizens or companies available for residents to use, resulting in greater use of public parks and recreation areas.
3.   Older parts of cities have fewer acres of parks due to the historic lack of land dedication or fees when the area was developed. Newer parts of the city often has more acreage in parks per 1,000 people due to ordinances in place.
4.   Competition with developers over lands for recreation vs. other uses.
5.   Perceptions from elected officials that maintenance costs of parks are prohibitive for the future budget.
6.   Technology (web-based information) has made access to these lands easier and has vastly increased the demand for special areas to handle particular needs (off-road vehicles, horse trails etc).

Despite strong statements from national leaders citing the need for more recreational areas, acquiring needed parklands has become increasingly difficult, particularly in urban areas where needs are greater, but where conflicting demands are formidable due to development pressures. Unfortunately, local political pressure from developers who argue that the land has a "higher and best use" as a housing or a strip mall can then lead to elected officials declaring that the ongoing maintenance costs are reasons to deny the acquisition of additional parklands. In addition, some citizens feel that additional parkland and the ongoing maintenance are costs are prohibitive. While others in the community may feel that the open space adjacent to their own homes may bring undesirable people close to their property and increased crime.

There are some positive aspects to the land acquisition situation, however. Land is often zoned for recreation because experience has proven this to be the best use. For example, flood plains are an example of areas where other uses are not practical because of periodic flooding. Recreational uses on such lands can adjust to the inconvenience without danger to human life or serious economic loss.

Figure 11.1 presents the ways in which land acquisition is presented in this chapter (adapted from Lankford, Lankford, & Wheeler 2011). It is important to note that parks and recreation plans suggest and authorize acquisition of parks and open space as an implementing measure. Further, the plans are used for the capital improvement programs.

Figure 11.1. Parkland and Open Space Acquisition Methods

The use of partnerships are strong in communities that have cultivated engagement. Other means by which the agency may acquire lands is through cooperative and negotiated agreements and by ordinances and land use zoning.

PARTNERSHIPS FOR LAND ACQUISITION

Thorough planning and civic engagement creates strong public and private partnerships with citizens and nonprofit groups. There is no standard template for involving public and private donors. The right approach varies by locale and public support. For example, as noted by Harnik (2003), the City of Seattle, through its parks and recreation planning process and acquisition program has over 335 contracts with nonprofit organizations for "adopt a park" programs and for securing funding for parks. Furthermore, the City of Philadelphia has reported 138 "friends of parks" groups. Not only do these groups maintain parks, they advocate for funding and for acquisition of parks and open space.

Many examples also exist of governmental collaborations. The City of New York collaborated with the Department of Transportation to convert paved areas into pocket parks and greet areas. The City of Fresno, California Department of Parks, After School, Recreation, and Community Services (PARCS) partners with schools for after-school programs in the schools and school grounds.

Another opportunity for acquiring lands for a park system has resulted from the general decline in railroading, resulting in the disuse and abandonment of tracks in the United States. Citizens have recognized the recreation potential in this unexpected resource and have worked to acquire abandoned railroad rights-of-way. These long, narrow, often scenic strips of land have proven to be excellent sites for public hiking, cross-country skiing, and biking trails.

In terms of railroad rights-of-way, the Rails-to-Trails Conservancy has led the way in the United States. Headquartered in Washington, D.C., with regional offices in California, Ohio, and Pennsylvania, and a state office in Florida, Rails-to-Trails Conservancy connects, builds, protects and promotes rail-trails and their far-reaching benefits.

Another positive influential nonprofit association, American Trails, has also advocated for trails and greenways. Their mission states

American Trails is pursuing a national infrastructure of trails and greenways that serve a full range of activities. Through education, partnerships, and timely information resources, we promote the creation, conservation, and broad enjoyment of quality trails and greenways that offer places of solace, health, fitness, recreation and transportation for all Americans. (http://www.americantrails.org/about.html)

American Trails envisions having trails and greenways within 15 minutes of every American home, serving both urban and rural landscapes. They advocate the following:

- An Interconnected National System of Trails and Greenways—used regularly by Americans and foreign visitors
- Myriad trails and greenways uses—with a full range of activities, both nonmotorized and motorized
- Quality trail and greenway experiences—that enable the appreciation of natural beauty, cultural and historic connections, and bring people back in touch with special places in the outdoors
- Trails and greenways that promote the conservation of resources—with a system that optimizes wildlife preservation and land and water stewardship
- Trails and greenways that promote economic development—enhancing property values, business opportunities, tourism and marketability of communities
- A trail and greenway system that is durable—affordable to maintain with a sustainable commitment of resources

The Trust of Public Land (TPL) is another unique resource for land management agencies. The Trust for Public Land provides the following ways for threatened lands to be purchased and then transferred to government ownership:

- It builds bridges with important conservation partners, both private and public, to help create solutions for land conservation.
- It is the primary link between TPL, government, and other nonprofits (Parks Foundation).
- It provides information and guidance about policy and funding resources to a wide range of interested parties, including local and state land trust activists and government officials, and other conservation groups.
- It works with governments to secure funding and authorizations related to land conservation.
- It provides guidance and assistance to TPL regional offices, as well as other local land trusts, community groups, and government offices, regarding federal funding and policy initiatives.

Trust for Public Lands also provides the following conservation services to aid parks acquisition efforts. The Trust for Public Land conserves land for human enjoyment and wellbeing, from inner city to wilderness. TPL's five initiatives are listed below (Trust for Public Land, 2015).

- **Parks for People.** TPL works in cities and suburbs across America to ensure that everyone—in particular, every child—enjoys close-to-home access to a park, playground, or natural area.
- **Working Lands.** TPL protects farms, ranches, and forests that support land-based livelihoods and rural ways of life.
- **Natural Lands.** TPL conserves places of natural beauty that preserve wilderness for our children's children to explore and that support wildlife habitat.
- **Heritage Lands.** TPL protects places of historic and cultural importance that keep us in touch with the past and who we are as a people.
- **Land and Water.** TPL preserves lands that protect clean water and the natural beauty of our coasts and waterways.

TPL worked with the City of Austin, Texas, to obtain the development rights of Barton Springs (the city aquifer recharge source) and deed it over to the City for a regional park. TPL is also active in Hawaii, where they obtain development rights for coastal areas and deed them over to counties for parks and public use. Another example of the impact of TPL is seen in the New Jersey Department of Environmental Protection (DEP) Green Acres Program. Like many other states, it provides the following example of combining scenic easements, zoning, and regulatory measures to protect parks and open space.

The goal of protecting the scenic quality of Route 57 can be accomplished in a number of ways. Local master planning and conservation zoning may be used to steer future growth away from sensitive view-sheds. Design guidelines may be used to encourage compact community forms and attractive building types that harmonize with the surrounding landscape. Scenic overlay zoning may also help municipalities limit visual disturbances by regulating such elements as building heights, parking, and commercial signs.

In some cases, certain views may be so highly valued by community residents that consideration can also be given to the outright acquisition of land for preservation purposes. Alternatively, landowners may be willing to grant scenic easements that protect views while allowing current activities to continue on a parcel. Public sector programs that may assist with the acquisition of specific parcels of land along Route 57 include NJDEP's Green Acres Program and Warren County's Department of Land Preservation. Private land trusts are another resource. Resources for acquiring preservation easements include the State Agriculture Development Committee's "Planning Incentive Grants" (PIGs), which target active farmland. Some of these programs require that the land in question be part of a municipal open space or farmland preservation plan. (New Jersey Department of Environmental Protection, 2010).

OTHER COMMON TOOLS FOR PARKS AND OPEN SPACE ACQUISITION—
FEE AND LESS THAN FEE EXAMPLES

There are several ways recreation or park agencies can acquire land. These include outright purchase, donation, stipulated deed, condemnation, easements, dedications, fee in lieu and/or park development fee, and transfer of property or development rights. The following techniques are used by city, county, special district, and state parks and recreation agencies to acquire lands. Often more than one technique is used to acquire parks and open space lands. For example, Table 11.1 presents what the City of Boulder, Colorado utilizes to expand what is considered a model parkland and open space system.

Table 11.1

City of Boulder, Colorado

- Partnerships with government and nonprofits
- Fee acquisition of lands
- Conservation easements and development rights agreements
- Trail easements
- Dedications of parkland and open space
- Condemnation of lands
- Grants
- Partnerships

Source: City of Boulder Colorado, 2014

The following example of the City of Seattle (2006) acquisition program highlights the use of some of the tools for a city to gain ownership. Notice the emphasis on form, design, greenways, and in-fill strategies (to discourage sprawl and provide parks closer to all neighborhoods). Using the guiding principles of the original 1903 Olmsted Plan, the city will expand open space acquisitions, park development, and creation of new or improved boulevards and trails to serve as park connectors. The plan advocates the acquisition and voluntary preservation of real property to expand Seattle's inventory of open spaces and parklands, and reclaiming urban property to serve as small neighborhood parks and major regional parks. The plan also calls for acquiring key private properties within greenspaces (greenbelts and natural areas) and other primarily natural areas such as stream corridors, and wetlands will be acquired to preserve such areas. The priority for the expansion of the open space network is for areas of the city subject to population growth, including urban villages targeted for the largest share of residential growth, and those areas not adequately served at present according to the population-based goals for open space. The following methods are allowed under the plan to acquire and preserve open space:

- Use of public funds and grants, donations, and community self-help
- Acquisition of life estates, where appropriate, to protect current owners
- Acquisition of voluntary conservation easements or similar mechanisms for preserving the open space qualities

- Dedication or leasing from other public agencies, including the Seattle School District
- If no other options are available, condemnation or removal of existing development will be pursued to preserve or re-create open space in highly developed areas lacking open space, although elimination of existing housing stock is generally to be avoided
- Encourage the private sector to join in providing adequate open space for residential developments and public open space for commercial developments

Cooperative and Negotiated Agreements

The following section highlights the types of cooperative and negotiated agreements that are commonplace in acquisition programs. These involve agreements between private landowners, developers and the city, county, or special district.

Cooperative agreements. Legal instruments defining administrative arrangements between two or more parties (public, nonprofit, or private). They can result in the exchange of services or benefits such as access to managing natural or cultural resources, sharing responsibility for maintenance of structures and facilities, providing public access, management of wildlife or other resources, and providing law enforcement.

Conservation bank. A conservation bank is used to protect privately or publicly owned lands that contain endangered, threatened, or at-risk species. With a conservation bank, credits are established for the specific habitat or species that occurs on a site. In exchange for permanently protecting the banked lands, the bank sells habitat credits to developers and others who need to compensate for the environmental impacts of a project. The bank uses the funds to protect the environmental resources it holds. Conservation banks are typically used when it makes more sense for a developer to purchase conservation credits than to protect part of the area being developed (for example, when on-site conservation would result in small, isolated sites). Not all states endorse conservation banks. A conservation bank is funded through an endowment created by participating landowners who deposit funds to maintain and manage the protected lands, which generates interest for management of the conservation bank.

Donations. This is the giving of land, interest in land, or money for the purchase of land to the federal government by a state, individual, corporation, trust, or foundation. Agencies often make known their need for recreation lands through contacts in order to attract donors. Some states, counties and cities have established park foundations to seek and receive donations. These foundations can be of great assistance to an agency, as they help people realize the rewards associated with this sort of generosity. It is suggested that recreation and park agencies become well acquainted with the programs and personnel of natural land, nonprofit land conservation organizations such as The Trust for Public Lands and The Nature Conservancy.

Exchanges. An exchange of land or interests in land is a "trade" of real property between the government and an owner of nongovernment land. Usually the properties must be equal in value, approximately equal in value, or can be equalized with cash payments. Land exchanges are included in this list because they are the tool often used by the federal, state, county and special district level to acquire lands for resource benefits as well as to improve land ownership configuration for management efficiencies. These are usually funded within existing agency appropriations.

Land trusts. A land trust is a nonprofit organization that, as all or part of its mission, actively works to conserve land by undertaking or assisting in land or conservation easement acquisition or by its stewardship of such land or easements. The trusts have proven to be very effective tools in conserving land. The trusts help interested landowners find ways to protect their land in the face of ever-growing development pressure. A land trust can be used to protect land that a community values; and the land can be farmland or scenic, recreational, or environmentally significant areas. The Trust for Public Land facilitates the development of these arrangements.

Leasing. A contract by which one party conveys land (or other property) for a term of years (or life) for a specific amount of rent or compensation. Fee title is retained by the agency or owner. This arrangement is usually for a set period of time and for a specific purpose. The rental fee is commonly based on the value of the property and paid on an annual basis. An example would be the county leasing land from the state government for recreational use. Another example is the utilization of land belonging to the U.S. Bureau of Land Management or U.S. Forest Service for ski areas.

Stipulated deed. This is the method commonly used to give land to an agency when there are conditions as to what may or may not be done with the land. An example would be the donation of a parcel of land that must be used for recreation or it would revert to the owner. This would preclude using this parcel for sale or trade in order to consolidate holdings or lessen management problems. For example, the City of Fresno was given land by the federal government (former office and storage site) for use as a park only.

Transfer of lands or management responsibilities. Transfer of jurisdiction between agencies and among local, county, state, provincial, and federal governments is a process frequently used in order to follow legislative mandates or to adequately represent all types of areas in systems planning. Hundreds of parks exist today as a result of the transfer process. The planning, acquisition, and management of each level of park is different with varying legal mandates.

Use permits. These are issued usually at little or no fee for an indefinite period of time, but with a provision for revocation. Typical situations would be use of the open space under electrical transmission lines for a trail of right-of-way or use of a bridge or pier for fishing.

Acquisition by Ordinances and Other Legal Instruments

This section presents tools for acquisition of lands that utilize exactions (land dedication, payments of fees-in-lieu of lands, and impact fees), condemning properties, and easements. Grants and out-right purchase of lands are also included in this section due to the legal and administrative nature (requiring resolutions, ordinances and capital budget approvals) for the use of these tools.

Condemnation

Sometimes an agency must institute condemnation proceedings. The actual condemnation process involves one or both of two actions. The first is establishing the right of eminent domain, which means, in essence, seeking a court ruling that states that the government entity needs the area for the welfare of the public. Some reasons why an agency might need the land for the public good and thus decide to institute such proceedings are discussed below.

Identified resources. The first reason for condemnation is based on the agency's master plan, as discussed earlier in this chapter. An identified resource refers to land that has already been selected as suitable and necessary to implement the agency plan, and for the public good.

Inholdings. For various reasons, an agency may find itself with a private parcel inside the boundaries of one of its holdings. The owner might choose to develop a facility not in keeping with the park atmosphere or might prevent the park agency from accomplishing a logical development. To eliminate such problems, attempts to acquire the in holding are made through condemnation.

Natural boundaries. Rivers, mountains, or lakes form natural boundaries for many land areas. Unfortunately, all too frequently an existing park's boundaries are artificially set; that is, they do not follow the natural boundaries. For instance, they may stop 30 feet (9 meters) from a wide river. Such intervening parcels of land cause many administrative problems, and agencies will sometimes condemn them to acquire them for access and continuity of management.

Threats of incompatible use. The possibility or actuality of incompatible use dictates acquisition, such as the threat of a motorcar raceway next to a natural area. Managers can perform a particularly useful service here in recognizing those areas that would affect a given park if incompatible uses were established.

Dedication, development fees, and fees-in-lieu of land. Dedication (or exaction) is the process of shifting forward to new development the cost of infrastructure, the need for which is generated by new residents. Parkland and or development of recreation facilities can be exacted from the developer as land, cash-in-lieu of land, and/or impact fees as a condition of subdivision map approval. Many states have laws or dedication ordinances allowing a local or county agency to require land for parks based on a formula of number of bedrooms in the housing development. Illinois and California have led the way with this acquisition method. Recreational areas and parklands are often designed as part of subdivisions and land developments. Municipalities are authorized under their codes (if approved by the state government) to require property developers to dedicate public open space within proposed subdivisions and land developments. An applicant or developer may also agree with a municipality to construct recreational facilities, pay to the municipality a fee to be used instead of dedicating land (i.e., "fee-in-lieu") or a combination of land dedication, construction of recreational facilities, or the payment of the fee. The dedicated parkland or the payment of the fee is to be used by the municipality to ensure that future residents of the subdivision or land development have adequate park and recreational opportunities.

For example, the Minneapolis Parkland Dedication Ordinance, which took effect on January 1, 2014, has as its purpose to assure there will be adequate parkland to meet the needs of residents and workers. The ordinance requires that new residential and commercial developments either (1) dedicate a reasonable amount of land to the MPRB for public use, (2) propose a privately owned park or plaza for public use, or (3) pay a fee to the Park Board in lieu of land dedication. Land dedications must be approved by both the city and the Minneapolis Park and Recreation Board (MPRB). When the fee is chosen, the MPRB will use the funds for land acquisition and development or for improvement of existing parkland within one-half mile of the development. It cannot be used for ongoing maintenance (City of Minneapolis, 2014).

Easement Acquisitions (Interests in Land)

Acquisition of a right of way or privilege to use the land for a specific purpose calls for easement purchases. Often, the arrangement allows the owners a right to use certain aspects of his/her property, yet still provide public use on the property. Easement acquisitions include the following:

Access easements. Also called rights-of-way; this is the right a person has to travel over a designated portion of another person's land.

Conservation easements. Acquired for conservation purposes and used to protect resource values on non-federal lands by restricting the type and amount of development or activities on land that is subject to the easement. The term "conservation easement" is often used generically to describe a scenic easement, open space easement, historic preservation easement, agricultural preservation easement, etc. Restrictions on non-public lands usually specify the activities in which the owner may not engage, such as felling trees, building structures, subdividing, excavating or draining the property.

Prescriptive easements. These are gained when an agency claims and is awarded the use of a parcel of land on the basis of a number of years of similar use by the public. For example, walking rights over a beach or across open space might be secured by such an easement.

Scenic easements. These are similar to development rights, but they differ in that the owner is paid the amount necessary to preclude any changes that would detract from the scenic aspect. Such an easement might involve a setback on a bluff overlooking a whitewater river, private land adjacent to a park, or an inholding next to a roadway. An examination of the U.S. Forest Service National Scenic Byways would be an example of these easements at the larger scale. There are many local and state examples as well. The National Scenic Byways Program is a voluntary, community-based program administered through the Federal Highway Administration (FHWA) to recognize, protect, and promote America's most outstanding roads. Through their state departments of transportation, communities can apply for designation as a State or National Scenic Byway for funding from the FHWA.

Grants

The federal government provides financial assistance to states, local governments, or nonprofit organizations for land acquisition, planning, development of outdoor recreation facilities, and/or for acquisition and protection of natural or cultural resources. LWCF provides some grants, as do federal agencies to local governments on occasion for threatened lands. The recreation and parks agency must have an approved plan that is adopted by resolution of the elected body. A traditional source of funding over the years has been the Land and Water Conservation Fund (LWCF, P.L. 88-578). This fund was established for acquisition of lands or for other uses (determined by Congress) to ensure public access to outdoor recreational resources and to provide protection of critical resources. The NPS, FWS, FS, and BLM all utilize LWCF to support their agency goals and Departmental objectives. Each agency has created its own ranking system based on its mission to determine which projects should receive the highest priority for acquisition. These ranking systems are the primary tools by which agencies establish their annual land acquisition budget request. Local city, county and special districts also access funding through LWCF. The requirement is for each state to have an approved Statewide Comprehensive Outdoor Recreation Plan (SCORP) that identifies needs, deficiencies, and demands.

Outright Purchase of Lands

Areas are acquired in fee title when all rights in the area are obtained. If the area is purchased in less than fee title, this implies some restrictions on rights. Frequently, for example, mineral rights are at issue. Bonds are one of the means by which parks agencies can acquire land. Consider the East Bay Regional Park District's newest measure, Measure WW.

Of the $500 million raised by Measure WW, $375 million (75%) will fund regional parks acquisitions and capital projects, with $26.2 million (7%) held in reserve for unanticipated future needs and opportunities. In addition, $125 million (25%) of proceeds will go to cities, special parks and recreation districts, and county service areas for their parks and recreation services. Livermore voters are not part of this extension tax as Murray Township was not within the East Bay Regional Park District's jurisdiction in the initial bond measure. The Park District continues to serve this community through new acquisitions of parklands.

Transfer and Purchase of Development Rights

Purchases of development rights works when a local government wants to protect open space, but keep land in active use (farms, etc.). This method assures the continuation of present use and does not involve purchase of the land. For instance, an agency might purchase development right from the owners of a golf course. That use, golf, and no other, would then prevail on that land. This is commonly done on farm lands to ensure the continuation of agricultural use. Another form (transfer of development rights) is allowance of developers to increase densities elsewhere, and keep an area for parkland. This process secures the development rights of a property (basically preserves it in parks and open space) and moves those development rights to another property to be sold by the landowner for higher densities.

Zoning and Land Use

Land use regulations consist of zoning and subdivision controls, development standards, and fiscal impact assessments (described earlier under exactions). These tools are basic to a comprehensive parks system. Zoning is based on the power of state and local governments to protect public, health, safety, and welfare by regulating the use of land. Local zoning can be used to limit the density, type, location, and character of private development. A type of zoning is the overlay zone can be used to protect particular natural, cultural, or built features in a community that are under pressure from development. Such zones can be used to carry out a variety of community objectives: to protect the character of a neighborhood, downtown, waterfront, or road corridor; to protect a scenic view, an aquifer recharge area, natural slopes, wetlands, and watersheds. Regulating the size of developments, density, clustering, and form allows the government to set aside adequate park space relative to the proposed project and its impact on the community parks and recreation system.

ACQUISITION AND THE CAPITAL IMPROVEMENT PROGRAM

Upon acquisition of the land envisioned in the recreation and parks plan, and the planners have provided a site plan document, a tangible structure or some other modification of the area will become a reality. Sometimes these areas have little or no development, based on the resources and needs of the community. For example, linear greenways serving as wildlife corridors and floodplain management might only have trails.

Once the plan is adopted, lands acquired, a program to financing the costs of construction is the next development. Here final project features are illustrated and estimated construction costs are projected. At this point, too, the agency starts perfecting its capital budget for legislative review.

The capital budget request deals with monies for acquisition and development of new areas and facilities as well as major renovations and repairs to extend the life of existing facilities. (This is in contrast to the operational budget, which is the day-to-day money used to run the agency.) The development part of the capital budget is usually set forth in a long-range capital needs program of six to 10 years; the specific capital budget request spans one or two years. The specific request requires much more specificity and should prove the need along with details on the proposed design and development plan. For example, the City of Eugene, Oregon uses the following techniques to fund capital improvements. Of particular note is the reliance on some of the same acquisition methods (Table 11.2).

Table 11.2

City of Eugene, Oregon Capital Improvement Funding Strategies

Source	Advantages & Limitations
CAPITAL PROJECTS AND OPERATIONS	
General Fund	• Wide flexibility. • Funds are constrained due to property tax limitations. • All City departments compete for these funds.
Road Fund	• Dependent on taxes collected • Limitation on the types of projects that may be funded – principally projects within the road right-of-way • Declining funding
Stormwater/ Wastewater Fees	• Projects must meet the goals of the stormwater and wastewater utilities. • A limited range of recreation projects that can qualify for use of these funds. • Cannot be used for general park improvements or operations.
Wetlands Mitigation Bank	• Limited to wetlands projects • Dependent on sale of credits to developers
Local Option Levy	• Wide flexibility. • Short duration – up to 10 years. • Must receive voter approval. Except during general elections in even-numbered years, a double majority is needed. A majority of voters must turn out, and a majority must vote in favor. Must be frequently re-approved or funding is eliminated. • Subject to the $10/$1,000 cap on general government property taxes.
Public/Government Grant Programs	• Voter approval is not required. • Wide range of grant programs provides funding for a broad range of projects and activities. • Each source has specific eligibility requirements and approval criteria. Matching projects to appropriate grant sources is not always easy. • Application, project reporting, and grant management requirements can be extensive for some programs. • Usually there are matching requirements.

Table 11.2 (cont.)

Source	Advantages & Limitations
Private Grants and Foundations	• Wide range of foundations provides funding for a broad range of projects and activities. • Requires continued monitoring to keep current with opportunities. • Each source has specific eligibility requirements and approval criteria, and matching projects to appropriate funding sources is not always easy. • Some sources do not provide grants to government agencies. • Highly competitive. • Funds may come with conditions (such as naming a facility).
Public/Private Partnerships	• Can be used to build, fund, or operate a facility. • May permit City to obtain a facility that would otherwise not be possible. • City may have to trade off some control of the project or facility.
Program Fees/Facility Charges	• Unlimited use, although funds are typically reinvested into the program/facility to cover program costs or facility maintenance. • Some programs or facilities can be designed to recover costs, or even to generate a profit. However, these programs are limited. The market should be considered in setting fees, as well as program affordability and accessibility. • Few programs and fee-based facilities (e.g., aquatic centers) generate significant amounts of revenue, and affordability affects the ability to increase fees.
CAPITAL PROJECTS ONLY	
System Development Charges	• Good source of capital improvement funding. • Must be used to fund capacity improvements or new parks, with a nexus to providing service to accommodate new development. • Cannot be used for operations or maintenance funding.
Donations	• Wide flexibility. • Usually must be solicited. • May come with strings or requirements.

SUMMARY

Few decisions made in recreation and parks systems are more long lasting or obvious than those made in the acquisition and development of parks and open space lands. This chapter discussed the relationships between planning and acquiring parks and open space lands. Regulations using ordinances and other legal means such as zoning and land use controls are often standard and predominate means by which to acquire lands. Importantly, the exactions such as fees in-lieu of lands, parkland dedications, and development impact fees are tied to zoning and subdivision regulations. These are often challenged by developers as unfair or increasing costs of development. However, the cost is passed on to the buyer ($200-$1,000 per dwelling unit) who will use the parks and facilities.

Raising money for land purchases and for capital improvements is successful when full collaborations and partnerships exist in a community. It is challenging to raise money over time. However, creating opportunities for organizations such as Trust for Public Land or Rails to Trails present unique opportunities for some communities. Cooperative agreements such as land trusts, leasing, transfer of properties, etc. also rely on collaborations and partnerships. In any case, having strong civic engagement programs enhances these techniques.

Using a variety of methods in a comprehensive manner has proven successful in a number of communities. Of importance to the success of any program is program structure and administration, planning, and having implementing measures for regulatory compliance.

This chapter illustrated the ways in which parks and recreation agencies acquire lands. These tools for land acquisition consist of actions that have granted the locality the authority to exact fees, parkland or other means to secure much needed open space. Also described in this chapter are a variety of methods using agreements, partnerships and transfers. Examples of acquisition programs using a variety of these methods were presented.

DISCUSSION QUESTIONS

1. Why is there a recreational space problem?
2. Why is it becoming difficult to acquire lands, beyond just fiscal resources?
3. How can Rails-to-Trails Conservancy work with your local parks and recreation agency?
4. How can Trust of Public Land work with your local parks and recreation agency?
5. Describe the City of Seattle acquisition program.
6. Compare your community to the City of Seattle program.
7. What are some cooperative and negotiated agreement acquisition examples?
8. Describe and then review and discuss a local recreation master plan acquisition program.
9. What ways can parks and open space lands be acquired?
10. What is a parkland dedication ordinance? What does in-lieu of fees mean?

REFERENCES

American Trails. (n.d.). About American trails. Retrieved from http://www.americantrails.org/mission.html

City of Bellevue. (2010). Bellevue parks and open space system plan. Parks and Community Services. Retrieved from www.bellevuewa.gov/parks-community-services.htm

City of Boulder. (2013). Open Space and Mountain Parks Acquisition Update. Retrieved from 2013-2019_OSMP_Acquisition_Plan_Update, August 1, 2015.

City of Minneapolis. (2014). Parkland dedication ordinance. Retrieved from https://www.municode.com/library/mn/minneapolis/codes/code_of_ordinances?nodeId=PAREBOCOOR_CH15PADE

City of Seattle. (2006). Seattle's Park and Recreation 2006 Development Plan, Retrieved from http://www.seattle.gov/parks/Publications/Development/Plan2006.pd

Crompton, J. L. (1999). *Financing and acquiring park and recreation resources.* Champaign, IL: Human Kinetics.

Duerksen, C., & Snyder, C. (2005). *Nature-friendly communities: Habitat protection and land use planning.* Washington, D.C.: Island Press.

Lankford, S., Lankford, J., & Wheeler, D. (2011). *An introduction to park management.* Urbana, IL: Sagamore.

New Jersey Department of Environmental Protection, Land Acquisitions and Easements: Route 57 Corridor Plan, (2010). Retrieved from http://www.state.nj.us/transportation/works/studies/rt57/pdf/LandAcquisitionandScenicEasements.pdf

Rails to Trails. (2014). About. Retrieved from http://www.railstotrails.org/ourWork/index.html

Scenic America. (2010). Scenic byways. Retrieved from http://www.scenic.org/byways.

Trust for Public Land. (2015). 2015 city park facts. Retrieved from https://www.tpl.org/2015-city-park-facts#sm.001jtpmsd1a0md3z10fhcgtvoewdy

Vaughen, L. P. (2000). Take me to the river. Byways and corridor management plans. *Parks & Recreation, 35*(1), 62–72.

Chapter Twelve

Programming

CHAPTER OBJECTIVES

- To gain an appreciation of the many approaches to community parks and recreation programming
- To understand the connection and differences between programming areas and formats
- To recognize the importance of writing program goals and objectives
- To be able to articulate the role of program evaluation in comprehensive parks and recreation program development
- To gain an understanding of community parks programing and the role of different types of parks that can exist in communities

INTRODUCTION

Programming is central as a primary focus of any parks and recreation department. Crafting well-designed parks and recreation programs that meet a wide array of leisure needs and interests across the lifespan may be the most important goal of any parks and recreation department. Such programs also should address the divergent racial, cultural, and ethnic interests of the community and provide numerous benefits to its members. Play spaces and areas such as parks and playgrounds provide opportunities for individuals to experience casual, spontaneous, leisure interests, or play, whereas more highly developed activities may take place in recreation centers and other facilities that are specifically designed to host highly organized and structured programs. The range and scope of parks and recreation programs are limitless and ever changing, depending on the evolving leisure interests of community members. Therein lies the great challenge as well as opportunity in parks and recreation programming.

Edginton and Chen (2014) have written that the leisure experience can be viewed as existing on a continuum. At one end of the continuum are more casual activities. Community parks and recreation departments provide and promote such casual activities by providing places and spaces that enable individuals to engage in more spontaneous drop-in self-directed types of leisure experience. At the other end of the continuum are more structured types of leisure experiences, wherein individuals may participate in, for example, a program of instruction where specific knowledge and skills are learned. Programming offered by community parks and recreation departments is offered across this continuum in various program formats and content areas.

A cursory review of the work of professionals whose primary responsibility is in the area of recreation programming reveals the multi-dimensional nature of their responsibilities. Figure 12.1 serves as an example of a job description for a recreation superintendent from the City of Pearland (Texas) (July 28-Aug. 9 of 2015). In addition to the management and administrative responsibilities, one can see that "knowledge of comprehensive recreation program development"—programming—is an essential job function.

General Statement of Job:

Manage the recreation division which includes athletics, seniors, programming at Recreation Center and Natatorium, Westside Event Center, adaptive recreation and aquatics. Work with subordinate staff to establish goals for the divisions. Manages divisions and performs duties personally or through subordinate's supervisors.

Essential Functions:

- Hire, train, lead, develop, discipline and supervise full time and part-time staff in Recreation Division and work with staff to develop goals and ensure that they are being met.

- Preparation and administration of budgets in the Recreation Division: develop divisions preliminary budget and administer final budget; recommend revenues and expenditures; and monitor and track expenditures.

- Develop and maintain relations with other recreation providers in the region.

- Maintains close contact with community groups regarding recreation programs and services as well as volunteer and partnership opportunities.

- Determines community needs and works with staff to create programs that fill those needs.

- Develops technical and statistical monthly/quarterly reports and presentations for senior management, Parks & Recreation Board of Directors and City Council.

Knowledge, Skills, and Abilities:

- Ability to read, analyze, and interpret general business periodicals, professional journals, technical procedures, or governmental regulations. Ability to write reports, business correspondence, and procedure manuals; Ability to effectively present information and respond to questions from groups of managers, clients, customers, and the general public.

- Knowledge of the philosophies, principles and practices of public recreation.

- Knowledge of comprehensive recreation program development, promotion and management.

- Knowledge of conceptual foundations of play, recreation and leisure.

- Ability to solve practical problems and deal with a variety of concrete variables in situations where only limited standardization exists. Ability to interpret a variety of instructions furnished in written, oral, diagram, or schedule form.

Figure 12.1. Recreation Superintendent Job Description from the City of Pearland (Texas). *Source:* Retrieved from https://pearland.applicantpro.com/jobs/253008-4700.html

In this chapter, the broader concept of programing for community parks and recreation will be explained, while Chapters 13 and 14 outline programming related to youth and adults and seniors, respectively. The first part of this chapter presents core elements of programming for community parks and recreation: leisure programming approaches, program areas/formats, goals and objectives, program philosophy, physical areas and facilities, and evaluation. The middle part of this chapter provides five examples of different community parks and recreation programming approaches. The last part of this chapter will describe community parks programming.

ESSENTIAL ELEMENTS OF PROGRAMMING

According to Edginton, Hudson, Dieser, and Edginton (2004), leisure programming is a process that enables individuals to experience leisure. These authors explain that "Leisure programs often structure social opportunities between individuals, create physical environments that facilitate leisure, and provide individuals opportunities to enjoy the natural environment. Leisure programs can be vibrant, dynamic, uplifting or they can be passive, relaxing, quiet" (p. 32). Edginton and colleagues states that essential elements of programming in community parks and recreation include leisure programming approaches, program areas/formats, goals and objectives, program philosophy, physical areas and facilities, and evaluation.

Leisure Programming Approaches

Many approaches to leisure programming have been identified, and Table 12.1 presents 34 such approaches. From a historical perspective, Driver (2008a) underscored that theories of leisure programming have moved from activity-based programming of the 1970s (provided activities to people), to experience-based programming of the 1980s (concentrated on providing better leisure experiences that occur behind recreation activities), to benefits-based and outcome-focused programming of the 21st century (focused on the individual and community benefit of leisure services). Parks and recreation professionals should always use programming theories to direct comprehensive recreation program development and later in this chapter five examples will be provided from various community parks and recreation agencies that have integrated theories of programming with theories of leisure.

Program Areas and Formats

Edginton, Hudson, Dieser, and Edginton (2004) articulate that a hallmark feature of leisure programming is the program design elements of areas and formats. Whereas program area is how leisure program activities are categorized or classified (e.g., aquatics, visual arts, sports), program format is the way in which a leisure experience is organized and structured for delivery to the customer (e.g., classes, interest groups, competition). Table 12.2 presents 12 programs areas and eight program formats.

Table 12.1

Leisure Programming Approaches

Programming Approaches	Description	Reference
Traditional approach	Provides services that have been offered in the past, relying on former successes	(Danford & Shirley, 1964)
Current practice approach	Uses current trends to understand program needs	(Danford & Shirley, 1964)
Expressed desires approach	Uses participant information for program development	(Danford & Shirley, 1964)
Authoritarian approach	Professional executives make decisions regarding program design	(Danford & Shirley, 1964)
Reaction plan	Professionals wait and respond to demands generated by participants	(Tillman, 1974)
Investigation plan	Uses fact-finding methods to determine needs	(Tillman, 1974)
Creative plan	Promotes an interactive relationship between the participant and the professional for joint problem solving/sharing	(Tillman, 1974)
Cafeteria approach	Creates menu of services and many program opportunities	(Murphy, 1975)
Prescriptive approach	Professionals diagnose the needs of participants, improving their leisure functioning	(Murphy, 1975)
Trickle-down theory	Bureaucratic activities result in services trickled down through the organization	(Edginton & Hanson, 1976)

Table 12.1 (cont.)

Programming Approaches	Description	Reference
Educated guess theory	Professional hunches are used to plan programs	(Edginton & Hanson, 1976)
Community leadership input theory	Advisory and policy-making boards assist in program planning	(Edginton & Hanson, 1976)
Identification of need theory	Involves analyzing demographic information to determine need	(Edginton & Hanson, 1976)
Offer what people want theory	Involves reflecting "what participants want"; promotes communication and interaction between professionals and participants	(Edginton & Hanson, 1976)
Indigenous development theory	Promotes grassroots program development that uses community resources	(Edginton & Hanson, 1976)
Interactive discovery	Encourages joint problem solving; no subordinate/superior relationship; rather, a process of assisting others without imposing a value system	(Edginton & Hanson, 1976)
Sociopolitical approach	Recognizes the influence of social and political pressures on the program planning process	(Kraus, 1985)
Synergistic approach	Several organizations and agencies working together can offer better leisure experiences to a community or group that can anyone organization or agency working alone	(Carpenter & Howe, 1985)

Table 12.1 (cont.)

Programming Approaches	Description	Reference
Facilitative approach	Views participants as increasingly self-directed in their desires to increase and review their leisure functioning and pursuits	(Carpenter & Howe, 1985)
Consultive/contractual approach	Promotes the hiring of independent contractors and consultants who provide recreation opportunity	(Carpenter & Howe, 1985)
Quality of life or amenity approach	Promotes leisure programs as a way of improving community life	(Kraus, 1990)
Marketing approach	Views programming in an economic context; a commodity to be aggressively promoted	(Kraus, 1990)
Human services approach	Promotes a social ethic, views programs as purpose-ful; links together community health-related programs	(Kraus, 1990)
Prescriptive approach	Sees programming as an instrumental activity; a form of therapy	(Kraus, 1990)
Environmental/aesthetic/ preservationist approach	Views programming as a mechanism to preserve the natural environment and protect historical heritage	(Kraus, 1990)
Hedonistic/individualistic approach	Stresses the pursuit of excitement and pleasure as focus of leisure programs; promotes creative expression	(Kraus, 1990)
Programming by objectives	Establishes use of performance/behavioral objectives to guide program development	(Farrell & Lundegren, 1991)

Table 12.1 (cont.)

Programming Approaches	Description	Reference
Programming by desires of participants	Built on the assumption that participant needs can be identified and linked to program development	(Farrell & Lundegren, 1991)
Programming by perceived needs of participants	Promotes anticipatory planning and understanding the interest of individuals	(Farrell & Lundegren, 1991)
Programming by external requirements	Promotes utilization of normative standards or external criteria (e.g., CARPRA standards)	(Farrell & Lundegren, 1991)
Participant-Centered Programming Planning	Six stage model of pre-design Program planning, goals and Objectives, design elements, Implementation, and evaluation	(Edginton & Edginton, 1994)
Symbolic interaction theory	Focuses on programming the leisure experience and the queuing of objects in social settings	(Rossman, 1995)
Benefits-based programming (BBP)	Focuses on sharply defining the benefits and positive outcomes of leisure service	(Kraus, 1997)
Outcome-focused paragon	Similar to BBP with more science and evidenced based empirical support of benefits where professionals identify benefits but also reference scientific support from academic literature	(Driver, 2008a, 2008b)

Expanded and adapted from Edginton, C. R., Hudson, S. D., & Ford, P. M. (1999). *Leadership for recreation and leisure programs and settings.* Champaign, IL: Sagamore.

Table 12.2

Programs Areas and Formats

Program areas: How leisure program activities are categorized or classified

- Visual arts: Decorative arts including graphic and plastic forms, along with crafts. (e.g., oil paintings, sewing wood carving).
- New arts: Use of 21st century technology (e.g., computer art, electronic music).
- Performing arts (subdivided into drama, dance, and music): Artistic expression in which the individual is the mode of expression (e.g., acting, dancing, barbershop quartets).
- Literary: Emphasize literary, mental, and linguistic activities (e.g., study foreign languages, creative writing, book reviews and discussion).
- Outdoor recreation: Activities that occur in natural or wilderness environments (e.g., camping, hiking, fishing).
- Social recreation: Activities that are created in order to bring about interaction between individuals (e.g., playground party, cooperative games, concert in the park).
- Hobbies: Activities pursued with interest over an extended period of time (e.g., coin or doll collecting, antiques, cooking, gardening).
- Travel and tourism: Movement of persons from their immediate surroundings and places of residence to other locations for the purpose of interacting with the physical and social environment (e.g., car-driving to see nature, trips to different cultural groups)
- Volunteer: Utilizing skills and abilities during free time for the purpose of giving to others (e.g., coaching, meals-on-wheels, interpreter at historical societies).
- Wellness: Physical fitness activities and programs related to health behaviors (e.g., physical fitness, smoking cessation, stress management, leisure education).
- Aquatics: Activities that take place in an around both natural and artificial water areas (e.g., swimming, water aerobics, scuba diving).
- Sports, games, and athletics: Any physiological activity that requires gross and fine motor muscle control may be categorized with this cluster (e.g., golf, rifle shooting, softball).

Program format: The way in which a leisure experience is organized and structured for delivery to the customer.

- Classes: highly structured teaching and learning situation (e.g., finger painting, hockey skills).
- Competition: Involves the act of a person or persons competing with one another in some form of a contest or match, or against a standard (e.g., annual open tennis or racket-ball tournament).
- Club: A group of people organized for some particular purpose (e.g., cooking, rugby, quilting group).
- Drop-in or rental: Do not have to follow a particular schedule and need very little supervision or no leadership (e.g., open gymnasium time, rental of a facility for large family reunion).

Table 12.2 (cont.)

- Special events: An unusual activity (e.g., puppet show in a park, Spanish night at a recreation center).
- Outreach: Expand and extend services to a broader segment of society (e.g., home-based activities for people who cannot leave their home due to health and medical conditions).
- Interest group: A collection of individuals that has formed around an activity, issue, or program aim. Similar to a club but with less structure (e.g., environmental or astronomy youth group).
- Workshop/conference: Intense content conducted over a relatively short period of time (e.g., cultural arts conference).

Source: Edginton et al. (2004)

It is important to note that although each program area and format is explained separately, each of these program areas or formats can overlap (dance, for example, can simultaneously be a performing art program area, wellness program area, and social recreation program area). Furthermore, within each program area the list of recreation activities can be vast. Edginton and colleagues list over 70 types of drama activities (e.g., charades, clowning, film making, improvisation theater, magic tricks, mobile theater, musical comedy, puppetry, and storytelling) and over 35 types dance programs (e.g., aerobic, ballroom, clog, ethnic, folk, jazz, rap, rock-and-roll, square, and tap).

A program area, and the resulting leisure experience, can be vastly different depending on format delivery. Edginton and colleagues, for example, explain that sports (program area) differs in experience when delivered as a class (beginning golf class), competition (softball tournament), club (soccer club), drop in (tennis courts) special event (5K run), outreach (roller blade mobile), workshop/conference (workshop for volunteer youth coaches), and interest group (sport boosters). Furthermore, there can be overlap between differing program formats. Figure 12.2, which presents the 10th annual Bucktown Apple Pie contest that occurs at Holstein Park (Chicago Park District), supported by the Friends of Holstein Park as a fund-raising event toward improving Holstein Park (see http://friendsofholsteinpark.com/about/), combines a friendly competition format with a special event and club formatting. Readers are encouraged to see the program matrix of program areas and formats from the academic labor of Edginton, Hudson, Dieser, and Edginton (2004, p. 302–303) for a more in-depth understanding of how program area can be a completely different leisure experience based on format provisions.

Goals and Objectives

Comprehensive recreation program development begins with the articulation of program goals and objectives. Goals are general or broad statements of intent, and objectives are specific outcomes that are measurable (Edginton et al., 2004). Although different authors (e.g., Russell & Jamieson, 2008) use different terminology to explain how to write objectives, in essence, objectives usually contain three components. First, well-written objectives identify a behavior. Second, the condition or conditions under which the behavior will take place—sometimes known as the restrictions—are identified. Third, the criteria of a successful performance—the minimum standard of correctness—are identified.

Figure 12.2. 10th Annual Bucktown Apple Pie Contest at Holstein Park (Chicago Park District). *Source:* Bucktown Apple Pie Contest/Friends of Holstein Park (Chicago). Retrieved from http://www.bucktownapplepiecontest.com/

Objectives, the specific outcomes that are measured or learned, can be written within a cognitive domain (e.g., knowledge of the rules to basketball), psychomotor domain (e.g., developing basketball skills), or affective domain (e.g., valuing the concept of sportsmanship). If the goal of a swimming program is to develop swimming skills (broad statement of intent), a measurable objective to develop this goal, within the psychomotor domain, could be "After two weeks of lessons (condition), the participant will swim the backstroke (behavior) one length of the pool as judged appropriately by the swim instructor (criteria)." In this example, the length of time involved in swimming lessons serves as the restrictions (condition), the backstroke serves as the action or behavior and performing the backstroke the length of the pool, based on professional observation as evaluation, serves as the minimum standard or criteria of correctness. If the goal of a parks and recreation youth bowling club is to develop bowling skills, a measurable objective to develop this goal, within the cognitive domain, could be "Upon request and within five minutes (condition), the participant will demonstrate knowledge of common bowling courtesies (behavior) by verbally stating five of the following seven courtesies (criteria); (the seven courtesies include [1] when two bowlers are ready to bowl at the same time, the bowler on the right goes first, [2] take turn immediately, [3] wait for ball near the return rack, [4] respect foul line, [5] do not use powder on shoes, [6] refrain from conversation with bowlers preparing to deliver the ball, and [7] refrain from commenting on the other bowlers' style). In regard to a goal of historical restoration of an older park band structure, a measurable objective could be "Within two years (condition) to accurately restore the interior and the exterior of the band shelter (behavior) to its original condition (criteria) utilizing accepted industry restoration conventions, standards, and practices."

Programming Philosophy

According to Edginton et al. (2004) leisure programming should also be based on a programming philosophy that acknowledges a basic set of beliefs and values and identifies leisure programming approaches that will be utilized (see Table 12.1). These beliefs are shaped into tenets that guide the development of a philosophy. In turn, the adoption of a set of tenets will influence the operational methods selected by the professional to create and distribute leisure services. Edginton and colleagues posit nine tenets of a philosophy of programming: (1) every customer has a right to pursue recreation and leisure in a manner that relates to individual needs; (2) leisure programmers should have an understanding of the needs and expectations of customers; (3) programming should offer a full spectrum of activities, (4) leisure is freedom to explore and express oneself,; (5) all individuals should have an equal opportunity to pursue leisure; (6) inherent in the leisure experience is the pursuit of happiness; (7) leisure programs should be safe, accessible, affordable, and pleasing; (8) customers should be viewed holistically and not as a commodity to be quantified; and (9) every customer has a right be treated in a dignified manner with full respect to diversity (e.g. gender, sexual orientation, religion, ability). The City of Riverside (California) Parks, Recreation and Community Services youth sports philosophy statement has following tenets: (1) work hard at sport, (2) play fair, (3) win or lose with dignity, and (4) give something back to communities (http://www.riversideca.gov/park_rec/pdf/Youth-Sports-Philosophy.pdf).

Physical Areas and Facilities

According to Edginton et al. (2004), part of leisure programming is to ensure physical areas and facilities align to leisure programs and services: "The location, the design, the availability, and the accessibility of any facility is what contributes to its usability for both structured and spontaneous participation in leisure activities" (p. 191). Physical areas and facilities can include everything from an open space, ballfields, golf course, to the recreation center or swimming pool building, to park structures, such as a band shelter, playground, or lake.

According to Harper (2009), program planning should consist of a facility inventory that periodically analyzes the supply and suitability of physical areas and facilities. Harper posits that facility inventory should consist of the following nine steps: (1) physical description (e.g., overall depiction of site, including components and features); (2) current use, users, and use of facilities (e.g., note unmet facility requirements); (3) long-term potential for use (e.g., trends analysis linked to facilities); (4) service radius/reach (e.g., consumer proximity to physical areas and facilities); (5) qualitative analysis of areas and facilities (e.g., examination of physical deteriorating facilities); (6) classification systems (e.g., assessment of level of play or activity); (7) condition assessment (e.g., life expectancy of various facilities), (8) potential for expansion (e.g., open space next to golf course that can be turned into a planetarium), and (9) capacity (e.g., the number of users that can effectively be accommodated in a given space). Farrell and Lundegren (1991) remind us that parks and recreation programmers can use their imagination and brainstorm how a specific physical area or facilities can be used for different leisure activities. They posit that a golf course, for example, can also be used for cross-country running or skiing, Frisbee, arboretum, sledding/tobogganing, orienteering, bird watching, summer concerts, or stargazing, and a site for a planetarium.

Program Evaluation

Evaluation is judging the worth of programs and services on the basis of an analysis of systematically collected evidence (Rossman & Schlatter, 2015). Whereas quantitative evaluation is based on collecting and using numerical calculations or statistics (e.g., using a survey where participants can only answer by circling a number response) qualitative evaluation refer to the use of words for data collection and result in patterns ascertained through analyses (e.g., interviewing or observing participants involved in a parks and recreation program (Edginton et al., 2004). Mixed-method evaluation consists of both quantitative and qualitative data, such as a survey in which the first part consisting of circling a number response but the latter part consisting of open-ended questions where participants can answer by writing in a holistic and narrative fashion. Whereas formative evaluation is a method for evaluating while the program activities are in progress or occurring, summative evaluation is a method of evaluating a program at the end of the program activities (Edginton et al., 2004).

EXAMPLES OF PROGRAM APPROACHES

As already noted in this chapter, Table 12.1 outlines 34 different programming approaches used in community parks and recreation. The section below provides five different programming approaches used in various community parks and recreation agencies.

Benefits-Based Programming/Outcomes-Focused Paragon at the Columbia (Missouri) Parks and Recreation

Benefits-based programming focuses on sharply defining the benefits and positive outcomes of leisure services (Kraus, 1997). Rossman and Schlatter (2015) outlined a four component benefits-based programming model, which include (1) target issues: focusing on social issues and problems (e.g., youth at risk, poverty); (2) activity components: writing goals and objectives, identifying activities to achieve goals and objectives, processing activities with recreation participants, and monitoring the achievement of objectives; (3) benefits outcome: summarizing the achievement of target goals; and (4) benefits-based awareness: communicating the successes (outcomes) to the general public, funding sources, and stakeholders. Driver (2008a, 2008b) summarized that benefits-based programming has evolved into a outcome-focused paragon that provides scientific documentation of the benefits of parks and recreation services and should be viewed as a science-based approach to leisure service delivery. Communication methods, to articulate the beneficial outcomes of leisure, can include news releases, social media promotion, annual reports, website pages, and so forth. Figure 12.3, from the City of Columbia (Missouri) Parks and Recreation (see http://www.gocolumbiamo.com/ParksandRec/About_Us/benefits.php#Aquatics%20-%20Senior%20Benefits) shows benefits-based awareness and outcome-focused statements/links of how this agency is communicating the many benefits of parks and recreation. That is to say, the City of Columbia (Missouri) Parks and Recreation website aligns with the outcomes-focused paragon by proving links that lead viewers to science- and evidenced-based empirical support of the benefits of leisure from the academic literature (e.g., expert opinion, a nationwide study conducted at Pennsylvania State University regarding the benefits of local recreation and park service).

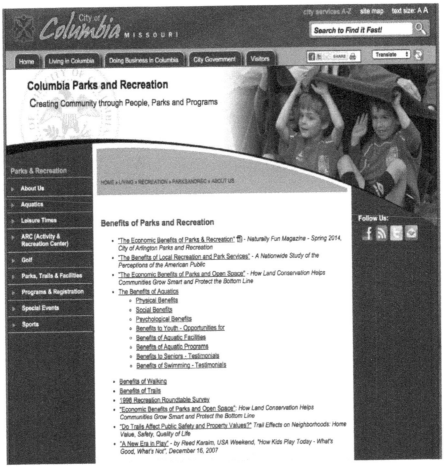

Figure 12.3. City of Columbia, Missouri, Benefits of Parks and Recreation. *Source:* Retrieved from http://www.gocolumbiamo.com/ParksandRec/About_Us/benefits.php#Aquatics%20-%20Senior%20Benefits

Cafeteria Programming at the Montpelier (Vermont) Recreation Department

Cafeteria programming designs a menu or smorgasbord of recreation activities or program opportunities (Murphy, 1975) usually based on the concept that people can choose. Figure 12.4, from the Montpelier (Vermont) Recreation Department 2017 spring and summer brochure, provides a menu or listing of adult recreation activities and programs.

SPRING AND SUMMER ADULT PROGRAMS

TAE KWON DO 4527B
This is an instructional class for those interested in learning the art of Tae Kwon Do. Parents who participate in class with their child will get a discount of 50% off.

WHO: Ages 7 to adult.
WHEN: Mondays and Thursdays
DATES: March 13 – May 25
Skip 4/17 and 4/20
TIME: 4527-B   9 years – adults
6:30 p.m.-7:30 p.m.   Mondays Small gym
Thursdays Large gym
WHERE: Union Elementary School
FEE: Residents Child: $70.00 Adult: $35.00
Non-Residents Child: $100.00 Adult: $50.00
INSTRUCTOR: Matthew Girouard- Black Belt in TKD
Minimum: 10 Maximum 20
All participants must purchase AAU insurance through TKD instructor at the cost of $14.00 per year. This will allow participant to partake in additional TKD competitive events. An additional $35.00 will be charged for TKD uniform.

HIIT KICK
HITT Kick is a high intensity interval training inspired in Tae Kwon Do and Kickboxing combat training. 50 minutes of hitting targets, kicking, punching, pylometrics and floor exercises. Release stress, get fit, be stronger and happier! This class is fast paced and advanced but all levels are welcome.

SESSION 1: 12 CLASSES 4528A
WHO: Adults 18+
DATES: March 9 – April 27
Skip April 6, 18, 20
WHEN: Tuesdays and Thursdays
WHERE: Union Elementary School Small Gym
TIME: Tuesdays 5:15 pm – 6:15 pm
Thursdays 5:30 pm – 6:30 pm
FEE: Resident: $72.00 Non-Resident: $108.00
WALK-INS: Resident: $9.00 Non-Resident: $12.00

SESSION 2: 14 CLASSES 4528B
WHO: Adults 18+
DATES: May 2 – June 15
WHEN: Tuesdays and Thursdays
WHERE: Union Elementary School Small Gym
TIME: Tuesdays 5:15 pm – 6:15 pm
Thursdays 5:30 pm – 6:30 pm
FEE: Resident:$84.00 Non-Resident: $126.00
WALK-INS: Resident: $9.00 Non-Resident: $12.00

FITNESS HOOPING
De Stress and get fit after the holidays and try a new Fitness Class with Carol Becker, Physical Therapist and a Certified Body Hoop instructor. Carol uses large 2 lb "Hula" Hoops for a fun, rejuvenating, Head-to-Toe work out.
If you don't think that you can "Hula" hoop, don't worry. Carol will teach you.
Check it out at www.fitnesshooping.com

FITNESS HOOPING
SPRING SESSION – 4514A
WHO: Adults Men and Women
WHEN: Thursday Evenings
DATES: March 9, 16, 23, 30, April 6, 13
TIME: 7:00 pm – 8:00 pm
WHERE: Montpelier Recreation Department
FEE: Resident: $60.00 Non- Resident: $90.00
Min. 5 Participants

ZUMBA
A total work out combining all elements of fitness – cardio, muscle conditioning, balance and flexibility. Zumba is for all ages from teen and beyond and for all levels.
INSTRUCTORS: Bobbyjo Dyer & Mary Bowser – Experience and energetic Zumba instructors.

SPRING ZUMBA SESSION 4531A
WHO: Adults Men and Women Age 16 and up
WHEN: Wednesday Evenings
DATES: March 8 – April 12
TIME: 5:30 pm – 6:30 pm
WHERE: Union Elementary School Small Gym
FEE: Resident: $18.00 Non- Resident: $27.00
Walkins Welcome Resident: $5 Non-Resident: $7.50
Minimum: 2 Participants Maximum: 15 Participants

ADULT DRAWING CLASSES-
BEGINNERS TO ADVANCED 4409A
Drawing class will consist of learning various drawing techniques – gesture drawing, contour line drawing, etc. Value studies will be developed through the use of a number of shading techniques. Perspective drawings will also be incorporated in the work. The works of the masters will be used during class. Still life objects will be brought in for our drawing studies. Bring in any photographs or drawings to class. Beginners to advance.
MATERIALS LIST:
Drawing Pad: medium 14"x17" suitable for pencil, ink, charcoal, wet medium
Drawing Pencils: 6B, 2B, H, 2H and 6H
Eraser: Kneaded eraser and a hard eraser
Ruler
WHEN: Wednesday evenings
TIME: 6:30 – 8:30
DATES: March 8 – April 12
WHERE: Union School Art Room
FEE: Resident: $95.00 for six sessions
Non-Resident: $135.00 for six sessions
INSTRUCTOR: Terry Hodgdon - Art Teacher for thirty-three years
Minimum: 4 Maximum: 10

DISCOVER THE JOY OF
BALLROOM DANCING
6 Week dance Sessions with Dance Instructors Samir & Eleni Elabd.
WALTZ & FOXTROT 4535A
WHEN: Tuesday evenings
TIME: 6:00 – 7:00
DATES: April 25 – May 30
WHERE: Union School
FEE: Residents: 72.00 per Person, 135.00 per couple
Non-Residents: 85.00 per person,162.00 per couple
MINIMUM: 16 MAXIMUM: 32

RUMBA & SWING 4535B
WHEN: Tuesday evenings
TIME: 7:00 – 8:00
DATES: April 25 – May 30
WHERE: Union School
FEE: Residents: 72.00 per Person, 135.00 per couple
Non-Residents: 85.00 per person,162.00 per couple
MINIMUM: 16 MAXIMUM: 32

Figure 12.4. Montpelier (Vermont) Recreation Department 2017 spring and summer brochure *Source:* Montpelier (Vermont) Recreation Department. *Source:* Retrieved from http://www.montpelierrec.org/DocumentCenter/Home/View/3686

SPRING AND SUMMER ADULT PROGRAMS

DRAWING FOR THE TERRIFIED 4410A

These classes are for beginners as well as those with some drawing experience who feel they might benefit from more instruction. They are based on the premise that drawing can be an acquired skill, not just a talent, and that most can learn how to draw if they spend the time and energy needed. Since drawing is foundational for representational painting, those who paint in watercolor and oil can also profit by taking these classes. Some of the topics to be covered are: Drawing to Learn, Materials used in drawing, Learning to see, Learning about graphite, charcoal and inks, Perspective, Creating 3D Volume on a 2D page, Defining form with light and Composition. The classes are a collaborative learning experience and will include individual assistance from the instructor, as well as class critiques. Come prepared to draw, share your work and have a good time!

WHO: Adults
WHEN: Tuesday Evenings
TIME: 5:30pm-8:00pm
DATES: May 2, 9, 16 & 23.
WHERE: T. W. Wood Gallery, 46 Barre St Montpelier
FEE: $130.00
INSTRUCTOR: Michael Strauss UVM Professor emeritus and author Michael Strauss began his artistic life drawing the crystals, shells, plants and insects he collected from around his home and from the landscape he explored along the coast and in the Sierras. Michael continues to draw, paint and take photographs of the things that interest him most, the people and places here in Vermont and in his travels around the world. His artwork has been exhibited across Vermont. mjstruass.com

ADULT PICKLEBALL 2508-A

A cross between badminton, tennis and ping-pong. Pickleball is a fast growing sport
that is perfect for all ages! Join the fun in Montpelier!

WHO: Men & Women Adults
WHEN: Monday 9:00 – 11:30am & 1:15-3:00pm
Tuesday 1:15-3:00pm
Wednesday 1:15 -3:00pm
Thursday 9:00-11:30am & 1:15 -3pm
Friday 9:00-11:30
DATES: Until Friday May 5th, 2016
WHERE: Montpelier Recreation Department Gym
DAILY FEE: Residents: $2.00 Non-Residents: $3.00

SPRING YOGA 4430A

WHO: Adults Men and Women Age 16 and up
WHEN: Tuesday Evenings
DATES: March 28 – June 6 (Skip April 18th)
TIME: 6:30 pm – 8 pm
WHERE: Union Elementary School Small Gym
FEE: Resident: $90.00 Non- Resident: $130.00
Minimum: 9 Participants Maximum: 16 Participants

SUMMER TAE KWON DO 1506B

Beginners are welcome and encouraged to join these classes. This is a class for people who want to learn the art of Tae Kwon Do. This will be an instructional class.

WHO: Youth and Adult
WHEN: Mondays and Thursdays
DATES: June 1 – June29
TIME: **1506-B** 9 years – adults
6:30 p.m.-7:30 p.m.-
WHERE: Union Elementary Gym & Montpelier Recreation Department (Switch once school ends)
FEE: Residents Child: $31.50   Adult: $16.00
Non-Residents Child: $48.00 Adult: $22.50
INSTRUCTOR: Matthew Girouard- Black Belt in TKD
Minimum: 10 Maximum: 20
All participants must purchase AAU insurance through TKD instructor at the cost of $14.00 per year. This will allow participant to partake in additional TKD competitive events. An additional $35.00 will be charged for TKD uniform.

SPRING AND SUMMER ADULT TENNIS LESSONS

VERMONT TENNIS ACADEMY – ADULT LESSONS

DIRECTOR: Scott Barker
The Vermont Tennis Academy is designed to help beginners to advanced players reach their maximum potential in a very short period of time. The Academy offers low and high performance tennis training for all ages and abilities. Scott's experience as a tennis professional includes teaching beginners, intermediates, and advanced players as well as high school, college, and professional level players. Scott has won over 60 combined singles and doubles tournaments and has worked with former world champions: John McEnroe, Jimmy Conners, Bjorn Borg and Stan Smith.

* All participants will be divided into groups by age and skill level.
* The Academy offers match play statistics, ball speed clinics, as well as match strategy.
*Absolutely all participants MUST be registered before arriving to lessons or camps. Participants that are not registered at the time will not be permitted to participate and will be excused from tennis. There are no exceptions. This is for each participant's safety and well-being. Registration are accepted at the Montpelier Recreation Department. No registrations are collected at the courts.

ADULT TENNIS LESSONS

Activity #	Dates	When	Time - 1 hour lesson	Age Groups	Resident Fee	Non-Resident Fee
2333-A	April 27 - May 18	Thursdays	5:00 pm - 6:00 pm	Adults	$50.00	$75.00
2333-B	May 25 1- June 15	Thursdays	5:00 pm - 6:00 pm	Adults	$50.00	$75.00
1333-A	June 22 - July 13	Thursdays	5:00 pm - 6:00 pm	Adults	$50.00	$75.00
1333-B	July 20 - August 10	Thursdays	5:00 pm - 6:00 pm	Adults	$50.00	$75.00
1333-C	August 17 - Sept. 7	Thursdays	5:00 pm - 6:00 pm	Adults	$50.00	$75.00

Figure 12.4. (cont.)

Human Services and Synergistic Approach at Seattle (Washington) Parks and Recreation

The human services approach to leisure programming promotes a social ethic and views programs as purposefully linked to community and health-related programs (Kraus, 1990). The synergistic approach to leisure programming occurs when several organizations work together to offer better leisure experiences to the community than if any one organization worked alone (Carpenter & Howe, 1985). The Seattle (Washington) Parks and Recreation Good Food program provides access to healthy food, opportunities for active recreation, and environmental awareness and supports the Parks' strategic plan of Healthy Parks, Healthy You, and Race and Social Justice Initiatives. Partnering with 18 nonprofit and governmental organizations, Seattle Parks and Recreation has dedicated one million square feet of parkland to growing food via its 12 community gardens, 3 urban farms, 30 p-patch gardens and 8 park orchards. Furthermore, this program offers low-cost educational opportunities to people who are poor so that they can grow, cook, and eat nutritious foods grown in local parks. The Good Food program produced 18,000 pounds of food that were donated to food banks (see http://www.seattle.gov/parks/goodfood/ and http://www.seattle.gov/parks/environment/OurCity.htm). The overall goals and priorities of this leisure program are to provide (1) access to healthy food and active recreation opportunities, (2) community stewardship of parkland used for food production, (3) coordinated recreation and learning opportunities focused on the Urban Food System, and (4) outreach and engagement of youth, seniors, and underserved communities (http://www.seattle.gov/parks/goodfood/).

Traditional Approach at Pawtucket (Rhode Island) Parks and Recreation

The traditional approach to programming provides a leisure experiences that have been offered in the past, thus relying on former successes (Danford & Shirley, 1964). Due to the fact that the Pawtucket (Rhode Island) Parks and Recreation Department annual Halloween Festival in Slater Park is scheduled for Friday and Saturday nights through the month of October (see Figure 12.5) year after year, it follows a traditional approach to leisure programming.

Programming by Desires of Participants at Seattle (Washington) Parks and Recreation

In 2015, an estimated 5.3 million Americans of all ages had Alzheimer's disease, with an estimated 5.1 million people aged 65 or older (Alzheimer's Association, 2015 see http://www.alz.org/facts/#quickFacts). To offer leisure programs for people with dementia,[1] in the summer of 2015, Seattle (Washington) Parks and Recreation partnered with Greenwood Senior Center, the Alzheimer's Association, Aegis on Madison, Elderwise and Outdoors for All, to offer a variety of "dementia-friendly" recreation programs, such as fitness classes, watercolor painting, snowshoe hiking, walking group, and opportunities to volunteer at the food bank. What makes this program align to the theory of programming by desires of participants is that the planning process consisted of people with dementia being actively involved in identifying meaningful leisure that Seattle (Washington) Parks and Recreation transformed into leisure programming programs.

PROGRAMMING IN COMMUNITY PARKS

Just as leisure programming is a process that enables individuals to experience leisure, park programming also enables individuals to experience leisure, recreation, and play in community park settings. Jones and Wills's (2005) historical research on the invention of city parks locates King Sennacherib, who assumed the Assyrian throne in 705 BC, as one of

---

[1] According to the American Psychiatric Association (2013) Alzheimer's disease is a type of dementia. In Chapter 16 of this book, it is classified as a medical disability.

HALLOWEEN FESTIVAL IN SLATER PARK

Fright Night in the Park offers a variety of
activities for children of all ages on Friday & Saturday
nights in October at Slater Memorial Park
**** Because these events are outdoor, times of operation are tentative
based upon weather conditions See Facebook's "Slater Park Haunted
Tunnel" for the most up-to-date information**

For the older ones -
**<u>not recommended for children 12 years or younger</u>

THE HAUNTED TUNNEL at DAGGETT FARM

The Haunted Tunnel is not to be missed an
surely not for the "faint of heart!"
Visit the
Slater Park Haunted Tunnel
Facebook Page & the *Haunted
Tunnel at Daggett Farm* as seen on YouTube f
an interactive tour.
Open: 6:30 to 8:30 p.m.   Cost: $8.0(
Where: Daggett Farm in Slater Park

For the YOUNGER ones...
PUMPKINS IN THE PARK

OPEN: 6:30 to 9:00 p.m.
Cost $4 Preschool = free
Across from the Carousel under the
"NEW" Slater Park
Pavilion
Carousel will also be open until 8 pm
during these events

*Figure 12.5.*Pawtucket (Rhode Island) Parks and Recreation Department Halloween Festival in Slater Park. *Source:* Retrieved from http://www.pawtucketlibrary.org/2015-FallPrograms.pdf

the first rulers who created parks when he constructed the city of Nineveh (the capital city of a vast empire from Palestine to Asia Minor). Jones and Wills explain how the Greek and Roman empires also created city parks for practicing athletes and strolling philosopher, as such, community parks were used as an exercise yard and debate society, respectfully. These historians located Frederick Law Olmsted's creation of Central Park in New York during the 1850s and 1860s as the "applicability of the park idea to New World shores" (p. 47).

In the contemporary era, LaPage (2007) provided a programming structure of the different types of leisure behaviors and activities that can occur in city parks, or in different areas of a larger community park. A park that is basically a small neighborhood tot lot and open space provides differing leisure opportunities than a large park that offers multiple structures, such as tennis and basketball courts, large playground structures, area for disc/

Frisbee golf, biking and walking trails, bird observation area, and a lake for boating and fishing. Parks and recreation agencies need to think deeply about the types of leisure activities that could and should occur in city parks before construction and LaPage's programming framework provides this type of professional reflection. According to LaPage there are eight ethical and societal reasons for community parks:

- **Promote peace, inspiration, meaning-making, and solitude:** A park with open space and spaced-out benches, with few physical structures and beautiful landscaping can help people leave a crowded and fast-paced world in order to have solitude and reflect about life (a form of classical leisure).
- **Encourage health:** A park with multiple structures that allow physical movement, such as jogging and biking trails, tennis and basketball courts, and soccer pitches can be places of cardiovascular health. Likewise, community parks that also provide outdoor fitness equipment in the parks (e.g., outdoor elliptical structure) also encourage healthy exercise in park settings.
- **Classroom of learning:** Urban park rangers have used the natural environment and different ecosystems in community parks to teach youth about nature.
- **Allow social justice and hope:** Parks can be used for city and national demonstrations to change social policy. As explained in Chapter 3 of this book, parks can be a place to help people who are homeless, thus instilling a sense of hope.
- **Stimulate economic engines:** Large parks are economic engines for cities as places for large festivals or part of a broader tourism strategic plan.
- **Historical markers of a community:** Parks can be powerful reminders of local, state, and national history.
- **Create cultural and community identity:** Parks can be cultural and community gathering spaces that highlight community identity and solidarity.
- **Nature-based and environmental responsibility:** Parks can help people realize they are part of a large ecology and understand their broader responsibility to flora and fauna.

Beyond this list, parks can also be created for animals, such as dog parks.

To outline the programming structure of the different types of leisure behaviors and activities that can occur in different types of community parks, two examples are featured next. Vinyard Park, located in Freehold Borough (New Jersey) is a small park that is a historical marker of community that simultaneously promotes inspiration and solitude. Figure 12.6 explains the historical background of Vinyard Park that has links to the American singer-songwriter Bruce Springsteen and two past youth mentors who helped him become a modern-day celebrity. Figure 12.7 shows a picture of this smaller neighborhood park. Figure 12.8 present Millennium Park in Chicago, which was specifically designed to be an economic engine as part of city council-driven ambiguous tourism strategy to make Chicago a hot international travel destination (Bennett, 2010; Gilfoyle, 2006). It covers 25 acres, and this enormous park offers a wide array of leisure activities, such as the Jay Pritzker Pavilion (bandshell with a capacity to hold 11,000 people), Cloud Gate (public sculpture made up of 168 stainless steel plates welded and measures 33 by 66 by 42 feet and weighs 110 tons), Crown Fountain (interactive public art and video sculpture, which cost $17 million, is 50 feet tall and provides digital videos), the Lurie Garden (2.4-acre garden that has a $10 million endowment maintenance and upkeep), and various other attractions.

Bruce Springsteen is arguably one of American's greatest singer-songwriters. He has sold over 120 million albums worldwide and has earned, among other honors, 20 Grammy awards, two Golden Globes, and an Oscar. In 1999, he was inducted into the Rock n Roll Hall of Fame, and in 2009 performed at the inauguration of Barack Obama as the 44th president. In the mid-1960s, when Bruce Springsteen was a teenager, he and a group of friends from Freehold (NJ), formed the band, The Castiles. It was at this time that Gordon "Tex" and Marion Vinyard opened their house and hearts to a group of "misfits" and began youth mentoring. Tex and Marion Vinyard created a community of belonging to a group of youth that many people thought were irrelevant and problematic. Tex began acting as the Castiles volunteer manager—a youth rock n roll scout leader—and found them shows in the community. Tex and Marion, who had no children of their own, changed their modest home into an informal music school; a "safe haven" for young musicians to hang out (keeping them off the streets) in order to practice their craft in a community of creative discovery with nurturing support from the Vinyards. The downstairs of their home had been turned into a rock band rehearsal studio with amps and drums set up in their living room with Marion preparing food for band members. On May 18, 2002, Vinyard Park was dedicated in the Freehold Borough to Marion and her late husband, Tex. The park was built on the site of the Vinyards' old house at 39 Center Street. Following the unveiling of Vinyard Park, the event moved into the new YMCA of Western Monmouth County with a special focus on the teen center with an implicit focus on how parks and recreation can contribute to youth development. At this ceremony, Springsteen recalled how "Tex was . . . someone who opened his house completely, opened his heart completely, opened his wallet to us . . . and allowed us to come in and turn it up as loud as we wanted." Vinyard Park is a small neighborhood park that has a dozen benches with a wonderful tree line providing shade for solitude and quite reflection, along with a small playground. It serves as a historical reminder how two everyday people, Tex and Marion Vinyard, made a huge difference in their community by creating community and belonging for a group of "misfits." Vinyard Park is a place for inspiration, solitude, and hope, as its literal geographical history tells a story of community and belonging and its present day use simultaneously creates community and belonging, along with solitude and inspiration.

Figure 12.6. Historical Overview of Vinyard Park Freehold Borough (New Jersey).
Source: Dieser (2015)

Figure 12.7. Vinyard Park, Freehold Borough, New Jersey. *Photo taken by author Rodney B. Dieser*

SUMMARY

Programming for community parks and recreation is a complex process that consists of many paramount elements. Parks and recreation programmers should have knowledge of the conceptual foundations of play, recreation, and leisure, along with knowledge related to programming approaches, program areas/formats, goals and objectives, program philosophy, physical areas and facilities, and evaluation. Parks and recreation programmers should also have an understanding of the eight ethical and societal reasons for community parks and how different park designs have a direct influence on the types of leisure behaviors and activities that can occur in city parks. The purpose of this chapter was to explain the broader concept of programing for community parks and recreation while the next two chapters outline programming related to youth and adults and seniors, respectfully.

Figure 12.8. Millennium Park in Chicago. *Source: Reiss 2014*

DISCUSSION QUESTIONS

1. Explain the difference between program areas and program format. Further, explain how a program area, and the resulting leisure experience, can be vastly different depending on format delivery.
2. Write a program goal and two measurable objectives related to a community parks and recreation area that you have an interest in future employment.

3. Describe how Columbia (Missouri) Parks and Recreation used benefits-based programming/outcomes-focused paragon and was able to communicate the benefits/outcomes of parks and recreation to various stakeholders in the community.

4. Describe how Seattle (Washington) Parks and Recreation Good Foods program integrated the human services approach to leisure programming and the synergistic approach.

5. Examine your own community and identify the different types of programming of community parks. For example, are there any parks that promote inspiration, meaning-making, and solitude? Are there parks that stimulate economic engines or are classrooms of learning?

6. In the last five years, there have been a number of "Occupy Wall Street" demonstrations throughout the United States, and many have occurred in community parks. Should parks be places that allow social justice and community protests? Defend your answer.

7. Examine the 34 approaches of leisure programming in Table 12.1 and list the top three approaches that resonate with you. Explain why these three approaches are relevant to you.

8. Do you think smaller parks, such as the example of Vinyard Park in this chapter, are important to have in communities? If you were going to use the benefits-based programming/outcomes-focused paragon approach to leisure programming, how might you articulate the beneficial aspects of a community space for inspiration, solitude, personal and historical reflection, inspiration, and hope?

9. Describe the difference between quantitative and qualitative program evaluation and the strengths and weaknesses of each evaluative approach.

10. In regard to using your imagination to brainstorm how a specific physical area or facility can be used for different leisure activities, brainstorm different types of leisure activities that could occur on a program area/facility that consists of five official size outdoor tennis courts (what other activities could be done on these tennis courts beyond tennis?).

REFERENCES

Bennett, L. (2010). *The third city: Chicago and American urbanism*. Chicago, IL: University of Chicago Press.

Carpenter, G., & Howe, C. Z. (1985). *Programming leisure experiences*. Englewood Cliffs, NJ: Prentice Hall.

Danford, H., & Shirley, M. (1964). *Creative leadership in recreation*. Boston, MA: Allyn and Bacon.

Dieser, R. B. (2015). Music and the power of community: Celebrating the 40th anniversary of Bruce Springsteen's "Born to Run," Gordon "Tex" and Marion Vinyard, and Vinyard park. *Parks & Recreation, 50*(8), 52–53.

Driver, B. L. (2008a). What is outcome-focused management? In B. L. Driver (Ed.), *Managing to optimize the beneficial outcomes of recreation* (pp. 19–37). State College, PA: Venture.

Driver, B. L. (2008b). Why outcome-focused management is needed. In B. L. Driver (Ed.), *Managing to optimize the beneficial outcomes of recreation* (pp. 1–17). State College, PA: Venture.

Edginton, C. R., & Chen, P. (2014). *Leisure as transformation*. Urbana, IL: Sagamore.

Edginton, C. R., DeGraaf, D. G., R., Dieser, R. B., & Edginton, S. R. (2006). *Leisure and life satisfaction: Foundational perspectives* (4th ed.). Boston, MA: WCB McGraw-Hill.

Edginton, C. R., & Hanson, C. J. (1976). Appraising leisure service delivery. *Parks & Recreation, 11*(3), 44–45.

Edginton, C. R., Hudson, S. R., Dieser, R. B., & Edginton, S. R. (2004). *Leisure programming: A service-centered and benefits approach* (4th ed). Boston, MA: WCB McGraw-Hill.

Edginton, C. R., Hudson, S. D., & Ford, P. M. (1999). *Leadership for recreation and leisure programs and settings.* Champaign, IL: Sagamore.

Edginton, S. R., & Edginton, C. R. (1994). *Youth programs: Promoting quality services.* Urbana, IL: Sagamore.

Farrell, P., & Lundegren, H. M. (1991). *The process of recreation programming: Theory and technique* (3rd ed.). State College, PA: Venture.

Gilfoyle, T. J. (2006). *Millennium park: Creating a Chicago landmark.* Chicago, IL: University of Chicago Press.

Harper, J. (2009). *Planning for recreation and park facilities: Predesign, process, principles, and strategies.* State College, PA: Venture.

Jones, K. R., & Wills, J. (2005). *The invention of the park: From the Garden of Eden to Disney's magic kingdom.* Malden, MA: Polity.

Kraus, R. G. (1985). *Recreation program planning today.* Glenview, IL: Scott Foresman.

Kraus, R. G. (1990). *Recreation and leisure in modern society* (4th ed.). Boston, MA: Jones and Bartlett.

Kraus, R. G. (1997). *Recreation programming: A benefits-driven approach.* Boston, MA: Allyn and Bacon.

LaPage, W. (2007). *Parks for life: Moving the goal posts, changing the rules, and expanding the field.* State College, PA: Venture.

Murphy, J. F. (1975). *Recreation and leisure services: A humanistic perspective.* Dubuque, IA: Wm. C. Brown.

Reiss, D. (2014, August 1). 10 Years of Millennium Park history. Lifestyle. Retrieved from http://michiganavemag.com/10-years-of-millennium-park-history

Rossman, J. R. (1995). *Recreation programming: Designing leisure experiences* (2nd ed). Champaign, IL: Sagamore.

Rossman, J. R., & Schlatter, B. E. (2015). *Recreation programming: Designing and staging leisure experiences* (7th ed). Urbana, IL: Sagamore.

Russell, R. V. (2009). *Pastimes: The context of contemporary leisure* (4th ed). Champaign, IL: Sagamore.

Russell, R. V., & Jamieson, L. M. (2009). *Leisure program planning and delivery.* Champaign, IL: Human kinetics.

Tillman, A. (1974). *The program book for recreation professionals.* Palto Alto, CA: National Press Books.

Chapter Thirteen

Services for Children and Youth

CHAPTER OBJECTIVES

- To gain an understanding of the uniqueness of programming for children and youth from a linear and developmental perspective
- To highlight child- and youth-centered programming and the components associated with the program planning process
- To discuss the various program areas and the impact on program content
- To gain an awareness of the array of program benefits that can be used in the structure and organization of community-based youth recreation programs
- To gain an awareness of organizational patterns in providing child and youth services by community parks and recreation departments

INTRODUCTION

Children and youth programs have been the mainstay of public parks and recreation services for more than a century. Sand garden programs in the late 1800s in Boston and playgrounds in New York City provide testament to the importance of programs focused on children and youth. Organized playgrounds that today have given way to before- and after-school care programs and day camps are a part of the program offerings of every community parks and recreation department in the United States. Today, programs and services for children and youth remain a significant component of any public parks and recreation departments.

Children and youth remain the most important asset to communities; they embody our dreams and hopes for the future (Edginton, 1997). They conceptualize, create, and develop new advancements that have moved global society in new directions. Discussing youth, Boyle has pointed out, "Today's youth will have a significant role in bringing about changes in technology, demography, economy, and politics" (Boyle, 2000, as cited in Delgado, 2002). The time spent investing in the development of children and youth benefits the communities where they grow up, and a major center of opportunity for growth is the community-based recreation center.

Public parks and recreation agencies serve as catalysts for the overall development of a community's children and youth population. The programs and services that are offered by the community-based parks and recreation agency may involve multiple philosophies, strategies, and programmatic principles. Public parks and recreation staff members pull ideas and concepts from areas such as sociology, psychology, physical education, recreation, and education. The amalgamation of unique perspectives from the aforementioned fields allows community-based parks and recreation organizations to develop programs and services that vary in curricular design and presentation. This is a unique and important facet of a public parks and recreation agency's offerings; "one size does not fit all," and administrators have the flexibility to implement programs and services that can reach children and youth in various ways.

In this chapter, we will discuss the nature of child and youth programming and present guidelines and a model for child and youth-centered program planning. In addition, we will include a short discussion of the process of building ownership and empowerment. Last, various program areas can be incorporated into the work of parks and recreation departments will be presented.

PROGRAMMING FOR CHILDREN AND YOUTH

Community-based parks and recreation programs, from highly structured to little or no structure, serve as vehicles for personal development of children and youth. Children and youth desire to build their personal and social skills; these opportunities can promote positive behavior within the community and reduce the potential for at-risk behavior (Carnegie Corporation of New York, 1992). As programs and services are created, there are essential pieces to consider as the design and implementation processes take shape. Those pieces include (a) the physical and psychological impact of participation; (b) a developmentally appropriate program structure, (c) the emotional and moral support from staff members, (d) opportunities for children and adolescents to experience supportive adult relationships, (e) opportunities for all children and youth to learn how to form lasting relationships with others, (f) opportunities for children and youth to feel a sense of belonging and positive self-worth, (g) opportunities for skill building and mastery, (h) opportunities to develop self-confidence in one's abilities, (i) opportunities to contribute to one's community, and (j) opportunities for leadership and involvement in the child and youth's community (Gambone & Arbreton, 1997).

There should be a linkage within public parks and recreation programs between the context of the program and the basic needs of children and youth. Understanding the needs of children and youth, then building programs and services around these needs will help steer the efforts of staff members. These basic needs should include the following: (a) social interaction, (b) safety and structure, (c) a sense of belonging, (d) creative expression, (e) positive self-worth, (f) sharing and giving to others, (g) physical activity, (h) interdependence, (i) competence and achievement, and (j) individualism and identity (Edginton & Edginton, 1994; Pittman, 1991; Scales, 1991). For children and youth, meeting these needs are benefits of program involvement, and they can serve as the goal(s) for program and service development.

How Does the Context of Time Influence Children and Youth Programs and Services?

Looking at the context of time in association with a program or service for children and youth involves viewing the process of participation in conjunction with its goals and objectives. There are two ways to view child and youth participation in relationship to the context of time—linearly and developmentally. Linear program participation means specific program goals and objectives should be accomplished within a specific timeframe or period. For example, in teaching swimming at a community-based parks and recreation center, there are specific behaviors to be demonstrated by a child or youth coupled with achievement or mastery of a skill that can be measured within a designated time period. Using a linear design to program participation downplays the fact that child and youth development differs among individuals. The alternative approach to swimming would be developmental. This approach would focus on each person's developmental needs and not how much time there is to achieve specific behaviors. Success would be if a child or youth learns how to swim, rather than meeting a prescribed set of goals and objectives over a specific time period.

Both linear and developmental approaches should be employed when developing public parks and recreation programs for children and youth. Multiple variables may influence the decision to go with a linear or developmental approach to programming. The mission of the community-based parks and recreation agency may stipulate using a linear developmental approach. Accrediting bodies often establish standards for child and youth programming that must be included in the design of the program. Lastly, consideration should be given regarding the quantity versus the quality of services; the design of some programs may focus on providing greatest good for the greatest number of children and youth as opposed to individualizing services.

CHILD- AND YOUTH-CENTERED PROGRAMMING

Community-based parks and recreation programming should provide opportunities for children and youth to be a part of the planning process in order to develop meaningful and effective programs. Empowering young people to help in the planning process demonstrates trust, and encourages healthy social interactions with both adults and peers. Programs that assist children and youth in developing self-confidence and resilience while on their personal development path are considered highly effective. These programs "… provide opportunities for values to be developed, beliefs to be considered, and behaviors to be shaped" (Edginton & Edginton, 1994, p.111). The program planning process should prioritize children's and youths' needs and highlight ways to involve them in program development.

CHILDREN TODAY

The term *child* or *children* refers to a person who is beyond infancy. Children are generally aged 6–11 and in grades 1–6. Although a number of parks and recreation departments provide daycare services that address the needs of infants up to grade 1, from the standpoint of parks and recreation programing, children services would be focused on the population in the aforementioned age range. The focus of these types of programs is often known as school-aged services. These definitions are not hard and fast and there is a great deal of flexibility in the way in which services are organized and provided by parks and recreation services.

According to the U.S. Census Bureau (2014), the number of children between the ages of 6–11 is 23.0 million. This figure is projected to increase slightly to 25.5 million by 2049. This reflects a significant increase from 1950, when the figure stood at 15.3 million. Of this number, 12.6 million are males, and 12 million are females. Approximately 21% of children today live in households below the poverty level and a similar percentage of individuals live in households receiving supplemental security income, public assistance income, or food stamps (U.S. Census Bureau, 2014).

When the need does arise in the community, parks and recreation departments have provided programs and services for children under six years of age. Play programs, art and music classes, swim programs, and special events are just a few opportunities that allow preschool-aged children (and in some cases parents) to get involved and begin developing skills for a healthy, active lifestyle.

LIFESTYLE PROFILE OF CHILDREN

Characteristics of children today reflect in many respects their predecessor generation, the millennial generation. They are technologically well versed, connected through the use of social media, and capable of independent, self-directed behaviors. They have grown up in environments where options and choice have been a major way of play and learning. This generation of children are not millennials, but no designation has been developed yet to define this demographic. Some have suggested that this is a new Generation Y, and their tag line will be defined in the future.

ORGANIZATIONAL PATTERNS FOR CHILDREN'S PROGRAMS

There is no universal strategy for organizing children's programs and services in parks and recreation departments across the United States. There are many and varied approaches that are undertaken by parks and recreation departments to plan, organize, and deliver children's activities. In some departments, responsibilities are clustered administratively with other functions. For example, the size and scope of programs and services to be offered may have an influence on the ways in which supervisory and administrative patterns are established. In other situations, programs may be tucked into other responsibilities. For example, a recreation center director may have as a part of his or responsibilities the provision of children's programs along with the provision of events, leagues, and adult instructional activities as well as the drop-in programs of the facility. Further, one might find that the supervision of sports programs may include the organization of both youth and adult sport leagues.

Many positions working with children within parks and recreation departments are part-time jobs paying hourly wages. Such positions require individuals to have a high school diploma supplemented by college course work recreation or related fields. Positions also require individuals to have some experience working with children and the ability to be cleared with appropriate certifications and record checks. These might include first aid and CPR. Appropriate clearances for working with children may include a back ground criminal record check, drug testing, and other relevant investigation.

An example of traditional job descriptions for recreation leaders whose work is focused on children is found in Figures 13.1 and 13.2. These position descriptions require the indi-

RECREATION OPEATIONS COORDINATOR
(Youth Services)
366

DEPARTMENT: Community Services/Recreation Services

NATURE OF WORK:

Performs complex responsible professional and supervisory/administrative work in planning and implementing recreation programs. Oversees and directs the operation of a County-wide and center-based program units which includes supervision of full-time staff. Duties are performed under the general supervision of the Superintendent of Recreation.

ESSENTIAL FUNCTIONS OF THE JOB:

Oversees the planning and implementation of a County-wide program of recreational activities for all segments, groups, ages, and interest levels. Monitors program activities.

Supervises the work of assigned staff; provides guidance and training to full-time employees; interviews and hires staff; conducts performance evaluations, counseling, employee selection, and disciplinary actions. Ensures staff enforces County policies related to hiring, training, safety, and evaluations.

Establishes and enforces of unit rules, regulations, and procedures.

Conducts research and analysis of need for programs and works with staff on program design, content and delivery. Conducts research, analyzes information, and prepares reports on special projects, as assigned.

Coordinates with school staff and principals to develop partnerships, coordinate facility usage, and promoted partnered activities.

Represents the Division on interagency councils and committees and community agencies and groups, both public and private. Establishes cooperative programming with other agencies, departments, and human service organizations. Works with community groups and leaders, to develop programs needs and promote volunteer group involvement in program implementation.

Coordinates help from other County departments as needed; participates in Division and County planning teams as required.

Works with management team in developing Division short- and long-range goals through youth services, parks and recreation, and County strategic plans. Develops plans for implementation of strategic goals through program areas.

Writes proposals and grants for outside funding opportunities; prepares monthly and quarterly financial grant reports.

Develops and implements marketing strategy of program unit to include all media resources, Division brochure, and other marketing outlets in cooperation with Division Communications Coordinator.

Figure 13.1. James City County (VA) Department of Community Services/ Parks and Recreation, Job Description for Recreation Operations Coordinator –Youth Services

Updates program design and content to keep unit within mandated State standards (licensing) where required.

Performs duties of the Superintendent of Recreation in their absence.

Coordinates with Division of Social Services and other agencies for the inclusion of emergency and long-term placement care of children in school-age program.

Maintains confidentiality of all staff and children's records in accordance with Commonwealth of Virginia Department of Social Services minimum standards for licensed child care centers.

Practices continuous learning through individual study, classroom training, seminars, and conferences.

Performs work safely in accordance with department safety procedures and the County Safety Program. Operates equipment safely and reports any unsafe work condition or practice to Supervisor.

Prepares unit budget; manages unit revenues and expenditures and prepares financial reports.

Monitors recreation services budget. Prepares financial reports and maintains records of material, staff hours, equipment, and operating costs. Prepares purchase orders and materials and supply requisitions. Prepares short and long-range revenue/expenditure projections. Responsible for meeting revenue projections. Tracks revenue/expenditures to assure appropriate allocation of funds.

Directs program evaluation process to include program delivery, customer service, and effectiveness; makes recommendations for change and implements changes as authorized. Develops plan to implement appropriate changes to program areas.

Figure 13.1 (cont.)

vidual to direct a program for children in arts and crafts, games, sport activities and special events as well as accompany children on field trips and supervise their daily camp or playground activities.

CHILDREN'S PROGRAM BENEFITS

There are a number of benefits for children and youth via participation in community recreation programs and services. Youth who are involved in programs designed around physical activity are able to develop gross and fine motor skills. Activities that adults may see as simple—such as throwing a ball—require practice and concentration. Children who have the opportunity to practice these skills in individual and team sports environments are able to refine the motor skills associated with these actions.

Children can also develop and refine their cognitive skills when participating in public parks and recreation programs and services. Learning how to make decisions is a complex process; some children may not understand that a decision they make could not only affect them but other children as well. Supportive leaders who nurture healthy cognitive and decision-making skills, and design a program curriculum that explorative and purposeful are setting children up for later success in life. Programs that encourage academic achievement, extracurricular involvement, citizenship, leadership, mentoring, and life skills development are just a few thematic examples associated with recreation programs for youth.

Youth also have the opportunity to practice socializing with other children, as well as learn to deal with their emotions through involvement in recreation programs and services. Elements of socialization, such as sharing, teamwork, conversing with others, and sportsmanship, can be found in a variety of ways through community recreation agencies'

LIVERMORE AREA RECREATION AND PARK DISTRICT

PART-TIME JOB DESCRIPTION

JOB TITLE: EXTENDED STUDENT SERVICES PROGRAM AIDE

DIVISION: Recreation   CLASSIFICATION CODE: PT-238
REPORTS TO: ESS Coordinator   FLSA STATUS: NON-EXEMPT
DATE ADOPTED: 3/14/07

POSITION SUMMARY

Under immediate supervision, assists in providing child development education services to elementary school aged children enrolled in the Extended Student Services (ESS) Program; helps children participate in recreational, educational and social activities; assists with meeting children's nutritional and other care needs; helps maintain required records and documentation; and performs related work as required.

DISTINGUISHING CHARACTERISTICS

This is the first working level in the ESS Program series. Incumbents need not have prior knowledge of and experience with child development programs/rules/regulations, though some background in child development or education is desirable. Incumbents are not given independent responsibility for a group of children, but always perform duties under the immediate supervision of higher-level staff.

ESSENTIAL DUTIES AND RESPONSIBILITIES:

Incumbents may not perform all duties. Duties include but are not limited to the following:

- Assists with providing child development activities for elementary school aged children; assists with implementing recreational, educational and social activities designed to provide a stimulating and supportive learning environment for children.
- May assist in providing tutorial and/or remedial activities in small groups.
- Helps provide basic nutritional services to children; serves meals and/or snacks based on established guidelines; performs cleanup and food storage duties; may shop for snack supplies.
- Helps maintain facilities in a clean and orderly condition.
- Helps prepare teaching, craft, and other materials; participates in and encourages play activities with the children.
- May participate in staff meetings, family conferences and other special meetings; observes and monitors family conditions and notifies superiors of concerns as appropriate.
- Assists with maintaining required and appropriate documentation, including observation notes, logs, and other records.
- May participate in public relations, outreach and community education activities.
- Attends staff trainings, workshops and courses related to child development.
- At all times, demonstrates cooperative behavior with colleagues, supervisors and the public.
- Performs other duties as assigned.

Figure 13.2. Livermore Area (CA) Recreation and Park District – Job Description for Extended Student Services Program Aide.

offerings for youth. Children have the chance to build lasting friendships with their peers through program participation.

TYPICAL CHILDREN'S PROGRAMMING

There are many different types of children's programs and services provided by community parks and recreation departments. It is challenging to establish a definitive framework for the myriad activities that may be provided by a parks and recreation department. A framework for comprehending the vast array of children's programs and services is presented in Table 13.1. As one can see viewing this table, there are 14 categories (and perhaps many more) of children's programs. When one stops to consider the many and varied exam-

Table 13.1

Public Parks and Recreation Programs and Activities for Children

Categories of Children's Programs	Some Examples of Activities
Fitness/Health	Physical activities, nutrition education, pick-up sports, dual and individual sports, team sports, skill clinics
Performing/Cultural Arts	Dance, drama, music, instructional programs, performances, clinics
Social Activities	Play days, parties, clubs, special interest areas, low organized games, cooperative and initiative games, charades
Trips/Tours	Museums, amusement parks, historical sites, cultural attractions, theater, aquariums, zoos, botanical gardens, theater
Day/Residence	Arts and crafts, games, songs, skits, camp crafts, water activities, theme-based activities, clubs, special interest groups, hiking, orienteering
Before- and After-School Care	Arts, crafts, songs, games, skits, tutorial, remedial instruction, field trips, drama, clubs, music, dancing, special interest areas
Team Sport Leagues	Soccer, baseball, T-ball, basketball, softball, hockey, bowling, double dutch, football, lacrosse, cheerleading, volleyball, water polo, tournaments
Individual Sport and Instruction	Tennis, gymnastics, golf, martial arts, bowling, racquetball, track, wrestling, ice skating, table tennis, archery, tournaments
Instructional Activities	Sports, drama, dance, music, arts and crafts, technology, health
Self-Directed Drop-in/Pick-up Activities	Choice areas, literary, arts, sports, computer, open recreation
Civic/Service Learning	Volunteer, community engagement, community cleanup
Character Education	Academic achievement, academic integrity, bullying prevention, sports, character development
Life Skill Development	Academic, negotiation, leadership, time management, stress management, problem solving
Aquatics	Learn to swim, canoe, kayaking, boating, sailing, diving, competitive swim

ples of activities within these categories, it is evident that the potential range and dynamic of programs and services for programs is extensive. Few parks and recreation departments address all of these areas although it would not be unusual for a good portion of these to be provided in one way or another by a community parks and recreation department.

ISSUES AND CHILDREN'S PROGRAMMING

Currently, there are a few items of concern as children participate in public parks and recreation programming: (a) bullying and cyberbullying, (b) "helicopter parenting," (c) a reduction in personal communication between children and significant adults in their lives, and (d) the influence of technology. Bullying refers to intentional, oppressive behavior against another person that causes physical and/or psychological harm (Olweus, 1993). Cyberbullying includes bullying through email, instant messaging, in a chat room, on a website, or through digital messages or images sent to a cell phone (Martin, 2005). Children may be more likely to experience bullying at school, but the public parks and recreation center still needs to emphasize positive social interactions and relationships between youth involved in programs (Nansel, Overpeck, Haynie, Ruan, & Scheidt, 2003). There are important steps that can be taken to reduce bullying and cyberbullying. Staff members can respond to bullying consistently and appropriately, wherever it occurs, inclusive of following up with parents to keep them informed. If bullying is suspected, make sure to thoroughly investigate the complaints when they occur, and refrain from disregarding the comments as "kids playing" or "joking around." Staff members should keep in mind the less structured and positive focus of programs can be encouraging for the development of relationships between themselves and children, leading to healthy interactions for all in the program or activity.

The term "helicopter parent" has been used since the late 1960s to describe the overfocused nature some parents may have when guiding their children (Ginott, 1969). Although the intentions are good, many parents are overly involved in their children's activities; this may be due to one or more reasons, including (a) fear of poor consequences or results from the child's efforts, (b) feelings of anxiety from an adult perspective, (c) overcompensation due to developmental issues during the adult's childhood, and (d) parental peer pressure. Public parks and recreation administrators who can design play areas or programs encouraging the whole family's involvement, such as parent/child activities or areas for parents to watch their children participate (but from a comfortable distance), aid in the reduction of helicopter parents' tendencies (Floyd et al., 2011).

The technological revolution has led to an increase in digital face time and a reduction in personal face time. Although the expediency associated with digital technology has led to quicker acquisition of knowledge and information, as well as instantaneous communication, the personal interactions developed between youth and significant adults remain at the core of positive development. Public parks and recreation programs that encourage high-quality interactions between staff members and youth and provide challenging activities leading to positive life events and accomplishments are beneficial to the development of children's life satisfaction (Park, 2004). The life skills and growth associated with youth development are still shown to be influenced by rich, high-quality relationships developed with role model adults, such as public parks and recreation staff and professionals.

The usage of social networking sites, cell phones, iPhones, and other social media platforms has globally connected people in a multitude of ways. These tools do have an impact on the development of relationships among youth, and the types of activities done while online can influence the sustainability of friendships and relationships (Blais, Craig, Pepler, & Connolly, 2008). The daily usage of technology and the Internet has community parks and recreation professionals concerned with children's physical and psychological safety, integration in schools, ability to develop life skills, and overall physical health (Witt & Caldwell, 2010). Public parks and recreation programs that collaborate with children in accomplishing desirable goals and make activity choices fun and interesting are better suited to work with the "digital natives" that are enrolled (Prensky, 2006). Staff members who can provide immediate and useful feedback to youth, as well as provide concrete examples of how a child improves in the program (referred to as "leveling up") are adopting successful practices for working with children under their supervision.

YOUTH TODAY

Equally as challenging as defining children or childhood is that of defining the term *youth*. Often the terms *child* and *youth* overlap one another and are used interchangeably. However, generally speaking, we can think of youth as "occurring between puberty and the legal age of one's adult life" (Edginton & Baptiste, 2015, p. 106). This might include individuals aged 12 to 18, although this is certainly not a fixed range of ages. Other terms associated with youth include *teen, teenager,* and *adolescent.* The term *adolescent* was coined by G. Stanley Hall (1904), a famous psychologist and early leader of the play movement.

The U.S. Census Bureau (2014) reports that the number of youth between the ages of 12–18 exceeds 24 million. This figure will increase slightly to 25.5 million by 2049. This reflects a substantial increase when compared with 1950, when the figure stood at 12.9 million. Of this recently reported number, 14.9 million are males, and 14.2 million are females. In 2015, the number of youth in America is slightly larger percentagewise than individual's ages 0-5 and 6-11 and by the year 2050 will be statistically the same (U.S. Census Bureau, 2014).

LIFESTYLE PROFILE OF YOUTH

The Millennial Generation reflects individuals born between 1980 and 2000. Some of the traits that characterize their behavior are that they are capable of multitasking, they are extremely connected to one another through the use of social media, and they are technologically savvy. They are viewed as individuals who seek instant gratification and recognition. Millennials are individuals who thrive in a team-oriented and transparent environment. Millennials also have a strong predisposition for assisting others and crave meaning in their lives. They are able to handle transformation and change in their environments.

ORGANIZATIONAL PATTERNS FOR PROVIDING YOUTH PROGRAMS

Similar to the provision of children's programs by community parks and recreation departments, there is no universal organizational pattern for providing such services. Youth programs can be aligned with other administrative functions or they can be organized as a separate organizational activity within a parks and recreation department. Again, the size of the community and the scope and nature of programs will have a direct impact on the organizational patterns of a given parks and recreation department. Often, when a community parks and recreation department operates a teen facility, it will have an individual whose responsibility it is to provide oversight for this facility, which will include program planning and implementation (Figure 13.3). This position is responsible for the planning, supervision and implementation of a comprehensive recreation program focusing on a va-

Job Description
After School Program Site Supervisor

GENERAL DESCRIPTION:
The After School Program Site Supervisor employed by the Sunset Empire Park and Recreation District provides leadership in the form of instruction or supervision to specific programs or activities. This may involve providing leadership on a one-to-one basis or working with groups of individuals as the instructor in programs or activities. The After School Program Site Supervisor also serves as the main point of contact for parents and the school district.

SUPERVISION RECEIVED:
This position comes under the direct supervision of a Recreation Coordinator of the Sunset Empire Park and Recreation District or an individual assigned by the General Manager to supervise the duties of the After School Program Site Supervisor. The After School Program Site Supervisor is responsible for following and carrying out all of the workplace expectations and policies of the Sunset Empire Park and Recreation District.

SUPERVISION EXERCISED:
The After School Program Site Supervisor directly supervises other staff members and has the responsibility of supervising Recreation Leaders or volunteers assisting in the organization and implementation of a program or activities.

ESSENTIAL DUTIES:
The essential duties for the After School Program Site Supervisor include but are not limited to:
- To supervise site Recreation Leaders and/or volunteers.
- To ensure activities and site are safe for participants and staff.
- To determine appropriate staff ratios and communicate with Recreation Coordinator to this end.
- To provide, organization, leading, and instructing individuals and groups in specified programs.
- To prepare instructional objectives and lesson plans.
- To supervise and implement safe practices as it relates to participants, programs, and facilities.
- To maintain program areas by cleaning up after activities.
- To positively and successfully perform within work team dynamics.
- To issue, receive, maintain, and inventory recreation equipment and supplies.
- To maintain attendance, and activity records and make required reports.
- To enhance the program or activities via participant solicitation or feedback.
- To make recommendations to the Recreation Coordinator regarding program enhancement and any concerns regarding operations.
- Other duties as assigned by the Recreation Coordinator or General Manager.

QUALIFICATIONS:

Knowledge of:
- Specific program or activity to which is instructed.
- Use of tools and supplies in the application of the program.
- Working with youth or adults with varying degrees of ability.
- General understanding of youth development and proper disciplinary actions.
- Education & practical training in sports, fitness, games, crafts, cooking, science, outdoor recreation and other recreational and cultural activities.

EXPERIENCE & TRAINING:
1-2 years of experience working with children.
Must be 14 years of age or older.
Previous experience in the leading or instruction of various ages and abilities preferred.

Figure 13.3. Job description, after-school youth center program supervisor

riety of program activities including tennis, aquatics, cultural arts, physical activities, and other special interest activities.

YOUTH PROGRAM BENEFITS

As Witt and Caldwell (2010) pointed out, youth benefit from participation in public parks and recreation programs in multiple ways. These programs aid in reducing juvenile delinquency and violent behaviors; developing self-confidence, optimism, and initiative; increasing civic responsibility; and helping to reduce parental stress. Overall, public parks and recreation programs provide supervised, positive outlets for youth during their out-of-school time. Youth who are involved in these programs have been shown to have lower involvement in gang violence, reduced participation in unhealthy behaviors (e.g., smoking), and higher rates of civic volunteering. Staff members who develop activities that challenge youth in fostering sound life skills, as well as foster healthy identity development are enabling young people to become strong, healthy adults.

TYPICAL YOUTH PROGRAMS

The National Collaboration for Youth (2001) suggests that there are a wide array of programs that could be provided by youth service organizations including leadership development, character enrichment activities, mentoring activities, community youth centers and clubs, after-school, weekend, and summer programs, sports and recreation, health promotion, academic enrichment, camping and environmental enrichment, workforce preparation, community service, civic participation, special interests groups, and youth-led programs. Edginton and de Oliveira (1995) have offered a program framework for youth development that includes the following areas: academic enrichment, leisure activities, health promotion program, peer mentoring, life-skill building, vocational/career, leadership development, service learning (community/civic), outreach services, and clubs/special interest groups.

Peer Mentoring

A popular approach to youth programming is known as peer mentoring, and a common way of establishing community-based recreation youth programs. Essentially, these programs involve youth meeting other youth who are equal in rank, ability, or value. A peer mentor is usually an individual trusted by another who provides wise counsel, assistance, instruction, guidance, or other useful information. Edginton and de Oliveira (1995:26) wrote that ". . . the concept of mentoring can be thought of as a process where the individual provides wise and trusted advice to another. A mentor is often seen as an individual with special levels of knowledge, skill, and/or experience." Key elements in mentorship programs are the development of a respectful, trusting relationship between youth (Figure 13.4).

Academic Enrichment

Public parks and recreation youth development programs often assist youth in advancing their knowledge, skills, or ability. This may be done through educational or learning activities. These learning activities can be organized in either a formal or informal fashion. Edginton and de Oliveira (1995) noted that such learning environments contribute

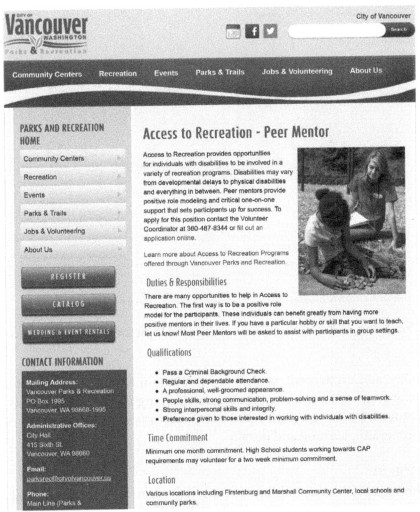

Figure 13.4. Peer Mentoring Program of the Vancouver-Clark (WA) Parks & Recreation Department

to growth and knowledge, critical thinking, and cognitive abilities. They write ". . . such programs may assist youth by proficiency, improvement, and by adding to enriching their knowledge or skill programs" (Edginton & de Oliveira,1995, p. 22). Such programs are often provided in a parallel and collaborative fashion with other learning environments, such as school or the home. When this collaboration occurs, these types of programs can be very powerful learning experiences for youth. Another approach would be to provide remedial programs that help uplift the level of youth in selected academic or scholastic areas. Youth learn at varying rates, and as a result may not reach predetermined academic standards. Remedial programs help students gain proficiency, meet minimum standards, and advance their knowledge and skills (Figure 13.5).

Leadership Development

Many community-based recreation youth programs are focused on the theme of developing leaders; efforts include building leadership competencies and abilities and finding the potential for youth to practice leadership. They further note that leadership involves

YOUTH SPORTS AND RECREATION

ABOUT A.S.A.P.

The Houston Parks and Recreation Department (H.P.A.R.D.) provides programming and recreational sports opportunities for children ages 4 to 18 in a safe, secure and supervised environment.

Youth programming is available year-round through H.P.A.R.D.'s Community Centers. Activities include after-school and summer enrichment programming, after-school and summer food service for youth, teen mentoring and academic support and much more.

A variety of free recreational sports are available. Participants receive equipment, uniforms, facility usage and expert coaching free of charge. League play is organized and directed by experienced youth sports professionals. H.P.A.R.D. staff and volunteers provide coaching assistance, encouragement and support to the children participating in our programs.

We invite you to visit your neighborhood H.P.A.R.D. **Community Center (communitycenters/communitycenters.html)** to find out more.

Figure 13.5. Houston, TX Parks and Recreation Department Enrichment Program for Youth

passion, flexibility, and excitement, as well as the wisdom to answer followers' needs and wants in such a way as to promote a common goal. Helping youth develop or discover their potential for leadership through public parks and recreation programs should be a prime goal of within program planning and design.

Health Promotion

Health promotion is an overarching concept that encourages positive health behaviors and lifestyle. There are various interpretations of health promotion due to the focus associated with various disciplines and fields. Health promotion can be viewed as a holistic enjoyment of life (Edginton, Hanson, Edginton, & Hudson, 1998), perseverance focused on desirable health practices and an optimal lifestyle (Schlaadt, 1983), methods of intervention to curtail undesirable health-related behaviors (U.S. Department of Health and Human Services, 1990), and supportive efforts encompassing physical, emotional, intellectual, spiritual, interpersonal and social, and environmental well-being. Community-based recreation youth programs provide opportunities for young people to gain information on such topics as drugs and substance abuse, alcohol consumption, sexual behavior, family dynamics, interpersonal relationships, fitness, stress management, dietary nutrition, and lifestyle changes. One example of a health promotion program is one known as TEEN (Total Education and Enrichment Network), which is operated by the City of Phoenix (Arizona) Parks, Recreation and Library Department. This program serves youth aged 18–21 and addresses the perils of substance abuse, teenage pregnancy, early parenthood, gangs, and dropping out of school.

Clubs and Interest Groups

Youth often "hang together" in groups. They are motivated by their desire to be with each other and to pursue common interests. From a youth program perspective, the creation of clubs and interest groups can facilitate the need for youth to be with one another and engage in common activities. Clubs and interest groups provide youth with an opportunity to enhance their skills, develop physically and mentally, promote teamwork, build self-confidence, personal reliance, and build a sense of pride. As Fine and Mechling (1993) have proposed regarding the formulation of groups by youth, they provide a sense of place and importance, a sense of belonging, loyalty, selfless rendering of service and even sacrifice for others, peer-sponsored morality, significant amounts of enjoyment, as well as goal-directed activity. Edginton et al. (1998) suggested that a club is ". . . a group of persons organized for some particular purpose. . .formed on the basis of age group, activity interest, or for some exchange of information and ideas" (Edginton et al., p. 172). In a similar fashion, they suggest that ". . . an interest group is a collection of individuals that has formed around an activity, issue, or program area" (Edginton et al., p. 173). Figure 13.6 highlights a leadership development program from the Washington, D.C. Department of Parks and Recreation.

Service Learning

Service learning programs provide opportunities for youth to support community needs in a meaningful and worthwhile way. These programs allow youth to give of themselves altruistically, as well as personally grow and develop, from meaningful opportunities and life experiences. Service learning has been generally defined as a form of intentionally guided community service that involves youth combining meaningful volunteer service with ongoing reflection (National Center for Early Adolescence, 2001). Most forms of service learning involve action followed by reflection; this is known as praxis.

There are numerous benefits for youth who engage in service learning via community-based recreation programs. Edginton and de Oliveira (1995) noted that

service learning programs engage youth in prosocial behaviors, helping them to develop healthy interpersonal skills, foster emotional growth, encourage care and responsibility, gain an understanding of community service, increase the ability to work with others, assist in the development of career objectives, expand willingness to learn and assist in the development of a sense of self. (p. 24)

Supreme Teen Clubs

Supreme Teen Clubs were established by the DC Department of Parks and Recreation's (DPR) Office of Teen Programs to offer District teenagers a holistic, quality youth development program that will assist them in gaining the necessary skills to ensure greater opportunities for personal success.

Supreme teen clubs seek to engage DC youth in dialogue about the issues that affect them and discuss the best method to address those issues.

Figure 13.6. Supreme Teen Clubs – Washington, D.C. Department of Parks and Recreation.

Schine (1990) proposed that the goal of adolescence is trying to answer the question "Who am I?" The beauty of service learning programs is they assist adolescents in discovering who they are, identity-wise. Still further, Edginton and Edginton (1995) have noted that ". . . service learning may be instrumental in helping youth learn to work with others, gain an understanding of community service, develop life skills, demonstrate caring and commitment, and other benefits" (p. 6).

Vocational and career. There are two ways of viewing the concept of vocation, or one's "calling" in life. Philosophically, youth are trying to discover their life's purpose when asking the questions, "What is my life's calling? What is my quest in life?" Theologically, a youth may be called to serve others, to act compassionately, to give of oneself in an altruistic fashion, or to be a caring and concerned individual. As youth begin to find their calling in life, community-based recreation programs assist in constructing a foundation for their self-concept and have a dramatic impact on the way in which one lives his or her life. The quest for a calling is ongoing; it is a life's quest that youth pursue with critical self-examination and inquiry throughout their lives into adulthood.

A second perspective of dealing with the concept of vocation and career is to think of it as finding one's self occupationally. For many individuals, a job is central to one's self-concept. When a person is asked who they are, it is often asked in the context of what he or she does for a living. Public parks and recreation programs can assist in preparing youth for the job market; in finding a career, an occupation, or a job. As youth search for a career, they need direction, counsel, information, and support. Community-based recreation programs aiding youth in preparing a resume, interviewing, and successfully engaging others in the workplace are critical opportunities for later success, employment-wise. Staff members can support youth in developing a variety of knowledge, skills, and competencies required for a successful entry level access into the job market (Figure 13.7).

Career Readiness Series
Jump Start Your Career Today: Discovering Internships and Volunteer Opportunities

For teens and adults starting a new career, internships and volunteer positions offer the valuable experience needed to land your dream job! By the end of the workshop, participants will be able to research and apply for positions related to their interests and aspirations. Workshop is held at the College Lakes Recreation Center.

How to Find the Perfect Summer Job
Saving up for a new phone or college? Finding a summer job can be difficult for a teenager. Participate in this workshop designed especially for teens in order to increase the likelihood that you will get an interview and be hired. The tips provided in this session come directly from the companies in Cumberland County who hire teens. Workshop is held at the Westover Recreation Center.
14+, Tuesday, May 5, 6-7 p.m., free

Fayetteville–Cumberland Parks and Recreation is proud to partner with the Office of College Access Programs at Fayetteville State University to bring these workshops to our community, free of charge! The Office of College Access Programs' mission is to encourage and assist youth who are traditionally underrepresented in college with preparation for entry into and completion of a college degree. For more information on FCPR Youth development programs, call 433-1021.

Figure 13.7. Fayetteville-Cumberland (NC) Parks & Recreation – Vocational and Career Youth Programs.

Life Skills

One of the important program areas addressed within public parks and recreation agencies is that of assisting youth in developing life skills that help meet daily challenges, as well as aiding them in their ongoing life journey through adolescence to adulthood. Pittman and Wright (1991) have written:

Life skills training . . . is the formal teaching of requisite skills for surviving, living with others, and succeeding in a complex society. Because of profound changes in our society over the past few decades, it can no longer be assumed that these skills are automatically learned.

...Adolescents need help in acquiring a range of social competencies to cope with academics, to meet fundamental challenges of forming stable human relationships, to maintain hope about their future, to understand and adopt health promoting behaviors, to make wise decisions about life options and to optimize use of social networks. (p. 3)

Adolescents need general problem-solving skills, planning, and decision-making skills, cognitive strategies for resisting peer or media influences, skills for increasing self-monitoring and self-regulation, and coping strategies to deal with everyday stresses.

Life skill development is an important component for community-based recreation programs for youth. According to Edginton and de Oliveira (1995) "...life skills include the ability to handle conflict, ability to make decisions and solve problems, ability to make positive and healthy choices, ability to value others, ability to achieve success in school/employment and other practical skills and knowledge" (p. 25).

Character Education

The facets of character building, moral education, and values development have all been important program features of public parks and recreation youth programs for over a century. Character education is a main focus of programs, helping identify and strengthen those characteristics that form the foundation for positive adult behaviors in an adult democratic society.

The Arts and Literary Programs

Youth are enthralled with programs associated with the arts (Figure 13.8). These community-based youth recreation programs include the performing arts (music, dance, drama), the visual arts (decorative arts and crafts), and the new arts (photography, computer graphics, radio and television). Literary programs include activities in categories such as writing, communications, reading, foreign studies, and discussion groups (Edginton et al., 1998).

Sports, Games, and Other Physical Activities

Sports, games, and fitness activities attract youth; regardless of the season or time of year, these offerings remain popular with youth. Sport is an activity that demands a combination "...of physical skill, endurance, purpose, and enthusiasm" (Edginton et al., 1998, p. 214). Sports, whether they are individual, dual, or team based, have more precise rules and regulations. Games require varying degrees of skill and ability for participation. Games vary in complexity, organization and skill level. Three basic games exist: (a)

Watercolor and Beyond:
Studio Workshop
Ages 15 and older

For those of you who are looking for a little extra time in the studio and would enjoy a more in-depth classroom discussion and time with classmates, this is the class for you. Students learn many of the same techniques as covered in the regular eight-week watercolor classes but have the luxury of time for class discussions, critiques, and additional one-on-one help. Bring a bag lunch for our 30-minute social break. Kits are available for purchase for $159. Three classes. Instructor: Emily Taylor

Day	Date	Time	Cost	Code
W	Sept. 16–30	10:30a.m.–2 p.m.	$82	456245-01
W	Oct. 7–21	10:30a.m.–2 p.m.	$82	456245-02

Figure 13.8. Arts and Literary Programs–Eden Prairie (MN) Parks and Recreation Programs.

low-organized, (b) table/board, and (c) mental. In recent years, there has been a greater emphasis on the importance of youth fitness due to the U.S. Surgeon General's report (Satcher, 2001) suggesting America's youth are unfit and increasingly obese. When social conditions are supportive, youth enjoy fitness activities and tend to participate more often. Youth will participate in programs at wellness and fitness centers, bowling centers, and in extracurricular activities where the environment encourages skill development, personal achievement, and even social ends, as contrasted with mandatory school-based programs or competitive athletic programs.

Adventure Education and Outdoor Pursuits

Childhood and adolescence are developmental stages in a young person's life when risk is "attractive." While the results associated with risky endeavors may not be evident or immediately understood, youth gravitate toward challenging, risky activities as a way to demonstrate their independence and maturity. Outdoor education and outdoor pursuits programs affiliated with public parks and recreation organizations provide opportunities for youth to be exposed to risk in but also the exhilaration that comes from being in the outdoors, interacting with nature. Many different terms are associated with this program area, including outdoor recreation, adventure tourism, conservation education, ecotourism, environmental education, environmental interpretation, natural history, nature education, and outdoor education. Outdoor activities that expose youth to some level of risk serve as a conduit for helping youth gain an awareness of self (especially in challenging situations), improve their social skills, and learn about the environment.

Discovery, Geography, and Science

These three terms have been combined and generally refer to public parks and recreation programs that encourage and allow youth to discover the physical environment. These program offerings enhance youths' understanding in the areas of biology, chemistry, geology, mathematics/computer science, and physics. The study of geography includes in-depth analysis of the earth's atmosphere and physical features, the distribution of populations and physical resources, land use, and industries. Through the process of discovery, youth are given the opportunity to investigate and explore scientific and geographic phenomena, subsequently developing insight and perspectives on the natural occurrences associated with these fields. Hands-on programs that allow youth to immerse themselves in the explorative process heighten an individual's appreciation, awareness, and value of the world in which they live (Figure 13.9).

Rocket Science!
Boys and Girls ages 8–14

Blast off in this thrilling class full of young aerospace engineers. Students in this class will use a wide variety of mediums, including, but not limited to, recycled plastic bottles, foam blocks, tape, cardboard, paper, newspaper, string, and glue. Using the recycled materials, young engineers will design and explore different methods of propulsion in learning about aerospace engineering. In addition, chemical engineering will be explored as a method of propulsion!

Figure 13.9. Discovery, Geography, Science Youth Program – Glastonbury (CT) Parks & Recreation.

Media Literacy Education

Dieser (2013) combined media literacy and leisure education and defined media literacy-based leisure education as (a) providing tools to help people (youth) critically analyze and interpret the meaning of media messages they encounter, and (b) link their interpretations to changing their leisure habits (e.g., lessening media consumption by becoming more involved in outdoor recreation). Mass media is a powerful societal force that greatly influences the relationship among leisure, lifestyle, and society (Edginton, DeGraff, Dieser, & Edginton, 2006) and includes all electronic or digital means and print or artistic visuals used to transmit messages. There is an abundant amount of re-search support that media literacy is successful in helping youth change their media and leisure behaviors (see Dieser 2013; Potter, 2011 for an overview of the research) and many organizations offer youth-based media literacy curriculum (e.g., Action Coalition for Media Education www.acme-coalition.org, New Mexico Media Literacy Project www.nmmlp.org). McCannon (2009) outlined that a popular media literacy technique is the counter-ad or anti-ad activity. This media literacy technique is based on teaching youth academic/science-based information (e.g., smoking cigarettes cause serious lung damage, such as cancer) and then having students create reversed and more truthful stories in advertisements. McCannon used the example of how Camel cigarettes have a highly sexualized woman smoking in one of their advertisements, with the words "pleasure to burn" on the cover. Students, then create a counter advertisement of a woman smoking (which can be done on a highly detail computer program or simply with a blank piece of paper and a pencil sketch) with the words "Lungs to burn" or "cancer your lungs to burn" in place of the phrase "pleasure to burn."

Table 13.2 offers a list of the aforementioned youth program categories and some typical activities.

Table 13.2

Public Parks and Recreation Programs for Youth

Categories of Youth Programs	Some Examples of Activities
Peer Mentoring	Tutorials, providing support, referrals, information sharing, role playing, job shadowing
Academic Enrichment	Tutorials, enrichment, advanced education, hands-on experiences
Leadership Development	Experiential learning, coaching, visioning
Health Promotion	Activities that enhance one's health perspectives and enables them to improve their well-being
Clubs and Interest Groups	Academic, cultural, faith-based, service-oriented, political, social (sorority, fraternity), sports, special interest
Service Learning	Civic engagement, volunteering, community activities
Vocational and Career	Activities that promote career development (e.g., resume preparation, interviewing skills)
Life Skills	Academic, negotiation, leadership, time management, organizing, stress management, problem solving
Character Education	Academic achievement, academic integrity, bullying prevention, safety, sports, character development
The Arts and Literary Programs	Music, drama, dance, plastic and graphic arts, crafts, writing, book clubs, speech, debate
Sports/Games/Physical Activities	Basketball, hockey, soccer, football, volleyball, tennis, golf, lacrosse, field hockey
Adventure/Outdoor Education	Spelunking, hiking, orienteering, mountain biking
Life Skill Development	Geo mapping, geo games, astronomy, biology, nature interpretation
Aquatics	Advocacy projects, counter advertisement designs

ISSUES AND YOUTH PROGRAMMING

There are a few main issues associated with public parks and recreation youth programming (Quinn, 1999; Witt & Caldwell, 2010). The first is developing programs and services that are attractive and relevant to young people, inclusive of providing opportunities for youth in low-income communities. Youth who actively participate in out-of-school public parks and recreation programs state that they enjoy "fun and friends" and "voice and choice." Staff members and administrators should work to create programs that encourage relationship-building and provide youth the opportunity to help plan activities for the day.

The impact of income level on youth participation in programs and activities is significant. Forty-four percent (44%) of families that are at or below the poverty level reported having a youth who participated in out-of-school programs or activities; this number jumps to 73% for families that are above the poverty level (Anderson-Moore, Murphy, Bandy, & Cooper, 2014). As highlighted in Chapter 8, it is important to provide public parks and recreation programs and services; if the need is evident, youth programs can be supported by grants to address specific issues. For example, as part of the Los Angeles (California) Department of Recreation and Parks Mission, LA Kids includes free programs and services to low-income areas so that youth have equal access to participation (http://laparks.org/LAKIDS/).

The second issue revolves around securing adequate funds for youth programs, including developing partnerships with other community-based groups to offset the costs. As mentioned in Chapter 8, funding for public parks and recreation is often met with skepticism, particularly when an increase in funds is needed for renovation or addition of facilities and programs. If community parks and recreation agencies' youth programs are disregarded or underfunded, the consequences can be dire. In many communities, these programs are the only source of positive influence for youth—stagnant funding or cutting funds reduces the potency of staff members' efforts, and can push youth down paths that are detrimental to development. A worst-case scenario is outlined in Figure 13.10.

The normally unassuming Bill Henry stood up at tonight City Council meeting and bluntly and passionately said—after a week in which Baltimore has been in the national spotlight over the Freddie Gray case—that city government has invested its resources unwisely for the last 25 years.

While the Police Department's budget has tripled since 1991, funding for programs that improve the lives of young people—such as recreation centers, libraries, after-school programs, and summer jobs—has stagnated or been slashed, the councilman representing North Baltimore's 4th district asserted.

Budget-wise, the police department "has been eating its lunch for a generation," he declared. Citing a police officer's comment that kids don't go to rec centers because they are "in awful shape," Henry said, "They are in awful shape because we haven't put any money in them in any serious amounts for a quarter of a century."

In 1991, "we spent $37 million on the Department of Recreation and Parks, and we spent $165 million on the Police Department. A quarter of a century later, we have almost doubled the overall city government budget, we have almost tripled the police department's budget, and we spend less today on recreation centers than we spent then."

How do these budget numbers relate to the looting and arson of last Monday that started when mostly teenagers threw rocks at officers at the mall and then marked angrily and violently down Pennsylvania Avenue? Henry said the city has "purposely disinvested" in young people "in favor of investing in catching and caging them."

Bill Henry speaks about he city's disinvestment in youth-oriented programs. "For years, we have been trying to police our way out of a situation that we cannot police our way out of," he said.

"We cannot continue to give more than half the money we raise from property taxes to one agency to do one part of a big job. And that job of public safety involves giving kids meaningful things to do so they are not out in the street causing trouble."

He said that the mayor and the board will vote on the budget that does not include enough money for the summer youth jobs or after-school programs. Henry said he is trying to convince the mayor to allocate $4 million more for after-school programs.

Figure 13.10. Closing Rec Centers and Slashing Youth Programs Were Root Causes of Riot, Councilman Asserts, Baltimore (MD).

SUMMARY

The concept of child and youth development has extended beyond the traditional educational realm into the public sector (Hamilton, Hamilton, & Pittman, 2004). Programs and services directed toward children and youth are a staple of a public parks and recreation organization's yearly plan. The importance of having quality opportunities, as well as staff members who are well versed in leading children and youth, are integral parts of a public parks and recreation departments' programs and services "palette." Administrators recognize that children and youth programs are no longer about "rolling the ball out in the gym" and letting children and youth do what they want; the personal development that occurs in children and youth when they participate in these programs speaks volumes of the importance of having a sound staff, vision, and design programmatically.

The benefits that result from public parks and recreation programs for youth can be nearly limitless. There are immediate and long-term results that bode well for development, including increased levels of self-confidence, healthy friendships and relationships, skill development, and the opportunity to practice decision-making. Administrators and staff members also play important roles in the design of programs; effective leadership exponentially enhances the positive results of public parks and recreation programs for children and youth.

Moving forward, there are a handful of items that are important to keep in mind when designing programs and services for young people. Relevant, attractive activities that challenge children and youth should be a consideration in program implementation when serving the generations of the 21st Century. Incorporating tools of the digital revolution in programmatic design is another way to reach today's youth. These steps are just a few examples of what public parks and recreation staff members can contemplate when creating programs and services that connect with youth and positively impact their growth and development.

DISCUSSION QUESTIONS

1. What are the two different ways to view child and youth participation in programs in relationship to time?
2. Give an example of a public parks and recreation program or service that is linearly designed.
3. Give an example of a public parks and recreation program or service that is developmentally designed.
4. List some of the characteristics associated with the current generation of children.
5. What are some of the key functions connected to youth services job positions in the public parks and recreation sector?
6. What are some of the benefits for children who participate in public parks and recreation programs?
7. Identify two to three categories of children's programs and activities from a local public parks and recreation agency.
8. What are two to three issues associated with children's programming?
9. Identify two to three categories of youth programs and activities from a local public parks and recreation agency.
10. What are two to three issues associated with youth programming?

REFERENCES

Anderson Moore, K., Murphy, D., Bandy, T., & Cooper, P. M. (2014). *Participation in out-of-school time and activities.* Publication #2014-13, Bethesda, MD: Child Trends.

Blais, J. J., Craig, W. M., Pepler, D., & Connolly, J. (2008). Adolescents online: The importance of Internet activity choices to salient relationships. *Journal of Youth and Adolescence, 37,* 522–536.

Carnegie Corporation of New York. (1992). *A matter of time: Risk and opportunity in the nonschool hours.* Carnegie Corporation of New York: Carnegie Council of Adolescent Development.

City of Los Angeles Department of Recreation and Parks. (n.d.). About LA Kids. Retrieved from http://laparks.org/LAKIDS/

Delgado, M. (2002). *New frontiers for youth development in the Twenty-First Century: Revitalizing and broadening youth development.* New York, NY: Columbia University Press.

Eden Prairie. (2015). Parks and recreation programs, Fall 2015. Retrieved from http://www.edenprairie.org/home/showdocument?id=3758

Edginton, C. R., DeGraaf, D. G. R., Dieser, R. B., & Edginton, S. R. (2006). *Leisure and life satisfaction: Foundational perspectives* (4th ed). Boston, MA: WCB McGraw-Hill.

Edginton, C. R., & de Oliveira, W. (1995). Youth development: A program framework. *PERS Review Hong Kong, 1*(2), 22–27.

Edginton, S. R., & Edginton, C. R. (1994). *Youth programs: Promoting quality services.* Champaign, IL: Sagamore.

Edginton, S. R., & Edginton, C. R. (1995). *Youth outreach and service excellence.* U.S. Army Child and Youth Services.

Edginton, C. R., & Jn Baptiste, T. (2015). Youth, youth development, youth work: Key concepts and perspectives. *International Leisure Review, 1,* 103–124.

Farrell, P., & Lundegren, H. M. (1991). *The process of recreation programming.* State College, PA: Venture.

Fayetteville-Cumberland Parks and Recreation (2015). Youth development–Career readiness series. Retrieved from http://www.fcpr.us/youth_development.aspx

Fine, G. A., & Mechling, J. (1993). Child saving and children's cultures at century's end. In S. B. Health & M. E. McLaughlin (Eds.), *Identity and inner-city youth* (pp. 120–146). New York, NY: Teachers College.

Floyd, M., Moore, R., Bocarro, J., Smith, W., Baran, P., Cosco, N., Edwards, M., Suau, L. & Fang, K. (2011). Park-based physical activity among children and adolescents. *American Journal of Preventive Medicine, 41*(3), 258–265.

Gambone, M. A., & Arbreton, A. J. A. (1997). *Safe havens: The contributions of youth organizations to healthy adolescent development.* Philadelphia, PA: Public/Private Ventures. Retrieved from www.aspe.hhs.gov/hsp/positiveyouthdev99.

Ginott, H. (1969). *Between parent and teenager.* New York, NY: The MacMillan Co.

Hall, G. S. (1904). *Adolescence: Its psychology and its relations to physiology, anthropology, sociology, sex, crime, religion, and education* (Vols. I & II). New York, NY: D. Appleton & Co.

Martin, K. S. (2005). Cyber-bullying: Creating a culture of respect in a cyber-world. *Children and Youth, 13,* 224–228.

McCannon, R. (2009). Media literacy/media education: Solution to big media? In V. C. Strasburger, B. J. Wilson, & A. B. Jordan (Eds.), *Children, adolescents, and the media* (2nd ed., pp. 519–569). Thousand Oaks, CA: Sage.

Nansel, T. R., Overpeck, M. D., Haynie, D. L., Ruan, W. J., & Scheidt, P. C. (2003). Relationships between bullying and violence among U.S. youth. *Archives of Pediatric Adolescent Medicine, 157,* 348–353.

National Collaboration for Youth. (2001). National youth development agenda. Retrieved from http://www.nydic.org/nydic/statements.html

Olweus, D. (1993). *Bullying at school: What we know and what we can do.* Oxford, UK: Basil Blackwell.

Park, N. (2004). The role of subjective well-being in positive youth development. *The Annals of the American Academy, 591,* 25–39.

Pittman, K. J. (1991). *Promoting youth development: Strengthening the role of youth serving and community organizations.* New York, NY: Center for Youth Development and Policy Research.

Pittman, K. J., & Wright, M. (1991). *A rationale for enhancing the role of the non-school voluntary sector in youth development.* Washington, D.C.: Center for Youth Development & Research, Academy for Educational Development.

Potter, W. J. (2011). *Media literacy* (5th ed.). Thousand Oaks, CA: Sage.

Prensky, M. (2006). Listen to the natives. *Educational Leadership,* 8–13.

Quinn, J. (1999). Where need meets opportunity: Youth development programs for early teens. *The Future of Children, 9*(2), 96–116.

Satcher, D. (2001). *Surgeon General's call to action to decrease overweight and obesity.* Washington, DC: Department of Health and Human Services.

Scales, P. (1991). *A portrait of youth adolescents in the 1990s.* Carrboro, NC: Center for Early Adolescence.

Schine, J. A. (1990). A rationale for youth community service. *Social Policy, 20*(4), 5–11.

Schlaadt, R.G. (1983). Wellness or lifestyle management. *The ACHPER National Journal, 100,* 19–22.

U.S. Census Bureau. (2014). *Current Population Reports, Estimates of the population of the United States by single years of age, color, and sex: 1900 to 1959* (Series P-25, No. 311).

Washington, D.C. Department of Parks and Recreation. (n.d.). Supreme teen clubs. Retrieved from http://dpr.dc.gov/service/supreme-teen-clubs

Witt, P., & Caldwell, L. (2010). *The rationale for recreation services for youth: An evidenced-based approach.* Ashburn, VA: National Recreation and Park Association.

Chapter Fourteen

Services for Adults and Seniors

CHAPTER OBJECTIVES

- To highlight the various stages associated with adulthood and the keys to programs and services for each age group
- To emphasize the impact older adults, particularly Baby Boomers and seniors, have on the development of community recreation programs and services
- To provide insight on the impact that older adult populations will have on public parks and recreation programming
- To understand the importance of intergenerational programs in community recreation program planning
- To examine future trends associated with programming adults and seniors

INTRODUCTION

Adulthood is considered the point in one's life when identity is formalized and established (Edginton, Jordan, DeGraaf, & Edginton, 2002). The transition to adulthood can be sudden or gradual, depending on the events that occur in a person's life. Marriage, raising children, and full-time employment are just a few of the significant benchmarks that may happen as a person matures.

Adulthood is also the time when individuals begin to put their lives in perspective, asking questions such as "How can I make a difference?" or "What do I still want to do in life?" Community parks and recreation agencies provide programs for adults during the latter part of one's lifespan that can answer both of those primary questions. Such programs allow adults to stay active and engage in a healthy lifestyle, as well as positively impact younger generations in the community.

In this chapter, programs for adults and seniors (older adults) will be discussed. First, the various stages of adulthood will be explained, including how public parks and recreation programs can be tailored to suit adults at each stage. An analysis of how community parks and recreation agencies can best serve adults, particularly the Baby Boomer population, will follow. In closing, examples of effective programs for adults at various stages on the developmental spectrum will be highlighted, as well as the importance of intergenerational programs for adults and youth.

PROGRAMMATIC GUIDELINES

As the United States has entered the 21st century, the average life expectancy has continued to climb. Men and women are living longer, and although the average age of retirement has decreased, it is not uncommon to see adults working into their early 70s (Beckner, 2012; Crompton, 2013). As a person moves from young adulthood to middle, late, and older adulthood, the focus of recreation program participation may shift (Edginton et al., 2002). Table 14.1 illustrates various programs and services provided by community recreation agencies during adulthood.

Table 14.1

Recreational Programs and Services for Adults

Categories of Adults' Programs and Services	Examples of Activities
Fitness/Health	Walking, jogging, swimming, hiking, zen, svelte, yoga, meditation, barre FX, dog/owner exercise classes, 5K and 10K runs, marathons, triathlons, Zumba Gold, cross-country skiing, Pilates, tai chi, nutrition classes
Performing/Cultural/Fine Arts	Pottery classes, ceramics, cooking classes, wine tasting classes, dance classes, quilting, painting, jewelry making, theatrical performances
Social Activities	Wii, crafts, karaoke, holiday celebrations (4th of July, Labor Day), concerts, intergenerational mentoring
Travel/Tourism	Day/Overnight Trips, International Tours
Team Sports Leagues	Softball, volleyball, pickleball, kickball, ping pong, basketball, hockey, flag football, lacrosse, soccer, billiards
Individual Sport and Instruction	Rock climbing, tennis, golf, fishing, racquetball, ice skating, martial arts, track & field
Instructional Activities	Woodworking, horseback riding, digital photography, CPR/First Aid, estate planning, financial instruction, home decorating and DIY
Civic Engagement	Gardening, volunteering, historical celebrations
Aquatics	Water aerobics, inner tube water polo, aquatic fitness

Early Adulthood

At the early adult stage in life (ages 21–30), recreation program participation may be limited due to growth in the family and economic constrictions. Community parks and recreation agencies can provide programs for couples and young families that encourage interactions and focus on shared commitments. Parents in this stage in life may want to try new experiences with their children; public parks and recreation agencies can offer a variety of programmatic opportunities that enhance cohesion among family members. Examples of public parks and recreation programs for this stage may include outdoor pursuits (i.e., rock climbing), team and individual sports (i.e., softball, volleyball, tennis, golf), and social activities.

Middle Adulthood

Middle adulthood (ages 31–50) is a time when individuals see physical changes in their bodies, and programs that encourage physical activity and movement can be at the forefront of maintaining a healthy lifestyle emotionally, mentally, and physically. Community recreation agencies that can offer programs in a variety of ways (i.e., different days, times, settings) will help adults in this stage create a balanced lifestyle, especially with the increase in family commitments. Leisure and recreation programs at this stage in life that can challenge a person with novel experiences will help enhance their commitment and focus on the "day-to-day operations" of their daily family routine (Zabriskie & McCormick, 2003). Examples of programs include team and individual sports (both as a participant and a spectator), gardening, and hobbies (i.e., crafts, art, music).

Late Adulthood

Late adulthood (ages 51–65) is a time when individuals see movement within the family. Children may leave the home and head off to college or begin a full-time profession; "empty nest syndrome" may set in with parents. While children departing may be a significant change in the family dynamic, it also allows the parents to reconnect with each other. Parents may also see an increase in free time, as well as confusion about one's identity, since a significant portion of their lives has been focused on child-rearing. Effective community parks and recreation programs for this age group involve more self-direction by the participants; leaders can assist in initiating activities, but adults in this age group want to drive the pace of their involvement. Public parks and recreation programs for this group should also include meaningful recreation and leisure pursuits as individuals are entering retirement. Examples of effective programs include more individual sports (i.e., fishing, walking, swimming, hiking), travel and tourism programs, as well as the aforementioned hobbies.

Older Adulthood

Older adulthood, (ages 66+) is a time of reflection; as Erikson (1963) pointed out, integrity is the primary goal in older adulthood. Integrity at this stage includes a sense of "wholeness" or satisfaction with the life one has lived. As older adults reflect on their accomplishments in life, a concern for younger generations emerges (Jordan, 1996). Public parks and recreation programs that are intergenerational in nature allow older adults to positively impact their community's youth, passing on the tools for success as young people grow. Many community parks and recreation agencies have created effective programs that prioritize older adults, either through full-time or part-time volunteering.

Many of the community parks and recreation programs and services offered for individuals in the young and middle adulthood stages of life (adults under the age of 50) are aimed at developing a healthy work-life balance or enriching one's life. Once a young adult achieves full-time professional status, gets married, or has children, there can be a sense of "power loss." In the past, concern was focused on one person—the individual. Schedules were more flexible, and there may have been fewer life obligations and commitments. Programs targeting this portion of the adult population are often laced with phrases such as "gain control of your life" or "take back your power." These programs may serve as a catalyst for the development of routines that can serve to support a healthy balance of work, family, and other daily obligations.

As alluded to, young and middle adults may recognize a change in their physical appearance as they age, including changes in athletic abilities. For decades, community parks and recreation agencies have been providing sports leagues and tournaments for adults as a way to continue to enjoy the competition, camaraderie, and social interaction that comes with participation in athletics. For some adults, these athletic opportunities also trigger nostalgic memories of their youth, which help craft the recreational endeavor into a positive experience. Sports such as pickleball, volleyball, softball, kickball, tennis, ping pong, basketball, racquetball, hockey, flag football, lacrosse, and soccer are staples of public parks and recreation sports offerings. Leagues are developed that are same-sex or coed and often have a playoff system or format to determine champions in each sport.

Recreational classes for adults are instructive ways that individuals can develop and refine skills, as well as become involved in a leisure pursuit that may turn into a hobby. The City of Beachwood, Ohio, has created a plethora of adult programs and classes aimed at enhancing one's life (http://www.beachwoodohio.com/DocumentCenter/View/968). Pottery classes, woodworking, group fitness, Zen, Svelte, Yoga, Barre FX, dog/owner exercise classes, horseback riding, cooking classes, wine tasting classes, and dance classes (i.e., line, swing, salsa, rumba, cha-cha, foxtrot, waltz) are a few of the offerings for adults. A few of the classes have varying challenge levels, which appeals to adults with a variety of skill levels. These classes are led either by experienced public parks and recreation staff members or experienced instructors brought in by the agency.

The Aurora Center for Active Adults (ACAA) in Aurora, Colorado, offers programs for adults under the age of 50 in a different capacity (https://www.auroragov.org/ThingsToDo/Recreation/Centers/AuroraCenterforActiveAdults/). The target population for the ACAA is adults over 50 years of age; adults under the age of 50 years can sign up for classes as long as there are slots not filled by the priority age groups. This opportunity allows younger adults to still participate and recreate, as well as create intergenerational relationships with older adults. There are also drop-in capabilities for all adults; adults under the age of 50 can still use the facility; they just pay a little more than the target population of adults ($4/day as opposed to $3/day). Admission includes usage of weight rooms, treadmills, NuStep, exercise bikes, and elliptical machines, as well as fitness classes, billiards, Wii, bingo, quilting, and crafts.

Special events are also common programs and services offered for young and middle adults. These opportunities are one-time events and can attract many adults in these two age ranges because of the ease in committing to one day instead of multiple days for a recreational event. Events such as 5K and 10K runs, marathons, and triathlons are being incorporated into public parks and recreation agencies' event calendars on a regular basis (http://slco.org/recreation/admin/adultSports/adultSports.html). These events may be sponsored by other community-based agencies and organizations as a method to offset the cost associated with the event.

THE IMPACT OF BABY BOOMERS ON SENIOR PROGRAMMING

Prior to the 21st century, the interpretation of parks and recreation for many older adults may have included attending church services, going on van or bus rides to view local flowers or scenery, or other primarily sedentary activities (Cochran, Stoll, & Kinziger, 2006). As some older adults may have seen a loss in independence and decline in mental or physical capabilities, the overarching assumption was this occurred with primarily all older adults. This assumption led to the design and implementation of less active programs and services for older adults and seniors.

As Kelly and Freysinger pointed out (2000), the term "frail elderly" was used to describe older adults and seniors at this time due to the belief in their involvement in activities. Over the past decade, there has been an interpretive evolution of what "old age" means from a media perspective. Previous images would illustrate older adults and seniors as being gray and stoop-shouldered, dependent and helpless, forgetful and confused, physically frail, out of touch with current events, and lonely or abandoned (Kelly & Freysinger, 2000). Now, it is common to see print, television, and digital media images highlighting older adults and seniors as being physically active and fit, athletically skilled, socially interactive, competent, adventurous, and risk-taking with their recreational endeavors (Briggs, 2013). To quote Kelly and Freysinger (2000, p. 119), "These images shape not only how old folks see themselves and their abilities, but also how they are perceived by others."

Pre-21st century beliefs and images of older adults and seniors as participants in recreational activities conjured images of disengagement from society and portrayed this disengagement as natural and healthy. These images influenced perceptions of others regarding recreational programming, and services such as fitness and exercise classes, travel opportunities, continuing education, volunteering, and athletic/artistic/intellectual performance were relatively low in quantity. Now, as we enter the second decade of the 21st century, there is a full-blown understanding that older adults and seniors are not frail, but highly active with the desire to be involved in community parks and recreation programs and services that are challenging, stimulate creativity, and foster socializing within one's age group and among other age groups.

As mentioned earlier, more adults are actively engaging in recreation and leisure programs into older adulthood. Currently, two generations are in the midst of this trend. The younger of the two age groups is the Baby Boomer generation. *Baby Boomer* was a term used to describe the large number of babies born after the end of World War II (Porter, 1951). This first wave of Baby Boomers celebrated their 65th birthdays in 2011; this is the generation that was born between 1946 and 1964 (Gillon, 2004). There are currently over 76 million adults in this generation, and as they enter retirement and a life of recreation and leisure, their expectations for involvement are unique. The Baby Boomer generation works hard, plays hard, and spends money wisely (Ziegler, 2002). Baby Boomers have high expectations for program participation, expect value for the money they spend on programs, want a high-quality program if they are going to spend money to be involved, and want options for convenience (Freedman, 1999). As Todd noted, there is a growing demand by Baby Boomers for recreational resources to remain physically fit and healthy even into retirement age (2004). The more traditional public parks and recreation programs that used to be conducted for this age range are unacceptable to the Baby Boomers; this generation of adults wants to be active, vibrant participants and not just recipients of programs and services (Sperazza & Banerjee, 2010a).

In order to fulfill their recreational needs, Baby Boomers are turning to active, adventurous programs and services (Riley & Stanley, 2006). Community parks and recreation programs that are intellectually and physically challenging, encourage personal growth, and support skill development are highly effective avenues for involvement. The Greeley Senior Activity Center, in conjunction with the Greeley, Colorado Leisure Services Department, offers a wide array of programs that meet the needs of older adults (http://greeleygov.com/activities/recreation/greeley-senior-activity-center). Examples include the following:

- Travel programs targeting historical sights and locations
- International and in-state overnight trips
- Day hikes
- Individual and team sports leagues and tournaments, such as table tennis and softball
- Development classes, such as fitness classes, AARP driver safety, computers, and ceramics
- Games, such as Bingo, Scrabble, Bunco, Pitch, Pinochle, and Bridge
- Nutritional lunches for individuals wanting to maintain a healthy dietary lifestyle

The generation preceding the Baby Boomers is generally referred to as seniors (Sperazza & Banerjee, 2010b). These adults were born between 1925-1945, and encompass those adults who are 65 years of age and older. By the year 2030, it is projected that there will be 70 million seniors in the United States, representing 20% of the overall population. Seniors are survivors of two major events in global history—the Great Depression and World War II—and value such things as hard work, tradition, hierarchical structure, discipline, family, honor, respect for authority, and uniformity (Brokaw, 1998). Many seniors engage in recreational activities that require little strenuous physical activity or exertion; some of those recreational activities include bingo, golf, cooking, and sewing (Cochran, Rothschadl, & Rudick, 2009).

Participation in parks and recreation programs and services carries different value for seniors than the Baby Boomer generation (Sperazza & Banerjee, 2010b). Seniors, in comparison to Baby Boomers, tend to not participate in recreational activities for competitive or educational purposes. Seniors do prioritize the physiological and social benefits of parks and recreation program participation higher than Baby Boomers. Lastly, more seniors than Baby Boomers indicated that participation in parks and recreation programs and services for relaxation was not important. Overall, parks and recreation program preferences for seniors include travel and tourism-based activities, health and wellness options, and the arts. Seniors also are less likely to prioritize volunteering or self-improvement programs and services.

Partnerships may also exist for community parks and recreation agencies when conceptualizing programs for Baby Boomers and seniors. These collaborative efforts allow third parties with expertise in specific recreation and leisure programmatic areas to aid in the program design and implementation process. For example, Healthways SilverSneakers© Fitness is a nationwide fitness and exercise program for active, older adults. The focus includes fitness, social interaction, and enjoyment when participating. A number of parks and recreation agencies have partnered with SilverSneakers© to provide effective programming for their older adult population, including Williamson County (Fairview, Tennessee); Winchester-Clark County (Winchester, Kentucky); Morrisville Aquatics and Fitness Center (Morrisville, North Carolina); and the Charles R. Drew Wellness Center (Columbia, South Carolina).

There are a number of suggested guidelines to consider when designing programs for older adults, particularly as the Baby Boomer generation enters this age range. These guidelines will also enhance professional practice when catering to older adults. First, focusing on the participatory benefits is crucial. Participants who felt the programmatic environment invited individual achievement, encouraged relaxation and social interaction with others, and stimulated creativity gained the most from their involvement in the program (Riley & Stanley, 2006). Participation rates and enrollment numbers will assist the public parks and recreation agency administrators in finding out who is being served, but numbers alone do not indicate if the participants are gaining any benefit from involvement (Henderson & Bialeschki, 2002). Setting up programs that are meaningfully related to one another will create a richer recreational experience for older adults who participate (Cochran, Rothschadl, & Rudick, 2009).

Second, having qualified, skilled staff members who understand and can connect with this age group will help in the longevity and success of the program. Instructors who can evaluate and provide specific guidance for participants, without doing the activity for them, will serve the program well. Teaching in a manner that encourages concept and technical skill development will serve participants well. Older adults enjoy rivalry and competition, so having program leaders who can work with participants in advanced-level programs and services will be a great benefit also (Tedrick, 2004).

Third, the objectives associated with the program must specific, attainable, and realistic for the participants. These attributes associated with the programmatic objectives should be relayed during the marketing and promotional campaign targeting older adults. Sperazza and Banerjee (2010a) refer to this approach as viewing programs and services through a "Boomer lens." This approach incorporates the mindset of looking at public parks and recreation programs through the eyes of Baby Boomers. Ways to do this include modifying mission statements and goals to reflect Boomers' desires for recreational programs or developing URL links on the community parks and recreation website to help Boomers feel welcome and included. Most successful public parks and recreation programs for older adults contribute to the maintenance and development of mental, physical, and social competencies (Godbey, Graefe, & James, 1992). If a community is having difficulty with targeting the needs of older adults, engaging in a needs assessment and surveying the population may help unearth what is wanted out of public parks and recreation programs.

WHY PRIORITIZE OLDER ADULT RECREATION PROGRAMMING?

The changing demographics associated with the population in the United States have caused public parks and recreation agencies to begin prioritizing programs and services for older adults and seniors. Community parks and recreation departments often operate senior centers or facilities. These facilities often serve to provide drop-in programs that promote social interaction. In addition, these types of centers provide a place for staging trips and tours, instructional activities, forums, lectures, and service opportunities. Further, these spaces often host meal functions. Such facilities often provide spaces for opportunities for the organization of senior councils or boards to help in the development of programs and services. They become the hub of life for many senior adults with their daily schedule revolving around the programs and services provided, as well as the opportunity for social interaction and engagement with their peers. The city of Cedar Falls, Iowa Senior Citizen Center provides "organized card clubs, organized billiards/pool games or tournaments, and other events scheduled from 8 a.m.–4 p.m. on non-holiday weekdays when available." (http://www.cedarfalls.com/communitycenter.

Lynn (2011) highlighted The Summit in Grand Prairie, Texas, dubbed "the first Baby Boomer facility in America," as a unique facility, one designed for adults aged 50 and older. Since the opening of the The Summit in 2010, there are over 5,000 active members, and the facility has become a hub of activity within the community and a central component of development within Grand Prairie. The Malley Senior Recreational Center in Englewood, Colorado, is another example of a facility primarily developed for seniors. In 2011, the Center was recognized as the national NuStep Pinnacle Award recipient, recognizing the excellence in older adult wellness programs and the commitment to transforming lives and promoting optimal health and wellness regardless of age (City of Englewood, 2015).

As Crompton (2013) pointed out, the increase in this portion of the population alone is not the only reason to prioritize older adult programming. There are five other important items associated with seniors' status that suggest community parks and recreation agencies should consider moving this age group to the forefront of their programmatic plans. These include: (a) an extension of active retirement time, (b) enhanced discretionary income, (c) contributions to the economic development of a community, (d) enhanced leisure literacy, and (e) disproportionate political influence.

Extended Retirement Time

Current demographic trends indicate that older adults and seniors are leaving the work force earlier in life, therefore retirement and the time associated with it is increasing. The Baby Boomer generation's average retirement time in years has doubled since 1950, going from roughly 11 years to 21 years for men, and 12.5 years to 25 years for women (Leonesio, Bridges, Gesumaria, & Del Bene, 2012). This dramatic increase in free time leads to more opportunities for engagement in public parks and recreation programs and services.

Enhanced Discretionary Income

There are currently four sources of income for older adults and seniors: Social Security; earnings; private pensions; and assets, such as interest, dividends, and rent (Crompton, 2013). The income growth for seniors has continued to increase over the past decade, even as other younger age groups' income levels have dipped. Notably, there was a 10% increase for individuals ages 55–64, and for those adults over 65 years of age, there was 45% increase. These income increases are important for the public parks and recreation administrators to digest. Older adults tend to have a lower cost of living than all other age groups; child-rearing costs and other work-related costs are relatively nonexistent. Other significant expenses, such as mortgages, have been paid off. Lastly, a growing trend illustrates that many older adults have freezes placed on their property taxes paid once they reach 65 years of age. All of these points regarding older adults' finances and expenditures lead to the conclusion that more seniors have more money to spend on recreation and leisure programs.

Contributions to the Economic Development of a Community

Aside from income, older adults have the largest amount of net assets when compared with any other age group. Understanding the ability of seniors to contribute to the local economy via their net assets can positively impact the revenue generated within a community. Crompton coined the term GRAMPIES to describe this age group—the Growing number of Retired Active Monied People In Excellent Shape (Crompton, 2001). Attracting and retaining seniors involves developing programs and services that encourage socialization, personal development, and a healthy active lifestyle. Community parks and recreation agencies that can do this will take steps toward generating revenue via older adults' economic contributions.

Enhanced Leisure Literacy

A rewarding experience for seniors is the opportunity to enjoy their post-work years. The current groups of older adults were exposed to more recreation and leisure pursuits than their parents and grandparents. These recreational avenues remain stable throughout the lifespan, and present-day seniors want more active recreational opportunities from their community parks and recreation agencies. As mentioned before, retention of older adults is predicated upon agencies taking steps to address these recreational needs. Communities that disregard or fail to act on the recreational needs of seniors will potentially lose seniors' participation in programs and services.

Disproportionate Political Influence

Finally, "gray power" is the political and social influence of seniors and older adults (Shankar, 1989). Their influence on political decision-making is noticeable and will continue to grow with the Baby Boomer generation's involvement in voting and community agenda items. Older adults have more time to delve into election of officials, investigate government budget proposals, and represent communities in meetings and open forums. Voting and representation in elections is highest within this age group, and a vested interest in their government officials yields significant turnout by seniors. One of the byproducts of "gray power" is the ability of seniors to voice their recreational needs to government representatives, potentially influencing public parks and recreation centers' programming.

INTERGENERATIONAL PROGRAMS

As outlined above, the Baby Boomer generation will soon embody one of the largest population groups within the United States. As public parks and recreation agencies move forward and develop programs that target this population, it is still inherent to create services that continue to connect older adults within their community. An unfortunate occurrence associated with individuals in this age range is isolation; whether it is physical, emotional, or psychological, there is a concern regarding isolation due to relocation of living, transportation constraints, or level of activity (Harris, 2007; U.S. Public Health Service, 2009).

Intergenerational programs are a unique way to facilitate the connectedness for older adults with others in the community while fostering a sense of generativity and integrity that is a part of the positive process of aging. As Belgrave (2012) pointed out, younger and older generations tend to interact within their peer groups, limiting nonfamilial cross-age interactions. Research on intergenerational programming has shown a number of improvements in the age groups involved, including positive cross-age attitudes, cross-age interactions, and enhanced psychological well-being in older adults (Belgrave & Darrow, 2010; Bowers, 1998; Darrow, Johnson, & Ollenberger, 1994; Frego, 1995; VanWeelden & Whipple, 2004). By fostering intergenerational programs, public parks and recreation agencies provide opportunities for cross-age relationships to develop between younger and older generations, promote harmony within the community, and increase social identity (Riley & Stanley, 2006).

Four intergenerational program models exist that can be implemented by community parks and recreation agencies that are interested in developing these services: (a) an older generation serving a younger generation, (b) a younger generation serving an older generation, (c) a younger and older generation learning together, and (d) a younger and older generation recreating together (Belgrave, 2012). When an older generation serves a younger generation, the older adults act as mentors, teaching and guiding youth via their skills or expertise in a specific area. When a younger generation serves an older generation, the opposite occurs; the youth teach and guide the older adults. When both age groups are learning together, there is mutually beneficial growth by each group. When both groups use a recreation model, the two age groups work together, learn together, and then demonstrate what was learned via the experience (Belgrave, Darrow, Walworth, & Wlodarczyk, 2011).

As life expectancy has increased, the stereotypical conception of older and younger generations will shift. Referring again to The Summit facility affiliated with Grand Prairie, Texas Parks and Recreation, a unique development occurred once the facility opened. Enrollment has included adults between the ages of 50-100 years, and the staff has seen the older adults taking the 50-year-olds "under their wings." These types of mentoring relationships are intergenerational, and highlight a paradigm shift in the traditional thought process of generations—in this case, 50 years of age is young!

SENIOR PROGRAMMER POSITIONS

The shifting perceptions by older adults of how to spend their recreation and leisure time has created a niche market in the workforce. Community parks and recreation agencies are now hiring full-time recreation specialists who have expertise in designing senior programs. Examples of what public parks and recreation agencies are looking for in staff members who specialize in developing programs for older and adults and seniors are illustrated in Figures 14.1 and 14.2.

These positions are a change from previous hiring for senior programs; existing staff members with little to no experience working with seniors were asked to create and implement services and activities. Senior Programs Recreation Specialists are asked to engage in a number of essential duties, including, but not limited to, the following:

- Organizing programs (i.e., seminars, classes, seasonal events, special events, trips), inclusive of advertising and placing equipment orders
- Supervising aquatic facilities and programs
- Working cooperatively with volunteers and community organizations to improve services
- Developing public relations and marketing materials
- Building effective marketing partnerships with media outlets
- Training part-time staff who may assist with senior programs
- Securing instructors, entertainers, and vendors for programs
- Coordinate intergenerational programs with schools, businesses and other agencies
- Implement fund-raising efforts, as well as manage program budgets

NEWPORT NEWS, VA
CITY OF OPPORTUNITY

JOB DESCRIPTION
MATURE ADULT CENTER SUPERVISOR
(COMMUNITY RECREATION DIVISION)
PARKS, RECREATION AND TOURISM

Human Resources Department
700 Town Center Drive, Suite 200
Newport News, VA 23606
Phone: (757) 926-1800
Fax: (757) 926-1825

GENERAL STATEMENT OF RESPONSIBILITIES

Under limited supervision, this position assists with the programming and operations of recreational programs at a Mature Adult Center. Reports to a Recreation Program Coordinator or Recreation Program Supervisor.

ESSENTIAL JOB FUNCTIONS

Plans and conducts recreational activities for mature adults to include physical, educational, cognitive activities, seminars, seasonal events and local trips which address the needs and interests of people age 50 and over.

Assists with monitoring facilities and activities to maintain structure, safety, and a clean environment. Sets up and breaks down equipment for various events and activities.

Performs a variety of administrative support work such as word processing, creating spreadsheets, data entry or retrieval. Transports program participants as needed.

Performs other duties as assigned.

PERFORMANCE STANDARD

Employees at all levels are expected to effectively work together to meet the needs of the community and the organization through work behaviors demonstrating the City's Values. Employees are also expected to lead by example and demonstrate the highest level of ethics.

REQUIRED KNOWLEDGE

- Recreational Programming – Extensive knowledge of recreational programming and recreational facility operations with a focus on mature adults and Gerontology.
- Safety – Knowledge of occupational hazards, safety precautions, and safety regulations related to recreational activities and other work related precautions.
- Customer Service – Knowledge of principles and processes for providing customer service. This includes setting and meeting quality standards for services, and evaluation of customer satisfaction.
- Technology – Knowledge of general office equipment and personal computers and related security software and equipment.

Figure 14.1. Senior Programmer Job Description, Newport News, (VA) Community Recreation Division

REQUIRED SKILLS

- <u>Judgment/Decision Making</u> – Evaluates the best method of research and then exercises appropriate judgment in establishing priorities and resolving complex matters. Considers the relative costs and benefits of potential actions to choose the most appropriate one.
- <u>Interpersonal Relationships</u> – Develops and maintains cooperative and professional relationships with employees and all levels of management to include representatives from other departments and organizations.
- <u>Time Management</u> – Plan and organize daily work routine. Establishes priorities for the completion of work in accordance with sound time-management methodology to meet strict deadlines.

REQUIRED ABILITIES

- <u>Communication</u> – Excellent ability to communicate complex ideas and proposals effectively so others will understand to include preparation of reports, agendas, and policies. Excellent ability to listen and understand information and ideas presented verbally or in writing. Ability to handle a variety of employee relations issues with tact, confidentiality and diplomacy.
- <u>Mathematics</u> – Ability to perform basic arithmetic applications.

EDUCATION AND EXPERIENCE

Requires a high school diploma and 1 year of program related experience or an equivalent combination of education and experience.

ADDITIONAL REQUIREMENTS

An acceptable general background check to include a local and state criminal history and sex offender registry check.

A valid driver's license with an acceptable driving record.

PHYSICAL REQUIREMENTS

- Tasks require the ability to exert moderate, though not constant physical effort.
- Some combination of climbing and balancing to include climbing ladders, stooping, kneeling, crouching, and crawling.
- Some lifting, carrying, pushing and/or pulling of objects and materials of moderate weight (12 – 20 pounds).

SENSORY REQUIREMENTS

- Some tasks require the ability to perceive and discriminate sounds and visual cues or signals.
- Some tasks require the ability to communicate orally.

ENVIRONMENTAL EXPOSURES

Performance of essential functions may require exposure to adverse environmental conditions, such as dust, pollen, temperature and weather extremes, traffic hazards, violent individuals, infectious disease, or rude/irate customers.

Figure 14.1. cont.

JOB DESCRIPTION

City of Patterson

Human Resources

RECREATION SPECIALIST
(SENIOR PROGRAMS)
HOURLY RATE: $9.50-11.50

JOB SUMMARY

*Class specifications are intended to present a descriptive list of the range of duties performed by employees in the class. Specifications are **not** intended to reflect all duties performed within the job.*

Under supervision of the Recreation Coordinator or Recreation Director, the Recreation Specialist will implement a wide range of programs that foster community development in senior center activities. This position will require assistance of general office duties and may include supervision of volunteers and staff. The Specialist will be committed to professional development within their position and perform related duties as assigned. This position is established for up to 28 hours per week and will be working weekday evenings and weekends.

SUPERVISION RECEIVED AND EXERCISED

Receives supervision from the Recreation Coordinator or Recreation Director.

This position may supervise volunteers and staff.

ESSENTIAL DUTIES

Essential and other important responsibilities may include, but are not limited to, the following:

➤ Organize a wide range of Senior adult programs including: advertising events, creating events and activities and placing equipment orders etc..
➤ Work cooperatively with volunteers and community organizations to build coalitions that will improve services and programs.
➤ Develop public relations materials and alliances with the media for the marketing of programs and the benefits of recreational programs to the participants and the community.
➤ Perform related duties as assigned.
➤ Assist with training and retention of P/T recreation staff

Figure 14.2. Senior Programmer Job Description, Patterson, California Recreation and Community Services Department

---

MIMIMUM QUALIFICATIONS

Knowledge of: Routine office practices and procedures. Knowledge of recreation programming principals and event planning. Excellent communication skills working with adults and volunteers.

Ability to: Understand and carry out oral and written directions. Ability to communicate courteously and effectively with the general public. Ability to speak Spanish is desirable but not required.

Education: Must have a High School Diploma or GED equivalent.

EXPERIENCE AND CERTIFICATION(S)

Any combination of experience and training what would likely provide the required knowledge and abilities is qualifying. A typical way to obtain the knowledge and abilities would be:

➤ Experience: Previous experience programming activities and events with Senior Adults, community groups, volunteers preferred.

License or Certificate:

➤ Completion of First Aid *
➤ CPR certification *

NECESSARY SPECIAL REQUIREMENTS

➤ Must be 18 years of age or older.
➤ Must posses a valid class C driver's license.
➤ Must successfully pass a pre-employment medical examination, including a drug screen, fingerprint, background check, and reference check.
➤ Must be able to provide proof of U.S. citizenship or legal right to work in the United States.

* Completion of a first aid, CPR, and Certified Coaches Administrators course within one year of employment.

Figure 14.2. cont.

Qualifications for Senior Programs Recreation Specialists extend beyond "being good with older people." Common requirements for these positions include the following:

- Knowledge of recreation programming principles, inclusive of special event design and management
- Positive customer service and public speaking skills
- Strong accounting and budgeting techniques
- An educational degree in gerontology, human development, recreation, or a related field

Public parks and recreation agency administrators who hire Senior Programs Recreation Specialists are being proactive and setting their organization up for success. Employing staff members who have previous experience working with seniors and older adults is beneficial in program design and implementation. If an organization can develop high-quality programs and services with effective leaders that are in line with seniors' expectations for an active, healthy lifestyle, it is a "win-win" scenario for the public parks and recreation agency, the seniors, and the larger local community.

SUMMARY

The evolutionary nature of public parks and recreation programs for adults and seniors has taken a unique path to prioritization in the field. Participants are looking for recreational opportunities that allow them to enjoy the different phases of adulthood as they create a healthy balance in work and life commitments. These outlets can be individual or group-oriented, competitive or recreational, educational or social, or a little bit of each—as long as they are beneficial to the person.

As community parks and recreation administrators and staff members develop programs for adults, population statistics show that older adults will soon be one of the largest age groups in the United States. This group of individuals is looking for activities that challenge them holistically—mind, body, and soul. Gone are the stereotypical assumptions of passive involvement by older adults; they remain active, energetic, and purposefully driven. They continue to drink from the "cup of life," tasting every opportunistic drop of the enriching and fulfilling programs that are provided by public parks and recreation agencies. Agencies that are capable of crafting programs and services, and even develop facilities that cater to older adults, are tapping into a boon for their organization financially. The benefit extends to the community if the programs are intergenerational in nature.

In order to meet the recreational needs of Baby Boomers and seniors, public parks and recreation agencies should seek to employ individuals with expertise and experience working with this portion of the population. Administrators recognize the importance of situationally specific qualities in staff members, as well as an overall adherence to the agency's mission, when searching for leaders of programs for adults and seniors. The right combination of leadership, program design, and variance in programmatic offerings will meet the needs of adults of all ages, as well as further stabilize the public parks and recreation agency as a torchbearer for growth and sustainability of the community as a whole.

DISCUSSION QUESTIONS

1. Highlight two to three categories and examples of adult programs and services at a local public parks and recreation agency.
2. What are some of the trends associated with older adult and senior programming?
3. What are the characteristics of the Baby Boomer generation?
4. What are some of the reasons to prioritize older adult programming in the public parks and recreation field?
5. What are benefits of intergenerational public parks and recreation programs?
6. Discuss one of the stages of adulthood, significant changes in this stage, and the types of public parks and recreation programs that are beneficial for this stage.
7. How has program design for older adults and seniors evolved over the past decade?
8. How do partnerships benefit older adult and senior programs?
9. What are the four sources of income for older adults and seniors, and why is it important for public parks and recreation administrators to know these income sources?
10. What are some of the essential job duties associated with Recreation Specialist – Senior Programs positions?

REFERENCES

Aurora, Colorado. (2015). Your city, your community, your home. Retrieved from https://www.auroragov.org/ThingsToDo/Recreation/Centers/AuroraCenterforActiveAdults/.

Beckner, B. (2012). Are seniors a core target audience for your programs and services? *Parks & Recreation, 47*(5), 52.

Belgrave, M. (2012). Implementing music therapy-based intergenerational programs in the community. *The International Journal of the Arts in Society, 6*(6), 1–9.

Belgrave, M., & Darrow, A. A. (2010). The effect of participation in intergenerational music activities on cross-age attitudes, positive nonverbal behaviors, and behaviors of engagement. In L. E. Schraer-Joiner (Ed.), *Proceedings of the 18th International Seminar of the Commission on Music in Special Education, Music Therapy, and Music Medicine.* Nedlands, WA: International Society for Music Education.

Belgrave, M., Darrow, A. A., Walworth, D., & Wlodarczyk, N. (2011). *Music therapy and geriatric populations: A handbook for practicing music therapists and healthcare professionals.* Silver Springs, MD: American Music Therapy Association.

Bowers, J. (1998). Effects of an intergenerational choir for community-based seniors and college students on age-related attitudes. *Journal of Music Therapy, 35,* 2–18.

Briggs, D. (2013). Identification of motivation in senior individuals who engage in the adventure experience of ice climbing. Unpublished doctoral dissertation: University of Northern Iowa.

Brokaw, T. (1998). *The greatest generation.* New York, NY: Random House.

City of Beachwood, Ohio. (2015). Recreation guide: Recreation programs for adults and children. Retrieved from http://www.beachwoodohio.com/DocumentCenter/View/968.

City of Greeley, Colorado. (February/March 2011). City of Greeley Leisure Services Department: Great from the ground up. Northern Colorado Business Report, 12.

City of Englewood, Colorado. (2015). Malley Senior Recreation Center. Retrieved from http://www.englewoodgov.org/inside-city-hall/city-departments/parks-and-recreation/malley-senior-recreation-center.

Cochran, L. J., Rothschadl, A., & Rudick, J. L. (2009). *Leisure programming for Baby Boomers.* Champaign, IL: Human Kinetics.

Cochran, L. J., Stoll, S., & Kinziger, M. (2006). Looking through a new lens: How to find leisure programming success with the Baby Boomer generation. *Parks & Recreation, 41*(1), 44–49.

Crompton, J. L. (November 2001). *Parks and Economic Development.* PAS Report No. 502. Chicago, IL: APA.

Crompton, J. (2013). Are your seniors moving to center stage? *Parks & Recreation, 48*(12), 36–41.

Darrow, A. A., Johnson, C. M., & Ollenberger, T. (1994). The effect of participation in an intergenerational choir on teens' and older persons' cross-age attitudes. *Journal of Music Therapy, 31,* 119–134.

Edginton, C. R., Jordan, D. J., DeGraaf, D. G., & Edginton, S. R. (2002). *Leisure and life satisfaction: Foundational perspectives* (3rd ed.). New York, NY: McGraw-Hill.

Erikson, E. (1963). *Childhood and society.* New York, NY: W.W. Horton.

Freedman, M. (1999). *Prime time: How Baby Boomers will revolutionize retirement and transform America.* New York, NY: Public Affairs.

Frego, R. D. (1995). Uniting the generations with music programs. *Music Educators Journal, 81*(16), 17–19.

Gillon, S. (2004). *Boomer nation: The largest and richest generation ever and how it changed America*. New York, NY: Free Press.

Godbey, G., Graefe, A., & James, S. D. (1992). *The benefits of local recreation and park services: A nationwide study of perceptions of the American public*. Arlington, VA: National Recreation and Park Association.

Harris, Y. (2007). Depression as a risk factor for nursing home admission among older individuals. *Journal of American Medical Director's Association, 8*(1), 14–20.

Henderson, K. A., & Bialeschki, D. (2002). *Evaluating leisure services: Making enlightened decisions*. State College, PA: Venture.

Jordan, D. J. (1996). *Leadership in leisure services: Making a difference*. State College, PA: Venture.

Kelly, J. R., & Freysinger, V. J. (2000). *21st century leisure: Current issues*. Needham Heights, MA: Allyn & Bacon.

Leonesio, M. V., Bridges, B., Gesumaria, R., & Del Bene, L. (2012). The increasing labor force participation of older workers and its effect on the income of the aged. *Social Security Bulletin, 72*(1), 59–77.

Lynn, A. (2011). Partners in design. *Parks & Recreation, 46*(3), 46–52.

Newport News, Virginia Community Recreation Division. (2015). Job description: Mature adult center supervisor. Community Recreation Division, Parks, Recreation and Tourism. Retrieved from http://www.nngov.com/DocumentCenter/Home/View/2945

Patterson, California Recreation and Community Services Department. (2015). Job description: City of Patterson Human Resources, Senior Program Specialist. Retrieved from http://www.ci.patterson.ca.us/DocumentCenter/Home/View/92

Porter, S. (May 4, 1951). Babies equal boom, *New York Post*.

Riley, K., & Stanley, M. A. (2006). Research update: Art programs for older adults. *Parks & Recreation, 41*(2), 22–27.

Salt Lake County. (2015). Salt Lake County: Salt Lake County Parks and Recreation. Retrieved from http://slco.org/recreation/admin/adultSports/adultSports.html

Shankar A. Y. (1989). Gray power: Agenda for future research. *Canadian Journal on Aging, 8*, 118–127.

Sperazza, L. J., & Banerjee, P. (2010a). Baby Boomers and seniors: Understanding their leisure values enhances programs. *Activities, Adaptation & Aging, 34*, 196–215.

Sperazza, L. J., & Banerjee, P. (2010b). Baby Boomers and seniors: A leisure value study. *Journal of Unconventional Parks, Tourism and Recreation Research, 3*(1), 15–21.

Tedrick, T. (2004). Seniors set sight on being competitive. *Parks & Recreation, 39*(8), 28–33.

Todd, C. (2004). *Perception is reality*. Presented at the National Recreation and Park Association Congress, Reno, NV.

U.S. Public Health Service. (2009). *Report of the Surgeon General's conference on older adults and mental health: A national section agenda*. Washington, DC: U.S. Department of Health and Human Services.

VanWeelden, K., & Whipple, J. (2004). Effect of field experiences on music therapy students' perceptions of choral music for geriatric wellness programs. *Journal of Music Therapy, 41*, 340–352.

Zabriskie, R. B., & McCormick, B. P. (2003). Parent and child perspectives of family leisure involvement and satisfaction with family life. *Journal of Leisure Research, 35*(2), 165–189.

Ziegler, J. (2002). Recreating retirement: How will Baby Boomers reshape leisure in their 60s? *Parks & Recreation, 37*(10), 56–61.

Chapter Fifteen

Event Management

CHAPTER OBJECTIVES

- To understand the role of the parks and recreation agency relative to community special events
- To appreciate the range of community special events that parks and recreation agencies manage and/or sponsor
- To provide insight into the responsibilities and difficulties of community event management
- To understand that community special events bring benefits to both the resident and visitor population
- To gain an appreciation of the elements that must be considered when organizing events

INTRODUCTION

The role that parks and recreation agencies play in a community has expanded over the years. Not only do these agencies provide services for the resident population, they also play a key role coordinating, facilitating, and managing special events and festivals for the community. Often these events are designed to attract tourists for economic reasons. Parks and recreation organizations play a central role in some communities and a supporting role in others. Holding special events and festivals in a community, depending on the scope, normally does not require special facilities. Therefore, communities of any size can hold these events in existing parks, town squares, pavilions, and other public facilities. Many communities rely on the parks and recreation department and their sports complexes to hold tournaments that attract visitors from out of town.

Communities hold special events and festivals for many reasons, which include enhancing the local image of the place and providing economic benefits for businesses and the community. Visitors' motivations to attend a festival or event are among the first considerations to account for organizing a festival. Attendees to festivals and events are motivated by learning about a place, supporting events and community, socialization, and novelty. Businesses engage in the sponsorship of special events and festivals in order to promote their business, but also to give back to the community and support others. Government involvement supports local businesses, and provides some funding (albeit a minimum at most times) for the ongoing support of these events.

Special events are occasions drawing individuals together to enjoy a recreation or educational experience that is meaningful, significant, and relevant to their well-being (Edginton, O'Neill, & O'Neill, 1999). Events and festivals are many and varied. Music and art festivals are popular, as well as food-and-beverage-based events. In fact, the development of food tourism as a generator of income and enhancement of community pride and identity has emerged as an objective of many communities. For example, a study of small communities and their food-based community festivals in Northeast Iowa found that the total economic impact was $2,638,811, with an additional tourist spending of $1 generating $1.61 of output in the economy of selected counties in Northeast Iowa (Cela, Lankford, & Lankford 2007; Lankford, Cela, & Lankford, 2005).

This chapter provides information on the typologies for special events and festivals. The role that parks and recreation departments play in holding the events is also discussed, as well as the benefits of holding these events. Information on the factors of success for community special events is also described. Examples of parks and recreation agency supported or sponsored events are contrasted.

PURPOSE OF SPECIAL EVENTS

Parks and recreation agencies are utilizing special events to provide more variety to the programs offered, and to highlight the community and its assets. Special events are targeted for the community, visitors, or both. Edginton, O'Neill, and O'Neill (1999) notes that a special event has four characteristics:

- A specifically planned and focused event
- A singular occurrence, an extraordinary activity of some importance, deviating from the routine, an event outside the normal program of activities of the agency, an opportunity for a recreation experience outside the normal range of choices or beyond the everyday experience
- A "crowd" participating, either by specific invitation or open invitation
- A publicized occurrence of finite length

It should be noted that event planning, programming, and management are a function of the recreation programming process. Parks and recreation professionals are well suited to plan, manage, collaborate and partner with community groups to stage these events. Edginton and O'Neill (1999) further elaborate on the purposes of special events, to include the following three areas: affect of the organization, promotion of community, and economic benefits. Figure 15.1 (adapted from Edginton and O'Neill) delineates how these three purposes impact an organization and community.

A study representing city administrators, planners, recreation directors, and tourism and convention professionals sought to identify perceptions of community based tourism and special events. Respondents represented 48 communities across the U.S. of various siz-

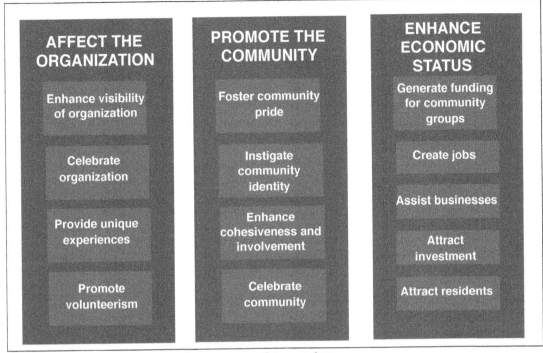

Figure 15.1. Functions and Purpose of Special Events

Table 15.1

Perceived Importance of Benefits of Special Events for Communities

How important are the following benefits to your community as a result of special events?	Very Important	Important	Not Important
Improvement of local economy	84.9%	15.1%	
Increased employment opportunities	66%	32.1%	1.9%
Improvement of quality of life	49.1%	50.9%	
Development of community pride	37.7%	60.4%	1.9%
Promotion of cultural exchange	30.2%	52.8%	17%
Preservation of cultural identity of host population	28.3%	50.9%	20.8%
Increased quality of attractions/recreational opportunities	56.6%	43.4%	

Source: UNI-STEP; 2012-2013 Community-Based Tourism Survey and Nelson, 2014

es, all known to have a tourism industry that was considered community oriented. As one can see in Table 15.1, the improvement of the local economy, employment, and increased quality of recreational attractions were the viewed as the primary benefits (UNI STEP, 2013) of special events, which resulted in tourists visitations. Interestingly, the purpose of festivals as proposed by Edginton and O'Neill (1999) in Figure 15.1 is supported by these perceived benefits in terms of economics, community identity and recreational opportunities.

TYPOLOGIES OF SPECIAL EVENTS

Edginton and O'Neill (1999) details the types of special events, which include the following:

- Fairs, expositions and shows are considered hall mark events. These include events such as county and state fairs, hobby and craft shows, garden shows, pet shows, art expositions, business and trade events.
- Holiday celebrations, festivals, music festivals, and parades that focus on folk festivals, cultural and heritage events, and carnivals.
- Sports competitions such as golf events, tournaments for youth and adult amateur for soccer, softball, etc., marathons and mini marathons, fishing, hunting and boat races. Included would be spectator events such as college and professional sports, dog and horse racing etc.
- Performing arts such as dance, music drama including folk festivals and community theatre.

Figure 15.2 provides a representation of these typologies.

An example of one of these events is the Mendocino (California) Music Festival (http://mendocinomusic.org/about/). Partners and organizers include the Mendocino Recreation Association, and the Mendocino Chamber of Commerce. The two week festival in July operates on donations, over 200 volunteers. Community members offer living arrangements for musicians through the "house a musician." The event was established in 1986, which is a blend of music by consisting of orchestra concerts, Big Band, chamber music ensembles, dance, blues, jazz, world, folk, bluegrass and popular contemporary music. Daytime concerts include lecture/recitals at the Piano Series, a performance by participants in the Emerging Artists Program, and small concerts in intimate venues throughout the historic towns of Mendocino and Fort Bragg (http://mendocinomusic.org/about/).

COMMUNITY CELEBRATIONS
- Festivals–arts, music
- Fairs and carnivals
- Cultural and historical
- Religious

BUSINESS AND EDUCATION
- Meetings and conventions
- Conferences
- Seminars

SPORTS
- Amateur
- Professional
- Recreational

PRIVATE
- Weddings
- Reunions
- Socials

Figure 15.2. Typology of Community Events and Festivals. *Source:* Adapted from Getz & Frisby (1991)

The Mendocino County Chamber of Commerce, in conjunction with the parks and recreation department, and California State Parks, also collaborates with local communities to offer festivals celebrating the California Coastal National Monument. This celebration involves the North Coast Brewing Company, and various festivals (crab feeds, wine festivals, Mendocino Music Festival, whale festivals, film festivals, beer festivals, art festivals, and parades) to raise funding and awareness. Included are also promotion of events including hiking and bike trails, cinemas, water sports, and ocean/ beach activities.

It is instructive to understand why visitors are attracted to communities. A study by the Sustainable Tourism and Environment Program (STEP) at the University of Northern Iowa of small, medium, and large tourism-based communities notes a variety of reasons that visitors come to the communities. Communities were purposely selected based on their dependence on tourism as an economic strategy. It is interesting to note the various reasons, and then think about amenities and attractions. Scenery, parks, gardens, outdoor recreation, and recreation top the list. Of importance is that sports, museums, shopping, and food are listed, yet they are not the main attractions in the selected communities (See Figure 15.3).

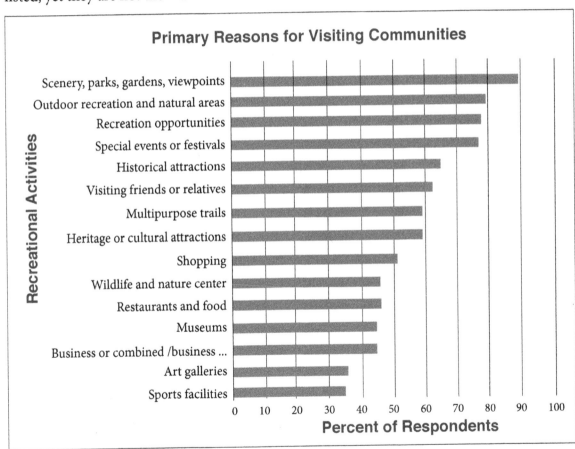

Figure 15.3. Reasons to Visit Community. *Source:* UNI-STEP; 2012–2013 Community Based Tourism Survey and Nelson (2014)

Table 15.2 compares popular community-based special events and festivals and their amenities. Interestingly, a review of the table suggests that each community has identified primary and secondary amenity attractions. For example, Hot Springs, Arkansas's primary attraction is the hot springs and bathhouses, which now comprise a national park. Of particular interest is the interdependency among the tourism industry, community, businesses, and parks and recreation agencies who work to ensure an improved quality of life for area residents (Hawkins & Cunningham, 1996), while enhancing the visitor product. As one can see in Table 15.2, the success of a community special events is a result of public and private partnerships. It is important to note that these events are held in public parks, facilities, and spaces.

Table 15.2

Examples of Community Based Special Events and Festivals

State	City	Example Festivals for Visitors and Community	Website
AR	Hot Springs	Festivals: Hot Springs Music Festival, Hot Springs Fishing Challenge	http://www.hotsprings.org
CA	Mendocino	Festivals: Two week music festival drawing national and international artists	http://mendocinomusic.org/about/
CA	San Francisco	Festival: Outside Lands Music Festival	http://www.sfoutsidelands.com/the-park/attractions
CO	Aspen	Festivals: Winter X Games, JAS Aspen June Snowmass Experience, tribal dances, food and wine festivals, writing festivals	http://www.colorado.com/cities-and-towns/aspen
CO	Glenwood Springs	Festivals: Strawberry Days Festival, ghost walk event	http://www.visitglenwood.com
IA	Amana Colonies	Festivals: Culinary, Car Clubs, Oktoberfest, Maipole dancers for Maifest (German heritage celebration)	http://www.amanacolonies.com
IA	Decorah	Festivals: Oneota Film Festival, Tractor Days, Nordic Fest, Lawn Chair Nights for concerts, Rendezvous Days	http://www.visitdecorah.com
IL	Galena	Festivals: hot air balloon race, art festivals, vintage orchestra, Oktoberfest, county fair, pub crawls, parades, pottery tours, ice sculpting festivals, dance festivals, 50's themed festivals, wine lovers	http://www.visitgalena.org/index.cfm
IL	Springfield	Festivals: Historic events, Abraham Lincoln tributes	http://www.visitspringfielddillinois.com
MI	Traverse City	Festivals: music festivals, film festivals, microbrew festivals, wine and art festivals	http://www.traversecity.com/summer/things-to-do/events/festivals/
MN	Wabash	Festivals: SeptOberFest, Riverboat Days, Grumpy Old Men Festival, Watermelon Festival	http://www.exploremississippibluffs.com/wabasha/
MN	Washington County	Festival: Lake Elmo Blue Grass Festival	http://www.co.washington.mn.us/index.aspx?NID=1559
OR	Ashland	Festivals: Shakespeare festival, Crab Fest, holiday festivals, honey festival, multicultural festivals, film, food, wine and brew festivals, walkathons, running relays	https://www.osfashland.org
OR	Champoeg	Festival: Folk Dance Festival at Historic Barn	http://oregonstateparks.org/index.cfm?do=parkPage.dsp_parkPage&parkId=79
WA	Leavenworth	Festivals: International celebrations, music festivals, Kinder Fest (Bavarian Village Celebration, River Salmon Festival, Autumn Leaf Festival, Quilt Festival, Rockfest (climbing)	http://www.leavenworth.org
WA	Walla Walla	Festivals: Sweet Onion Festival, Stopover music festival	http://www.wallawalla.org
WI	Mineral Point	Festivals: Cornish Festival, Book Festival, film festivals, county fair, "city-wide garage sales"	http://mineralpoint.com

An interesting example and profile of a community-based festival involves a public university, city parks and recreation, and a nonprofit is the College Hill Arts Festival held in Cedar Falls, Iowa. Now celebrating its 39th anniversary, the College Hill Arts Festival was conceived in 1979 and came alive with 30 or so local and northeast Iowa artists showcasing their original artwork. Today this top-ranked, national arts festival features 75 talented artists who turn the corner of West 23rd & College Street on the campus of the University of Northern Iowa into a living museum. These artists have come to Cedar Falls from all over the United States to give festival patrons the very best art experience possible. These juried artists exhibit and sell their original artwork in categories, including ceramics, fiber, wood, jewelry, metal sculpture, painting, photography, and glass. The festival, staffed entirely by volunteers, has become a very unique opportunity to connect nationally known artists and the Cedar Valley community in an effort to create a top-quality juried art festival and to make fine art easily accessible to the public.

Nationally recognized artist Gary Kelley became a festival supporter in 1985 by creating his first College Hill Arts Festival poster. Kelley's annual creations have become "must haves" for festival supporters, and he has won numerous national awards for his festival designs. Complementing the artists' exhibits are a variety of musical groups performing on stage, hands-on creative activities for children sponsored by the Hearst Center for the Arts, plus balloon sculptures and face painting—all free—and a variety of food vendors to entice festival attendees. And, unique to festivals, the College Hill Arts Festival features a Young Art Collectors Gallery, with original artwork created by the exhibiting artists with prices of $10 or less, which encourages youth aged 14 and under to make independent decisions about art based on their own feelings. The 2014 festival was ranked in the top 300 events nationwide by *Art Fair Source Book*. In addition, for nine out of the last 10 years, the College Hill Arts Festival has been named by *Sunshine Artist* magazine to their list of 100 Best Fine Art & Design Shows in the United States (Bartlett, 2015; and adapted from Lankford, Grybovych, & Lankford, 2015).

FACTORS OF SUCCESS AND MANAGEMENT FOR COMMUNITY SPECIAL EVENTS

Collaboration and coordination of special events and festivals involves multiple organizations and volunteers. The importance of building and maintaining partnerships in the community cannot be overstated. By communicating goals to partners, a community can gather more support (fiscal, human resources etc.) for the events. See Figure 15.1 for an example of the types of interests that are represented in community based festivals and events (adapted from Lankford, Grybovych, & Lankford, 2015).

A study recently demonstrated the role that the parks and recreation agency plays in supporting special events in a community (Table 15.3). Various stakeholders collaborate to make a successful event and festival. Not surprisingly, the visitor convention bureau always collaborates followed by the chamber of commerce. Of particular interest is that the parks

Table 15.3

Stakeholder Collaboration in Promoting Special Events and Festivals

Which stakeholders collaborate toward a successful visitor industry in your community?	Always Collaborate	Sometimes	Never
Parks and recreation	67.3%	30.8%	1.9%
Visitor convention bureau/visitor center/tourism office	90.2%	7.8%	2%
Chamber of commerce	58.5%	34%	7.5%
Economic development authority	50%	37.5%	12.5%
Main street organization	42.2%	31.1%	26.7%
Community festival group	48%	38%	14%

Source: UNI-STEP; 2013 Community-Based Tourism Survey

and recreation department always or sometimes (97.3%) collaborates for community tourism. This finding suggests that the role of the local government is particularly important and supportive of tourism efforts (UNI-STEP, 2013).

In another study (see Table 15.4), Saunders (2005) researched the factors that make community festivals successful. Based on the work of Wilson et al. (2001), Saunders tested the following factors by examining festivals and events in small, medium and large communities (27 communities).

Table 15.4

Factors of Success for Rural Community Tourism and Festivals (In Order of Importance)

Wilson et.al. (2001) Community Tourism	Saunders (2005) Festivals
A Complete Tourism Package	Widespread Community Support for Tourism and the Festival
Good Leadership	Volunteers
Support & Participation of Local Government	Festival Management
Sufficient Funds for Tourism Development	Coordination and Cooperation With Businesses
Strategic Planning	Sufficient Funding
Coordination and Cooperation between Businesses and Local Leadership	Support and Coordination from Local Government
Coordination and Cooperation between Rural tourism Entrepreneurs	Choice of Festival Activities
Information and Technical Assistance for Development and Promotion	Strategic Planning
Supportive Convention & Visitors Bureau	Supportive Convention & Visitors Bureau
Widespread Community Support for Tourism	Information & Technical Assistance
	Cooperation with Professionals
	Complete Visitor Package

Importantly, one can see that coordination, cooperation, community government, and community support are the basis for successful community-based tourism and festivals. This list of factors may be a tool for communities in assessing their current position with regard to developing tourism. Wilson et al. (2001) defined success as "a community tourism attraction that has established an effective infrastructure to support tourism development." The authors also defined unsuccessful communities as "one with substantial natural/cultural resources, but that has not established the economic, political, and community-based infrastructure necessary to support tourism development. Saunders (2005) clearly identified that community support, volunteers, festival management, funding, local government support, and planning were essential elements to successful special events and festivals. Of particular interest the role and expertise that parks and recreation organizations provide in staging such events.

MANAGING AND PLANNING SUCCESSFUL EVENTS

Before a parks and recreation agency moves forward in the planning stage of an event, it should have clear goals, objectives, and a vision statement. Important questions to consider include the following:

- Why is the event being held?
- Who will the stakeholders (those who are interested or involved in the event) be?
- When will the event be held?
- Where will the event be staged?
- What is the event content or product/experience sought?
- How will the event be evaluated?

The City of Maple Ridge Parks and Leisure Department in British Columbia has provided a checklist (see Table 15.5) for planning a community-wide event (City of Maple Ridge, 2015). This checklist provided by the Parks and Leisure Department begins with considerations that are a least five months out from the event, and concludes with an "after" action phase. One should note that evaluation of the event is not on this list. It is important that surveys be collected during the event to document satisfaction, visitor characteristics and economic impacts for the community. Volunteers would randomly select individuals to fill out a one page survey for the evaluation. A focus group could also be formed after the event to evaluate the event or aspects of the event. It is important that the survey data be made available to the event manager, planner, volunteers, and parks and recreation agency as soon as practical.

Another example of event management is from the City of San Diego, California. The city has developed an extensive permit system for city special events and festivals. This example demonstrates to event organizers the permits required to conduct the event within the city limits. San Diego prides itself on its special events, from major conventions and international sporting events to community-based festivals, parades, and athletic events. The city hosts thousands of events each year with a goal to enhance the vitality, quality of life, and economic prosperity of San Diego through the support of special events in San Diego (City of San Diego, 2015). Table 15.6 provides the framework set forth in the guide for event promoters and organizers. Of particular interest is that permits are required for many of the items listed below, or detailed plans that would be approved by the city. As one can see, many of the items listed are basically a planning process or guide to event management.

Table 15.5

Community Event Planning Checklist

At Least 5 Months Before the Event	4 Months Before the Event
• Form event planning committee • Establish a regular meeting location and dates (e.g., every two weeks) • Determine the purpose of the event and brainstorm activities • Choose a tentative date and location • Check availability of event venue and consider restrictions (e.g., seating capacity) • Identify the intended audience • Determine possible event sponsors and grant funders • Create sponsor levels and amounts	• Decide on a theme and title of the event • Decide on activities (e.g., performers, speakers, displays, food vendors, crafts, parade) • Hold auditions for entertainers • Determine roles and responsibilities for committee members (e.g., promotions, food, speakers, stage, equipment, and logistics) • Establish an initial budget • Research insurance requirements • Apply for special permits, licenses, insurance, etc. (e.g., food vendor and road closure permits) • Create a fund-raising plan and begin contacting possible funders • Book the Community Event Kit Trailer • Decide on a rain plan if the event is outdoors
3 Months Before the Event	**2 Months Before the Event**
• Develop an advertising and publicity plan • Gather cost estimates and finalize the budget • Request logos from corporate sponsors • Design a site map of your event. Include power sources, water hookup, activity and stage locations, parking, volunteer, and general information booth • Plan for first aid, security, electrical, water equipment, recycling, porta-potties • Contract entertainment and sound production • Create a food vendors' application form and post online • Consider accessibility to event (e.g., wheelchair accessible parking)	• Submit a Special Event Application • Submit a food vendor information to Health Unit • Prepare ads, posters, Facebook pages, and other promotions • Design a volunteer application form • Contact the Community Volunteer Centre with volunteer information • Begin advertising volunteer positions • Design a safety plan. Consider first aid, lost and found center, traffic plan, security, fire lanes • Develop a green plan (e.g., bike parking, advertise bus routes, recycling plan)
1 Month Before the Event	**3 Weeks Before the Event**
• Notify emergency and transit services of any road closures. Advertise road closure in local newspaper • Design press releases • Prepare signage for event (e.g., stage schedule) • Finalize entertainment schedule and contracts • Submit safety and site plan for municipal approval	• Design a volunteer schedule and list of tasks • Begin to schedule volunteers for 2- or 4-hour shifts • Plan volunteer refreshments and appreciation • Prepare volunteers' ID (e.g., t-shirts, aprons, or name tags)

Table 15.5 (cont.)

2 Weeks Before the Event	1 Week Before the Event
• Submit press releases to local media, radio stations, public service announcers • Host a site walk-through of event with committee members • Host a volunteer information and training session	• Confirm number of volunteers, entertainers, sound production, and other staff • Schedule pick up/ delivery of any rented or loaned equipment • Write checks for payments to be made on event day • Prepare speaking notes for emcee
Day of Event	**Week After the Event**
• Set up registration and volunteer center area • Register volunteers and assign tasks • Meet with key organizers for a communication session (pre-event) • Reserve parking for loading zone, VIPs, accessible parking, Event Trailer • Check entrances to ensure clear, safe and unobstructed access to facticity • Set up equipment (e.g., tents, traffic cones, barricades, signage) • Set up stage and sound equipment • Decorate • Implement traffic and safety plan • Greet entertainers and vendors, assist with set up • After event, take down decorations, clean up garbage, tear down stage and other equipment • Return supplies to source locations	• Send thank-you notes • Reconcile all invoices • Meet with the event planning committee to evaluate the event

Table 15.6

City of San Diego California Event Management Permit System Requirements

Venue Design	Type of Event
• Event Components (such as music and other activities) • VIP/Dignitary Presence • Cash Management • Storm Water Management • Insurance Requirements • Americans with Disabilities (ADA) Compliance • Illegal Vendors • Cost-Reduction Strategies	• Setup and Dismantle Plan • Alcohol Management • Security Responsibilities • Recycling/Trash Plans • Traffic Management Plan • Community Support/Issues • Additional Required Permits/Approvals • Other

Edginton, O'Neill, and O'Neill (1999) note that special events require careful and extensive planning to be successful. The following section will detail these considerations. Specifically, they recommend consideration of the following aspects:

- Staffing
- Scheduling
- Location
- Financing and budget, as well as sponsorships
- Marketing and media relations
- Risk management and legal considerations
- Event production
- Evaluation

Staffing

Three levels of staffing are required for successful events, which include an overall event manager (or director), the planning and management team, and the committees.

The parks and recreation organization must appoint, designate, or hire a person to provide leadership, supervision, and coordination of the event. Often, larger parks and recreation organizations have a staff member who assumes this role on a full-time basis. Smaller parks and recreation organizations utilize staff time as events are scheduled. The manager (director) has oversight that includes volunteer coordination and oversight, fund-raising and budgeting, communications, marketing and promotion, event production, and evaluation. The role is one of coordination, monitoring, and guidance of the process for these events. The manager ensures the goals and objectives are being met by the event, as well as any community concerns that may arise from hosting large and intrusive events.

The event manager is responsible for the formation of an event management team. Ideally, the team has persons with expertise in finance, budgeting, marketing, communications, and public relations, permits and vendor compliance, and evaluation. The team members would be responsible for formation of volunteer committees who also have interest in and expertise with these skills. Edginton, O'Neill, and O'Neill (1999) suggest committees should be formed to have responsibilities for the following:

- **Finance,** to develop and monitor a budget. This committee works with the parks and recreation agency, a treasurer and coordinates with the committees on sponsorship and concessions/vendors.
- **Marketing, promotion, and media relations** committee prepares a marketing plan, to include promotion and advertising. Importantly the community monitors community relations using the media.
- **Crowd control and safety** committee is concerned with behaviors that may arise, such as alcohol use, drugs, traffic, signage and transportation issues etc. This committee coordinates with the parks and recreation, police, fire and medical representatives of the community.
- **Production and event management** committee is responsible for the staging of the event or festival. There may be subcommittees representing entertainment, maintenance, food and beverage, volunteers, activities, prizes and awards, judges, or VIP liaisons.

It should be noted that most all community events rely heavily on volunteers. Management of the volunteer process is crucial to the success of any volunteer effort. Fortunately, parks and recreation organizations rely on and are experienced with using volunteers in the delivery of services. An active event is a major community event and will need adequate numbers of volunteers in order to be successful. There should be a safety and information meeting approximately one week before the event so volunteers are informed of their rights and responsibilities, have timelines for the event and emergency contact information. At the safety meeting, include training on incident reporting and traffic issues.

Scheduling

The event manager and the event planning committee, in coordination with the parks and recreation agency and other organizations, must schedule the event so that sponsors, community members, and visitors are best served. Scheduling requires a collaborative approach with other agencies, communities, and businesses so that competition is avoided and maximum participation and support are increased. Avoiding holidays, school, and other community functions are also considerations. Considering school holidays that may increase family visitations to the event is also important. In addition, if there are competing events, there may be a lack of facilities available to adequately stage the event. Finally, the day and time of week may be a consideration for families and youth.

Location of Event

Consideration of rental fees, maintenance, and supervision costs is important when considering the location of the event. For example, important questions to answer consist of sound systems, parking, access for handicap, crowd control (fencing, barriers, etc.), sanitary facilities, and seating or facility capacity.

Finances

Event planners and organizers must address the question of budget for the event and the source of the funds. The parks and recreation agency would provide a line item for the sponsorship of the event. The organizers, working with a treasurer, would establish and maintain fiscal controls of the budget. Oversight of committee expenditures, supplies, and vendors and services is the responsibility of the event manager. A procedure for expending and reporting the budget must be established.

Revenue sources can come from a variety of public, nonprofit, and private organizations, including individual donations. In addition tickets and fees (entry fee, dinner fee, etc.) are considered revenue sources. Often, ticket sales constitutes the largest portion of revenue. When public parks and recreation agencies sponsor events, ticket sales etc. are usually offered at cost of offering the event or sometimes at a loss, when it is considered a community program. Since the governmental unit does collect taxes for the provision of recreation programs, this is considered standard practice to offer the event at no or reduced costs for the community.

Grants are sometimes available to host an event. Arts councils, private foundations, and individuals will sometimes provide grant funding for an event. Often, event organizers obtain several sponsors for the event. These usually are businesses who want to create a positive image of their business and the community. In-kind services are also considered revenue. This may be in the form of the local electricians union doing all the electrical work as a contribution, or the local businesses supplying prizes for drawings (again advertising their business and product).

Marketing and Media Relations

Effective marketing and promotion of the event is important for the budget and covering costs of the event. Marketing is especially important in events since they are periodic events. Publicity, advertising, and personal contact by staff, volunteers, and others in the community will help promote the event. Often, media outlets will provide services in-kind for the event, thereby helping with the budget, but also promoting the event.

Risk Management and Legal Considerations

Not only is a risk management plan essential, it is required by many governmental units. The plan allows the manager of the event to predetermine areas of potential risk. Without a risk management plan, the sponsoring agency places themselves at risk of legal liability, as well as at risk for personal injury of participants. The plan would cover weather (lighting, tornado), power failures, crowd control, unruly patron behavior, fire, traffic, security, public safety (fire safety, emergencies, and evacuations), ADA access, OSHA, health regulations for food and beverages, and documentation of permits as required by the governmental unit. This plan is coordinated with the police, fire, ambulance medical unit, hospitals etc., for implementation. A committee is normally charged with developing this plan and ensuring that it is implemented.

Event Production

Event production consists of a committee or number of committees who address the following components of an event:

- Decorations (banners, signs, plantings)
- Entertainment (assures quality including talent, appearance, and content appropriate to event)
- Operations and Maintenance (set up, clean up, seating, removal of equipment, trash etc.)
- Signage (collects, inventories, and stores all signs for event)
- Transportation (parking, bus shuttles, handicap access, etc.)
- Concessions (food and beverage and supervision of vendors)
- Parking and Traffic (coordinates with police a parking and traffic plan)
- Children's Activities (as appropriate for entertainment and child care)
- Prizes and Awards

Evaluation of Event

Probably the least understood and most often dismissed aspect of event management is the evaluation of the event. There should be a formal, predetermined, one- or two-page survey used to collect responses from participants. Collection of responses would be over the entire event period on random days, times, and locations. The survey should cover items important to the organizers, as well as the economic impacts and the levels of satisfaction with the event. A report should be written and presented to the organizing group, who would then use the findings to improve the next event.

SUMMARY

Many cities and counties actively promote and hold festivals and community events. Festivals and community events are closely associated with municipal parks and recreation agencies. Communities hold special events and festivals for many reasons, which include enhancing the image of the community, providing economic benefits, and celebrating the culture or history. Events create more social benefits than social costs when properly planned and managed. There is also evidence that when parks and recreation agencies hold smaller scaled events (for example marathons, Senior Games, soccer, softball, etc.), they are considered more sustainable from a social, economic, and environmental perspective (Gibson, Kaplanidou, & Kang, 2012). Often these events are family oriented, attracting moderate numbers of people, yet bringing some benefits to the community.

Events have distinctive characteristics, such as a specific planned event, a singular occurrence outside of normal recreation programs, and a finite length for the event. The function and purpose of the event varies by community, but generally influences and shapes the organization (affect), promotes the community, and enhances the economic situation. Studies have shown that benefits of special events support these functions and purposes.

Typologies for community events generally can be categorized as community celebrations (festivals, fairs, parades, concerts, etc.), business and educational events (conferences and meetings), sports (amateur, recreation, and professional), and private events (weddings and reunions). Studies have noted that attending a community special event is ranked in the top five reasons to visit a community or region.

Community events widely vary, as was demonstrated in Table 15.2. It is important to consider that no matter what the type of event, it usually involves the public parks and recreation areas, facilities and organization at some point. Collaboration and partnerships between government, businesses, resident groups and festival organizers are necessary for successful events. Studies have demonstrated that parks and recreation agencies are involved in over 95% of community events in some fashion.

DISCUSSION QUESTIONS

1. Why do communities hold special events and festivals?
2. What types of festivals can you name and describe in your community?
3. What are the four characteristics of special events?
4. What are the functions and purposes of special events?
5. What are the benefits of special events and festivals?
6. Describe the typology of special events and list events in your community that fit that typology.
7. Compare and contrast the reasons why people visit a community. How does that compare to your community?
8. List the community stakeholders in your community who are involved in event planning and management.
9. What are the factors for success for special events?
10. What are the essential eight planning considerations for successful special events?

REFERENCES

Bartlett, M. S. (2015). University of Northern Iowa. Personal communication, July 10, 2015.

Cela, A., Knowles-Lankford, J., & Lankford, S. (2007). Local food festivals in northeast Iowa communities: A visitor and economic impact study. *Managing Leisure, 12*(2 & 3), 171–186.

City of Maple Ridge Parks and Leisure. (2015). Planning a special event. Retrieved from http://mrpmparksandleisure.ca/DocumentCenter/View/65

City of San Diego. (2015). Special event planning guide. Retrieved from http://www.sandiego.gov/specialevents/pdf/planningguide.pdf

Edginton, C., O'Neill, C. R., & O'Neill, J. (1999). Program, services, and event management. In B. van der Smissen, M. Moiseichik, V. Hartenburg, & L. Twardzik (Eds.), *Management of park and recreation agencies* (pp. 175–232). Ashburn, VA: National Recreation & Park Association.

Getz, D., & Frisby, W. (1991). Developing a municipal policy for festivals and events. *Recreation Canada,* October 1991.

Gibson, H., Kaplanidou, K., & Kang, S. J. (2012). Small-scale event sport tourism: A case study in sustainable tourism. *Sport Management Review, 15*(2), 160–170.

Hawkins, D. E. & Cunningham, J. D. (1996). It is Never Never Land when interest groups prevail: Disney's America Project, Prince William County, USA. *Practicing responsible tourism: International case studies in tourism planning, policy, and development* (pp. 350–365). New York, NY: John Wiley and Sons.

Lankford, S., Cela, A., & Lankford, J. (2005). Place-based food tourism in Northeast Iowa. Sustainable Tourism and Environment Program. University of Northern Iowa. Retrieved from http://www.uni.edu/step/reports/place_based_food.pdf

Lankford, S., Grybovych, O., & Lankford, J. (In press). *An introduction to community- based tourism.* Urbana, IL: Sagamore Publishing.

Nelson, M. (2014). Characteristics of community-based tourism practices: A stakeholder perspective. AMA Research Paper, University of Northern Iowa.

Saunders, K. (2005). Factors of Success for Northeast Iowa Community Festivals. A MA Research Paper, University of Northern Iowa. Retrieved from http://www.uni.edu/step/reports/festivals_success.pdf

UNI STEP (2013). *Characteristics of community-based tourism practices: A stakeholder perspective.* University of Northern Iowa Sustainable Tourism and Environment.

Wilson, S., Fesenmaier, D. R., Fesenmaier, J., & Van Es, J. C. (2001). Factors for success in rural tourism eevelopment. *Journal of Travel Research, 40,* 132–138.

Chapter Sixteen

Community-Based Therapeutic Recreation/ Inclusive Recreation

CHAPTER OBJECTIVES

- To recognize current demographics related to people with disabilities in the United States
- To comprehend the nature and spectrum of disability and human variation
- To gain an appreciation of the historical linkage between community parks and recreation and therapeutic recreation through Hull House and the social settlement movement
- To gain an understanding of inclusion and how accessibility, accommodations, and adaptations are the three prerequisites of inclusion
- To understand the role of special recreation and special recreation districts in community parks and recreation inclusive practice

INTRODUCTION

The U.S. Census Bureau (Brault, 2012) identified 18.7% of the civilian noninstitutionalized population, aged 15 or older, as having a disability in 2010, with 12.6% having a severe disability. This report underscored that 6.2% of adults have a disability related to seeing, hearing, or speaking; 12.6% have limitations associated with ambulatory activities of the lower body (e.g., walking); 8.2% have limitations associated with upper body functioning (e.g., grasping objects); 6.3% experienced difficulty with some kind of cognitive, mental, or emotional functioning; and 3.9% have difficulty with at least one activity of daily living (e.g., getting in and out of bed, eating, toileting). Only 41.1% of adults with disabilities aged 21 to 64 were employed and 10.8% of adults with disabilities experience persistent poverty (Brault, 2012).

According to McAvoy (2008), there are three reasons why the parks and recreation profession should include people with disabilities. First, it is the law. Of the many laws created to protect people with disabilities, the most well known is the Americans with Disabilities Act (ADA) of 1990 (P.L. 101-336), which mandates that all states and local public accommodations and services must be accessible to people with disabilities. Table 16.1 provides selected disability legislation beyond the ADA. Second, it makes marketing sense to serve these 56.7 million people (18.7% of the adult population). Third, it harkens to the basic philosophy of leisure services of providing personal freedom, justice, and equality to all people.

Table 16.1

Selected Disability Legislation

Architectural Barriers Act (1968): Prohibited architectural barriers in a federally owned or leased buildings.

Rehabilitation Act (1973): Prohibited discrimination in federal programs and services and in all other programs or services receiving federal funds.

Education of All Handicapped Children Act (1975): Required free, appropriate public education in the least restrictive setting.

Telecommunications for the Disabled Act (1981): Mandated telephone access for deaf and hard-of-hearing people at public places such as hospitals and police stations and all coin-operated telephones had to be hearing aid-compatible.

Individuals with Disabilities Education Act (IDEA) (1990): Congress renamed the Education of the Handicapped Act and reauthorized programs to improve support services to students with disabilities, especially in the areas of transition (to adult life beyond high school) and assistive technology.

Individuals with Disabilities Education Improvement Act (2004): Mandated that all park and recreation agencies and others that use schools or community settings must offer inclusive services that accommodate people with disabilities.

Sources: Dieser & Scholl (2010); McAvoy (2008)

In parks and recreation agencies, historically, therapeutic recreation specialists (TRSs)[1] have been hired to assist people with disabilities and train parks and recreation professionals toward inclusive practices, so that people with disabilities can experience leisure. Drawing from Sylvester, Voelkl, and Ellis (2001), therapeutic recreation is defined as a service that uses activity therapy, education, recreation, and leisure to promote health, well-being,

---

[1]In the broader field of leisure services, the term inclusion specialist or recreational therapist is often used simultaneously with therapeutic recreation specialist. It is beyond the scope of this chapter or book to explain the difference. In this chapter and book, the terms therapeutic recreation specialist and inclusion specialist will be used interchangeably.

and quality of life of persons who require specialized care because of illness, disability, or social condition (e.g., poverty).

The purpose of this chapter is two-fold. First, to explain how therapeutic recreation services can help community parks and recreation agencies meet the needs of people with disabilities or special needs. Second, to clarify how community-based therapeutic recreation and community parks and recreation are integrated professions. Community-based therapeutic recreation has much in common with, and should not be separated from, community parks and recreation services. In fact, part of this chapter will explain the historical overlap between community-based therapeutic recreation and community parks and recreation as both professional fields developed through the settlement movement in the late 1800s to the middle 1900s in the United States. But before providing this historical overview, this chapter begins with a broad overview of the nature and spectrum of disabilities.

THE NATURE AND SPECTRUM OF DISABILITY AND HUMAN VARIATION

Although many books on recreation for people with disabilities define disability as a specific impairment or deceit (e.g., Smith, Austin, Kennedy, Lee, & Hutchison, 2005), Anderson and Heyne's (2012) strengths-based approach to therapeutic recreation defines disability as a variation in the human condition, rather than a deficit, and outlines that an acceptance of human variation will ". . . widen the boundaries of what we [people] consider to be part of mainstream culture" (p. 20). The World Health Organization (2001) International Classification of Functioning, Disability, and Health (ICF), which has been integrated into therapeutic recreation practice (e.g., Sylvester, 2014, 2011; Van Puymbroeck, Porter, McCormick, & Singleton, 2009), and many other professions in the United States (e.g., education, social work), is a framework for defining human variation that recognizes the complexity and environmental factors of disability and functioning. Environment factors range from physical factors (such as climate, terrain, or building design) to social factors (such as attitudes of people without disabilities, institutions, and laws). According to the ICF the major components of functioning and disability are as follows (WHO, 2001):

- **Body functions.** The physiological functions of body systems (including psychological functions).
- **Body structures.** Anatomical parts of the body, such as organs, limbs, and their components.
- **Impairments.** Problems in body function and structure, such as significant deviation or loss.
- **Activity.** The execution of a task or action by an individual.
- **Participation.** Involvement in a life situation.
- **Activity limitations.** Difficulties an individual may have in executing activities.
- **Participation restrictions.** Problems an individual may experience in involvement in life situations.
- **Environmental factors.** The physical, social, and attitudinal environment in which people live and conduct their lives. These are either barriers to or facilitators of the person's functioning.

There are many different frameworks that classification types of disabilities. Drawing on many sources (e.g., American Psychiatric Association, 2013; Dattilo, 2012; Mobily

& MacNeil, 2002), the authors of this book offer the following overview of the types of disabilities, or variation of the human condition, which exit.

Physical Disabilities

Physical disabilities result from congenital conditions, accidents, or progressive neuromuscular diseases. These disabilities may include human variation such as spinal cord injury, spina bifida, amputation, muscular dystrophy, cardiac conditions, cystic fibrosis, paralysis, polio, and stroke.

Medical Disabilities

Medical disabilities are conditions affecting one or more of the body's systems. These include respiratory, immunological, neurological, and circulatory systems. For example, cerebral palsy, epilepsy, migraine headaches, and Alzheimer's disease are common neurological health conditions, while hypertension and heart disease are common circulatory conditions.

Mental Health Disabilities

This refers to a wide range of behavioral and/or psychological variation such as anxiety, mood swings, depression, posttraumatic stress, disordered eating, substance dependency, and/or a compromised assessment of reality.

Hearing Disabilities

Hearing disabilities prevent people from receiving sounds through the ear. If the loss is mild, the person has difficulty hearing faint or distant speech; if the hearing loss is severe, the person may not be able to distinguish any sounds. There are four types of hearing loss: (1) conductive, which is caused by diseases or obstructions in the outer or middle ear; (2) sensorineural, which results from damage to the inner ear; (3) mixed, which occurs in both the inner and outer or middle ear; and (4) central, which results from damage to the central nervous system.

Visual Disabilities

Three types of sight limitations include (1) total blindness, where a person learns and communicates via braille or other nonvisual media; (2) legal blindness, which indicates that a person has less than 20/200 vision in the more functional eye or a very limited field of vision (20 degrees at its widest point); and (3) low vision, which refers to a severe vision loss in distance and near vision.

Intellectual or Neurodevelopmental Disabilities

These disabilities interfere with the acquisition and use of listening, speaking, reading, writing, reasoning, or mathematical skills and typically have an onset in the developmental period. Examples include autism, attention-deficit/hyperactivity, and specific learning variations such as dyslexia

Figure 16.1 explains how the United States Census (Brault, 2012) classified disabilities into the three domains of communicative, mental, and physical.

Definition of Disability in the Communicative, Mental, and Physical Domains

This report categorizes types of disabilities into communicative, physical, and mental domains according to a set of criteria described here. While the characteristics of individuals with disabilities in a domain may be heterogeneous, the domains may group individuals with some common experiences. Because people can have more than one type of disability, they too may be identified as having disabilities in multiple domains.

For the purpose of this report, disability among children aged less than 15 years are not categorized into one of the three domains. Furthermore, it is possible for adults to have a disability for which the domain is not identified.

People who have disability in the communicative domain reported one or more of the following:

1. Was blind or had difficulty seeing.

2. Was deaf or had difficulty hearing.

3. Had difficulty having their speech understood.

People who have disability in the mental domain reported one or more of the following:

1. Had a learning disability, an intellectual disability, developmental disability or Alzheimer's disease, senility, or dementia.

2. Had some other mental or emotional condition that seriously interfered with everyday activities.

People who have disability in the physical domain reported one or more of the following:

1. Used a wheelchair, cane, crutches, or walker.

2. Had difficulty walking a quarter of a mile, climbing a flight of stairs, lifting something as heavy as a 10-pound bag of groceries, grasping objects, or getting in or out of bed.

3. Listed arthritis or rheumatism, back or spine problem, broken bone or fracture, cancer, cerebral palsy, diabetes, epilepsy, head or spinal cord injury, heart trouble or atherosclerosis, hernia or rupture, high blood pressure, kidney problems, lung or respiratory problem, missing limbs, paralysis, stiffness or deformity of limbs, stomach/digestive problems, stroke, thyroid problem, or tumor/cyst/growth as a condition contributing to a reported activity limitation.

Figure 16.1. United States Census Classification of People with Disabilities. *Source:* Brault (2012)

HISTORICAL LINK BETWEEN COMMUNITY PARKS AND RECREATION AND THERAPEUTIC RECREATION

One of the tragic aspects within the profession of therapeutic recreation in the modern era is the hyper focus on the clinical/medical orientation and scant attention that is focused on community-based therapeutic recreation (see Dieser, 2008; Mobily, 2015; Mobily, Walter, & Finley, 2015 for an excellent overview). Although the American Therapeutic Recreation Association (ATRA) has a "treatment network" dedicated to community-based practice, its overall focus is related to clinical/medical procedure and is fraught with medical terms, such as "treatment networks" rather than just the term "networks." ATRA interprets therapeutic recreation as "health care providers," and in listing 11 potential employment settings, only one is related to community recreation; the other settings are clinical/medical (e.g., free-standing rehabilitation hospitals, rehabilitation units in general hospitals, long-term care or skilled nursing facilities) (see https://www.atra-online.com/welcome/the-organization). Although 38% of certified therapeutic recreation specialists (CTRSs) work in hospital settings and 19% in skilled nursing settings, over 25% of CTRSs work in community-based settings, such as community parks and recreation agencies, schools, or community-based residential group homes (National Council for Therapeutic Recreation Certification, 2014).[2]

---

[2]Readers need to be mindful that the National Council for Therapeutic Recreation Certification statistics only refer to CTRSs. There are noncertified therapeutic recreation specialists and park and recreation professionals who also work in the area of providing leisure to people with disabilities and special needs in community settings.

Both Bedini (1995) and Dieser's (2008) historical research pinpoints that the "Play Ladies" of Hull House (settlement movement) were some of the first therapeutic recreation specialists. These Hull House leaders[3], the most famous being Jane Addams, are also considered pioneers in community recreation and important leaders in the play and recreation movement (Dieser, Harkema, Kowalski, Osuji, & Poppen, 2004; Edginton, DeGraaf, Dieser, Edginton, 2006; McBride, 1989; Wellman, Dustin, Henderson, & Moore, 2008; also see Chapter 2 of this book). In particular, Jane Addams provided inspiration for the early development of the Chicago Park District (Farrell, 1976), as the Hull House playground that was built in the spring of 1893 was the first public playground in Chicago (and one of the first in the United States). Through Addams' efforts, the Chicago playground commission became responsible for its management in 1906 (Woods & Kennedy, 1970). Moreover, Jane Addams helped with the original development of the Playground Association of American in 1906, served as its first vice president, and presented at the association's first Congress in 1907 (Edginton, DeGraaf, Dieser, & Edginton, 2006). In fact, many of the Settlement Houses throughout the United States had a paramount influence on the development of community parks and recreation settings and infrastructure (e.g., public play spaces and gymnasiums) that transitioned into early and rough parks and recreation commissions and agencies. The College Settlement in Mount Ivy, New York, created many parks, playgrounds, and centers/gymnasiums, for numerous recreation activities (e.g., athletics, singing and dance classes, social excursions) that evolved into the East Side Recreation Society in 1897. The Henry Street Settlement in New York City, specifically campaigned for public recreation, was instrumental in securing Seward Park and Corlears Hooks Park[4] with settlement residents/volunteers serving in the New York City Parks Department and on the executive committee of the Parks and Playground Association of New York (Woods & Kennedy, 1970). In addition, the Henry Street Settlement maintained the playground at the Stillman House, which was part of the African-American (Negro) section of New York City (Woods & Kennedy, 1970).

Jane Addams and Ellen Gates Starr opened Hull House in September of 1889, when they purchased the dilapidating house of Charles Hull[5] in a poor district of Chicago. In keeping with the settlement houses philosophy, which was to established agencies in city slums where settlement house residents/volunteers provided human services and engaged in social action on behalf and with people who had special needs (Mandell & Schram, 2012), Hull House provided services to people who require support and humane attention because of illness, disability, and social condition (e.g., homeless immigrants). When Jane Addams died in 1935, with the help of numerous Hull House leaders, Hull House expanded from Charles Hull's house to a 13-building complex, along with a 72-acre year-round out-

---

[3]These leaders included Edith and Grace Abbot, Louise deKoven Bowen, Alice Hamilton, Florence Kelley, Mary Keyser, Mary Rozet Smith, Helen Culver, Ellen Gates Starr, and Julia Lathrop. George Herbert Mead and John Dewey were sociologists at the University of Chicago who also provided support for Hull House.

[4]Both Seward Park and Corlears Hooks Park still exist today in the Manhattan part of New York City.

[5]In 1868, Charles Hull, a wealthy real estate developer, moved to another part of the city. Miraculously, Charles Hull's original home somehow survived the great Chicago fire of 1871, and after the fire, this area of Chicago (19th ward) became the roughest and filthiest area of Chicago, and soon the neighborhood was a crowded tenement section full of poor and starving immigrants (see Addams, 1910/1990, Miller, 1996).

door camp (Bowen Country Club). Many of the community recreation programs that Hull House provided were simultaneously community-based therapeutic recreation facilitation and intervention strategies. Jane Addams (1908/2002, 1909/1972, 1910/1981) advocated for inclusion of children with disabilities and special needs (e.g., homeless immigrants) into schools, community, and community recreation activities of Hull House. Inclusion is a common therapeutic recreation intervention in the modern era (Anderson & Heyne, 2012. Beyond inclusion, and drawing on Dieser (2008), the following is a sampling of Hull House community recreation programs that simultaneously were therapeutic recreation activities (the names of therapeutic recreation facilitation/intervention strategies are in bold). These community-based therapeutic recreation interventions were virtually inseparable from community parks and recreation programming formats and areas (see Chapter 12 in this book) and used a community development, social policy, and social action approach to organizing community resources (see Chapter 1 of this book).

- The coffee house, which served nonalcoholic beverages and free food, was a **therapeutic community** (and informal men's self-help group and community center), where men could talk about their frustrations while participating in recreation activities, such as billiards, cards, and reading/discussion of current events from newspapers and national magazines. From a community leisure programming perspective, the coffee shop would be social recreation (leisure area) within a club format (see Chapter 12 in this book).

- Many **expressive art programs** were facilitated by various Hull House residents, such as Ellen Gates Starr. The circulating art program consisted of pictures and paintings that poor and struggling families could check out and place on the walls of their tenement homes. This art program was a method to develop freedom and imagination (hope) of a different future life. Likewise, theater/drama, dances, and therapeutic writing were used to help people with special needs experience enjoyment, meaning, accomplishment, freedom, and self-determination. From a community leisure programming perspective, expressive arts would be arts/visual arts/performing arts (leisure area) from both a class and drop-in/rental format (see Chapter 12 in this book). Figure 16.2 explains Ellen Gates Starr Park located Chicago Park District.

- The reading of novels, plays, poetry, and short stories—**bibliotherapy**—was used to help struggling immigrants (1) understand that other people share similar problems (they are not alone in their struggles), (2) become aware of new insights, and (3) help them to structure their lives. From a community leisure programming perspective, bibliotherapy would be literary activity (leisure area) within an outreach and interest group format (see Chapter 12 in this book).

- The labor museum—a form of **leisure education intervention**—was an actual live working museum that allowed immigrants to work on and display their creative works (e.g., old world spinning and weaving, wood carving of doors and door handles) as a means to debunk the stereotypes that Americans held that immigrates were lazy and unskilled workers. Every day Chicagoans would drop in to watch immigrants working hard on their creative endeavors. From a community leisure programming perspective, leisure education would be related to new arts and possible even wellness (leisure area) within a drop-in format (see Chapter 12 in this book).

In 1996, the Chicago Park District began creating Ellen Gates Starr Park as part of an innovative partnership with the Board of Education. The park district acquired several parcels of land adjacent to Dett Elementary School including closing and greening over part of Maypole Avenue, to create a lovely 1.25-acre site with a playground, gardens, and recreational landscape. The project included a $75,000 donation from Blue Cross/Blue Shield for the community garden planted by elementary school students. This park was one of the first successes of the Campus Park Program. This innovative cooperative effort between the Chicago Park District, Board of Education, and City of Chicago, eventually resulted the replacement of asphalt with green space and recreational facilities at sites adjacent to more than 100 schools. The Chicago Park District named the park in honor of Ellen Gates Starr in 2004, as part of a system-wide initiative to recognize the achievements of significant Chicago women. Ellen Gates Starr (1859-1940), an associate and close friend of Jane Addams, was one of the nation's most important social reformers. Starr and Addams met at the Rockford Female Seminary. After one year, however, Starr did not have the financial means to remain at the Seminary and she left college to become a teacher in 1878. The two women continued their friendship, and in 1888, they traveled to Europe together. In England, Addams visited Thornbee Hall, one of the world's first settlements, providing social services to people who lived in the slums of East London. After the trip, Starr agreed to help Addams found America's first settlement, Hull House, which opened on W. Polk Ave. and S. Halsted Street in September 1889. Starr's interest in the arts resulted in progressive programs at Hull House, such as art classes and an art gallery available to the residents of the settlement house, other poor immigrants who lived in the area, as well as Chicago's cultural elite. Starr's interest in art also inspired her to found the Chicago Public School Art Society in 1894, and the Chicago Society of Arts and Crafts in 1897. Starr also fought tirelessly for women's and workers rights and became particularly involved in helping workers form unions and strike for better pay and improved working conditions. Dett School is approximately 3 miles away from Hull House, where Ellen Gates Starr lived until 1929, when she moved to New York after becoming paralyzed due to a surgical procedure.

Figure 16.2. Ellen Gates Starr Park in Chicago (Chicago Park District. *Source:* Retrieved from http://www.chicagoparkdistrict.com/parks/Ellen-Gates-Starr-Park/#8hcq4yg44f

- **Physical activities** were used as a means of catharsis and release of pent-up negative feelings through public gymnasiums, swimming pools, and for children/youth the Hull House playground. From a community leisure programming perspective, the physical activities would be athletics (leisure area) within a class, club, and competition format (see Chapter 12 in this book).

- Bowen Country Club was a year-round 72-acre outdoor camp for children, youth, adults, and families that was a form of **nature-based therapy and stress management.** Louise deKoven Bowen purchased and took direct leadership of this camp, which boasted a full range of facilities, including dormitories, activity buildings, a pool, and a dining hall. Hull House residents, both youth and entire families, would take the train approximately 50 miles north to get to the Bowen Country Club (present-day Waukegan, Illinois). From a community leisure programming perspective, the Bowen Country Club would be outdoor recreation (leisure area) within a class, special event, or interest group format (see Chapter 12 in this book). Figure 16.3 explains the current land use of the original Bowen Country Club site.

In 1963, the Waukegan, IL Park District purchased the Hull House Bowen Country Club, transformed it into a public park, and renamed it Bowen Park. This park has a ubiquitous range of recreation facilities, such as the Lilac Cottage, which is the home of the John L. Raymond Historic Research Library and the Waukegan Historical Museum (headquarters for the Waukegan Historical Society). Bowen Park houses the Grosche Baseball Field, Waukegan Skate Park, and is home to the Jack Benny Center for the Arts. The Jane Addams Center, which can hold up to 100 people, is also located in Bowen Park and is often used as a rental facility for family reunions, group parties, Sunday services, and community meetings.

In keeping with Louise deKoven Bowen's enjoyment an education from nature and nature-based play ethic in 2008, the Bowen Playground Forest was created within Bowen Park at the cost of $1 million, This interactive playground offers tiered play areas combined with several environmental learning stations that represent a forest ecosystem. Vibrant and easy-to-read interpretive signage highlights each play area, such as the forest outlook tower, which represents the forest canopy. Children can climb to the top of the tower an slide down the 40-foot tunnel slides to the forest floor. The area between the forest canopy and the forest floor is packed full of activities, such as the spider web climber and the owl overlook. The lower part of the playground represents the forest floor, where children can splash in the water spray area, observe animal footprints, sit on the fungi bench, and play beneath the giant trillium.

Figure 16.3. Bowen Park and the Original Hull-House Bowen Country Club Site (Dieser, 2008; Hornig, 2008; Waukegan (Illinois) Park District. *Source:* Retrieved from http://www.waukeganparks.org/parks/parks/bowen_playground.html; Waukegan (Illinois) Park District, http://www.waukeganparks.org/about/history.htm

INCLUSION THROUGH ACCESSIBILITY, ACCOMMODATIONS, ADAPTATIONS

Inclusion is an attitude and behavior, on the part of parks and recreation professionals, of providing the needed adaptations, accommodations, and support (physical and social) so that people with disabilities can participate in leisure opportunities with friends, family, and community members as an equal participant (Hironaka-Jutea & Crawford, 2010). There are many types of inclusion models that parks and recreation agencies can use. Anderson and Kress (2003) outline a seven-step process of inclusion: program promotion, registration and assessment, accommodations and supports, staff training, program implementation, documentation, and evaluation.

An outstanding inclusion strategy that parks and recreation agencies can use is to hire a therapeutic recreation specialist or inclusion specialist in the dual role of helping people with disabilities experience leisure and training parks and recreation professionals on inclusive practices (e.g., accessibility, accommodations, and adaptations). The City of Bloomington (Indiana) Parks and Recreation Department's normative registration forms have an inclusive service request section, a specific adult and child version inclusion questionnaire (Figure 16.4 is the adult inclusion questionnaire), and a full-time inclusive recreation coordinator who help people with disabilities experience leisure and trains parks and recreation staff toward inclusive practices (see https://bloomington.in.gov/inclusive). In a similar vein, the Together We Play program is an inclusive model used in Cedar Falls and Waterloo (Iowa) in which a therapeutic recreation specialist function as a leisure resource specialists to a multitude of community recreation leaders in order to help people with disabilities experience leisure (Scholl, Dieser, & Schilling, 2005). The Together We Play program provides services for inclusive recreation to (1) children and youth with disabilities, (2) parents who have children with disabilities, (3) community recreation and after-school agencies, and (4) referral agencies. The Together We Play model is presented in Figure 16.5.

CITY OF BLOOMINGTON
parks and recreation
Inclusion Questionnaire

Program Ready:
In order to support the success and safety of individuals registered and participating in Bloomington Parks and Recreation programs, it is important that participants are indeed "program ready." To assist in determining if a person is "program ready," the following criteria have been developed:
- Participant is able to participate independently or with reasonable accommodations.
- Participant is age appropriate.
- Participants may be aged up or down by one grade level in some situations.
- Participant is able to take direction and instruction from a staff person.
- Participant is comfortable with, and able to interact in, a group environment.
- Participant interacts and participates in a manner that is physically and emotionally safe for themselves and others.
- Participant is able to participate in self-care (toileting, feeding, etc.) independently or with minimal verbal prompting.

This form is intended to assist in identifying reasonable accommodations which may be beneficial for successful participation in Bloomington Parks and Recreation Department programs. **To adequately meet your needs, we require registration for each program and reasonable accommodation requests be made at least two weeks prior to the program registration deadline. In some cases, reasonable accommodations may take longer to arrange.**

Please complete as thoroughly as possible.

PARTICIPANT INFORMATION (to be completed by parent/guardian if participant is under 18)

Name _____ Date of Birth _____ Grade ____

Address _____ City _____ Zip _____ Phone _____

Parent/Guardian (if applicable) _____ Phone_____

Email _____

Recreation Interests
Please identify any interests the participant has:

Community Examples: traveling	Outdoors hiking, fishing	Physical ice skating, golf, tennis	Wellness tai chi, yoga, relaxation	Educational language, outdoors, financial	Hobbies music, dance, reading	Creative sewing, painting, stained glass

Are there any hobbies or activities the participant is interested in learning?_____

Which Bloomington Parks Recreation activities has the participant registered for in the past? _____

Figure 16.4. The Adult Inclusion Questionnaire of the City of Bloomington (Indiana) Parks and Recreation. *Source:* Retrieved from https://bloomington.in.gov/inclusive

Social (please check all that apply)

____ Shows interest in others
____ Will play/interact cooperatively with others
____ Is tolerant of others, not easily agitated or annoyed
____ Can listen and follow direction
____ Is aware of safety concerns (traffic, staying with group, using sharp objects, etc.)

____ Will sit quietly to watch a program, movie, etc
____ Can identify and take responsibility for
        personal belongings

Comments/Areas of difficulty: _____
_____

Other Information

Circle each diagnosis that applies to the participant and/or identify any condition not listed.

Amputation
Arthritis
Attention Deficit Disorder
Autism Spectrum Disorder
Behavioral Disorder
_____
Cerebral Palsy
Deaf

Down Syndrome
Epilepsy
Hard of Hearing
Learning Disability:
_____
Intellectual Disability:
mild, moderate, severe
Multiple Sclerosis

Muscular Dystrophy
Psychiatric Disability
Spina Bifida
Spinal Cord Injury Level:
_____
Traumatic Brain Injury
Vision Impairment
Other_____

Does participant have seizures?   YES   NO   If yes, please indicate type and describe: _____
_____

Date of most recent seizure: _____

Does anything trigger the seizures?_____

Medications

Medication	Time	Dosage	Purpose	Side Effects/Contraindications

Allergies (include food/medication/other) activity restrictions, special diets or other medical concerns:_____
_____
_____

Communication Skills

How does the participant communicate? (Circle the ones that apply)

Speech   Read Lips   Communication Board   Sign Language   Computerized Device

Any communication devices that are used at home or work are also needed in recreation settings. Please provide any resources available, including but not limited to: communication board/books, computer devices, etc.

Figure 16.4. (cont.)

How can staff assist the participant in communicating needs? _____
_____
_____

Feeding Skills
Does the participant eat and drink independently? YES NO If no, what type of assistance or adaptive equipment is needed? _____

Mobility Skills
Does participant walk independently?   YES   NO   If no, please identify any mobility devices used or assistance needed: _____

Describe transfer techniques used: _____
_____

If the participant uses a wheelchair, is a wheelchair lift required? YES NO   Explain:_____
_____

Restroom Skills
_____ Wears Attends/Depends   _____ Uses toilet independently
_____ Indicates need to use toilet   _____ Washes hands independently
_____ Uses toilet with physical assistance

Concerns/Restrictions
Activity concerns or restrictions related to health/social issues:_____
_____

Do you feel your child requires one-to-one supervision?   YES   NO
(Level of supervision will ultimately be determined by the Inclusive Recreation Coordinator.)

Additional Comments: (please attach additional sheets if necessary)

This assessment expires one year from date of the assessment or in the event of significant change. Termination of inclusive recreation services must be completed through the Inclusive Recreation Coordinator. At no time may a participant or parent/guardian terminate inclusive recreation services without consulting the Inclusive Recreation Coordinator.

_____   _____
Signature (parent/guardian if participant is under 18 or under legal guardianship)   Date

Please return to Bloomington Parks and Recreation:
401 N. Morton, Ste 250
P.O. Box 848
Bloomington, IN 47402
Phone: 812-349-3747
Fax: 812-349-3785

 INCLUSIVE RECREATION

Figure 16.4. (cont.)

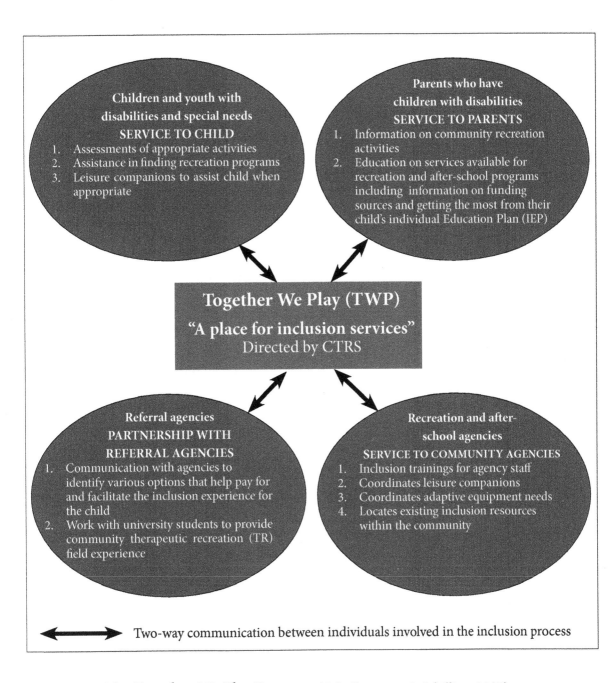

Figure 16.5. The Together We Play Program (Scholl, Dieser, & Schilling, 2005)

According to Long and Robertson (2010), the three prerequisites of inclusion are accessibility, accommodation, and adaptation. Whereas accommodation is defined as the removal of barriers that might otherwise prevent leisure participation, adaptation is when qualified professionals manage variables and services in order to meet the unique needs of people with disabilities and achieve desired outcomes (Long & Robertson, 2010). Although readers are encouraged to revisit Chapter 3 in this book to refamiliarize themselves with leisure constraint theory, the following are common structural constraints (leisure barriers) that people with disabilities experience (Dieser, 2013; Hironaka-Jutea & Crawford, 2010):

- **Attitudinal.** A negative predisposition toward people with disabilities by people without disabilities.
- **Economic.** Lack of money to participant in leisure.
- **Transportation.** Lack of usable or affordable methods of transportation to parks and recreation settings.
- **Architectural.** Structures that present obstacles for people to enjoy.
- **Ineffective organization policy.** Shortage of inclusion policies for people with disabilities such as not offering a sliding scale fee to help people with disabilities who have an economic barrier.
- **Health.** A health condition limits participation in leisure, such as a person with muscular dystrophy lacking muscular endurance and strength to participate in leisure.
- **Programmatic accommodations.** When the needs of people with disabilities are not taken into consideration in parks and recreation programming.

Parks and recreation professionals can make rule adaptations, thus providing accommodations, to various leisure activities. Drawing from Davis (2010) Figure 16.6 explains some rule adaptations related to wheelchair basketball, wheelchair soccer, sitting volleyball, and beep ball.

Accessibility is provided via universal design, and universal design is a broad-spectrum approach by making products, communications, and environments usable for all people (Anderson & Heyne, 2012). Although there are excellent examples of parks and recreation agencies committed to inclusive practice, such as the City of Bloomington (Indiana) Parks and Recreation Department noted previously, there are examples of parks and recreation agencies that do not provide accessibility.

Olsen and Dieser's (2012) investigation of 57 community parks with playground structures in two neighboring cities (combined population of 102,000 people) reported that (1) only 5% of play areas had an accessible route that connected the playground equipment to the park entrance or parking area, (2) only 11% of play areas had some type of designated accessible parking, (3) only 14% of play areas had some type of accessible shade (shade structure, tree), (4) only 32% of the community playgrounds were compliant with the ADA recommendation of the ratio between ground-level play components and elevated play components, and (5) less than half (44%) of the playground sites met the correct ADA requirement for ramps and transfer systems (and 5% of the playground structures did not have either a ramp or transfer system at all). This study reminds us accessibility to certain parks and recreation setting is still a very real problem in some communities.

	Traditional Sport	Disability Sport
Basketball compared with wheelchair basketball		
Passing (chest, bounce, baseball)	All passing done with hands; pass can be made while player is moving or stationary.	Same as in traditional sport
Dribbling (stationary, moving)	Traveling is prohibited (moving while in possession of the ball and not dribbling with each step).	Traveling: Players are allowed two touches to the hand rim of their wheelchair while in possession of the ball; after two pushes, player much pass, dribble, or shoot the ball.
Shooting (free throw, field goals)	Free-throw shooting: feet must be behind the free-throw line.	Free-throw shooting; small wheels in front of wheelchair (casters) are allowed to be over the free throw line; larger rear wheels must remain behind the line.
Soccer compared with wheelchair soccer		
Passing (stationary, moving)	All passing done with the feet.	All passing done with the hands.
Dribbling (stationary, moving)	All dribbling done with the feet.	Dribbling skills performed similar to basketball; however a player must pass, dribble, or shoot the ball within 3 seconds of possession; once they do so, a new 3-second period starts.
Throw-ins	Players use two-hand overhead throw, keeping both feet on ground and out of bounds.	Players use two-hands overhead throw, keep all wheels behind the line.
Volleyball compared with sitting volleyball		
Serve (underhand, overhand)	Both feet remain behind the serving line.	Buttocks must stay behind the serving line; legs may be inside the court
Passing (underhand, overhand)	Pass can be made from on our off the court.	Player must remain seated on floor and cannot lift buttocks to gain advantage during play.
Setting	Players must have simultaneous contact with finders as ball leaves both hands; feet can be off the floor during setting	Players must remain seated on the floor and cannot lift buttocks to gain advantage during play.
Blocking	Players cannot block an oncoming sere	Players are allowed to block at net during
Softball compared to beep ball		
Hitting	Pitcher and catcher are from fielding team	Pitcher and catcher are from hitting team; both players are sighted.
Fielding	Players use gloves when throwing to bases for outs	Gloves are optional; no throwing to bases for outs; fielding players record outs by gaining control of a hit ball and raising it up in the air.
Base running	Players must run all three bases and touch home plate to score a run	Only two bases are used and each has speakers mounted inside to elicit noise; player hitting the ball must reach the beeping base before the fielding player secures ball; if this occurs, a run is scored.

Figure 16.6. Rule Comparison Between Traditional and Disability Sports
(Davis, 2010)

SPECIAL RECREATION AS INCLUSION

The broad concept of inclusion can also take the form of special recreation. Whereas inclusive recreation generally means equal and joint participation of people with and without disabilities, special recreation occurs when people with disabilities participate in recreation with other people with disabilities (usually separate from people without disabilities). Perhaps Special Olympics is the most common example of special recreation programming (see Figure 16.7 for an explanation of Special Olympics). However, parks and recreation special recreation districts offer an array of special recreation programming, such as the Crystal Lake Park District of the Northern Illinois Special Recreation Association offering youth with disabilities various day camps related to canoeing, archery, nature hikes, and creative art projects (see http://crystallakeparks.org/Programs/day-camp.asp).

The Mission of the Special Olympics is to provide year-round sports training and athletic competition in a variety of Olympic-type sports for children and adults with intellectual disabilities, giving them continuing opportunities to develop physical fitness with their families, other Special Olympics athletes and the community.

Special Olympics is the world's largest sports organization for people with intellectual disabilities with more than 4.5 million athletes in 170 countries and millions more volunteers and supporters. We are also a global social movement.

Figure 16.7. Mission and Overview of Special Olympics. Special Olympics. *Source:* Retrieved from http://www.specialolympics.org/

The Special Recreation Association Network of Illinois lists 33 Special Recreation Cooperatives in Illinois serving 206 Communities that represent 158 park districts, 44 municipalities, and one township (see http://www.specialrecreation.org/find-my-services). The Western DuPage Special Recreation Association (see http://www.wdsra.com/Inclusion/about-inclusion-faq.htm#), a cooperative extension of nine park districts in the Western suburbs of Chicago, provides both special recreation (e.g., day camps related to specific disabilities, Special Olympics) and inclusive recreational opportunities for individuals with special needs. The beginning step starts on the registration forms when a person with a disability can explain his/her disability and needed accommodations and is encouraged to contact the Manager of Inclusion at least two weeks prior to the beginning of the recreation program in order to determine support needed and types of adaptations and accommodations. Figure 16.8 presents the mission and overview of the Chicago Park District special recreation program.

ACCESSIBLE PLAYGROUNDS AND AQUATIC ENVIRONMENTS

There are many excellent resources related to accessibility that parks and recreation professionals can use to help them provide inclusive leisure services. For example, the North Carolina Office on Disability and Health in collaboration with the Center for Universal Design (2008) provide an excellent guide and checklist to accessibility to health clubs and fitness facilities that any community recreation agency could use that covers a plethora of facility areas such as parking outside the building, locker room, exercise equipment, and customer services (see http://fpg.unc.edu/sites/fpg.unc.edu/files/resources/other-

The mission of the Chicago Park District special recreation program is to provide a diverse range of recreational opportunities for children and adults with disabilities. These include the following programs and services: Adaptive Sports, Paralympic Sports, Special Olympics, recreation and leisure programs for deaf/hard of hearing and/or blind/visually impaired individuals, ranging from introductory levels to competitive sports. There are two locations with year-round programs for deaf/hard of hearing individuals. There are 16 locations that work with individuals with intellectual disabilities. One location offers programs with a primary focus to work with youth at risk. All special recreation field staff and inclusion aids are trained in behavior management and adaptive sport skills. Participation assessments are completed when requested to assure an individual with a disability will be successful in any program the Chicago Park District Offers.

The Chicago Park District special recreation program has developed a partnership with schools and agencies that work with individuals with disabilities, focusing on the expansion of services for physical and sensory disabilities, with a goal to create a Chicago Park District Paralympic team. Leagues and competitions for youth at risk, a program with the alternative schools within the City of Chicago, are also coordinated through special recreation program. This successful outreach offers the recreational opportunities needed for this population.

Figure 16.8. Mission and Overview of the Chicago Park District special recreation program. *Source:* Retrieved from http://www.chicagoparkdistrict.com/departments/programming/community-recreation/special-recreation/

resources/NCODH_RemovingBarriersToHealthClubs.pdf). Likewise, Dillenschneider and Burkhour (2010) present a sampling of accessibility elements that are located in traditional parks and recreation agencies, such as picnic areas and tables, sports fields and courts, fishing docks, beach areas, nature centers and zoos, and skiing and sledding hills. To provide a beginning overview of inclusive practice within a parks and recreation setting, below are selected elements that should be considered when creating an inclusive playground or aquatic center.

According to Olsen and Dieser (2012) and Burkhour and Almon (2010), accessible playgrounds should have the following:

- **Accessible route.** Pathways that allow children to move throughout the playground and connect to accessible play components. Accessible routes should be a continuous route free of rocks, sand, debris and bumps that may prohibit children from movement throughout the playground. Accessible routes must connect to the parking lot, the sidewalk, buildings (e.g., restrooms), and to the playground equipment.
- **Accessible surfaces.** Surfacing material should allow wheeled components to get around the playground. Some loose-fill materials, such as sand and pea gravel, are definitely not accessible.
- **Ground-level play components.** These components can be approached or exited at ground level by the accessible route. Examples include swings, standalone climbers and sand diggers. When more than one ground level play component is present, it is required to be on an accessible route.
- **Entry points and seats.** Play components, such as slides, spring rockers, or swings, must be at a transferable height. The entry point or seat height must be a minimum of 11 in (28 cm) and a maximum of 24 in. (61 cm) above the required clear ground or floor space (that's the place a child could leave there wheelchair or walker). This play

component must also have a means of support for transfer, such as handholds or gripping surfaces, to help a child move onto the play component.

- **Play tables.** In regard to height and clearance, children need to be able to pull up and under any play tables (e.g., with a wheelchair) and reach all the stuff to do like the water spout on a water table. This space must be at least 24 in. (61 cm) high so knees slide right under.
- **Maneuvering space and clear or ground space.** A play component must have a maneuvering space (measuring 60 x 60 in. [152 x 152 cm]) so a kid using a wheelchair can get there, play, turn around, and go to something else. The user must have a clear ground space (measuring 30 x 48 in [76 x 122 cm]) to sit or stand in to play with the component (like next to the spring rocker or swing); these spaces must be on the same level as the accessible play component and can overlap.

According to Baun (2010) and Lepore, Gayle, and Stevens (2007) accessible aquatic environments should have the following:

- **Pool entry.** There are six types: Sloped entries, gradually slopped stairs, portable stairs, portable lift devise, aquatek platforms, and person to person transfer with a mat placed over the edge of the pool deck.
- **Basic accessibility guidelines for swimming pools.** Swimming pools with less than 300 linear feet (91.4 meters) of pool wall: The primary means of entry must be either a sloped entry into the water or a pool lift that is capable of being operated independently by a person with a disability. Swimming pools with more than 300 linear feet (91.4 meters) of pool wall: A minimum of two means of accessibility are required; the primary means must be either a sloped entry into the water or an independently operated pool lift, whereas the secondary means can be a lift, sloped entry, transfer wall, transfer system, or pool stairs. It is recommended that the secondary means not duplicate the primary means.
- **Locker rooms and restrooms in aquatic centers.** Install nonskid carpet from the shower area to the pool ladder to aid participants in balance, crutch traction, orientation, or mobility. Provide disability-accessible family and caregiver restrooms and changing areas so that caregivers of the opposite gender can assist.
- **Aquatic equipment.** Provide flotation devices for people who cannot stand on the pool bottom, for instance, people who are paraplegia. Provide a water chair and include upper-body movements in water aerobics classes to accommodate people with lower-body impairments.

Baun (2010) and Lepore, Gayle, and Stevens (2007) also suggest additional special accommodations in aquatic centers, such as the following:

- Allow a person who has a urine bag to wear long, baggy shorts over his/her swimsuit to avoid embarrassment.
- Allow participants with obesity and those with financial challenges to wear shorts and a top rather than a bathing suit.
- Allow an aide to participate in a program with a person who needs support; do not charge a fee for the aide to participate.
- Designate an area on the pool deck for assistive companions, guide dogs, crutches, wheelchairs, and other support and mobility equipment.

- Provide special services such as braille or computer disk for registrations, handouts, and certificates.

SUMMARY

In the United States 18.7% of the civilian noninstitutionalized population, aged 15 or older, has a disability (Brault, 2012). Beyond the legal rights that people with disabilities have under the ADA, it makes marketing sense, and links to a moral professionalism, to serve these 56.7 million people and treat them as equal members of society. Inclusion is an attitude and behavior on the part of parks and recreation professionals, of providing accessibility, adaptations, and accommodations so that people with disabilities can participate in leisure opportunities with friends, family, and community members as an equal participant.

An outstanding inclusion strategy that parks and recreation agencies can use is to hire a therapeutic recreation specialist or inclusion specialist in the dual role of helping people with disabilities experience leisure and training parks and recreation professionals on inclusive practices (e.g., accessibility, accommodations, and adaptations). The partnership between therapeutic recreation/inclusive recreation and community parks and recreation has a long, historical relationship that dates back to both professions developing, simultaneously, from the social settlement movement in the United States. The broad concept of inclusion can also take the form of special recreation and special recreation districts.

DISCUSSION QUESTIONS

1. What conclusions can you draw about the U.S. Census Bureau Statistics related to people with disabilities? In addition, explain why the parks and recreation profession should include people with disabilities.
2. Explain the nature and spectrum of disabilities or human variation. Furthermore, why is it important to view disabilities through a strengths-based approach?
3. Describe how community parks and recreation is linked historically to community-based therapeutic recreation. Further, explain how Hull House and other settlement house programs were simultaneously community parks and recreation and community-based therapeutic recreation entities and helped create both professions.
4. Define inclusion and further articulate how accessibility, accommodations, and adaptations are the three prerequisites of inclusion.
5. Explain the similarities and differences between special recreation and inclusive recreation and further explain how special recreation is a type of inclusion.
6. Visit a local park in your community to evaluate if they have the selected elements of universal design identified in this chapter (e.g., accessible routes and surfaces).
7. Visit a local aquatic center/swimming pool in your community to evaluate if it has the selected elements of universal design identified in this chapter (e.g., pool entry, designate an area on the pool deck for assistive companions or guide dogs).
8. Interview a person with a disability to learn about his or her experiences related to access to parks and recreation settings and programs.
9. How can you use the I-Triad and advisory boards, which you read about in Chapter 3 of this book, to serve people with disabilities?

10. Explain why hiring a therapeutic recreation specialist or inclusion specialist at a local community parks and recreation agencies is paramount. Using the Together We Play model, explain how an inclusion specialist can provide services to multiple people beyond the person who has disabilities.

REFERENCES

Addams, J. (1908/2002). The home and the special child. In J. B. Elshtain (Ed.), *The Jane Addams reader* (pp. 224–228). New York, NY: Basic Books. (Reprinted from *Journal of Proceedings and Addresses*, pp. 99–102, by National Education Association).

Addams, J. (1909/1972). *The spirit of youth and the city street.* Urbana and Chicago, IL: University of Illinois Press.

Addams, J. (1910/1981). *Twenty years at Hull House.* New York, NY: Signet.

American Psychiatric Association. (2013). *Diagnostic and statistical manual of mental disorders* (5th ed.). Washington, DC: Author.

Anderson, L., & Heyne, L. (2012). *Therapeutic recreation practice: A strengths approach.* State College, PA: Venture.

Anderson, L., & Kress, C. (2003). *Including people with disabilities in parks and recreation opportunities.* State College, PA: Venture.

Baun, M. P. (2010).Inclusive aquatics. In Human Kinetics (Ed.), *Inclusive recreation: Programs and services for diverse populations* (pp. 249–278). Champaign, IL: Human Kinetics.

Bedini, L. A. (1995). The "Play Ladies": The first therapeutic recreation specialists. *Journal of Physical Education, Recreation and Dance, 66*(8), 32–35.

Brault, M. W. (2012). Americans with disabilities 2010: Household economic studies (Report No. P7131). Retrieved from U.S. Department of Commerce website http://www.census.gov/prod/2012pubs/p70-131.pdf

Burkhour, C., & Almon, J. (2010). Play and playgrounds. In Human Kinetics (Ed.), *Inclusiv recreation: Programs and services for diverse populations* (pp. 3–18). Champaign, IL:Human Kinetics.

Dattilo, J. (2012). *Inclusive leisure services* (3rd ed.). State College, PA: Venture.

Davis, R. (2010). Inclusive sports. In Human Kinetics (Ed.), *Inclusive recreation: Programs and services for diverse populations* (pp. 3–18). Champaign, IL: Human Kinetics.

Dieser, R. B. (2008). History of therapeutic recreation. In T. Robertson & T. Long (Eds.), *Foundations of therapeutic recreation* (pp. 13–30). Champaign, IL: Human Kinetics.

Dieser, R. B. (2008, May). Past voices from the Hull House Joseph T. Bowen Country Club, 1911-1953: Initial research findings of relatedness, enjoyment of nature, and leisure as social values of youth outdoor recreation and wilderness experiences. Paper presented at the Canadian Congress of Leisure Research, Montreal, Quebec, Canada.

Dieser, R. B., (2013). *Leisure education: A person-centered, system-directed, social policy perspective.* Urbana, IL: Sagamore.

Dieser, R. B., Harkema, R. P., Kowalski, C., Ijeoma, O., & Poppen, L. L. (2004). The portrait of a pioneer: A look back at 115 years of Jane Addams work at Hull House, her legacy still lives on. *Parks & Recreation, 39*(9), 128–137.

Dieser, R. B., & Scholl, K. (2010). Inclusive recreation history and legislation, In Human Kinetics (Ed.), *Inclusive recreation: Programs and services for diverse populations* (pp. 19–38). Champaign, IL: Human Kinetics.

Dillenschneider, C., & Burkhour, C. (2010). Universal design in recreation. In Human Kinetics (Ed.), *Inclusive recreation: Programs and services for diverse populations* (pp. 137–158).Champaign, IL: Human Kinetics.

Edginton, C. R., DeGraaf, D. G., Dieser, R. B., & Edginton, S. (2006). *Leisure and life satisfaction: Foundational perspectives* (4th ed.). Boston, MA: McGraw-Hill.

Farrell, J. (1967). *Beloved lady: A history of Jane Addams' ideals on reform and peace.* Baltimore, MD: John Hopkins Press.

Hironaka-Juteau, J. H., & Crawford, T. (2010). Introduction to inclusion. In Human Kinetics (Ed.), *Inclusive recreation: Programs and services for diverse populations* (pp. 3–18). Champaign, IL: Human Kinetics

Hornig, E. F. (2008). Forest findings: Bridging the gap between children and nature. *Parks & Recreation, 43*(12), 46–51.

Lepore, M., Gayle, G. W., & Stevens, S. (2007). *Adapted aquatics programming* (2nd ed.). Champaign, IL: Human Kinestics.

Long, T., & Robertson, T. (2010). Inclusion concepts, processes, and models. In Human Kinetics (Ed.), *Inclusive recreation: Programs and services for diverse populations* (pp. 61–78). Champaign, IL: Human Kinetics.

Mandell, B. R., & Schram, B. (2012). *An introduction to human services: Policy and practice* (12th ed.). New York, NY: Pearson.

McAvoy, L. H. (2008). Disability as diversity. In M. T. Allison & I. E. Schneider (Eds.), *Diversity and the recreation profession: Organizational perspectives* (rev. ed., pp. 39–64). State College, PA: Venture.

McBride, P. (1989). Jane Addams. In H. Ibrahim (Ed.), *Pioneers in leisure and recreation* (pp. 53–64). Reston, VA: American Alliance for Health, Physical Education, Recreation, and Dance.

Miller, D. L. (1996). *City of the century: The epic of Chicago and the making of America.* New York, NY: Simon & Schuster.

Mobily, K. E. (2015). Should U.S. recreation therapy be replicated globally? An opportunity to do better. Part II. *World Leisure Journal, 57*(1), 57–68.

Mobily, K. E., & MacNeil, R. D. (2002). *Therapeutic recreation and the nature of disabilities.* State College, PA: Venture.

Mobily, K. E., Walter, K. B., & Finley, S. E. (2015). Deconstruction of TR/RT: Does TR/RT contribute to the negative construction of disability? Part I. *World Leisure Journal, 57*(1), 46–56.

National Council for Therapeutic Recreation Certification. (2014). CTRS professional profile. Retrieved from http://nctrc.org/documents/CTRSProfileBrochure.pdf

North Carolina Office on Disability and Health in collaboration with the Center for Universal Design. (2008). Removing barriers to health clubs and fitness facilities: A guide foraccommodating all members, including people with disabilities and older adults. Retrieved from http://fpg.unc.edu/sites/fpg.unc.edu/files/resources/other-resources/NCODH_RemovingBarriersToHealthClubs.pdf

Olsen, H., & Dieser, R. B. (2012). I am hoping you can point me in the right direction regarding playground accessibility": A case study of a community that lacked social policy toward playground accessibility. *World Leisure Journal, 54*(3), 269–279.

Scholl, K., Dieser, R. B., & Schilling, A. (2005). Implementing an ecological approach to therapeutic recreation: A collaborative inclusion service model. *Therapeutic Recreation Journal, 39*(4), 299–311.

Smith, R. W., Austin, D. R., Kennedy, D. W., Lee, Y., & Hutchison, P. (2005). *Inclusive and special recreation: Opportunities for persons with disabilities* (5th ed.). Boston, MA: McGraw Hill.

Sylvester, C. (2011). Therapeutic recreation, the International Classification of Functioning, and the capability approach. *Therapeutic Recreation Journal, 45*(2), 85–104.

Sylvester, C. (2014). Therapeutic recreation and disability studies: Seeking an alliance. *Therapeutic Recreation Journal, 48*(1), 46–60.

Sylvester, C., Voelkl, J. E., & Ellis, G. D. (2001). *Therapeutic recreation programming: Theory and practice.* State College, PA: Venture.

Van Puymbroeck, M., Porter, H. R., McCormick, B. P., & Singleton, J. (2009). The role of the International Classification of Functioning, Disability and Health(IFC) in therapeutic recreation practice, research, and education. In N. J. Stumbo (Ed.), *Professional issue in therapeutic recreation: On competence and outcomes* (2nd ed., pp. 43–58). Urbana, IL: Sagamore.

Wellman, D., Dustin, D., Henderson, K., & Moore, R. (2008). *Service living: Building community through public parks and recreation.* State College, PA: Venture.

Woods, R. A., & Kennedy, A. J. (1970). *The rise of urban America: Handbook of settlements.* New York: Arno Press.

World Health Organization. (2001). *The International Classification of Functioning, Disability and Health* (ICF). Geneva: WHO.

Chapter Seventeen

Area and Facility Management

CHAPTER OBJECTIVES

- To gain an awareness of different types of parks and recreation areas
- To achieve knowledge of various types of parks and recreation facilities
- To understand factors associated with the planning and management of parks and recreation facilities
- To recognize staffing and supervisory patterns associated with parks and recreation areas and facilities
- To gain knowledge of universal design and accessibility associated with parks and recreation areas and facilities
- To understand safety and risk management patterns associated with parks and recreation areas and facilities

INTRODUCTION

Parks and recreation agencies develop, maintain, and operate a wide array of areas and facilities to meet the leisure needs and interests of the participants whom they serve. Areas and facilities can provide opportunities for passive and/or active recreation. They provide spaces and places for the staging of recreation programs and services. Areas and facilities can be highly developed and structured requiring a significant investment of the community's resources to not only develop but maintain. Such areas and facilities may in fact represent a significant portion of the community's assets.

The areas and facilities operated and managed by parks and recreation agency are key factors that promote and contribute to the livability and quality of life of a community. They provide opportunities for individuals to experience leisure by participating in recreation programs and services. A community's parks and recreation areas and facilities may also contribute to a community's appreciation of beauty. Clearly parks, parkways and greenbelts all enhance the environmental value of a community. Attractively designed parks and recreation facilities also may contribute in positive ways to providing pleasing features to a community's aesthetic value.

In this chapter, a discussion of the management of parks and recreation areas and facilities will be included. First a variety of types of areas and facilities that are often a part of parks and recreation agencies will be identified. The list provided is extensive but not inclusive of all of the different types of areas and facilities that may be associated with a parks and recreation department. Examples from parks and recreation departments from across the United States are included in this chapter. This is followed by a discussion of "Planning and Management Considerations" for areas and facilities. The next section of the chapter focuses on the topic of "Staffing and Supervision." Following is a discussion of "Universal Design and Accessibility." Finally, a discussion of "Safety and Risk Management" is included.

TYPES OF AREAS AND FACILITIES

There are many different types of areas and facilities operated and managed by community parks and recreation departments. Following is a discussion of parks and recreation areas and facilities, and Tables 17.1 and 17.2 provide descriptions and examples of numerous areas and facilities. Areas can be thought of as a space or surface that is utilized for recreation purposes. We often think of parks and recreation areas as including open space, parks, natural preserves, wetlands, and/or other sites which are used for recreation and/or preserved for a variety of purposes including the survival of wildlife and the natural environment. Table 17.1 provides descriptions of the more common parks and recreation areas. Facilities on the other hand, can be thought of as structures that enable some type of service to be provided. Parks and recreation facilities can be of single or a focused usage or can be developed for multipurpose use. There are many types of parks and recreation facilities, including but not limited to, recreation centers, museums, swimming pools, basketball courts, tennis courts, ice rinks, and senior centers. It should be pointed out that areas and facilities are often combined to create resources to enable leisure participation. Table 17.2 offers information and examples of some of the more common parks and recreation facilities.

PLANNING AND MANAGEMENT CONSIDERATIONS

This section of the chapter is devoted to the topic of planning and management considerations for community parks and recreation areas and facilities. Topics discussed include policies; funding and budgetary considerations; parks and facility planning considerations; visitor services; and safety, first aid, and emergencies.

Policies

Policy governs the way an agency shall conduct itself concerning a specific action in a specific situation. Policies emanate from legislative actions, court rulings, and agency self-determination. In some instances, policies are a response to social or political change, reflecting new directions, while in other instances, policy might represent a direction of change based on collective action by appointed, elected or staff personnel. In the broadest sense, policies are guidelines for action (Lankford, Lankford, & Wheeler, 2011). As a guideline, policies give a sense of direction, an assurance of consistency, and ensure that an agency carries out its mandate properly.

Table 17.1

Park and Recreation Areas- Descriptions and Examples

Areas	Description	Example(s)
Adventure Courses	This type of development may include a number of different types of activities and may feature opportunities for initiatives, games, rope climbing, rock climbing, climbing walls, obstacle courses, and zip-lines. These types of park and recreation areas are also known as adventure parks.	An example of this type of development is one operated by New York City Department of Parks & Recreation. Their Youth Adventure Course assists young people in "building trust, problem solving, team building, and overcoming fear in a safe, secure environment" (New York City Department of Parks & Recreation Youth Adventure Course). http://www.nycgovparks.org/programs/rangers/adventure-course/youth-adventure
Arboretums	One can think of an arboretum as a place that cultivates and displays trees, shrubs, and other plants. Arboretums provide for opportunities for passive recreation and enjoyment of natural beauty as well as for scientific and educational purposes. Arboretums vary in scope and size depending upon the ability of an agency to support their development.	The Washington Park Arboretum operated by the Seattle (Washington) Parks and Recreation Department is a project that emphasizes education, conservation, and recreation. This area includes numerous plant collections in a 230-acre park environment. http://www.seattle.gov/parks/projects/arboretum/trail.htm
Basketball Courts	This facility consists of a rectangular playing surface. Outdoor basketball courts are made from paving materials such as concrete or asphalt. Indoor basketball courts are made up of wood or bamboo or even some type of multi-use synthetic surface.	Miami Beach (Florida) Parks & Recreation Department Flamingo Park's basketball courts were selected as the "Best of Miami 2005 and 2009." These courts are available on a rental basis from 7:00 am to 2:00 pm. http://miamibeachfl.gov/parksandrecreation/scroll.aspx?id=1574 2#basketball
Beaches, Lakes, and Ponds	Bodies of water such as ponds, lakes, and even river fronts provide opportunities for recreation. Often park and recreation agencies are involved in staffing such resources to ensure safety. Popular activities associated with such areas includes swimming, boating, fishing, and other water sports such as skiing, knee boarding, etc.	The city of Lake Forest (Illinois) Parks and Recreation Department operates lakefront and beach activities and provides fishing piers, boat launches, walking paths, and concession operations. In addition, they offer numerous classes, camps, and rentals. http://www.cityoflakeforest.com/parks-and-recreation/lakefront-and-beach-activities/
Bike Paths	A bike path can be thought of as a trail or area that has been set aside or separated for the use of bicyclists. Often, communities will establish bike paths in conjunction with neighborhood city streets or sidewalks.	The city of Cedar Falls (Iowa) has on a continuous basis, broaden their sidewalks to accommodate not only individuals walking, but also for bicyclists. The city offers 80 miles of trails and bike paths that can be used for "non-motorized and non-equestrian activities, such as biking, hiking, cross-country skiing and skating" (Cedar Falls Iowa Trail Maps). http://www.cedarfalls.com/index.aspx?NID=730

Table 17.1 (cont.)

Boat Ramps	Boat ramps can be thought of as an area that enables for the storage and/or launch of boats of various types and shapes. Essentially, a boat ramp is an area on some type of body of water wherein boats can be transferred between the land and water.	The Lee County (Florida) Parks & Recreation Department operates seven boat ramps that can be accessed for various recreational purposes. http://www.leegov.com/parks/boat%20Ramps
Campgrounds	A campground can be thought of as an area which is used for camping. Usually, campgrounds afford opportunities for tent camping or to park a camper. Campgrounds often provide some resources such as electricity, toilets, and showers.	The Black Hawk County (Iowa) Conservation Commission operates several campgrounds which provide affordable access to such areas for individuals to enjoy their leisure. Among their numerous parks, campgrounds are included as well as river access, wildlife areas, bike trails, and other resources. http://www.mycountyparks.com/County/Black-Hawk.aspx
Disc Golf Courses	Disc golf is a game that involves tossing a Frisbee or similar type of equipment on a well-laid-out course usually in an open space such as a park.	The City of East Ridge (Tennessee) Parks and Recreation Department offers a 19-hole disc golf course as a part of their Camp Jordan Sports Complex. http://www.eastridgeparksandrec.com/Facilities-and-Rental-Information/Disk-Golf-Course.aspx Disc golf is a relatively inexpensive activity and can be enjoyed by all ages.
Fishing Dock/Pier	A fishing dock or pier can be thought of as a resource that is placed over the water to enhance access for individuals wishing to fish. Such fishing docks or piers are extended out from the land into a body of water. Such areas also serve as a way for mooring and launching boats.	The Queen Anne County (Maryland) Parks & Recreation has developed and operated several piers that can be used for various recreational uses. http://www.parksnrec.org/hiker-biker-trails/landings-piers/
Golf Courses	A golf course can be thought of as an area that has been developed to enable the playing of the game of golf. Usually golf courses include a series of nine or 18 holes and are developed to include tees, fairways, and putting greens. Golf courses also include natural or artificial hazards such as sand traps, ponds, and other.	The Bensenville (Illinois) Park District operates an 18-hole golf course known as the White Pines Golf Club. This course was established in 1928. http://www.whitepinesgolf.com/
Greenbelts	A greenbelt can be thought of as a parcel of land that includes woods, parks, or other open spaces that surrounds a community. As noted in Chapter 2, greenbelts have played an important role in the development of the community parks and recreation movement.	The Boston Metropolitan Park System was established in 1893 and created a greenbelt around that city. In addition, the Forest Preserve District of Cook County (Illinois) established in 1911 provided a buffer between the city environment and the countryside. Information regarding the Metropolitan Park System of Greater Boston can be found at http://www.nps.gov/nr/travel/massachusetts_conservation/metro_park_system_of_greater_boston.html. Likewise, information regarding the Cook County Forest Preserve District can be found at http://fpdcc.com/.

Table 17.1 (cont.)

Horticultural Gardens	This type of area involves the cultivation of various plants, flowers, shrubs, and trees. Horticultural gardens are often very formal and ornate in their design and presentation. A garden usually occupies a designated space that can be cultivated and enjoyed by the public.	The Missouri Botanical Garden is an excellent example of this type of resource. http://www.missouribotanicalgarden.org/ The Orcutt Ranch Horticultural Center formally known as the Center Rancho Sombra Del Roble is operated by the city of Los Angeles (California) Department of Recreation & Parks. The area includes many trees of interest, opportunities for fruit picking, and gardens. http://www.laparks.org/dos/horticulture/orcuttranch.htm
Multi-use Synthetic Turf Fields	Over the past several decades, multi-use synthetic turm fields have gained in popularity in a variety of recreational settings including stadiums, ball diamonds, and playgrounds. The first artificial turf known as Astro Turf was established in the 1960s for youth in the Astrodome. Artificial multi-use synthetic turf is widely used in sport facilities and although it has some drawbacks, is becoming increasingly preferred as a way of providing a playing surface for activities that normally take place on natural grass.	For example, the City of Los Angeles (California) Department of Recreation and Parks operates 21 synthetic fields. http://www.laparks.org/dos/synthetic.htm
Nature Preserves	A nature preserve can be thought of as an area that has been protected and is managed in such a way as to preserve its flora, fauna, and wildlife.	The City of Austin (Texas) Parks & Recreation Department operates a system of preserves of over 2,000 acres. Preserved lands provide for nature-based programs and "provides essential endangered species habitats, includes a unique natural feature such as a cave or stream, or provides a prime example of a specific type of ecosystem" (City of Austin Parks & Recreation Department Nature Preserves and Nature Based Programs). http://www.austintexas.gov/naturepreserves
Parks	A park can be thought of as an area that is usually free of structures and maintained to emphasize nature or ornamental horticulture. Whereas in the past, parks were provided in such a way as to emphasize passive recreation pursuits. Today, they often include other recreational resources such as ball diamonds, picnic shelters and playgrounds. Parks often include lawns, trails, wooded areas, and other open spaces.	The Minneapolis (Minnesota) Parks and Recreation operates an extensive system of parks including 134 parks and lakes. https://www.minneapolisparks.org/parks__destinations/parks__lakes/

Table 17.1 (cont.)

Parkways	A parkway is a thoroughfare that has been planted with grass, trees, shrubs, flowers, and other flora and fauna. Parkways originated in the late 1880s as a way of beautifying urban environments.	The City of Denver (Colorado) Parks and Recreation have developed a system of inter-connected parkways, parks, and neighborhoods. The system is the responsibility of the city's Department of Parks and Recreation and involves establishing right-of-way, set-backs, tree lawn (the space between the street and an individual's lawn that is planted with trees), median strips, and an individual's homeowner front yard. This integrated system provides for continuity of the landscape. https://www.denvergov.org/content/denvergov/en/denver-parks-and-recreation/parks/parkways.html
Softball/Base-ball Diamonds	These types of areas provide opportunities for participants to engage in the game of softball or baseball. As a park and recreation area, we can think of a softball/baseball diamond as a parcel of land or ground. Most park and recreation departments operate softball and baseball fields which are used for tournaments or leagues or even drop-in play.	The Columbia (Missouri) Parks and Recreation Department has developed 22 baseball/softball fields. These fields are "scheduled for youth and adult league games, tournaments, and youth and adult practices" See https://www.gocolumbiamo.com/ParksandRec/Parks_and_Faciliti es/Facility_Reservations/baseball-softball.php for a more extensive explanation of their program.
Tennis Courts	A rectangular area whose surface is either made up of concrete, clay, or grass, which enables two individuals or two pairs of players to engage in the game of tennis.	The San Francisco (California) Recreation and Parks Department manages 132 tennis courts located on playgrounds, parks, and at recreation centers. These courts can be accessed at no charge; however, there are 21 tennis courts located in Golden Gate Park that can be reserved for a small fee. See http://sfrecpark.org/recprogram/tennis-program/ for more information about the tennis court resources of the San Francisco Recreation and Parks Department.
Trails	A trail can be thought of as a path that participants can walk, jog, hike, or bike for a leisure experience.	A popular program is the Rails-to-Trails program, which is aimed at crafting a network of trails from former railroad lines. The Rails-to-Trails Conservancy has developed a program that has envisioned that 90% of all Americans will have a trail within three miles of their residency. http://www.railstotrails.org/ . The Bend (Oregon) Park & Recreation District manages 65 miles of trails. http://bendparksandrec.org/parks___trails/trail_list/

Table 17.1 (cont.)

Wetlands	A wetland can be thought of as an area that is often covered with shallow water or that the soil of the area is saturated with moisture. A marshy area or swamp often carries the designation of a wetland. Wetlands are important as the provide a refugee for fowl in their migration patterns. Agricultural land is often converted into wetlands to encourage habitat for various bird species.	Clark County (Nevada) Parks & Recreation Department operates a wetland park which provides "lush habitats for over 300 species of plants and animals while improving the quality of our water supply." http://www.clarkcountynv.gov/parks/Pages/cc-wetlands-park-homepage.aspx
Wildlife Preserve	Closely related to nature preserves and wetlands is that of a wildlife preserve. This area of land is established in order to protect a particular type of wildlife.	Bainbridge Island (Washington) Metro Park & Recreation District's Gazzam Lake Nature Preserve includes 444.6 acres. The park includes an upland forest, wetlands, and an extensive trail system. As an area untouched by human development, it provides wildlife habitat for a variety of species. http://www.biparks.org/biparks_site/parks/gazzam-lake.htm

17.2

Park and Recreation Facilities- Descriptions and Examples

Facilities	Description	Example(s)
Aquatic Complexes	Since the early 1900s, aquatic facilities have been a staple of municipal park and recreation agencies. Initially, such facilities were just for public bathing, fitness, and later served as a method to curb tensions during the summer months. Today, aquatic complexes have become increasingly sophisticated incorporating slides, whirlpools, lazy rivers, spray/sprinklers, geysers, bubbling water, as well as the opportunity to generate dynamic environments found in wave-generating swimming pools.	The Falls Aquatic Center, an aquatics facility operated by the city of Cedar Falls (Iowa), includes several appropriately-named water experiences including Safari Falls, Rock Falls, and Adventure Falls. The facility also includes a bucket dump. http://www.cedarfalls.com/index.aspx?NID=652. The Northshore Aquatic Complex operated by the St. Petersburg (Florida) Park & Recreation Department includes a 50-meter swimming pool, 25-meter warm-up pool, flume slides, zero-depth entry, and a baby pool. http://www.stpeteparksrec.org/north-shore-aquatic-complex.html
Art/Cultural Centers	This type of facility provides opportunities to showcase the arts and cultural activities. Such complexes may include a theater, meeting rooms, display areas, studios, practice rooms, and instructional areas.	Nashville (Tennessee) Parks and Recreation Department's Centennial Art Center (CAC) offers a Fine Art Gallery and studio areas for classes, workshops, and exhibition. http://www.nashville.gov/Parks-and-Recreation/Cultural-Arts.aspx
Band Shell	This facility is a concaved acoustically resonant structure that enables musical performances to be offered. Band shells are usually found located in a park setting.	For example, Baraboo (Wisconsin) Parks, Recreation, & Forestry Department operates a band shell in its Ochsner Park. http://www.cityofbaraboo.com/index.asp?Type=B_BASIC&SEC=%7BB55D077F-2005-4BE3-AABC-7447CCA3F2C6%7D&DE=%7B0EC46D87-B434-4436-BE4F-71FB47C26E45%7D
Fitness Centers	Fitness centers have gained in popularity over the past several decades. The increasing emphasis on leisure, health, and one's well-being have led to the growth of these kinds of facilities. Fitness centers often include a wide array of equipment and perhaps a jogging track and support services such as saunas, medicinal pools, massage, and locker rooms. Of course, fitness centers often provide a wide range of programs focused on strength and conditioning, aerobic exercise, Pilates, spinning, Zumba, and cardio exercises.	Bowling Green (Kentucky) Park & Recreation Department operates a fitness center which includes free weights, treadmills, stair climbers, ellipticals/cross trainers, and exercise bikes. http://www2.bgky.org/bgpr/fitness/
Ice Rinks	An ice rink is a space that may be provided on an indoor basis or outdoor basis. The ice rink contains an ice surface that provides for ice skating, ice hockey, broomball, and other related activities. Ice rinks are especially featured in colder climates, although it is not unusual for communities to operate indoor ice rinks in warmer areas.	The Maple Grove (Minnesota) Parks and Recreation Department operates 12 outdoor skating rinks. http://www.maplegrovemn.gov/parks-and-recreation/parks-and-trails/outdoor-skating-rinks/ The Park District of Oak Park (Illinois), Ridgeland Common Recreation Complex includes an indoor ice arena

17.2 (cont.)

Museums	This type of facility displays collections of historical, scientific, artistic, or cultural interest. Museums come in all shapes and sizes. Some are focused on specific areas of interest such as the arts or display of historical items. Others are broader in scope incorporating a wide variety of artifacts.	The Fayetteville-Cumberland (North Carolina) Parks & Recreation Department operates a "area transportation and local history museum." This museum includes displays of model trains, automobiles, airplanes, steamboats, and a recreated Station Agents Office. http://www.fcpr.us/transportation_museum.aspx
Picnic Shelters	Many, if not all park and recreation departments provide picnic shelters. These types of facilities are often located in park areas and serve as a rallying point for events such as family picnics, social events, and other activities. Picnic shelters are often covered and include barbecue pits, picnic tables, and electrical outlets. Often picnic shelters can be reserved for a small fee.	A good example of the provision of picnic shelters are those provided by Arlington (Virginia) Parks & Recreation Department http://parks.arlingtonva.us/picnic-shelters/. Some of the reservable picnic shelters of this agency can accommodate a capacity of 200 individuals. This agency has 30 picnic shelters available, 16 of which can be reserved for a fee.
Playgrounds	This type of facility has served as the background and even raison d'etre for the organization of the play movement. Playgrounds are usually outdoor areas that have been developed for children's play and include a variety of structures such as slides, climbing apparatus, swings, obstacle courses, and other types of equipment. Playgrounds can be designed as inclusive spaces with a high degree of accessibility. They can also be developed as age-appropriate spaces with emphasis placed on creating opportunities for younger and or older children. Still further adventure playgrounds create opportunity for children to build, rearrange, and/or manipulate the play environment. Playgrounds can also be structured to emphasize natural features of the landscape and/or draw into its design more natural elements such as the use of wood or other types of surfaces.	As a result of the efforts of the National Recreation and Park Association and the National Program for Playground Safety housed at the University of Northern Iowa, a great deal of advancement has been made in ensuring safe playgrounds through more effective supervision, the provision of safe surfaces, and the inclusion of safer types of playground equipment. The Howard County (Maryland) Recreation and Parks Department operates an extensive system of playgrounds including the provision of 34 sites. http://www.howardcountymd.gov/playgrounds.htm
Recreation Centers	These types of facilities provide space for the provision of recreation programs. Recreation centers may include meeting rooms, gymnasiums, theaters, studios, display areas and small cafes. Often park and recreation agencies may have a system of neighborhood recreation centers and/or a single facility may be highly developed and centralized within a community.	For example, the Arlington Heights (Illinois) Park District operates a series of neighborhood recreation centers throughout the community. http://www.ahpd.org/parks/parks--facilities-general-info/ Likewise the Salt Lake County (Utah) Parks and Recreation Department operates an extensive series of recreation centers. http://slco.org/recreation/admin/facilitylocations/recreationCenters.html

17.2 (cont.)

Senior Centers	These types of facilities serve as a hub of community activity, programs, and services for older adults. Senior citizen centers provide programs such as meal/nutrition programs; information assistance; health, fitness, and wellness; transportation; counseling; employment assistance; opportunities for volunteering; recreation programs; educational programs; and the opportunity for intergenerational activities. Such facilities may include open meeting spaces, club rooms, studios, lounge areas, cafeteria, libraries, game rooms and space for fitness and exercise. As Keller and Sprinkmeyer (2016 p. 52) write, "Senior centers are responding with new facilities and programs to meet the diverse, dynamic lifestyle and activities of older adults." They emphasize the importance of flexibility and the emergence of the virtual senior center.	The Gwinnett County (Georgia) Parks and Recreation Department operates senior centers that provide opportunities for "caring and supportive atmospheres for social, recreational and educational opportunities to the senior population (age 50 – up)." https://www.gwinnettcounty.com/portal/gwinnett/Departments/Community Services/ParksandRecreation/SeniorRecreationOfferings
Skate Parks	Skate parks have become increasingly popular with the rise of skateboarding. A skate park is an area that has been developed and designated to enable skateboarding to take place in a safe yet often dynamically designed environment. Skate parks often also facilitate recreation opportunities for BMX, scooters, wheelchairs, and inline skating.	The city of Boulder (Colorado) Parks and Recreation Department operates a skate park that provides unsupervised, skate-at-your-own-risk opportunities. The design of the skate park features an exciting "street-course" with the lure of rails, curbs and free-flowing forms and bowls." https://bouldercolorado.gov/parks-rec/skate-park-at-scott-carpenter-park
Stadiums	Stadiums provides opportunities for events of various types including sporting activities such as football, soccer, baseball, and rugby, as well as for the staging of concerts, rallies, pageants, plays, conferences, and other events. A stadium is a large structure that includes seating for spectators. Most stadiums are open to natural environments, although there are numerous indoor stadiums, especially those for professional or college football.	The city stadium complex operated by the Lynchburg (Virginia) Parks & Recreation Department includes seating for 10,000 individuals and provides opportunities for the staging of high school games and for the home games of the Lynchburg Hillcats minor league baseball team, an affiliate of the Atlanta Braves. http://www.lynchburgparksandrec.com/city-stadium-complex/
Zoos	A zoo is a place where animals are collected and displayed, usually in park-type setting. Animals are exhibited in a way that enables the public to enjoy viewing them in a safe fashion. These facilities come in all shapes and forms, including ones that are fully developed with extensive collections to ones that are less sophisticated, such as small petting zoos.	Located in Balboa Park the San Diego Zoo featured over 3,700 animals. Although operated by the nonprofit Zoological Society of San Diego, the zoo is located on park land leased from the city of San Diego. The city of Tucson (Arizona) Parks and Recreation department operates the Reid Park Zoo. Founded in 1965, this facility is dedicated "to encourage commitment to the conservation of biological diversity and to provide educational and fun experiences for visitors of all ages." https://www.tucsonaz.gov/parks/contact-parks-and-recreation

Most policies stem from the legislative branch of whatever level of government the agency operates within. Government, in response to societal and political pressures has become more complex. The legislative branch has conveyed to the agency more and more rule-making authority within the rather broad policies it has formulated. As a practical matter, this has resulted in a greater amount of policy being set by the agency or governmental executive. The formulation of policy is a matter of critical concern. Policy must be broad enough to provide latitude for responsive decision making, yet be specific enough to enable the decision makers to accurately reflect intent. Regulations have to apply to the majority of situations—to anticipate the worst case—they must address the problems they are designed to address.

Lankford, Lankford, and Wheeler (2011) note the following steps on policy formulation: 1) appoint a project leader who counsels with the elected and appointed officials, 2) develop a needs statement for the policy, 3) gather all pertinent facts and data on the issue, 4) draft policy document, 5) consult with city legal counsel on compliance with any other directives and the impact on other programs, 6) staff review of policy, and 7) present policy in public hearings and workshops.

Once the policy is adopted, copies of it are reproduced in sufficient quantity to assure its availability at parks and recreation facilities, as well as at headquarters, and also on web pages. It is equally important that time be given to policy matters during the regular in-service training programs so that all are aware of policies and know that they apply to everyone, from the top administration down. When new employees are hired, policies should be discussed with them as a regular part of introductory training.

Funding and Budgetary Considerations

In all probability, the procurement of sufficient funds will always be a challenge in parks and recreation. Parks and recreation organizations frequently lack a constituent lobby group. In times of tax revolt or budget reductions, this lack of representation is disastrous for parks and recreation funding. As California and Arizona State Parks can testify, there was also evidence of a lack of awareness and sympathy on the part of decision makers. Effective support for parks and recreation takes many years to build and needs politically competent resource people to continue building support (Lankford, Lankford, & Wheeler, 2011).

Funding categories. Some governmental units require that all agency-generated revenues be deposited in the general fund, while others permit the agency to use the revenues. Basically, all revenues are organized in one of the following categories.

General fund. Although the title may vary, all levels of government have a fund into which receipts flow. For the purposes of this chapter, consider the general fund as the depository for revenues that are not designated for any specific purpose and that may be expended in any way the legislative body decrees.

Dedicated funds. These, as the name implies, are funds that are dedicated to a specific use or a specific agency. For example, fees in-lieu of land dedication for park development must be spent to provide parks, trails, and facilities for the development. Revolving funds, as noted below, are another type of dedicated funds.

Revolving funds. Under certain circumstances, the legislative body will permit the agency to establish an account for revolving funds. These are funds the agency both generates and spends within general legislative authority. This is usually done to provide for the replacement of equipment or for programs if the income generated completely covers the cost of operating a particular activity or service.

Sources of revenue. All revenues are placed in one or more of three funds: general, dedicated, and revolving. Where and how are these revenues obtained?

Anticipated and unanticipated revenues. When an agency prepares its budget, it must estimate and identify planned expenditures and list all anticipated sources and amount of revenue. Revenues received in excess of the amount anticipated are not usually considered unanticipated and may not be expended by the agency. Only a new source of funds is considered as unanticipated. For example, the agency anticipates $40,000 from facility registration fees, all of which is deposited in the general fund. The agency has an extraordinarily busy year, increasing the revenues to $60,000. The $20,000 is not considered unanticipated revenue and may not be available to the agency.

Unanticipated revenues, then, are revenues from a source not contemplated at a budget time. For example, a windstorm fells a large number of trees in the park, producing harvestable timber. The revenues from salvaging that timber would be unanticipated. To enable salvage, the governing control agency will usually permit the agency to spend the unanticipated revenues up to the amount necessary to log, clean up, and replant, but this may not entail an amount in excess of the amount to be realized from the log sale.

Additional funding—nongovernmental. Though agencies normally handle funds only from governmental sources, there is a large and variable source of funds available from nongovernmental sources. An agency can always use additional funds to acquire, develop, and operate areas, facilities, and programs no matter how many dollars it is allotted from the legislative authority. Some of the other ways an agency might raise funds from commercial and noncommercial sources follow (adapted from Lankford, Lankford, & Wheeler, 2011).

Commercial vendors. In some cases, a working relationship with the private sector has shown to benefit parks and recreation agencies. The subject of concessions is of great importance. The term "concession," as it relates to park use, means a space or privilege within a park for a subsidiary business or service. Examples are overnight accommodations or places to buy food, rent canoes, or obtain rides accompanied by interpretation. These outlets are not only a potential source of income but also a key factor in major development and park and facility operations. For this reason, concessions are being handled as a major unit within fiscal management. These concessions are bid upon by the businesses and awarded the contract for a specified time based on performance. Here are a few examples of concessions.

- The production of outdoor recreation guides, park brochures, or agency films could be accomplished as a joint venture whereby the agency provides the text, the commercial firm provides the funds, and both receive credit. For example, the manufacturers or wholesalers of mountain bikes might well finance trail or safety brochures.
- The development and operation of a golf course could be managed as a commercial venture under agency rules and regulations.
- Granting a private developer a utility easement across public land could result in a needed development on the land in the future.
- The passage of an ordinance requiring that all new subdivisions set aside park areas, or money in lieu of these areas, can generate lands and funds for an agency.

Noncommercial. One of the major sources yet to be fully tapped for financial revenues for parks and recreation use is that of the noncommercial, nongovernmental organizations.

Within that resource are the foundations. A number of foundations fund parks and recreation programs. Some of these foundations are international; others allocate funds to recipients in a localized area only. A municipality, state, or province might choose to organize its own parks foundation. Some, such as the California State Park Foundation, serve only the sponsoring agency, while others, such as the Washington Parks Foundation, serve all parks and recreation agencies in a geographical area. In Canada, contact the local Provincial Community Service Branch. In addition to foundations, there are considerable financial resources in the proceeds from bequests and donations. These are usually within the community foundation system at the local or county level.

Grants. Grants are available from both governmental and nongovernmental sources. They may be used for capital or operation requirements. They are available to both public and nonpublic agencies.

Government grants. These might be federal grants to state or local agencies, state grants to state agencies, or state grants to a lower entity. The latter include those grants from a federal source administered through the states. There are two basic types of government grants. The first uses a formula for determining the amount. Grants from the Land and Water Conservation Funds, Historic Preservation Funds, and Boating Funds operate this way. Those that go directly from the federal government to the specific agency, such as the Dingell-Johnson Funds, use a formula as well. In the second type, no formula is used to determine the amount. With the advent of block grants from the federal government, the various lower levels of government have greater freedom of allocation.

Bonds. Bonds are interest-bearing certificates of debt issued by a corporation or government by which an agency gains immediate access to funds while committing itself to fulfillment of an obligation. Three categories of bonds are mentioned here, but bonds may have many variations and often bear the name of the issuing authority.

General obligation bonds. These bonds pledge full faith and credit of the municipality and are paid for by general taxation. General obligation bonds provide for the early acquisition and completion of development with payment prorated over several years, during which time the site is usable.

Revenue bonds. Revenue bonds are not used unless the financed projects return revenues. The revenues produced by specific earning assets are pledged and, as such, the issues are dependent on the governing authority to receive revenues from use of the facility constructed in an amount sufficient to pay the principal and interest. These bonds have the same advantage as general obligation bonds, but the disadvantage is having to make payment on schedule from the revenue received.

Special assessment bonds. These sorts of bonds are used where special benefits to property are equal to or greater than the assessment. These bonds are used and paid for by the residents of the local area, such as a sewer district. They are often called LIDs (local improvement districts), or tax increment finance. Like the general obligation bonds, they pledge full faith and credit of the governing agency.

Special tax levies. These are taxes levied against a special source, such as cigarettes or gasoline, for a special purpose, such as park development or boating access. This method supposedly has the advantage of enabling the agency to predict the amount of revenue and ensure the income over a long period of time.

Fees and charges. These can be levied for almost everything, depending on the past history and policy of an agency. Fees are commonly charged for showers, dog kennels, boat rentals, horseback rides, firewood permits, camping, parking, day-use entrance, guarded beaches, special equipment, special instruction, and activity entrance. Additional fees may be charged for out-of-area visitors. This decision will undoubtedly be made by the legislative authority.

Parks and Facility Planning Considerations

The culmination of a thorough planning process for facility development is reflected in the parks and recreation master plan. Some master plans present objectives in the broadest terms, serving only as guides to the development of more detailed plans, including facility location. Other master plans, for small parks, may be so specific that they spell out in detail the location and type of roads, trails, utilities, buildings, and other facilities. Often parks and recreation agencies combine these two types of plans and have specific plans for facility design and development within the general master plan. There must be consistency between the master plan and site-specific plans. The master plan guides site-specific plans; however, the development of site-specific plans can require a shift in the master plan.

When determining the kind and extent of facilities, the planner must consider the following factors:

- How is the site to be used?
- What is the amount and kind of land and water available?
- Will the land support the expected visitor load and activities without excessive deterioration?
- Can the proposed facilities be maintained with a modest increase in the personnel and materials budget, or will substantial increases in one or both be needed?

Parks and facilities include any modification of the landscape intended to facilitate access, use, and understanding of the park. All structures, roads, trails, signs, utilities, and parking lots, among other "improvements," are considered facilities. The location and design of facilities can help to interpret park resources; however, facility location and design can also contribute to the degradation of the resource. Facility location and design is one of the most important management techniques for the manager to guide the interface between visitors and the park. Careful consideration must be given to the location of every facility to maximize use and control for user behaviors. An understanding of facilities, their relationships, and their use is important to the design of new facilities or the remodel of existing facilities. The process used for facility design is critical to creating a visitor experience that complements the resource area.

Functions of facilities and design considerations. It is difficult to imagine the average park area without facilities. Facilities do the following:

- They serve the need of park visitors.
- They protect the park from visitor impact.
- They are necessary to the management and maintenance of the park.
- They create the park image, either favorable or unfavorable.

Although facilities may add to the appearance and function of a park, they also intrude on park resources. Facilities cost money to build, are expensive to maintain, and can be a focus for vandalism. Vandalism must be addressed by giving special consideration to the design, placement, and material make-up of facilities. Where possible, facilities should be constructed of materials indigenous to, as well as in harmony with, the natural environment. Facilities must not infringe on unique areas or be placed where there is unusual or endangered flora or fauna. In the past, too many parks were unduly manicured or overdeveloped simply because the park "looked better that way." The four facility functions listed earlier illustrate that facilities provide user satisfaction and serve as management tools. Using these as criteria, the planner might look at proposed facilities under the following headings (adapted from Lankford, Lankford, & Wheeler, 2011).

Suitability to site. Is there harmony between the proposed facility and the natural landscape? Is there harmony among the various facilities? How much of the natural setting will have to be altered to construct the facility?

Adaptability. Can the proposed facility be expanded to meet new demands at reasonable cost?

Suitability for maintenance. Will this design raise or lower maintenance costs? Has this design proven elsewhere to be relatively low in maintenance costs?

Safety. Do design and materials provide maximum safety for both visitors and staff?

Vandalism potential. Will the design leave the facility vulnerable to vandalism, or will it discourage vandalism? Will broken or defaced facilities be easily restored?

Access. Is the facility readily accessible to all visitors including persons with disabilities? Is traffic flow and directions obvious for both foot and vehicle traffic? Is night lighting adequate?

Energy efficiency. Is the facility designed for minimizing heat loss in cooler months? Does it make provision for cooling in the warm season? Are the energy requirements reasonable? Is lighting achieved with minimum wattage? Is solar an option?

Cost effectiveness. Is the design actually the least expensive, or would spending more on the construction be offset by reduced maintenance and vandalism costs as well as increased life of the facility?

Construction costs. Does the design entail unnecessary or expensive constructions costs, such as earth removal and grading? Are the materials difficult to secure?

Architectural character. Do the facilities and structures help interpret the nature of the site and the cultural heritage of the area? Is the design compatible with existing facilities?

Visitor Services

Parks and recreation facilities are places where informality prevails, and it is considered appropriate for strangers to interact with one another. This is an interesting feature of parks and recreation—the fact that although people seldom communicate with their neighbors at home, they smile and speak to strangers when in parks and recreation settings, where interaction is enjoyed and even sought.

Visitors are usually looking for a particular experience when they arrive at a park or facility. These anticipations are influenced by their background, previous experience with parks, and motivations for visiting a site. Not every activity can or should be provided in each park. Certain parks can better offer specific activities than other parks. It must be made clear to potential visitors which parks offer which activities and where in the park they are available. Cell phones and associated technology can provide maps and other information including reservations and amenities and even driving directions to attractions.

In addition visitor services may include concession operations which provide food, drink, and even souvenirs for visitors to parks and recreation areas and facilities.

Safety, First Aid and Emergencies

Parks and recreation organizations have the responsibility for the safety of both users and parks and recreation personnel. Every reasonable precaution should be taken to reduce or eliminate existing and potentially hazardous or defective conditions that might be sources of injury to persons and property. Operating procedures should provide for the detection and reduction of these conditions through an adequate program of inspection.

First aid, now sometimes called "first responder," is the immediate and temporary care given to a victim of an accident or sudden illness until the services of a physician can be obtained. Parks and recreation managers must acquaint themselves with the state and local situation and have a plan and supplies ready for emergency response. Trained personnel should be available, especially during the high-use season. It is important that the necessary information on the injury be obtained as soon as possible after the treatment so that the data are accurate. Accurate information is also needed about any treatment so managers will be able to properly represent the agency or themselves in a lawsuit. The employee must not prescribe treatment or medicine unless trained to do so. The victim or relatives should be provided with a list of local doctors and allowed to make the choice. Regular review and training should take place in all rescue and treatment procedures, and equipment and procedures should be state of the art if at all possible.

Regardless of how well the park or facility is planned, constructed, and operated, there are certain situations that cannot be circumvented. Emergencies, by their very nature, are unexpected but can be anticipated. They demand an immediate coordinated response on the part of parks and recreation personnel. These emergencies include fires, accidents, lost persons, group disturbances, and evacuation in the event of a fire, flood, severe storm threat, or other catastrophe. Emergency routes should be clearly identified and kept clear of obstacles. Inherent in any emergency is the need to act quickly. Preparation and training are critical to successful outcomes. Many organizations, such as law enforcement, EMS services, fire departments, and volunteer search and rescue teams, provide both expertise and training for park staff and others. They have extensive experience and can direct almost any rescue or emergency operation.

STAFFING AND SUPERVISION

Supervision is an action that involves providing oversight to the management of parks and recreation areas or facilities. The act of supervision may involve providing direction to others including staff and participants. Supervisory activities may also involve providing information, inspecting and/or maintaining resources, planning and scheduling, and ensuring that policies, procedures, rules, and regulations are followed. There are several types of supervision as follows.

Direct Supervision

This type of supervision related to community parks and recreation areas and facilities involves providing direct oversight to a program, area or facility. In this case, an individual engaged in the supervisory function may be assigned to monitor a specific area or facility and have the responsibility of performing a specific function. A lifeguard would be an example of an individual who is involved in direct supervision.

Indirect Supervision

Individuals engaged in indirect supervision are able to perform certain task or job responsibilities but under the direct supervision of a higher level manager. Thus an individual is responsible for carrying out an activity, yet higher level supervision is present. For example, individuals working in a concession stand operate with a degree of freedom and make transactions, yet may be be supervised to ensure that they are dealing with participants in a fair and honest manner.

General Supervision

This type of supervision involves providing oversight to a larger area or facility. For example, a supervisor for a drop-in recreation program may lead no specific activity yet ensure that the environment is safe and free of hazards. Also the supervisor may ensure that play behavior follows appropriate rules and regulations and those participants treat one another with respect.

Staffing refers to those positions involving individuals for specific job functions within a parks and recreation agency. Generally staffing involves selecting the right people and placing them in positions that amplify their strengths to carry out specific tasks. There are many models of staffing for parks and recreation area and facility management. As can be seen in the following examples, recreation service provision is central to the management of area and facilities. Often, areas and facilities are viewed as "revenue" producing and therefore have a manager or supervisor for these entrepreneurial activities, which is the case for Davenport, Iowa.

The organizational charts in Figures 17.1 and 17.2 depict the ways in which Davenport, Iowa, and Clayton, Missouri, have organized their parkss and recreation programs. Of interest here is the supervision of the facilities and parks. Davenport (Iowa) Department of Parks and Recreation has a parks section staffed by the senior parks manager who supervises the parks operations manager. The parks operations manager supervises staff in horticulture, safety, and shop coordinators. Both full-time and seasonal staff are included. The senior recreation manager oversees the facilities operations manager (who supervises seasonal workers) and the supervisors for performing arts, adaptive and inclusive recreation, environmental education, and sports and special events. The superintendent of revenue facilities overseas golf operations and staff and the supervisors for ice and turf and sports and special events. Interestingly, the sports and special events supervisor reports to the senior recreation manager but is also reporting to the superintendent of revenue facilities.

In contrast, the Clayton Missouri Parks and Recreation Department organizational chart (Figure 17.2) indicates that the recreation manager supervises the aquatic supervisor, athletic and facilities supervisors, and fitness supervisor. It would appear on this chart that facility managers are supervised by the membership services supervisor, while the superintendent of parks provides oversight to the park maintenance supervisor, horticulturist and field technicians and laborers. By contrast, the City of Minneapolis (Minnesota) Parks and Recreation Board considers the planning, environmental stewardship, and recreation services division as the "service delivery" group. It is apparent that facility management, supervision, and staffing are within and shared by these three distinct programs (See Figure 17.3).

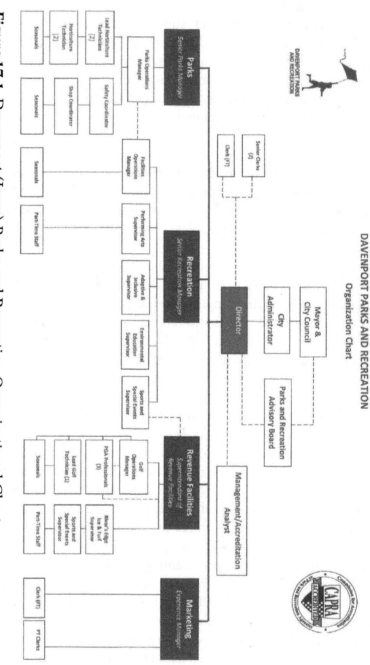

Figure 17.1. Davenport (Iowa) Parks and Recreation Organizational Chart

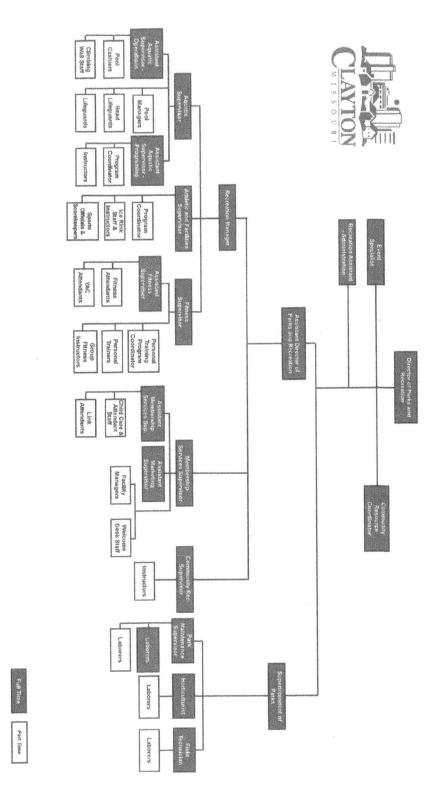

Figure 17.2. Clayton, Missouri Parks & Recreation Organizational Chart

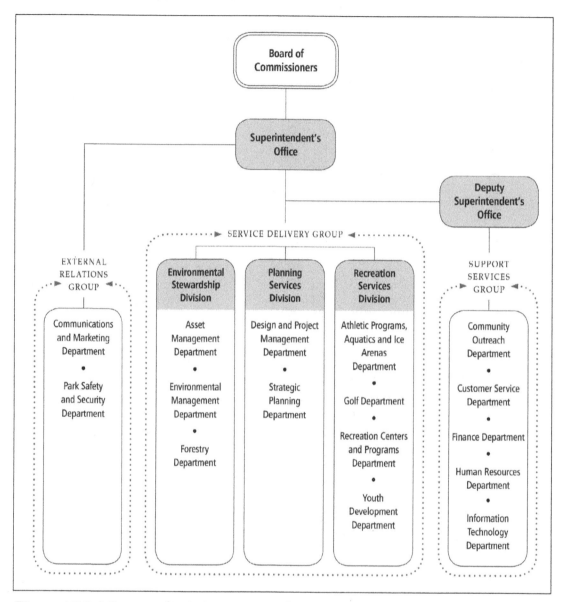

Figure 17.3. Minneapolis, Minnesota Parks & Recreation Board Organizational Chart

In any of the models, it should be apparent that full-time, part-time, and seasonal staff exist within all of the units of the parks and recreation system. Importantly, specialists exist for parks such as horticulturists, or pool managers for aquatics, etc. All of these positions require specialized training and certifications.

UNIVERSAL DESIGN AND ACCESSIBILITY

As outlined earlier in this book, the U.S. Census Bureau (Brault, 2012) identified 18.7% of the civilian noninstitutionalized population, aged 15 or older, as having a disability in 2010, with 12.6% having a severe disability. The authors posit that inclusion is an attitude and behavior, on the part of parks and recreation professionals, of providing the needed adaptations, accommodations, and support so that people with disabilities can participate in parks and recreation opportunities. Parks and recreation activities are appealing to a range of people with varying abilities. All areas in parks, forests, and reserves cannot be available to all visitors, but older facilities that are being refurbished and all new facilities being considered can eliminate most structural barriers by using universal design principles.

Universal design, also known as inclusive design, design-for-all, or human-centered design, provides a framework for designing places or products without special or separate accommodations. The universal design framework pushes parks and recreation facility planning and design beyond minimum accessibility guidelines. The National Center on Accessibility (www.ncaonline.org) has developed a one-hour e-course as an introduction to the principles of universal design for parks and recreation practitioners. Drawing on the work of Dillenschneider and Burkhour (2010), Table 17.3 presents universal design ideas that are related to accommodations for typical parkss and recreation areas and facilities.

The Architectural Barriers Act of 1968 notes, "Any building or facility, constructed in whole or part by federal funds must be made accessible to and usable by the physically handicapped." This Act was followed by Section 504 of the Rehabilitation Act of 1973 and the Americans with Disabilities Act (ADA) of 1990. In March 2010, the U.S. Department of Justice issued the 2010 ADA Standards for Accessible Design, Title II and Title III.

The Americans with Disabilities Act (ADA) requires the Department of Justice (the Department) to publish ADA design standards that are consistent with the guidelines published by the U.S. Architectural and Transportation Barriers Compliance Board (Access Board). The Department has adopted revised ADA design standards that include the relevant chapters of the Access Board's 2004 ADA/ABA Accessibility Guidelines as modified by specific provisions of the Department's revised rules implementing title II and title III of the ADA. To minimize compliance burdens on entities subject to more than one legal standard, these design standards have been harmonized with the Federal standards implementing the Architectural Barriers Act and with the private sector model codes that are adopted by most States. The changes to the design guidelines were adopted by the Access Board as a series of separate rules that were combined in the 2004 ADA/ABA guidelines. These rules addressed recreation facilities, play areas, state and local government facilities (detention facilities and courthouses), and, finally, the revision of the Access Board's 1991 guidelines. These changes have been adopted, with some modifications, as the 2010 Standards for Accessible Design (U.S. Department of Justice, 2010).

The 2010 Standards set minimum requirements—both scoping and technical—for newly designed and constructed or altered State and local government facilities, public accommodations, and commercial facilities to be readily accessible to and usable by individuals with disabilities. These ADA standards establish a revised reference point for Title II entities that choose to make structural changes to existing facilities to meet their program accessibility requirements; and it establishes a similar reference for Title III entities undertaking readily achievable barrier removal.

SAFETY AND RISK MANAGEMENT

Monitoring risk and creating safe areas and facilities for participants to recreate in is an integral part of the community parks and recreation management process. There are a number of steps that administrators and staff members can take to ensure that participants

Table 17.3

Area/Facility Accommodations

Area/Facility	Selected Accommodations
Trails/Walkways	• Make trails wide enough so two people can walk side by side or people can pass without stepping off the trail.
	• Use unitary trail surfaces such as concrete, boardwalk, or asphalt, or more natural surfaces such as very small, crushed aggregate or screenings that have been "stabilized," or natural soils enhanced with soil stabilizers so the trail surface remains firm and stable with little need for maintenance. Concrete and asphalt can be colored so the surface blends into the natural environment, and surfaces can be stamped to look like boardwalk or dirt with animal tracks or fallen leaf prints.
	• Use a contrasting color treatment of the surface and textured surface treatments such as brushed concrete at intersections or interpretive stations to cue people who have vision impairments that there is something to pay attention to at that spot. This type of visual and tactile cue can be helpful for people who have cognitive impairments, because it draws attention to change.
	• Make sure the cross-slopes (side-to-side) are nearly level, particularly where there is a change of direction on the route, and keep very gentle running slopes with no steep slopes. If some sections with steep slopes are unavoidable, provide large (greater than 5 x 5 feet [1.5 x 1.5 meters]), level landing areas at the beginning and end of each steeper trail section and at all turns and intersections.
	• Make sure all trails and routes are thoughtfully laid out to maximize the experience with minimal difficulty for all users. "Pick your way through the woods" in the most accessible route possible by looking for opportunities to achieve universal recreation accessibility that makes the experience more enjoyable by all people of all abilities together. Look for opportunities to lay out a route that has gentle slopes and level resting spots at interesting locations with a nice view of cooling shade. Easy slopes and resting areas are appreciated by families with children and older folks alike.
Picnic Areas/Pavilions **Picnic Tables/** **Grills/Fire Rings**	• Provide accessibility for all tables, grills, fire rings, and water pumps, so all people will be able to picnic at any table, cook on any grill, build a fire in any fire ring, and get water from any spigot. Remember, universally accessible designed elements are also usable by people who don't have a disability.
	• Locate all elements on accessible routes. Place elements so all of us can get to them carrying our picnic basket, pulling our cooler on wheels, pushing a child in a stroller, or using a walker or wheelchair.
	• Create level routes to picnic pavilions with no changes of level from pathway surface onto pavilion surfaces, and thoughtfully locate pavilions within easy access to accessible parking. It can be so frustrating to expend the energy to walk or roll to the pavilion and then not be able to get onto the concrete pad.
	• Design wide routes and clear spaces, with firm surfaces, all the way around all elements so someone with mobility limits can easily move around the element (tables, grills). This is particularly helpful to parents who have a disability and need to cook the food or tend the kids who are seated all around a picnic table.

Table 17.3 (cont.)

	• Provide a variety of table styles: some with clear sitting space on one or both sides, some with extended table tops on one or both ends that allow people to sit side by side or across from others or at the head of the table. The interesting thing is that many people who don't have disabilities also like these tables; they put their hibachi on the extended top and their cooler underneath, or some choose to sit in a comfortable lawn chair in the accessible, clear space instead of on the hard bench that is difficult to climb onto.
	• Include clear space all around each element, with firm level surfaces, and connect elements to a route so people can approach and use the grill or fire ring from the front, back, and either side; this also makes it easier to pull your cooler on wheels near the grill or the wagon with your firewood. A firm, level surface also reduces the chance that someone will trip over uneven surfaces and fall into a fire or onto a cooking surface. The accessible surface all the way around also gives you the opportunity to move out of the path of the smoke from a fire or grill.
	• Design grills so users can lower and raise the cooking surface with only one hand, which is great for those who have paralysis on one side or only have one arm as well as for someone holding a platter of burgers or a beverage in one hand while moving the food closer to the heat or out of the flames.
	• Include raised fire-building surfaces so you can place wood without leaning too far over from a standing or seated position. Not only are these easier to use, but many campground rangers tell us this design reduces injuries from accidentally stepping into the cooling embers of fires built on the ground or in low fire rings, and the higher fire-building surface in accessible fire rings helps keep small children away from the fire surface. A well-designed fire ring with a raised fire surface also gets the flames up high enough to move smoke up and away from those seated around the fire because the flames are about knee height, again enhancing the campfire experience for everyone.
Fishing Docks/Piers/ Observation Decks	• Provide lowered rails all the way around or no rail at all so everyone can fish from anywhere. However, be sure to provide edge protection to prevent users from inadvertently rolling off. Provide multiple fish-landing openings on all sides of the dock. Also provide benches (all of which have backs and arm rests) so anglers can sit or stand to fish. Benches should have clear space at one or both ends to enable an angler in a wheelchair to sit next to another person who is sitting on the bench; this improves the opportunity to exchange "fish tales."
	• Provide tackle box stands near the railing and make sure they are high enough and with clear space around them so an angler using a wheelchair can reach the items she needs. If you place the tackle box stand next to a bench, do so only on one bench end (not both) and only on the end of some benches, leaving one bench end clear space for sitting side by side with someone in a wheelchair. These tackle box stands also make it easier to reach items for the angler who is standing to fish at the rail because he doesn't have to bend all the way to the ground, which is helpful for the angler who may not be as limber as he used to be. Also, providing these tackle box stands encourages anglers to not set their smelly equipment on the bench.
	• Provide fishing opportunities such as overwater fishing from a deck or dock; shore fishing from firm, stable surfaces; and in-water fishing stations that have firm, stable, and accessible surfaces. Some people don't realize that anglers with disabilities, particularly those with mobility impairments, have the same interest as other anglers in a variety of fishing experiences.

Table 17.3 (cont.)

Sports Fields/Courts	These include fields for soccer, football, and baseball and courts for tennis, basketball, bocce, and horseshoes. • Provide accessible routes to both sides of all playing fields and all courts, not just end zones, so that coaches, players, and spectators have access to a variety of seating and viewing locations and areas to interact with the players when they are off the field of play. • Design accessible seating spaces both at ground level and elevated if risers or bleachers are provided so all spectators have the same viewing opportunities and experiences and can sit with family and friends. Scatter these accessible seating spaces throughout all viewing areas and levels with companion seating on both sides of the space. • Lower all service windows at all concession areas at the sports complex and provide menus in alternative formats such as large print or braille so everyone can independently get a snack. • Provide wide gate openings into all court areas (tennis, bocce, basketball) and skate parks to accommodate sports wheelchairs which have a wider wheel chamber. • Design routes to both horseshoe pits and along both sides of the route between pits so players can play from either end, retrieve thrown horseshoes, and change ends during play. • Provide level routes onto bocce courts with sitting benches at both ends where all players can rest.
Canoe, Kayak, Boat Launches	• Provide a wide route to the launch site so people can hand-wheel or carry boats on a wheeled dolly to the launch, pulling the boat next to them if they are in a wheelchair; this extra width provides room for two people to carry a boat with one person on each side. • Design accessible surface to water's edge and into the water at launch. • Provide gentle slopes for easier entry and exit when hand-wheeling a boat. • Include a rack to stabilize the boat at a transferable height and a mechanism or roller system so the participant can move the boat into the water while seated in the boat. • Provide transfer assistance such as overhead bars or slide board so someone can position her body weight over the center of the boat for a balanced entrance and exit. • Provide a winch system so participants can pull the boat out of the water and back into the rack to an exit or transfer that leads to a transfer system on the dock or shore that people can use to transfer back into a mobility-assistive device. • If there is a dock, provide a transfer system on the dock so someone seated on the dock can transfer to a boat in the water that is in a stabilizer rack. • Provide adapted boats such as kayaks or sailboats available for use or rent if others have the opportunity to rent water craft. • Design a shore station that has a platform (instead if a V rack) with a transfer system on the deck of the shore station, located next to a dock, so someone can roll or otherwise move onto the platform and it to the right level to transfer into a boat. • All of these design ideas also make it easier for older people to move into boats safely and allow parents to help young children in and out of boats by sitting and scooting.

Table 17.3 (cont.)

Archery Ranges	• Ensure that all shooting stations can be used from a seated or standing position. • Include accessible routes to the retrieval area for each target. • Provide targets that are usable with crossbows and modified bows so hunters and archers with disabilities can use the targets. • Include a backstop behind the target to limit retrieval distance of arrows that miss the target. • Design large maneuvering spaces at all shooting stations to accommodate archers with shooting assistants or who use individual mobility-assistive devices.
Beaches/Waterfronts	• Design routes over the beach and into the water; these routes can be portable, such as temporary matting, which can be taken in and out for beach cleaning and dragging or in the off-season. • Include beach routes that are wide enough for side-by-side walking and passing; this is good for a parent pushing a stroller while also holding the hand of a walking toddler. • At the end of the beach route have a "hanging-out" area at the water's edge large enough to get off the route end; this allows grandparents and others who find walking in the sand difficult a way to get to the water to watch and interact with people who are in the water. • Provide a transfer system at the water's edge so people can get to the ground level and into the water to play; this also helps families with young children who want an easy way to get to the water, and it gives the kids a surface to play on an lets them put their feet in the water without getting totally wet.
Nature Centers/ Museums/Cultural Sites/Zoos	• Ensure that all interpretive information is in a variety of alternative formats such as auditory, large print, braille, and pictures. • Use technology creatively, such as providing iPods for auditory descriptions (this gives the information directly to the person and won't disturb others), closed-loop assistive listening devices, and closed-circuit captioning of all interpretive presentations. • Place all displays at heights that allow sitting or standing viewing for all people, including children. • Ensure that all mechanisms are operable with one hand and do not require tight pinching, grasping, or twisting to operate.
Skiing/Sledding Hills	• Provide an accessible route to the top (no steps), maybe using a rope tow lift with the "magic carpet"; this is a carpet or mat-type surface that pulls the sled (with the participant in it) up the hill. • Include a level surface for sled mounting at hilltop. • If the location is staffed, provide ATV transport or have policy that allows personal ATV use by people with disabilities who can't get up the hill on their own. • Include a transfer at hill bottom to help people get off the sled and get into a chair or reach a walker.

Table 17.3 (cont.)

Restrooms	• Provide more than a minimum number. • Design multiple unisex and single-user toilet rooms and units so opposite-sex caregivers can assist; these are good for parents of young children of the opposite sex so kids aren't sent alone into a multiuser restroom. If all the toilets are single-user rooms, then several are available for either sex to use at any time so someone with a disability has as many options as anyone else. Another benefit of this design is that only one toilet room is closed at a time for cleaning, unlike the multi-user design where a whole gender's toilet room is closed. • Locate restrooms near areas of activity such as play areas, beaches, and fishing piers. • Ensure that all portable toilets are designed with accessibility in mind, again big enough for individual use or caregiver assist and also food for families with young children who need assistance.
Parking	• Provide more than minimum number of spots. • Connect each accessible parking spot directly to an accessible route at the head end of the parking space that takes users to the park elements and not into the traffic flow behind the vehicle. • Locate accessible parking spots near all the activity entrances (some near the beach, some near the playground, some near the bathhouse).

enjoy their experience. Having a sound safety and risk management plan in place will aid in identification of risk, as well as outlining the efforts needed to address unsafe situations so that participants are protected while recreating.

Waivers

Waivers are an effective tool, when designed properly, in communicating multiple pieces of information to users of community recreation areas and facilities. Waivers justify the activity's purpose, warn users of dangerous or risky behavior, and clear the public parks and recreation agency of fault that may arise from an accident (Edginton, Hudson, & Lankford, 2001; Hronek, Spengler, & Baker III, 2007). There are six main points to remember when community parks and recreation administrators are going to use waivers: (a) clear, concise writing that is easily understood by the participant; (b) obvious location so the participant recognizes the document is a waiver; (c) a signature is required by a participant who is a legal adult, or a parent/guardian of a minor; (d) specificity regarding what the waiver is covering; (e) the signature that is required must be done voluntarily; and (f) the waiver must support public policy. When waivers meet certain legal and written requirements, they are usually upheld by the court system if questioned in a lawsuit. An example of a waiver is included in Figure 17.4.

Participation Agreements

The most effective tool that community parks and recreation staff members can use to reduce risk and enhance safe practices of minors is the participation agreement (Hronek et al., 2007). On a whole, it is more risky to develop and implement community parks and recreation programs for youth than adults. This is because youth are still developing emotionally, socially, physically, and psychologically; motor skills are still forming, abstract reasoning is still being contrived, and at times, decision-making is more individual-centered (Witt & Caldwell, 2010). These ongoing developmental changes in youth often lead to participation behaviors that can put them and others at risk, and the youth may not even realize it. For these reasons, participation agreements are explicitly directed toward the parents and place the burden of responsibility on the parents to explain to the child the rules and policies for participation in a community parks and recreation program or activity. Public parks and recreation organizations have an obligation to protect youth, while designing programs and activities that attract youth.

Invitees, Licensees, and Trespassers

For many community parks and recreation agencies, the scope of services that are provided may include multiple recreational areas and facilities. Within the scope of services that are provided, there are traditionally three categories of users: invitees, licensees, and trespassers (Hronek et al., 2007). The standard of care associated with risk management and safe practices is related to the status of the user. An *invitee* is a participant who pays a fee for programs or services that occur in or on a community parks and recreation's property. The organization's responsibilities related to maintaining a standard of care for invitees include making sure proper repairs are done to facilities and equipment, identifying and alleviating hidden hazards, addressing known hazards, and conducting programs or activities with reasonable care.

RELEASE AND WAIVER OF LIABILITY FOR VOLUNTEERS

I want to volunteer my services to the City and County of Denver, Department of Parks and Recreation. I certify that I am in good mental and physical condition and I understand the inherent risks associated with acting as a volunteer including the risk of physical injury or death. I further understand that I risk aggravating any preexisting physical condition I may have and that I am hereby advised to consult with a physician prior to engaging in any major physical exertion as may occur in providing these volunteer services.

I understand that while my volunteer services will be at the direction of the Department of Parks and Recreation, its officers and employees, I am nevertheless not an employee of the City and County of Denver within the meaning of the Colorado Workers' Compensation Act or for any other purpose at the time of my performance of these volunteer services. I further understand that no employee/employer or master/servant relationship is created between myself and the City and County of Denver or the Department of Parks and Recreation and that I will receive no compensation of any kind for my participation as a volunteer.

In consideration of the City and County of Denver allowing me to participate as a volunteer, I agree not to sue and forever release, waive and discharge the City and County of Denver and its officers, employees, agents, representatives, and the various sponsoring agencies and entities (hereinafter referred collectively as "Releasees") from any and all liability to me or my personal representatives, assigns, heirs, children, dependents, spouse and relatives for any and all claims, causes of action, losses, judgments, costs, demands or damages that are caused by or arise from any injury to me (including death) or loss or damage to my property regardless of the cause(s) of such injury, loss or damage. I assume all risks associated with my participation as a volunteer. I understand to defend, indemnify, and hold harmless the Releasees from and against any and all liabilities, claims, liens, actions, causes of action, costs or expenses of any nature whatsoever arising from any damage, loss, or injury (including death) causes by me, in whole or part, or directly associated with my actions or inactions as a volunteer.

I understand that the City and County of Denver shall not be responsible for loss or theft of personal property, or damage to personal property caused by City employees and officers, other volunteers, or the public. I understand photos will be taken at this event and you have my permission of "free use of any photo's"

I hereby acknowledge that I have carefully read this entire document, that I fully understand its contents, that I am over the age of 18, that I am signing this document of my own free will and without coercion, and that I intend for this document to be legally binding. To the extent permitted by law, this document shall include my child or children and my capacity as guardian for my child or children if I am signing on behalf of my minor child or children who will participate as a volunteer(s).

PLEASE PRINT:

Name of Volunteer(s)_____ # of Adults or Youth Adults_____ Youth_____

Email:_____ Phone:_____

Company/Group: _____

Emergency Contact _____ Phone:_____

Signature_____ Date_____
(Signature of Adult Volunteer or Adult parent or Guardian of youth under 18)

The Denver Department of Parks and Recreation receives requests from other departments, agencies, associations, and groups requesting the names and mailing addresses of Parks and Recreation volunteers who may be interested in similar volunteer opportunities. Please indicate if you authorize the Parks and Recreation Department to share your name and mailing address with other departments, agencies, associations, and groups for other volunteer opportunities   YES   NO

Figure 17.4. Waiver for Voluntary Participation–Denver Department of Parks and Recreation

A *licensee* is a participant who has permission, either expressed or implied, to be on community parks and recreation property. The level of care that should be applied by the agency is reasonable in nature; in many instances, a licensee does not pay a fee as an invitee does for usage or program participation. The permission given to a licensee is not specific; it is usually general in nature and does not come with the preferred status of an invitee.

A *trespasser* is a nonpaying user who intentionally enters or uses a community parks and recreation organization's property, areas, or facilities. A trespasser is not given consent to be on the property. The obligation for standard of care by a community parks and recreation agency in relationship to a trespasser is that the agency needs to avoid gross misconduct, inclusive of intentional recklessness. Public parks and recreation administrators can take the steps to reduce trespassing; some examples include signage indicating areas or facilities that are closed or off-limits during certain hours; fencing to enclose the property; cameras, alarms, and other technological security devices; and staff security.

There are some community parks and recreation areas and facilities that can attract trespassers due to the special features or design. Waterparks, sports complexes, and golf courses are good examples of areas and facilities that may be considered attractive nuisances. These types of areas and facilities could pose foreseeable risk to adults and children, and it is in the public parks and recreation organization's best interest to take the necessary steps to exercise reasonable care and potentially eliminate the possibility of trespassing.

Addressing Risk within Community Parks and Recreation Services, Areas, and Facilities

The process of addressing risk should be looked at in a positive manner and not as a burden to community parks and recreation administrators and staff members. Hronek et al. (2007) have outlined a four-step risk management process that aids in developing safe programs and activities, as well as monitoring public parks and recreation areas and facilities. The four steps associated with the process are (1) risk identification, (2) risk evaluation, (3) risk treatment, and (4) risk implementation.

Risk identification. Risk identification can occur in relationship to participant safety, property loss, contracts, and personnel issues. Conducting area and facility audits are excellent measures to help target possible hazards associated with the public parks and recreation environment. It is important for community parks and recreation professionals on all levels of administration to continually educate themselves on what could be considered risky within area and facility design. These educational opportunities exist via networking with other professionals in the field, attending conferences, site visits to other public parks and recreation areas and facilities, and keeping abreast of the body of knowledge and research associated with risk, safety and liability in the parks and recreation profession.

Risk evaluation. Risk evaluation includes assessing the frequency and severity of incidents or accidents related to community parks and recreation services. Frequency deals with the potential or likelihood for an injury or accident to take place. Severity addresses the type of injury or accident that may occur via participation in a program or activity, or usage of an area or facility. Evaluating risk in a proactive, rather than reactive manner, allows administrators and staff members to take action before something unfortunate occurs.

Risk treatment. Risk treatment includes addressing the risky behavior or situation in one of four ways: (a) retention, (b) reduction, (c) transfer, or (d) avoidance. Risk retention can be done actively or passively (Edginton et al., 2001). Actively retaining risk involves a community parks and recreation agency recognizing that a service being provided may include elements that could lead to an incident or accident, and taking the proactive steps necessary to protect participants before engagement in the service. Passively retaining risk is a reactionary measure and usually happens after an incident or accident has occurred; the risk is retained due to oversight or error. Unfortunately, passive retention of risk is due to a lack of assessment regarding the level of risk associated with a service, and a hope that nothing will happen to individuals involved in the program or activity. Risk reduction involves eliminating elements of a service that could lead to risky endeavors by participants. Transfer of risk shifts the risk associated with a public parks and recreation service to another individual or organization. This can occur through insurance policies, contracts, or lease agreements. Finally, avoiding risk includes a cancellation or prohibition of services under the guise of the community parks and recreation organization's supervision.

Risk implementation. Risk implementation involves action taken as a direct result of the choice made when treating risk. For example, actions that reduce risk include repairing equipment, closing down a part or all of a public parks and recreation area or facility due to hazards, and proper signage warning of the risk associated with a service. Risk implementation can also include modifying or changing community parks and recreation policies and procedures associated with participant involvement or usage of areas and facilities. Community parks and recreation administrators, as well as staff members, who know about risk associated with their areas and facilities and take the steps necessary to address them and creating positive environments for all participants.

The Hazards Associated with Natural Areas and Facilities

Many community parks and recreation agencies have natural components under the umbrella of supervision (Hronek et al., 2007; Kaiser, 1999). Effectively managing these outdoor areas and facilities is two-fold; first, the public should be protected from natural hazards. Second, the public should also be protected from any manmade features that are associated with the natural areas. Addressing weather hazards and nature feature hazards are essential steps if these locales are going to be a part of the public parks and recreation agency (League of Minnesota Cities, 2014).

A body of water can be an enjoyable place for the public to recreate, but it also can be an attractive nuisance as well as a risky location for public parks and recreation services. Drowning and diving accidents can occur, the water temperature can fluctuate dramatically, and natural objects can prohibit safe recreational practices. It is the responsibility of the community parks and recreation administration to empower the staff members through the risk management process discussed earlier so that proper steps can be taken to develop positive recreational experiences.

The topography of a natural area can provide participants with breathtaking scenic views and unique programmatic recreational opportunities. Examples of appealing topographical areas include cliffs or overlooks, caves, mountains, and sand dunes. It is imperative that proper signage is in place regarding participant usage, and if needed physical barriers are constructed. While the assumption of risk associated with participation may be understood by participants, it is still important for a public parks and recreation agency to take steps to inform the public.

The flora, or vegetation, that is found in many community parks and recreation natural areas may be appealing to the eye but also hold hidden dangers. Toxic vegetation (i.e., poison ivy), barrier vegetation (i.e., cactus and bramble shrubs), and tree failure (i.e., falling trees, shallow rooting) are just a few examples of the dangers associated with flora that can be found in public parks and recreation natural areas. Inspecting and if needed, removing flora that can be hazardous to the public are proactive steps to enhancing healthy participation by users.

Finally, fauna are the animals that may inhabit community parks and recreation natural areas. There are many animals that are native to areas; the public should remember they are recreating in a delicate natural ecosystem and that some fauna may adversely react to humans. Stinging or poisonous insects or animals, animals that bite, and large carnivore and omnivores may occasionally come into contact with participants. In many instances, this interaction and the subsequent harm that may occur to a person are due to the animal being fearful or surprised while in the wild. Informing the public of animal locations in the public parks and recreation area, reiterating the dangers of purposely seeking out animals for amusement, and generally speaking of the importance of "leaving no trace" are steps that community parks and recreation administrators and staff members can take to encourage a healthy dichotomy between animals and humans in natural areas.

Security and Protection Issues

As Hronek et al. (2007) point out, law enforcement within the public parks and recreation setting has three basic purposes related to enforcement: (a) to protect people from other people, (b) to protect people from the environment, and (c) to protect the environment from the people. Within this discussion, the environment is considered the public parks and recreation areas and facilities under the supervision of the agency. While contemplating this topic within the recreation field, there is one characteristic of recreational experiences that can make law enforcement challenging within public parks and recreation areas and facilities—freedom (Nelson, 1999). Freedom can be a positive component to a participant's recreation experience—but it can also lead to dangerous and destructive behaviors. This is why it is important to have legal policies and procedures in place that regulate freedom associated with participation. Examples of policies regulating behavior between participants who use community parks and recreation areas and facilities are illustrated in Figure 17.5.

In the first purpose of enforcement, it is a community parks and recreation department's responsibility to protect people using their areas or facilities from the offensive behavior of others within the same area or facility. If a community parks and recreation agency chooses to not take steps to protect people from other individuals, then the organization can be targeted as liable for injury or damages. Regulations, ordinances, and statutes that govern behavior are used to protect participants' freedom at public parks and recreation areas and facilities.

As discussed earlier, examples of protecting people from the environment included proper signage outlining appropriate activities, closing certain public parks and recreation areas or facilities, and informational brochures or paraphernalia detailing what is proper behavior. While appropriate steps may be taken to protect people from the environment, those steps may not always work. There will always be individuals who ignore the warnings and act in a manner that leads to injury, damages, or death, and then try to sue the community parks and recreation agency for compensation. Being as proactive as possible when identifying risk and taking the proper steps to either reduce, transfer, or avoid risk are efforts that may help if litigation occurs.

Misusage of community parks and recreation areas and facilities by participants does occur; it is the organization's responsibility to attempt to curtail this type of behavior. Common societal problems, such as vandalism and overcrowding, have become regular occurrences in public parks and recreation areas and facilities. Protecting the environment from people can be done through visitor information programs or activities, limiting or restricting access to areas and facilities, managing the carrying capacity, requiring permits or licenses for usage, and regular treatment of natural flora areas.

4.16.030   Policy

The following are prohibited in any Park or Park Facility:

1. Violation of any City Park Regulation set out in Corvallis Municipal Code Chapter 5.01.

2. Intentionally causing public inconvenience, annoyance, or alarm or recklessly creating a risk of public inconvenience, annoyance, or alarm, by engaging in fighting or behaving in a violent, tumultuous, or threatening manner.

3. Possessing a weapon, except as permitted by Oregon Revised Statutes (ORS) 166.370.

4. Smoking as defined by Corvallis Municipal Code Section 5.03.080.160 or the use of chew, snuff, snus, and any other smokeless tobacco product, excluding Federal Drug Administration (FDA) approved nicotine-replacement therapy products for the purpose of tobacco cessation. Smoking also includes the use of an electronic smoking device which creates a vapor, in any manner or in any form. Electronic smoking device is defined as any electronic oral device, such as one composed of a heating element, battery, and/or electronic circuit, which provides a vapor of nicotine or any other substances and the use of inhalation which simulates smoking. The term shall include any such device, whether manufactured, distributed, marketed, or sold as an e-cigarette, ecigar, e-pipe, e-hookah, or under any other product name or descriptor and any cartridge or other component of the device or related product.

5. Consumption of alcohol, except as allowed by a permit issued as part of a facility or park rental (Corvallis Municipal Code Section 5.03.040.010.06).

Figure 17.5. Policies Regulating Behavior on Community Parks and Recreation Property, Corvallis (OR) City Council Policy Manual

SUMMARY

This chapter has provided information regarding various aspects of managing parks and recreation areas and facilities. A parks and recreation area can be thought of as a space or surface that is utilized for recreation purposes. In this chapter we identified, described, and provided examples of numerous areas, including adventure courses; arboretums; basketball courts; beaches, lakes, and ponds; bike paths; boat ramps; campgrounds; disc golf courses; fishing docks/piers; golf courses; greenbelts; horticultural gardens; multi-use synthetic turf fields; nature preserves; parks; parkways; softball/baseball diamonds; tennis courts; trails; wetlands; and wildlife preserves. Facilities are structures that enable some type of service to be provided. Featured in this chapter were the following parks and recreation facilities:

aquatic complexes, art and cultural centers, fitness centers, ice rinks, museums, picnic shelters, playgrounds, recreation centers, senior centers, skate parks, stadiums, and zoos.

This chapter discussed policies; funding and budgetary considerations; parks and facility planning considerations; visitor services; and safety, first aid, and emergencies. Policies can be thought of as guidelines an agency uses to conduct its operations. Policies emerge from legislative actions, court rulings, and agency self-determination. Funding for parks and recreation areas and facilities and their operations is often a challenge. There are many different types of funding categories, including general funds, dedicated funds, and revolving funds. Revenues can be derived from many different sources such as tax revenues, commercial partnerships, grants, bonds and fees, and charges.

When planning facilities, the following considerations must be addressed: (1) how the site is to be used; (2) what amount and kind of land and water are available; (3) will the land support the expected visitor load; (4) activities without excessive deterioration; and (5) can the proposed facilities be maintained with a modest increase in the personnel and materials budget, or will substantial increases in one or both be needed? Further, planning consideration must be given to the suitability of the site, adaptability, suitability for maintenance, safety, vandalism potential, access, energy efficiency, cost effectiveness, construction costs, and architectural character.

Another important element in planning areas and facilities is the need to consider the provision of visitor services. A host of amenities is often provided in various areas and facilities. This can range from concessions operations to providing maps and other types of information. Concerns for the safety of participants often requires knowledge of ways to reduce or eliminate hazards or effective conditions that may injure participants. Rescue and treatment procedures should be preplanned to enable responders to address various situations where a participant might become injured.

There are many models of staffing, supervising, and organizing for parks and recreation facility management. One model shows the recreation service division is central to the management of facilities. Sometimes the facilities are viewed as "revenue" producing, and therefore a manager or supervisor is responsible for these entrepreneurial activities. Facility management, supervision, and staffing may be shared across various divisions or units within the department. Importantly, the staffing is full-time, part-time, seasonal staff, and volunteers employed within all of the units of the parks and recreation system. Specialists exist for parks such as horticulturists or pool managers for aquatics, etc. All of these positions require specialized training and certifications.

Universal design offers a framework for developing areas and facilities without special or separate accommodations. Several legislative acts govern issues related to planning parks and recreation facilities that have been supported by the use of federal funds. To wit, the Architectural Barriers Act of 1968 states that, "Any building or facility, constructed in whole or part by federal funds must be made accessible to and usable by the physically handicapped." This Act was followed by Section 504 of the Rehabilitation Act of 1973 and the Americans with Disabilities Act (ADA) of 1990. In March 2010, the U.S. Department of Justice issued the 2010 ADA Standards for Accessible Design, Title II and Title III.

The monitoring and management of risk is an important part of the work of parks and recreation managers. First, and perhaps the most important issue is the need for a risk management plan and ways to mitigate these risks to address unsafe situations. This process usually involves the utilization of waivers, establishment of participation agreements, and the identification of scope of services that may include three types of users: invitees, licensees, and trespassers. There are four steps in addressing risk including; (1) risk identification, (2) risk evaluation, (3) risk treatment, and (4) risk implementation.

DISCUSSION QUESTIONS

1. Define parks and recreation areas. Provide examples and describe parks and recreation areas in your home community.
2. Define parks and recreation facilities. Provide examples and describe parks and recreation facilities in your home community.
3. Identify common parks and recreation areas and facilities. Locate additional examples online.
4. Identify a source of funding beyond taxes and fees and charges that your local parks and recreation department utilizes for building of facilities.
5. Discuss three "site suitability" factors and contrast them to a local example. What works well and what is problematic?
6. Describe how your local parks and recreation department has organized the staffing and supervision of facilities. Find an organizational chart and discuss the pros and cons of the current situation.
7. Discuss the pros and cons of having facility oversight as part of the recreation program unit of a parks and recreation department.
8. Identify and briefly describe the three categories of users associated with community parks and recreation areas and facilities.
9. What are the four ways that risk is treated in the public parks and recreation setting?
10. What are the three purposes of law enforcement in conjunction with community parks and recreation areas and facilities?

REFERENCES

Arlington (Virginia) Parks & Recreation Department. (2017). Picnic shelters. Retrieved on from http://parks.arlingtonva.us/picnic-shelters/

Austin (Texas) Parks & Recreation Department. (n.d.). Nature preserves and nature-based programs. Retrieved from http://www.austintexas.gov/naturepreserves

Bainbridge Island (Washington) Metro Park & Recreation District. (n.d.). Parks and trails finder. from http://www.biparks.org/biparks_site/parks/gazzam-lake.htm

Bensenville (Illinois) Park District White Pines Golf Club. (2017). Welcome. Retrieved from http://www.whitepinesgolf.com/

Black Hawk County (Iowa) Conservation Commission. (2017). About. Retrieved from http://www.mycountyparks.com/County/Black-Hawk.aspx

Bowling Green (Kentucky) Park & Recreation Department. Fitness facility. (2017). Retrieved from http://www2.bgky.org/bgpr/fitness/

Boulder (Colorado) Parks and Recreation Department. (2017). Skate parks. Retrieved from https://bouldercolorado.gov/parks-rec/skate-park-at-scott-carpenter-park

Brault, M. W. (2012). Americans with disabilities 2010: Household economic studies (Report No. P7131). Retrieved from U.S. Department of Commerce website http://www.census.gov/prod/2012pubs/p70-131.pdf

Cedar Falls Iowa. (n.d.). Trail maps. Retrieved from http://www.cedarfalls.com/index.aspx?NID=730

City of Clayton. (2016) Park and Recreation Organizational Chart. Retrieved from http://www.claytonmo.gov/home/showdocument?id=1882

City of Corvallis. (2014). Council policy manual. Policy Area 4 – Leisure and Cultural Activities. Code of Conduct for Patrons at Parks and Recreation Facilities, Events, and Programs. Retrieved from https://www.corvallisoregon.gov/modules/showdocument.aspx?documentid=339.

City of Davenport. (2012). Park and recreation organizational chart. Retrieved from http://www.cityofdavenportiowa.com/department/index.php?structureid=21

City of Minneapolis. (2016). Park and recreation organizational chart. Retrieved from https://www.minneapolisparks.org/about_us/leadership_and_structure/organizational_chart/

Clark County (Nevada) Parks & Recreation Department. (2017). Wetlands. Retrieved from http://www.clarkcountynv.gov/parks/Pages/cc-wetlands-park-homepage.aspx

Columbia (Missouri) Parks and Recreation Department. (2017). Baseball diamonds. Retrieved from https://www.gocolumbiamo.com/ParksandRec/Parks_and_Facilities/Facility_Reservations/baseball-softball.php

Denver (CO) Department of Parks and Recreation. (2012). Release and waiver of liability for volunteers – Department of Parks and Recreation. Retrieved from http://finconexpo.com/wp-content/uploads/2012/08/Volunteer-Parks-and-Rec-Waiver.pdf

Denver (Colorado) Department of Parks and Recreation. (2017). Parkways. Retrieved from https://www.denvergov.org/content/denvergov/en/denver-parks-and-recreation/parks/parkways.html

Dillenschneider, C., & Burkhour, C. (2010). Universal design in recreation. In Human Kinetics (Ed.), *Inclusive recreation: Programs and services for diverse populations* (pp. 137–158). Champaign, IL: Human Kinetics

East Ridge (Tennessee) Parks and Recreation Department Disc Golf Course. Retrieved from http://www.eastridgeparksandrec.com/page/show/2363308-disc-golf-course

Edginton, C. R., Hudson, S. D., & Lankford, S. V. (2001). *Managing recreation, parks, and leisure services: An introduction.* Urbana, IL: Sagamore.

Fayetteville-Cumberland (North Carolina) Parks & Recreation Department Museums. Retrieved from cpr.us/facilities/museums/transportation-museum

Gwinnett County (Georgia) Parks and Recreation Department. (2017). Senior centers. Retrieved from https://www.gwinnettcounty.com/portal/gwinnett/Departments/CommunityServices/ParksandRecreation/SeniorRecreationOfferings

Howard County (Maryland) Recreation and Parks Department Playgrounds. Retrieved https://www.howardcountymd.gov/Departments/Recreation-and-Parks/Parks-and-Planning/Playgrounds

Hronek, B. B., Spengler, J. O., & Baker III, T. (2007). *Legal liability in recreation, sports, and tourism.* Urbana, IL: Sagamore.

Kaiser, R. (1999). Risk management. In B. Van der Smissen, M. Moiseichik, V. J. Hartenburg, & L. F. Twardzik (Eds.)., *Management of parks and recreation agencies* (pp. 715–741). Ashburn, VA: National Recreation and Park Association.

Keller, M. J., & Sprinkmeyer, F. (2016, January). Reinventing senior centers: Virtually. *Parks & Recreation*, 50–53.

Lake Forest (Illinois) Department of Parks & Recreation. (n.d.). Lakefront and beach activities. Retrieved from http://www.cityoflakeforest.com/parks-and-recreation/lake-front-and-beach-activities/

Lankford, S., Lankford, J., & Wheeler, D. (2011). *An introduction to park management* (3rd ed.). Urbana, IL: Sagamore.

Lee County (Florida) Parks & Recreation. (2017). Boat ramps. Retrieved from http://www.leegov.com/parks/boat%20Ramps

Lynchburg (Virginia) Parks & Recreation Department. (n.d.). Stadiums. Retrieved from http://www.lynchburgparksandrec.com/city-stadium-complex/

Los Angeles (California) Department of Recreation and Parks Synthetic Fields. Retrieved from http://www.laparks.org/synthetic-turf-fields

Maple Grove (Minnesota) Parks and Recreation Department. (2017). Outdoor skating rinks. Retrieved from http://www.maplegrovemn.gov/parks-and-recreation/parks-and-trails/outdoor-skating-rinks/

Miami Beach (Florida) Parks & Recreation Department. (2017). Basketball courts. Retrieved from http://miamibeachfl.gov/parksandrecreation/scroll.aspx?id=15742#basketball

Minneapolis (Minnesota) Park & Recreation Board. (2017). Parks and lakes. Retrieved from https://www.minneapolisparks.org/parks__destinations/parks__lakes/

Missouri Botanical Garden. (n.d.). Visit. Retrieved from http://www.missouribotanicalgarden.org/

Nashville (Tennessee) Parks and Recreation Department. (2017). Cultural arts. Retrieved from http://www.nashville.gov/Parks-and-Recreation/Cultural-Arts.aspx

Nelson, C. M. (1999). Law enforcement. In B. Van der Smissen, M. Moiseichik, V. J. Hartenburg, & L. F. Twardzik (Eds.), *Management of parks and recreation agencies* (pp. 743–783). Ashburn, VA: National Recreation and Park Association.

New York City (New York) Department of Parks & Recreation. (n.d). Youth adventure course. Retrieved from http://www.nycgovparks.org/programs/rangers/adventure-course/youth-adventure

Queen Anne County (Maryland) Parks & Recreation Department. (n.d.). Piers and docks. Retrieved from http://www.parksnrec.org/hiker-biker-trails/landings-piers/

Rails-to-Trails Conservancy. (2016). About. Retrieved from http://www.railstotrails.org/

Salt Lake County (Utah) Parks and Recreation Department. (n.d.). Recreation centers. Retrieved from http://slco.org/recreation/admin/facilityLocations/recreationCenters.html

San Francisco (California) Recreation and Parks Department. (2017). Tennis courts. Retrieved from http://sfrecpark.org/recprogram/tennis-program/

Seattle Parks and Recreation and The Seattle School District No. 1 (2010). An agreement for the joint use of facilities between The Seattle School District No. 1 and Seattle Parks and Recreation, 2010-2015. Retrievedf from https://www.seattle.gov/Documents/Departments/ParksAndRecreation/PoliciesPlanning/JUA.pdf

St. Petersburg (Florida) Park & Recreation Department. (2014). Aquatic complex. Retrieved from http://www.stpeteparksrec.org/north-shore-aquatic-complex.html

The Falls Aquatic Center, Cedar Falls (Iowa). (n.d.). Retrieved from http://www.cedarfalls.com/index.aspx?NID=652

Witt, P., & Caldwell, L. (2010). *The rationale for recreation services for youth: An evidence-based approach.* Ashburn, VA: National Recreation and Park Association.

Chapter Eighteen

Trends, Issues, and Opportunities

CHAPTER OBJECTIVES

- To gain an awareness of community parks and recreation trends, issues, and opportunities
- To comprehend issues impacting on the provision of community parks and recreation services
- To gain an appreciation of the way in which issues impacting on community parks and recreations can become opportunities
- To gain knowledge of various examples of trends, issues, and opportunities in community parks and recreation
- To apply lessons learned in the chapter to one's local community

INTRODUCTION

The understanding of trends, issues, and opportunities can serve to provide important insights to assist in the provision and management of parks and recreation services. Such insights can provide a clearer understanding of the complexity of today's society and the ways in which parks and recreation agencies may contribute to the transformation of community life. Gaining an awareness of trends, issues, and opportunities can provide solutions and strategies to guide the provision of programs, services, as well the development of parks and recreation areas and facilities. When linked to a parks and recreation agency's vision, mission, goals, and objectives and analysis of trends, issues, and opportunities can provide a foundation for future planning.

One can think of a *trend* as a movement, tendency, or shift in which a parks and recreation program, service, area, or facility is shifting or moving. A trend is a general tendency that a course of events takes. Trends, unlike fads, are patterns that reflect gradual change over time. *Fads* are short-lived; actually many leisure pursuits are in vogue one moment and out in the next. An *issue* can be thought of as a problem or topic that requires some action; for example, the reduction of tax resources from the state or federal government is providing a challenge to parks and recreation agencies. The aging nature of our population creates a demand and the expansion for new services for senior citizens. Of course, trends and issues also create opportunities for parks and recreation agencies. Many parks and recreation managers often look at trends and issues not as problems but rather as opportunities for new development and resolution to challenges that may be occurring.

In this chapter, a number of trends, issues, and opportunities with implications for community parks and recreations are presented and discussed. An attempt has been made to tie various trends, issues, and opportunities to topics covered in each of the chapters. For example, discussion of promoting community livability and quality of life reflects the earlier conversation presented in Chapter 1. Still further, trends related to areas and facilities are tied to Chapter 17, which focused on areas and facilities management. The information presented is not intended to be a complete or comprehensive analysis of the trends, issues, and opportunities associated with community parks and recreation but rather highlight topics that may be of interest to the reader. These topics may warrant future investigation and analysis, especially when taken community by community.

DIGITAL INFLUENCE IN PUBLIC PARKS AND RECREATION

The digital age of the late 20th century has transformed each moment of a person's day. iPads, iPhones, Fitbits, and other digital innovations have streamlined the way the public works, socializes, and recreates. Public parks and recreation agencies are continuing to look forward in the planning, implementation, and evaluation of programs and services. Various components associated with a community parks and recreation agency's offerings are now digitally managed, and "hybrid" programs are being offered that include a digital component. Holding onto traditionally designed programs and services is important, but also recognizing the influx of the digital age and designing opportunities for users is paramount.

Several community parks and recreation agencies have taken steps to incorporate the digital influence into programs and services. For example, the San Francisco, California Recreation and Parks Department offers digital arts programs for participants of all ages (http://sfrecpark.org/recprogram/digital-visual-arts/). The programs involve the traditional components of creative expression, problem-solving, and imaginative design, but have merged with the digital art field. Professional instructors lead these programs and demonstrate how to digitally edit and design work.

The larger scope of operations for a community parks and recreation agency is also being impacted digitally. Many organizations have taken creative steps regarding the marketing and promotional design of materials and services. Countless community parks and recreation agencies have moved toward posting videos of events on their webpage. Many of these videos or other digital promotional tools (i.e., photos, testimonial interviews) highlight the benefits of participation in public parks and recreation agencies' programs and activities. It is still important to market and promote using the traditional outlets, such as television and print media, but the general public is "wired in" and these digital tools provide instantaneous coverage.

General usage of public parks and recreation agencies has been positively impacted by digital age (Anderson, 2016; National Recreation and Park Association, n.d.). For example, Foursquare is a popular location-based social network that allows users to "check-in" through a mobile application on their iPhone. Agencies that have locations such as gyms and multi-use centers benefit from using Foursquare. Users are privy to specials and deals via the community parks and recreation agency, check-in usage patterns can be tracked, and new customers can be established.

There is a prevailing sense that the digital influence and usage capabilities of the public are more inclined toward younger generations. While it is true that younger people may be more digitally savvy, it is also true that all generations have the ability to be involved in digitally based programs and activities. Numerous public parks and recreation agencies offer programs that educate users on the concept of social media and the merits of using social media platforms. These programmatic opportunities show the public that a community parks and recreation agency embraces the digital influence in society, and is willing to help others do so in hopes that all will benefit from it.

TRENDS IN LEISURE PROGRAMMING

Trends within leisure programming continue to include services that center around healthy, active lifestyles for all generations, at various stages in one's life. Sport training, prenatal fitness, life sports, and cross-training are just a few of the popular options that public parks and recreation agencies are developing. These programs can be seasonal or year-round, and help participants develop positive habits that lead to a holistically healthy lifestyle. For example, the Bend, Oregon Parks and Recreation District offers two types of classes—prenatal exercise classes and "Baby and Me" exercise classes. Both classes are strategically designed to provide the best options (i.e., pace, exercise, rigor) for participants (See Figure 18.1).

Prenatal and Baby & Me Classes

At Juniper we realize the importance of healthy moms (& dads, too!) and babies. You will find these fitness classes a great way to get exercise and meet other expectant and new parents.

Prenatal exercise classes consist of gentle paced cardio activity with strength and stretching exercises, to help keep you fit. Please come to your first fitness class 15 minutes early for an orientation. **Prenatal participants are welcome at any of our group exercise classes.** A doctor's approval is required before beginning any group fitness class. For more information or a personal consultation, call Carolyn or Monica at (541) 706-6188.

On-going, weekly drop-in classes offered for your convenience. Use your Fitness Pass. No registration required.

Prenatal Classes
Journey through this magical time together as you draw on the experiences, support and long lasting friendships of the group. The classes follow ACOG (American Council Obstetrics Gynecology) guidelines helping you maintain your fitness level. All of our classes are on-going. You can start at anytime! **Prenatal participants are welcome in the any of 40 water fitness classes a week. Find one that meets your schedule.**

Water Exercise   Classes offered 7 days a week throughout the day Water Exercise schedule
Prenatal Yoga   Tuesdays 5:30-6:30 pm

Baby & Me Classes
After your six week check-up, come exercise with your baby at your side in a supportive environment. We'll help you lose the baby weight, regain strength and tone your body. Exercising is fun with friends. Come meet other new moms! Dads are welcome too!

Baby & Me Cycle
Ages: 6 weeks to crawling
After your six week check-up, come cycle with your baby at your side in a supportive environment. We'll help you lose the baby weight, regain strength and tone your body. Exercising is fun with friends. Come meet other new moms! Dads are welcome too!
Thursday 10:30 – 11:15 am

Figure 18.1. Bend (OR) Parks and Recreation District Exercise Classes

Public parks and recreation programs and services that emphasize the importance of environmental awareness and education are also trending (Tipping, 2015). The focus of these opportunities is how participants can impact the environment; reducing permanent impact on ecosystems and how to "do one's part" regarding perpetuation of outdoor and nature areas are central programmatic components. Portland (OR) Parks and Recreation has developed Hands-on classes, guided walks, camps, volunteer opportunities, and special events to emphasize these points regarding environmental awareness and education (https://www.portlandoregon.gov/parks/38295).

TRENDS IN FINANCING PARKS AND RECREATION

The National Parks and Recreation 2015 Field Report has highlighted positive trends regarding public parks and recreation revenue. Revenue intake by public parks and recreation agencies has shown an increase in dollars, and there has also been a decrease in agencies that are reporting decreasing revenues (Tipping, 2015). Over the next few years, it is projected that these statistics will continue on their current paths. More agencies are taking steps to simultaneously increase revenue and reduce expenditures on operational and programmatic levels. Common steps that community parks and recreation agencies are taking include (a) improving energy efficiency within the organization, (b) increasing user fees for services, (c) reducing staff members, (d) tabling construction or renovation plans, and (e) adjusting operational hours.

Although Tipping (2015) showed that general revenue is gradually increasing with public parks and recreation agencies, the revenue needed for larger capital operations and developments is proving to be a challenge. Walls et al. (2009) surveyed parks and recreation directors and found that insufficient funds for land acquisition, capital expenditures, and construction of new facilities ranked as "significant," "major," or "huge" challenges to nearly 75% of the respondents. Funding for operations and maintenance of public parks and recreation areas and facilities was a serious concern as well. These statements shed light on the potential hurdles that community parks and recreation administrators face when trying to develop long-range strategic plans for positively impacting the communities they serve.

These statistics also indicate that in order to increase revenue, manage expenditures, and raise the funds needed for the capital acquisitions and developments, administrators should be able to take on various roles as the public representative for the organization. It is increasingly common that public parks and recreation administrators are becoming more proficient in fund-raising, working with donors, and creative partnerships (i.e., sponsorships) that lead to revenue generation. Building inroads with other agencies and organizations in a community, whether public, private, or nonprofit, lends to a collaboration that builds a dynamic community and helps share the burden of fiscal responsibility.

GENERATIONAL MARKETING

Public parks and recreation agencies are taking steps within their marketing and promotion campaigns to attract all generations of users. Traditional target markets (i.e., youth, active young adults) are now just as important as other generations of individuals, such as seniors. Community parks and recreation agencies also recognize the importance of highlighting family-based programs and services, since a strong emphasis is continually placed on a healthy family dynamic within the home. Lastly, intergenerational programs are popping up as part of a community parks and recreation organization's programmatic calendar.

As mentioned in Chapter 14, programs for seniors are becoming more commonplace in the public parks and recreation sector. As part of this trend, marketing that targets seniors is becoming a staple of community parks and recreation operations. Age is not a barrier for seniors; programs and services that provide healthy, active options for seniors attract new users. For example, Seattle, Washington Parks and Recreation has developed "Lifelong Recreation." This is a program that involves seniors and provides programmatic options to continue recreating as one ages (http://www.seattle.gov/Parks/Seniors/index.htm).

Marketing and promotional materials have usually been designed by administrators or staff members who are employed by the agency, but these tactics are changing. Users of public parks and recreation facilities, programs, and services are vital members of the marketing and promotion process, and in some cases, actively aid in the design of materials. Two examples help illustrate this trend. First, the Youth Advisory Committee of Montgomery County, Maryland Recreation plans, promotes, and implements activities specifically targeting teenagers (http://www.montgomerycountymd.gov/rec/thingstodo/youthdevelopment/yac.html).

Having the opportunity to collaborate on a marketing campaign allows young people to learn professional skills as well as attract other teenagers who can identify with the young leaders associated with the Youth Advisory Committee. Second, as mentioned earlier, Seattle, Washington Parks and Recreation's Lifelong Recreation program is designed with older generations in mind. The marketing video on the Seattle Parks and Recreation website shows participants involved in Lifelong Recreation engaging in the programs; these participants help craft the promotional materials used for Lifelong Recreation (http://www.seattlechannel.org/misc-video?videoid=x25776). Both of these examples demonstrate how the participant can be an active member of the program or service, as well as play a vital role in the marketing and promotional campaign for the public parks and recreation agency.

CROSS TRAINING OF STAFF

A significant challenge highlighted by park directors involved in Walls, Siikamaki, Darley, Ferris, and Maher's (2009) study was the problem associated with staffing facilities and training employees. This dilemma is exacerbated when there are key technical functions that staff members manage under the operations of the public parks and recreation agency, such as billing or payroll. As Administration and Staff Divisions are regularly changing, expanding, or shifting regarding classification, it is important that employees are up to speed with the integral functions of the organization. Compartmentalizing tasks and jobs within a community parks and recreation agency can be detrimental to growth of the organization; cross training staff members on multiple function areas can be a lifesaver. Cross training staff members cannot only provide opportunities for staff to "plug in" when other employees are unavailable, but it can also increase intra-departmental support, build inter-departmental relationships and positively impact the organizational culture as a whole. Inefficiencies are avoided, and the quality of services provided to users does not dip.

Other benefits exist in association with cross training staff members. Empowering staff members with the ability to handle a fluctuating workflow and diverse tasks associated with the organization can demonstrate a level of investment in the person. Staff members who feel that the public parks and recreation agency cares for them and believes in their professional development may be more likely to maintain their commitment to parks and recreation as a career. Diversification of training may lead to employee retention, which could address the challenge brought up by park directors in Walls et al.'s (2009) study. Creating silos that people work in is becoming archaic; the movement of cross training is the path of success in public parks and recreation. This concept of educating and training staff members aligns with the "T Professional" (Estrin, 2008).

The "T Professional" is a staff member who has expertise in one area as well as understanding of other areas associated with their profession. Having expertise in one area and a breadth of understanding of other areas allows the individual the opportunity to positively impact the bigger picture associated with the organization's mission. In conjunction with expertise and understanding, the staff member should also be aware of how the overall operations of the organization work, as well as what their personal abilities and goals are as an employee. Conversely, the "I Professional" is the individual who has a wealth of expertise and knowledge in one area, but is extremely limited regarding other areas of the organization. "I Professionals" have challenges if understanding in various areas of a profession is needed; it is difficult for "I Professionals" to be multifaceted and "wear many hats" in association with the organization's mission (University of Cambridge, 2007).

For the public parks and recreation field, "T Professionals" are becoming the linchpins that move agencies forward. Cross-trained staff members are professionals who can maneuver between various areas of the field within the organization (i.e., aquatics, youth programs, facility management) and help create a sustainable organization with a positive operating culture. Expertise is important, but the "plug-in" style of cross training that comes with employee management is vital.

COMMUNITY LIVABILITY AND QUALITY OF LIFE

Community parks and recreation departments play a key role in advancing community livability and quality of life. Such government units have as one of their primary functions, the greening and beautification of a community. In this way, parks and recreation departments contribute to the beautification and aesthetic enhancement or value of a community. In addition, community parks and recreation services help to "reenergize our relationships with one another—our sense of community" (Edginton, 2000, p. 31).

What is meant by community livability? What does the concept of improving the quality of life imply? The idea of community livability is a subjective one. From a philosophical perspective, promoting livability in the context of one's community is about making life worth living. To have livable communities implies not only a focus on the physical places within which one lives, but also can be viewed from a social perspective. Such physical and social environments contribute to one's well-being, happiness, and morale.

Quality of life, like community livability, is difficult to define and must be looked at from a subjective perspective. We usually think of quality of life as being concerned with the well-being of individuals and communities. Broadly, quality of life is concerned with elements that promote human happiness. These may include one's health, educational attainment, recreation opportunities, and feelings of belonging. Community parks and recreation departments are involved in crafting a series of opportunities for individuals, which may lead to happiness. Programs, services, areas, and facilities all may enhance one's well-being and happiness. Leisure is directly related to health. City parks, open spaces, and parkways all provide a respite from the hurried, rushed lives individuals are confronted with in today's society. Such natural resources often serve as a stress relief for individuals, enabling them to readjust and attune their lives to more natural life rhythms. In addition, there are many opportunities for growth and development as a result of participation in community parks and recreation services.

BUILDING COMMUNITY-EXPANDING SOCIAL CAPITAL

As Robert Putnam (2000) has noted in his book, *Bowling Alone: The Collapse and Revival of American Community*, that individuals and communities have lost a great deal of social capital over the past several decades. Social capital refers to one's networks, which are essential in order to build trust and reciprocity between individuals. Community parks and recreation departments provide numerous opportunities for people to engage in both social bonding and social bridging. Social bonding is a way of strengthening existing relationships between individuals. When children who are familiar with one another play together, they are building their social bonds. The same could be said about adults who participate in a team activity. Often such team members know each other in advance and form their team, thus again, strengthening their existing social bonds. On the other hand, community parks and recreation services also provide opportunities for individuals to bridge out, expanding their social networks in ways in which they make new acquaintances, friends, and in a sense, build new relationships. Social bonding involves strengthening one's existing relationships, whereas social bridging involves expanding one's social networks.

Why is expanding one's social capital important? We live in a society wherein individuals are increasingly socially isolated from one another. On one hand, technology provides a way of people being connected with one another. Yet, on the other hand, it also creates veneer-thin relationships. Parks and recreation programs provide an opportunity for individuals to develop deeper, more meaningful relationships with others. Programs and services provide opportunities for individuals to be connected to one another and in a sense, build community. Community life is one that is lived in association with others where people with common interests, aspirations, and values, live, work, and play together.

PARTNERSHIPS AND BUILDING COLLABORATIVE RELATIONSHIPS

Without question, the development of cooperative, collaborative partnerships is essential in the provision of community parks and recreation services. A partnership can be thought of as a relationship between organizations that enable programs to be provided collectively that would be difficult if one were to go at it alone. The crafting of partnerships creates many new opportunities to expand and enhance programs and services by sharing resources. Close cooperation between various agencies may enable them to conduct programs that would not be possible due to budget limitations, staffing, lack of facilities, and other factors.

Partnerships take many different forms. They can exist between public agencies or established with nonprofit organizations. Still further, partnerships and collaborative relationships can be established with the commercial sector. This latter type of partnership usually involves some type of sponsorship of activities or events. The Austin (Texas) Parks & Recreation Department features several types of partnerships on its website, including Adopt-a-Park, Community Projects, and Public-Private Partnerships. This department has provided definitions to each of these types of partnerships. For example, the Adopt-a-Park program enables individuals to become stewards and advocates for a park. Community Projects are very diverse and encourage partners to leverage the development of specific projects with other resources. Last, Public-Private Partnerships call for both profit and nonprofit organizations to work with the department to provide revenues for development (Austin Park & Recreation, 2016).

Two excellent examples that have emerged recently are reflected in the Fresno, California area. An imbalance in parks and open spaces when comparing south Fresno with the northern part of the community suggests that there was a great deal of social inequity. To address this challenge, the Fresno unified and central unified school districts will open school grounds for public use for the purpose of engaging in outdoor recreation activities (Ortiz-Briones, 2016). This cooperative agreement will make available 340 acres of green space especially to underserved populations. The mayor of the city of Fresno calls the new relationship a "fantastic partnership" (p. 1). Still another example of an outstanding partnership is that between the Department of Recreation Administration at Fresno State University's Sustainable Parks and Recreation Community Initiative and its attempt to link with nearly 50 city and parks and recreation districts in the San Joaquin Valley of California. The program provides opportunities for faculty and students to provide assistance to various community parks and recreation agencies. "Achieving sustainability can be challenging, especially for cities, counties, and special districts in the San Joaquin Valley who often grapple with tight budgets to meet community needs" (Fresno State College of Health and Human Services, 2016). This partnership creates the opportunity to link a university with community agencies to address challenges and issues.

BLURRING OF TRADITIONAL LIMITS ON WHAT PARKS AND RECREATION DOES

As society evolves and changes, the traditional boundaries of community parks and recreation programs are ever changing. As LERN (2016) has offered, "recreation programs are doing it all from recreation, sports, educational enrichment programs, fine arts, and performing arts focus… recreation's umbrella of programming focus and expertise continues to expand and grow" (p.1). Increasingly, community parks and recreation departments have developed programs that promote health and fitness as well as taking on greater responsibility for the before- and after-school care of children.

Not only are new programs being added to community parks and recreation departments, but organizations are often undergoing continuous restructuring in order to meet emerging needs. The Newport News (Virginia) is organized as a Department of Parks, Recreation, & Tourism. In addition to managing many parks, the organization also operates museums and a cultural arts center (Newport News Department of Parks, Recreation & Tourism, 2016). The city of Shoreline (Washington) is organized as a Parks, Recreation, & Cultural Services Department. Its mission statement is "…to provide life-enhancing experiences and promote a healthy community. To bring our culture to life and transfer it to the next generation" (Shoreline Parks, Recreation, & Cultural Services, 2016). The city of St. Louis (Missouri) organizes its services as a Department of Parks, Recreation, and Forestry. Although this is more classical with organizing services, it does blend together important complementary functions (Department of Parks, Recreation, and Forestry, 2016). The city of Fresno (California) organizes its services as a Department of Parks, After School, Recreation, and Community Services (Department of Parks, After School, Recreation, and Community Services, 2016). Similarly, the city of Jacksonville (Florida) organizes its services as a Department of Parks, Recreation, and Community Services. This organization provides a system of urban parks, open spaces, trails, athletic facilities, community and senior centers, beaches, golf courses, aquatic facilities, boat and kayak launches, nature preserves, along with an amphitheater, arboretum, and an equestrian center (Jacksonville Parks, Recreation, and Community Services Department, 2016).

AREAS AND FACILITIES

The use of community parks and recreation areas and facilities is projected to grow significantly. In a study reporting on the 2015 State of the Industry in *Parks & Recreation* (2015, p. 65), an annual increase in use of facilities was noted. Respondents indicated that there was a rise from 2012–2015 of 55.4% in 2012 to 63.1% in 2015. However, projections suggest a slight decline when comparing projections of 2016 with a reduction to 60.9%. Budgets for construction of areas facilities from 2014–2015 increased slightly. The most common areas and facilities reported in this study included playgrounds, park shelters such as picnic areas or gazebos, park restroom structures, walking and hiking trails, open spaces such as gardens and natural areas, bleachers and seating, outdoor sports courts, natural turf sports fields, concession areas, and classrooms and meeting rooms (2015, p. 67).

Respondents to this study reported that continued plants are underway to add additional features to areas and facilities. Some of the planned additions include the following:

- Splash play areas (23.4% of the respondents)
- Playgrounds (22.4% of the respondents)
- Dog parks (22% of the respondents)
- Fitness trails and outdoor fitness equipment (21.5% of the respondents)
- Hiking and walking trails (20.3% of the respondents)
- Bike trails (20.1% of the respondents)
- Park restroom structures (19.5% of the respondents)
- Park structures such as shelters and gazebos (17.7 % of the respondents)
- Synthetic turf sports fields (16.1% of the respondents)
- Wi-Fi services (14.4% of the respondents)

With the exception of splash play areas, dog parks, and Wi-Fi services, the areas and developments are focused on traditional community parks and recreation areas and facilities. Certainly, community parks and recreation agencies are giving value to technological advances such as us of mobile phones, laptop computers and other devices that may be brought into parks and recreation settings. In one way this seems antithetical to the idea of a park being a place for the serene enjoyment of nature. Yet, on the other hand, such a development recognizes the fact that individuals want to stay connected to their friends, family, and local, regional, national, and world events. Providing convenient access to one's technological devices may in fact rob them of the opportunity to build meaning by interacting with others personally face to face and the environment.

GLOBAL CLIMATE CHANGE

The Intergovernmental Panel on Climate Change (IPCC, 2014), the American-based Union of Concerned Scientists (see http://www.ucsusa.org/our-work/global-warming/science-and-impacts/global-warming-impacts#.VrI2i00UXcs), and various independent researchers (e.g., Bell & Ashwood, 2016; Koger & Winter, 2010), have outlined that future Americans will be impacted by global climate change. These impacts, according to the sources above, will include (1) an acceleration in the rise sea levels and coastal flooding, especially on the U.S. East Coast and Gulf of Mexico; (2) longer and more damaging wildfire seasons, especially in the western United States, (3) more frequent and intense heat waves; (4) costly and growing health impacts, especially connected to air pollution and allergy seasons; and (5) heavier precipitation and flooding.

In regard to future trends, parks and recreation agencies need to commit to actions that will decrease factors leading to global climate change (e.g., less use of greenhouse gases) and help remedy the impacts of global climate change. A starting step is awareness that community parks and recreation programs can contribute to environmental problems such as pollution and greenhouse gas use, but can also contribute to air quality and the reduction of greenhouse gasses. Drawing on an example from a sister profession—the National Park Service—Zion National Park in Utah has begun using a shuttle system to eliminate car driving in the park. By replacing over 5,000 cars with 21 buses, this park policy will remove 13,926 tons (28 million pounds) of greenhouse gasses emitted in the park, which is having a destructive effect on air quality, which then impedes the healthy development of flora and fauna (National Park Service, 2008). Community parks and recreation are no different than the National Park Service system in that management can contribute, remedy, or prevent global climate change.

Over 15 years ago, research by Akbari, Pomerantz, and Taha (2001) demonstrated that cool surfaces and shade trees reduce energy use (and less greenhouse gas emission) and improve air quality in urban areas, which obviously leads to healthier people. At the beginning of the new millennium, cities such as Chicago spent approximately $600 million on capital improvements, including rooftop gardens on various buildings which improve air quality and reduce energy use and use of greenhouse gases. The rooftop garden on City Hall in Chicago has over 20,000 plants and this city developed the Calumet Open Space Reserve which included 4000 acres of prairie, wetlands, and forest/tree areas (see http://www.artic.edu/webspaces/greeninitiatives/greenroofs/images/GuidetoRooftopGardening_v2.pdf or Daley, 2002). Figure 18.2 is the rooftop garden on the City Hall building in Chicago. Related to being thoughtful environmental stewards and improve air quality, from 1989 to 2006 Chicago added 120 new acres of park land, instituted a city-wide recycling plan, and planted more than 400,000 trees with community parks and recreation being one of the change agents (see Daley 2006). Imagine the consequences if each community parks and recreation agency duplicated what was occurring in Chicago and led a community movement to increase air quality and health by park and roof-top garden development in their communities. As outlined in Chapter 4 of this book, Harnik and Welle (2009) underscored that in Washington D.C. there are 4, 839 acres of tree cover in the city's 7,999 acres of park land, which remove 244 tons of combined pollution (e.g., carbon dioxide, nitrogen dioxide, sulfur dioxide, ozone, particulate matter) each year.

Figure 18.2. Rooftop garden on City Hall in Chicago

Community parks and recreation agencies need to invest in best practice and management related to environmental issues. According to the International Society of Sustainability Professionals (ISSP) (2008), the development of bicycle infrastructure is a paramount way to reduce greenhouse gases. As Rojek (2007) summarized, American's account for 5% of the world's population, they drive 30% of the world's cars and contribute to nearly 45% of the carbon dioxide pumped into the atmosphere each year. Bell and Ashwood (2016) noted that in the Netherlands, half of all trips are by bike or foot, compared to just 7% of all trips in the United States, and one reason is that the Netherlands has invested greatly in bicycle infrastructure. In Chicago's Millennium Park (see Chapter 3 in this book, which explains this park), there is a two-story, free of cost bike parking garage for hundreds of bikes, showers, lockers, and a bicycle rental and repair area. The following bicycle infrastructure recommendations suggested by the ISSP (2008) could easily be championed by community parks and recreation agencies as part a trend toward promoting both environmental health and personal health:

- **Bike Llnes**—to keep bikers safe when riding on busy roads
- **Bike boxes**—special pavement markings to keep bikers safe at dangerous intersections
- **Laws and outreach**—laws should protect bicyclists and outreach should inform people about these policies
- **Bike racks**—provide a place to put bikes, especially artistic ones
- Bike Lockers—provide storage for bikes, clothing, and other equipment; safe from weather or vandalism
- **Facilities with showers**—Provides showers so that bikers can be clean (e.g., biking to work)

As noted above, the consequence of global warming and climate change will be severe: storms, floods, and other environmental disasters, such as wildfires. Community parks and recreation agencies need to have short- and long-term plans related to protecting children after environmental disasters. Writing specifically to the parks and recreation profession, Thompson (2015) recently outlined the unique needs of children during disasters (e.g., mobility, reliance on caregivers such as recreation leaders) and how to support children after a disaster. Thompson suggested that after a natural disaster, youth-based parks and recreation programs should help children express their feelings, normalize and validate feelings, and that the daily routine of available recreation programs helps all people cope. Community parks and recreation leaders need to be trained in both disaster prevention and response.

Beyond global warning and climate change, community parks and recreation agencies need to also be aware of other environmental problems and issues. Writing right before the new millennium, Godbey (1997) summarized that one of the key global and local issues in the 21st century will be water scarcity. Godbey outlined the ethical dilemma that in the year 2025, many American golf courses will continue to use massive amounts of water related to leisure, yet it is projected that in this same year over one billion people worldwide will be living in areas subject to extreme water scarcity. This, in turn, leads to global anti-American sentiment among people and governments of developing countries as the water they need to literally survive is used in America for leisure purposes (Rojek, 2006). As underscored in Chapter 4 (see Figure 4.3) of this book, Kopp, Johnson, Klotz, and Miller (2015) and Snow (2001) provided management strategies to decrease negative environmental consequences (e.g., water usage) in golf courses. Community parks and recreation agencies need to be good stewards of the Earth and be global citizens by investing and implementing environmental-friendly practices, such as using less water resources.

MENTAL HEALTH

The United States leads the world in citizens with mental illness (Kessler & Üstün, 2008; World Health Organization, 2004). According to the 2014 National Survey on Drug Use and Health administered by the Substance Abuse and Mental Health Services Administration (SAMHSA), one in five American adults aged 18 or older (18.1% or 43.6 million adults) has a mental illness, with 4.1% (9.8 million adults) dealing with serious mental illness (SAMHSA, 2014). In fact, the United States Department of Labor (2015) has projected that employment of mental health counselors is projected to grow 19% from 2014 to 2024, much faster than the average for all occupations. What is relevant is that increasing the mental health of Americans is a future trends in the United States and has direct implications for community parks and recreation as leisure services can both prevent mental illness and increase overall mental health.

Although there are numerous and complex reasons why mental illness is projected to increase, one paramount factor is the trend of the new consumer culture connected to media. The new consumer culture, according to Schor (2004), are people who measure their worth and self-esteem by obtainment of consumer goods (e.g., purchasing expensive automobiles, athletic shoes, or golf clubs). Due to greater child marketing through Internet and media-based mediums, the new consumer culture is literally creating commercialized children/youth, who are exploited and controlled by corporate companies (e.g., the diet industry). Research clearly outlines that people who have commercialized identities experience greater depression, anxiety, and psychosomatic complains as commercialized identities undermine well-being (Schor, 2004). Seligman Reivich, Jaycox, and Gillham (2007) articulated that a key factor that has contributed to the epidemic of youth depression is the notion that consumerism becomes a way of life and antidote to struggles in life. Seligman and colleagues argue that consumerism focuses on a "feel-good" society, rather than a "do-well" (accomplishment) society, and that the focus on self and feeling good leaves people with hollow and meaningless lives. This aligns to Greenfeld's (2013) study, which outlines that the prevalence of mental illness in the United States is cultural in origin.

As one example, Durham (2008) has extended how consumeristic culture and its connection to leisure and media messages has had a destructive outcome on girls' and young women's self-worth as they desire a commercialized body image (e.g., how the diet, fashion, and plastic surgery industry targets children and adolescents in their marketing strategies). In fact, due to public and health trepidation that girls and young female adults continue to suffer from specific types of mental health disorders at higher rates, the American Psychological Association (APA) published a report that concluded that the increase in media portrays of women being sexually objectified will continue to augment mental health disorder in girls and women, along with impacting society and boys/men in a negative way (APA, 2007). Although not classified as "leisure," the APA report listed the primary cultural contributors of the sexualization of girls/women, and the resulting increase in mental health disorders, as television, music videos, music lyrics, movies, popular magazines, sports media, video/computer games, the Internet, advertisements, dolls, and cosmetics.

Community parks and recreation can provide myriad programs and services that can enhance mental health and prevent mental illness. The APA (2007) report suggested that athletics and extracurricular activities, such as drama club and marching band, can protect girls and women against buying into commercialized identities and body images by teaching them how to use their bodies and psychological energy toward accomplishment-based activities (e.g., performing well in a marching band or in community theater). Recently scholarship in the field of mental health counseling has acknowledged how different theories of leisure—namely flow theory and the serious leisure perspective—have an important role in increasing mental health (see Dieser, Christenson, & Davies-Gage, 2014). There is research evidence that exercise and human movement (e.g., walking in a park) promotes emotional and mental health (e.g., Fahey, Insel, & Roth, 2014; Otto & Smits, 2011). Dieser (2013), in merging leisure education with media literacy, advocated that all leisure service organizations, including community parks and recreation, use leisure education media literary as an approach to increase mental health by empowering individuals (especially youth) to step away from the media gaze developed by corporate companies. Media literacy, as a way of protecting children and adolescents from specific mental health disorders, is also advocated by the APA (2007).

Leisure education media literacy examines how media consumption as leisure influences the overall leisure experience, including personal and societal harm, and can help propel people toward healthy human development where leisure becomes part of meaningful and fulfilling lives (Dieser, 2013). Media includes everything from reading newspapers and comic books, to watching television, to interacting on Facebook or surfing the Internet. To counter the stereotypes of how Arab American women are portrayed in the media, Bing-Canar and Zerkel (1998) created a year-long media literacy youth program in the Arab Community Center of Chicago, in which Arab American teenage girls produced a video titled *Benaat Chicago (Daughters of Chicago): Growing up Arab and Female in Chicago,* which created an alternative media representation of Arab American girls and women.

That is, these young women devoted their leisure time to reclaim media space regarding Arab American representations from powerful media corporations. Dieser (2013) provides evidence, including his own case study research, related to how leisure education media literacy can change attitudes away from consumer culture to wellness activities. As one example, McCannon (2002, 2005) reported that a six-day media literacy program changed attitudes among youth about alcohol and tobacco advertisements, increased anger toward tobacco companies (related to how they exploited and target youth), and increased their desire to live a healthier lifestyle. Community parks and recreation agencies can begin to offer leisure education media literacy to help motivate youth and adults toward more community recreation and less commercialized pursuits.

OBESITY

More than one-third of adults and 17% of youth in the United States are obese (Ogden, Carroll, Kit, & Flegal, 2014). Furthermore, over 300,000 deaths annually can be attributed to obesity (Mokdad, Ford, Bowman, Dietz, Vinicor, & Bales, 2003). According to Lee, McAlexander, and Banda (2011) a paramount factor to reversing the obesity problem is the reversing of the obesogentic environment, which is the infrastructure of cities that encourage people to be inactive. Lee, McAlexander, and Banda specifically state that communities need greater parks, open spaces, walking trails, and bikeways for human movement and physical activities in order to combat the obesity problem. Lee and colleagues state that "Parks and open spaces are community features that provide an ideal setting for physical activity because they offer free or low-cost alternatives to other resources, making them accessible to most people" (p. 62). Beginning in 2011, the San Antonio (Texas) Parks and Recreation Department created fitness zones and fitness equipment through various parks. Fitness equipment allows users to perform the following exercises: stretches, power step, push-ups, squats, dips, and core and torso balance exercises with the goal of improving cardiovascular conditioning, muscle tone, and flexibility (MySanAntonio, 2017).

To prevent and remedy obesity, community parks and recreation agencies can create active living programs. The National Recreation and Park Association's health initiative titled "Hearts N' Parks" is, in essence, an active living lifestyle program. The Hearts N' Parks program, which runs through 11 states and over 50 parks and recreation programs, is specifically focused on educating community people and policy decision-makers that parks can be used for fitness activities and can be viewed as sites of cardiovascular health and human development. Moreover, the active living community model presented by Sallis, Cervero, Ascher, Henderson, Kraft, and Kerr (2006) focuses on teaching social policy makers that community change is needed in order to developing active living spaces (e.g., creating safe parks and neighborhoods for active movement), along with teaching people to link their leisure to active movement (e.g., use bike trails to get to school or work). In fact, Dieser (2013) underscores how all leisure service agencies need to provide leisure education when developing active living programs as a means to decreasing obesity.

DIVERSITY

In writing about the industries of the future, Ross (2016) stated that one of the most important trends is "multicultural fluency," and this has direct application to community parks and recreation agencies. As explained in Chapter 3, the U.S. Census Bureau's 2014 National Projections (Colby & Ortman, 2015) suggest that by 2044, more than half of all Americans will belong to a minority group (any group other than non-Hispanic White alone) and by 2060, nearly one in five of the nation's total population is projected to be foreign born. Table 3.1 in this book shows a very racially diverse United States by the year 2060. Between 2014 and 2060, the U.S. population is projected to increase from 319 million to 417 million, and in 2030, one in five Americans is predicted to be 65 or over. In 2015, an estimated 5.3 million Americans of all ages had Alzheimer's disease, with an estimated 5.1 million people aged 65 or older affected (Alzheimer's Association, 2015). Due to greater population and the aging of the baby boomers, Alzheimer's disease will continue to increase over the next decade. Furthermore, there will also be greater diversity in the future related to sexual orientation and religion. Serving people who are transgender, people who experience a mismatch between their gender identity or gender expression and their assigned sex, is one example of a population group that community parks and recreation agencies need to be ready to serve in the future. To this end, the *Brainerd Dispatch* (local newspaper in Brainerd, Minnesota) featured an article in April 2015 explaining that the Brainerd Parks and Recreation Board unanimously voted to adhere to the transgender policy adopted by the Minnesota State High School League when it comes to competitive youth sport programming due to an inquiry by a parent of a male child who identifies as a female, about registering for the softball league for girls aged 14-17 (Perkins, 2013).

Cultural and diversity competence is an issue relevant to all community parks and recreation agencies. Cultural and diversity competence means having a plan of action or strategies to ensure that people with diverse backgrounds are welcome in community parks and recreation settings. Chapter 3 of this book offers many suggestions related to the development of cultural and diversity competence, including how the I-triad can be used to increase cultural inclusion and cross-cultural training that any community parks and recreation agency can implement (see Table 3.3).

Community parks and recreation agencies in the future need to develop creative partnerships in order to provide services to diverse populations. As one example, in the summer of 2015, Seattle (Washington) Parks and Recreation partnered with Greenwood Senior Center, the Alzheimer's Association, Aegis on Madison, Elderwise and Outdoors for All, to offer a variety of "dementia-friendly" recreation programs such as fitness classes, watercolor painting, snowshoe hiking, walking group, and opportunities to volunteer at the food bank.

ACCOUNTABILITY

In the future, community parks and recreation agencies need to be held to a higher level of accountability. For years, community parks and recreation agencies have made arguments and claims related to the benefits of leisure services. This has included such assertions as community parks increase air quality, youth-based programs increase the self-esteem of youth and prevent juvenile delinquency, and that aerobic programs, open spaces, and walking trails can be places of cardiovascular health. Accountability is being answerable to claims that an agencies or person puts forth. A future trend in community parks and recreation is to marshal evidence—being answerable or accountable—related to the benefit claims that community parks and recreation agencies put forth.

Wholey (2015) summarized that the use of evaluation in government services such as community parks and recreation agencies is a form of accountability. As explained in Chapter 12 of this book, evaluation is an essential feature of programming and is needed in order to be accountable. In short, evaluation is judging the worth of programs and services on the basis of an analysis of systematically collected evidence (Rossman & Schlatter, 2015) and can be done using quantitative, qualitative, or mixed data. Benefits-based/outcome-focused paragon programming (see Chapter 12), which has a specific component related to evidence-based documentation of the benefits of parks and recreation services, is a programming framework that provides accountability. In the future, community parks and recreation agencies need to be more committed to the use of evaluation and benefits-based /outcome-focused paragon programming in order to be accountable to community members and relevant stakeholders.

RELEVANCE AND IMPORTANCE OF PARKS AND RECREATION PLANNING

It is imperative that parks and recreation managers and their staff members become more involved in local development efforts. The challenge is to help the general public, decision makers, and some city planners become aware of and appreciate the economic, social, community, and environmental benefits of parks and open space. Many times, opposition to more parks and open space note the ongoing maintenance as a liability. Yet, studies have shown the benefits and return on investment in communities who have placed a priority on adequate park and open space acreage to serve the needs of the community. For example, plans can guide an extensive and wide-ranging management decision-making processes to add value and relevancy to community parks and recreation program.

- Ensure the public health, welfare, and safety of the community
- Assess the current state of the parks and recreation system
- Guide the development of the parks and recreation system within a community
- Provide a foundation for financial security of the department
- Develop a tool for rational decision-making
- Engage the public in discussing issues and developing solutions
- Coordinate the various functions of the department and other municipal agencies
- Create feasible actions to translate the strategic concepts of the plan into actual implementation

As a profession, we must recognize that planning helps community parks and recreation agencies make critical decisions concerning ways to preserve significant natural and cultural resources for public enjoyment and balance competing demands for limited resources. Planning and plans also allow organizations to prioritize available funding and staff to provide most efficient delivery of services. Finally, planning helps to understand and address the varied and conflicting local interests and views of what is most important, affordable, and necessary. Often, the process of planning is more important than the actual plan produced. It is the interaction of staff, management, citizens, and decision-makers that makes planning useful in managing parks and recreation organizations.

Parks and recreation plans are not stand-alone documents. There are linkages between recreation planning and land use, transportation, open space, and housing at the community level. It is important that community parks and recreation professionals become involved in local development issues and projects. It is equally important that community parks and recreation professionals educate the decision makers on the value of recreation in the context of comprehensive community planning. This last point may be of future importance in that future of parks and recreation at the community level is susceptible to budget pressures before any of the other city services, and unduly so. Professionals need to be more vocal and more active in promoting the relevance and value of parks and recreation investments.

IMPORTANCE OF ENGAGING THE PUBLIC FOR PLANNING AND FUTURE DECISION-MAKING

Successful parks and recreation management is based on meaningful and collaborative citizen involvement. Engaging the citizens broadens the base of public support for the parks and recreation organization. Citizens can be involved in recreation and parks management by performing tasks under agency supervision, by participating in decision-making through planning teams and providing input, or by belonging to a special interest group. It is important to note that there are differences between the personal assistance offered by individual volunteers and members of special interest groups, those involved in an advisory role for plan and policy making. No matter the intent and level of involvement, these groups are considered stakeholders who have interests in the management, planning, funding, and maintenance of parks and recreation services. Plans, policies, and future direction are misguided without adequate and meaningful citizen engagement.

Citizen engagement and involvement in parks and recreation service delivery has been recognized as being of critical importance to the organization and community. The goals of citizen engagement are to revitalize civic culture, improve public discourse, and generate the political will to take action. The importance here is that planning that encourages civic engagement will strengthen social capital, which will enhance social sustainability. In communities where public controversy over plans is highly charged, little progress is made in implementing and realizing those plans. Where civic engagement is high, issues are discussed, and some effort is made to recognize concerns and mitigate impacts, significant progress is realized.

Parks and recreation organizations must be responsive to public opinion from beyond the volunteer ranks, and they should be legitimately active in forming that opinion. Involving citizens is the best way of both serving their needs and addressing inequities in the parks and recreation service delivery system. Involving citizens also is a principle of sustainable park management. The richer the citizen involvement is for parks and recreation management, the more likelihood that plans and programs are responsive to needs and address diverse viewpoints and problem-solving strategies.

ACQUISITION OF PARKS AND OPEN SPACE

It is important to note that parks and recreation plans suggest and authorize acquisition of parks and open space as an implementing measure. Further, the plans are used for capital improvement programs. The use of partnerships is strong in communities that have cultivated engagement. Other means by which the agency may acquire lands is through cooperative and negotiated agreements and by ordinances and land use zoning. Implementation strategies for recreation and parks master plans more often than not address land acquisition programs for expanding the parks and open space systems.

Parks and recreation agencies are under increasing pressure to acquire enough lands and contiguous parcels for greenways due to development pressures. In some communities, other uses for the land may preempt recreational use if a well-planned program of acquisition is not employed to secure suitable land. There are six important factors adding to the recreational space problem:

1. More and more residents are using park lands more frequently.
2. There is far less open space owned by private citizens or companies available for residents to use, resulting in greater use of public parks and recreation areas.
3. Older parts of cities have fewer acres of parks due to the historic lack of land dedication or fees when the area was developed. Newer parts of the city often have more acreage in parks per 1,000 people due to ordinances in place.
4. Competition with developers over lands for recreation vs. other uses.
5. Perceptions from elected officials that maintenance costs of parks are prohibitive for the future budget.
6. Technology (web-based information) has made access to these lands easier and has vastly increased the demand for special areas to handle particular needs (off-road vehicles, horse trails, etc).

Despite strong statements from national leaders citing the need for more recreational areas, acquiring needed parklands has become increasingly difficult, particularly in urban areas where needs are greater, but where conflicting demands are formidable due to development pressures. Unfortunately, local political pressure from developers who argue that the land has a "higher and best use" as a housing or a strip mall can then lead to elected officials declaring that the ongoing maintenance costs are reasons to deny the acquisition of additional park lands.

However, there are some positive aspects to the land-acquisition situation. Land often zoned for recreation has proven this to be the best use. For example, flood plains are an example of areas where other uses are not practical because of periodic flooding. Recreational uses on such lands can adjust to the inconvenience without danger to human life or serious economic loss.

There are several ways parks and recreation agencies can acquire land. These include outright purchase, donation, stipulated deed, condemnation, easements, dedications, fee in-lieu and/or park development fee, and transfer of property or development rights.

Few decisions made in park systems are more long lasting or obvious than those made in the acquisition and development of parks and open space lands. This chapter discussed the relationships between planning and acquiring parks and open space lands. Regulations using ordinances and other legal means such as zoning and land use controls are often standard and predominate means by which to acquire lands. Importantly, the exactions such as fees in-lieu of lands, park land dedications, and development impact fees are tied to zoning and subdivision regulations. These are often challenged by developers as unfair or increasing costs of development. However, the cost is passed on to the buyer ($200-$1,000 dollars per dwelling unit) who will use the parks and facilities.

Using a variety of methods in a comprehensive manner has proven successful in a number of communities. Of importance to the success of any program is program structure and administration, planning, and having implementing measures for regulatory compliance.

SUSTAINABILITY: AN AREA OF CONCERN FOR ALL

The concept of sustainable development is still ambiguous even in definition. The 1987 report of the United Nations World Commission on the Environment and Development popularized the term "sustainable development." The report "Our Common Future," also known as "The Brundtlund Report," broadly defined sustainable development as "development that meets the needs of the present without compromising the ability of future generations to meet their own needs" (United Nations, 1987). The National Parks Service has adopted this definition.

Parks and recreation organizations have an advantage over many organizations because the core of their mission includes principles of sustainability to maintain, improve, and guide the long-term health and well-being of the entire community and the elements on which they rely—the people, flora and fauna of earth, water, air. These fundamental principles allow us to question the range of user needs and demands. Ecosystem management can be seen as a means rather than an end to provide an avenue for land management agencies to work with an array of constituencies and operationalize the concept of sustainable development.

Many public parks and recreation organizations and the communities in which they operate have adopted efforts to identify policy and practices to effectively advance the economic, environmental and social objectives of a sustainable parks system. Sustainability efforts include administration, engineering, energy, water, air quality, health, interpretation services, operations and maintenance, park management, revenue enhancement, partnerships, habitat preservation, and transportation. Lankford, Lankford, and Wheeler (2017) note:

> Generally, dimensions of sustainability include but are not limited to: (a) energy, (b) wildlife habitat, (c) transportation, (d) education, (e) economy, and (f) citizen participation. These dimensions can help form the basis of park planning and management process. However, a thorough understanding of sustainable development and management cannot replace an intimate understanding of the place itself. (p. 378)

Issues of sustainability permeate how an organization operates from supporting alternative transportation for employees or members to asset management and investment, from establishing hours of operation to purchasing practices, from defining marketing efforts to physical structure design, from developing a fire management plan to developing a visitor education and interpretation plan. It is easy for one facet of an organization to work in opposition to another facet unless principles of sustainability permeate the organization. Adopting sustainable principles comprehensively is often extremely difficult because an organization relies on established systems that are not sustainable perpetuating the problem.

SUMMARY

Trends, issues, and opportunities facing community parks and recreation agencies are the subject of this chapter. A trend may be thought of as a movement, tendency, or shift in which a parks and recreation program, service, area or facility is heading. An issue can be defined as a problem or topic that requires some action. Issues often become opportunities that provide new meaning and direction to a parks and recreation organization. Parks and recreation agencies are best suited when they view issues and problems as opportunities. Such a perspective often gives way to new strategies and directions for an organization, resulting in new programs, services, areas, and facilities. Still further, such opportunities may involve the restructuring or reconceptualizing the way in which a community parks and recreation operates. Efforts aimed at reorganization often result in greater effectiveness and efficiency.

As the community parks and recreation field moves further into the 21st century, administrators and staff members are taking steps to synergize their programs and services with the digital influx in society. Potential users have the opportunity to be involved in progressive activities, emphasizing skill development, social relationships, and a healthy lifestyle. These services may target specific participant groups, such as families, or generations, such as older adults and seniors. These participant groups are also becoming vital members of the marketing and promotion of public parks and recreation programs, assisting with the design and implementation of campaigns. As the target market groups involved in services becomes more diverse, so does the skill set of staff members who serve them. Cross training and developing "T Professionals" are critical moves that can help develop a responsive, vibrant organizational culture with the public parks and recreation organization.

Parks and recreation managers and their staff should become more involved in local development efforts. The challenge is to help the general public, decision makers, and city planners become aware of and appreciate the economic, social, community, and environmental benefits of parks and open space. City administration opposed to more parks and open space use the ongoing maintenance as a financial liability. As a result, professionals and parks and recreation advocates need to be more vocal and more active in promoting the relevance and value of parks and recreation investments.

Parks and recreation agencies are under increasing pressure to acquire enough lands and contiguous parcels for greenways due to development pressures. Despite strong statements from national leaders citing the need for more recreational areas, acquiring needed local parklands has become increasingly difficult, particularly in urban areas where needs are greater, but where conflicting demands are formidable due to development pressures. However, there are some positive aspects to the land acquisition situation. Land often zoned for recreation has proven this to be the best use. For example, flood plains are an example of areas where other uses are not practical because of periodic flooding. Recreational uses on such lands can adjust to the inconvenience without danger to human life or serious economic loss. Methods of acquisition of park land include outright purchase, donation, stipulated deed, condemnation, easements, dedications, fee in-lieu and/or park development fee, and transfer of property or development rights.

Parks and recreation organizations have an advantage over many organizations because the core of their mission includes principles of sustainability to maintain, improve, and guide the long-term health and well-being of the entire community and the elements on which they rely—the people, flora and fauna of earth, water, and air. Many public parks and recreation organizations and the communities in which they operate have adopted policies and practices to effectively advance the economic, environmental, and social objectives of a sustainable parks system. Sustainability efforts have embraced administrative practices, engineering, energy, water, air quality, health, interpretation services, operations and maintenance, park management, revenue enhancement, partnerships, habitat preservation, and transportation.

DISCUSSION QUESTIONS

1. What is a trend? What is the value in engaging in a trend analysis?
2. Why is the exploration of community issues important for parks and recreation agencies?
3. How can a parks and recreation organization reframe issues into opportunities?
4. Why do you think the boundaries and organizational patterns of community parks and recreation departments are constantly evolving? What do you believe will be the ways in which such services will be organized in the future?
5. Discuss why it is important that parks and recreation professionals advocate for planning for parks and facilities.
6. Why is it important to engage the public in parks and recreation issues and concerns?
7. What pressures are there that impact the acquisition of park lands that are outside of control of the parks and recreation organization?
8. Identify the dimensions of sustainability. Discuss examples of these dimensions in practice in your community.
9. Identify 10 social, cultural, economic, or environmental trends impacting on the delivery of parks and recreation services.
10. Identify and define 10 issues from your local community that may be addressed by its parks and recreation department.

REFERENCES

Akbari, H., Pomerantz, M., & Taha, H. (2001) Cool *surfaces and shade trees to reduce energy use and improve air quality in urban areas. Solar Energy, 70*(3), 295–310.

Anderson, K. R. (2016). Safe and secure: New trends in sports facility security and safety. *Recreation Management, 17*(1), 32–34.

Austin (Texas) Parks & Recreation. (2016). Partnerships. Retrieved from https://austintex-as.gov/department/partnerships

Bell, M. M., & Ashwood, L. L. (2016). *An invitation to environmental sociology* (5th ed). Los Angeles, CA: Sage.

Bend (Oregon) Parks and Recreation District. (2015). Prenatal and Baby and Me Classes. Retrieved from http://bendparksandrec.org/juniper_swim__fitness/prenatal_postna-tal/

Colby, S. L., & Ortman, J. M. (2015). Projections of the size and composition of the U.S.Population: 2014 to 2060 (Report No. P25-1143). Retrieved from http://www.census.gov content/dam/Census/library/publications/2015/demo/p2511   pdf

Daley, R. M. (2002). Chicago invests in citizens. *Parks & Recreation, 37*(4), 40–47.

Daley, R. M. (2006). Chicago mayor talks parks: Mayor Daley opens up about park land, recreation and the importance of citizen involvement. *Parks & Recreation, 41*(5), 32–33.

Department of Parks, Recreation, and Forestry. (2016). Parks, recreation, and forestry. Retrieved from https://www.stlouis-mo.gov/government/departments/parks/

Dunnington, G. (2011). *The potential impacts of climate change on recreation in Vermont.* Climate change adaptation white paper series. Climate Team: Vermont Agency of Natural Resources.

Edginton, C. R. (2000) *Enhancing the livability of Iowa communities: The role of recreation, natural resource development, and tourism.* Cedar Falls, IA: University of Northern Iowa, 130.

Environmental Protection Agency. (December 4, 2015). Heat island effect: Heat mitigation strategies. Retrieved from http://www.epa.gov/heat-islands.

Estrin, J. (2008). *Closing the innovation gap: Reigniting the spark of creativity in a global economy.* New York, NY: McGraw-Hill.

Fahey, T. D., Insel, P. M., & Roth, W. T. (2014). *Fit and well: Core concepts and labs in physical fitness and wellness* (11th ed.). New York, NY: McGraw Hill.

Fresno State College of Health and Human Services. (2016). Department of Recreation Administration partners with city to look at sustainable parks system. Retrieved from http://fresnostatelivewellblog.com/2016/01/25/department-of-recreation-administration-partners-with-city-to-look-at-sustainable-parks-system/

Fresno (California) Department of Parks, After School, Recreation, and Community Services. (2016). Retrieved from http://www.fresno.gov/DiscoverFresno/ParksRecreationandCommunityServices/default.htm

Harnik, P., & Welle, B. (2009). *Measuring the economic value of a city park system.* The Trust for Public Land. Washington, D.C.: The Trust for Public Land.

Intergovernmental Panel on Climate Change. (2014). Climate Change 2014 Synthesis Report. Geneva, Switzerland. Retrieved from https://www.ipcc.ch/pdf/assessment-report/ar5/syr/SYR_AR5_FINAL_full.pdf

International Society of Sustainability Professionals. (2008). Cool trends: 10 things cities are doing now to reduce greenhouse gases. Retrieved from http://www.sustainabilityprofessionals.org/files/Cool%20Trends.pdf

Jacksonville (Florida) Parks, Recreation, and Community Services Department. (2016). Retrieved from http://www.coj.net/departments/parks-and-recreation.aspx

Kessler, R. C., & Üstün, T. B. (2008). *The WHO world mental health survey: Global perspectives on the epidemiology of mental disorders.* New York, NY: Cambridge University Press.

Kopp, K., Johnson, P. G., Klotz, E., & Miller, C. (2015, January). Water-use efficiency on golf courses in Utah. *Golf Course Magazine,* 114–117.

Kogrt, S. M., & Winter, D. D. N. (2010). *The psychology of environmental problems* (3rd ed.). New York, NY: Taylor and Francis.

Lankford, S., Lankford, J., & Wheeler, D. (2017). *An introduction to park management.* Urbana, IL: Sagamore.

Lee, R. E., McAlexander, K. M., & Banda, J. A. (2011). *Reversing the obesogenic environment.* Champaign, IL: Human Kinetics.

LERN. (2016). Top trends in recreation programming, marketing and management. Retrieved from http://www.lern.org/blog/2014/07/07/top-trends-in-recreation-programming-marketing-and-management/

McCannon, R. (2002). Media literacy: What? Why? How? In V. Strasburger & B. Wilson (Eds.), *Children, adolescents and the media* (pp. 327–367). Thousand Oaks, CA: Sage.

McCannon, R. (2005). Adolescent and media literacy. *Adolescent Medicine Clinics, 16*, 463–480.

Mental Health Foundation. (2013). Starting today: The future of mental health services. Retrieved from https://www.mentalhealth.org.uk/sites/default/files/starting-today.pdf

Mokdad, A. H., Ford, E. S., Bowman, B. A., Dietz, W. H., Vinicor, F., & Bales, V. S. (2003). Prevalence of obesity, diabetes, and obesity-related health risk factors, 2001. *Journal of the American Medical Association, 289*, 76–79.

Montgomery County, Maryland Recreation (2016). Montgomery County Recreation – Youth Development. Retrieved from http://www.montgomerycountymd.gov/rec/thingstodo/youthdevelopment/yac.html

MySanAntonio. (2017). New outdoor fitness equipment in city parks. Retrieved from http://www.mysanantonio.com/community/southside/news/article/New-outdoor-fitness-equipment-in-city-parks-950663.php

National Park Service. (2008). Zion National Park: Green transit – The Zion shuttle. Retrieved from www.nps.gov/zion/naturescience/green-transit-the-zion-shuttle.htm.

National Recreation and Parks Association. (n.d.). Issue Brief: Using social media marketing to promote physical activity and health and wellness in parks. Retrieved from https://www.nrpa.org/uploadedFiles/nrpaorg/Grants_and_Partners/Recreation_and_Health/Resources/Issue_Briefs/Social-Media.pdf.

National Recreation and Park Association. (2015). *NRPA's 2015 Field Report: A parks and recreation national database analysis.* Ashburn, VA: National Recreation and Park Association.

Newport News Department of Parks, Recreation & Tourism. (2016). Retrieved from https://www.nngov.com/parks-and-recreation

Ogden, C. L., Carroll, M. D., Kit, B. K., & Flegal, K. M. (2014). Prevalence of childhood and dult obesity in the United States, 2011-2012. *Journal of the American Medical Association, 311*(8), 806–814.

Ortiz-Briones, M. G. (2016). Fresno residents to have access to more open green space. from http://www.vidaenelvalle.com/news/state/california/fresno/article56110005.html

Otto, M. W., & Smits, J. A. J. (2011). *Exercise for mood and anxiety: Proven strategies for overcoming depression and enhancing well-being.* New York, NY: Oxford University Press.

Perkins, C. (2015). Brainerd parks board approves transgender policy. *Brainerd Dispatch.* Retrieved from http://www.brainerddispatch.com/news/3733841-brainerd-parks-board-approves-transgender-policy

Putnam, R. D. (2000). *Bowling alone: The collapse and revival of American community.* New York, NY: Simon & Schuster Paperbacks.

Rodgers, D. T. (1998). *Atlantic crossings: Social politics in a progressive age.* Cambridge, MA: The Belkamp Press of Harvard University Press.

Ross, A. (2016). *The industries of the future.* New York, NY: Simon & Schuster.

Rossman, J. R., & Schlatter, B. E. (2015). *Recreation programming: Designing and staging leisure experiences* (7th ed.). Urbana, IL: Sagamore.

Sallis, J. F., Cervero, R. B., Ascher, W., Henderson, K. A., Kraft, M. K., & Kerr, J.(2006). An ecological approach to creating active living communities. *Annual Review of Public Health, 27*, 297–322.

SAMHSA. (2014). Behavioral health trends in the United States. Retrieved from http://www.samhsa.gov/data/sites/default/files/NSDUH-FRR1-2014/NSDUH-FRR1-2014.pdf

San Francisco Recreation & Parks. (2016). Digital and visual arts program. Retrieved from http://sfrecpark.org/recprogram/digital-visual-arts.

Seattle (Washington) Parks and Recreation (2016). Lifelong recreation: Come play with us. Retrieved from (http://www.seattlechannel.org/misc-video?videoid=x25776).

Shoreline (Washington) Parks, Recreation, & Cultural Services. (2016). Mission statement. Retrieved from http://www.cityofshoreline.com/government/departments/parks-recreation-cultural-services.

Snow, J. T. (2001). Water conservation on golf courses. In International Turf Producers Foundation (Ed.), *Water eight: Conserving our water, preserving our environment* (pp. 48–51). Rolling Meadows, IL: International Turf Producers Foundation.

The City of Portland Oregon Parks and Recreation. (2015). Environmental education. Retrieved from https://www.portlandoregon.gov/parks/38295.

Tipping, E. (2015, June). A look at trends in parks and recreation. *Recreation Management, 16*(6), 60–69.

Thompson, S. (2015). A big threat to our little campers: Protecting children in disasters. *Parks & Recreation, 50*(12), 40–45.

United Nations World Commission on Environment and Development. (WCED). (1987). *Our common future.* Cary, NC: Oxford University Press.

United States Department of Labor. (2015). Mental health counselors and marriage and family therapists. Retrieved from https://www.bls.gov/ooh/community-and-social-service/mental-health-counselors-and-marriage-and-family-therapists.htm

University of Cambridge. (2007). *Succeeding through service innovation: A service perspective for education, research, business, and government.* Cambridge, UK: University of Cambridge Institute for Manufacturing.

Walls, M., Siikamaki, J., Darley, S., Ferris, J., & Maher, J. (2009). *Current challenges, funding, and popularity trends in local parks and recreation areas: Responses to a survey of park directors.* Washington, D.C.: Resources for the Future.

Wholey, J. S. (2015). Use of evaluation in government. In K. E. Newcomer, H. P. Hatry, & J. S. Wholey (Eds.), *Handbook of practical program evaluation* (4th ed., pp. 798–815). Hoboken, NJ: John Wiley & Sons.

World Health Organization. (2004). Prevalence, severity, and unmet need for treatment of mental disorders in the World Health Organization World Mental Health Surveys. *Journal of the American Medical Association, 291*(21), 2581–2590

Index

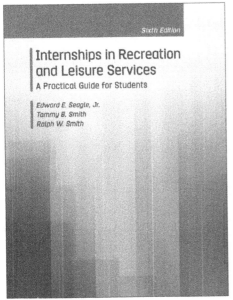